The Rainbow Challenge

THE
RAINBOW
CHALLENGE

The Jackson Campaign and the Future of U.S. Politics

Sheila D. Collins

Monthly Review Press
New York

Library of Congress Cataloging-in-Publication Data

Collins, Sheila D.
  The rainbow challenge

  Bibliography: p.
  Includes index.
  1. United States—Politics and government—1981–
2. Jackson, Jesse, 1941–   . 3. Afro-Americans—
Politics and government.   4. Presidents—United States—
Election—1984.   I. Title.
E876.C64   1986   324.973926   86-21778
ISBN 0-85345-690-9
ISBN 0-85345-691-7 (pbk.)

Monthly Review Press
155 West 23rd Street
New York, N.Y. 10011

Manufactured in the United States of America

10 9 8 7 6 5 4 3 2 1

For John,
beloved comrade in the struggle for justice and peace

Contents

Preface and Acknowledgments

Early in 1984, finding myself jobless, I volunteered for a week to work in the Jesse Jackson for President campaign in New Hampshire. That week stretched into seven marathon months of the most fascinating (and physically exhausting) work I have ever done. After New Hampshire, I did field organizing in New York, Detroit, and Philadelphia, before going to the national office in Washington, D.C., to become the campaign's national rainbow coordinator.

This book began as an attempt to understand the experience I had lived through and its implications for the future of race relations in American political life. It seemed to me that what I had experienced was never adequately conveyed by the news media, and was either dismissed or trivialized by most mainstream political analysts, with a few notable exceptions. Indeed, the Jackson phenomenon was treated, for the most part, as a kind of exotic sideshow, apart from the main business of governing the country, and as soon as it lost its appeal as entertainment, it was quickly forgotten.

Being part of a campaign that sought national power on behalf of a constituency that had never really been represented in the halls of Congress or the White House left an indelible impression on me. Those of us on the national staff were forced, by the nature of the campaign, to deal at the very highest and lowest levels of power and status in our society at the same time. It was a wrenching and illuminating experience.

To be with Jackson, for example, as he spoke before a national television audience parrying statistics and projecting national policies with Walter Mondale and Gary Hart, having just left a slum project in Harlem, was an experience of cultural dissonance to which few have the privilege of being exposed. That housing project was not simply a bit of "local color"—a backdrop for a "photo opportunity"—but home to Jackson's aunt. Such projects across the country are where so many of the potential "American electorate" are forced to raise children, make love, and face death. I knew something of the courage and suffering contained in those ugly brick buildings with their chain-link fences, for I had lived for almost ten years during the 1960s in a contiguous neighborhood—East Harlem—and for several years after that was professionally involved with groups of poor people who were struggling for social justice and human dignity in many different kinds of slums: in the rural Mississippi Delta, on Indian reservations in the Southwest, in decaying industrial cities in the Northeast and Midwest. Thus, I think I was able to grasp at least some of the profundity of Jackson's oft-used slogan "From the outhouse to the White House, our time has come!" and to understand the aspirations of those he referred to as the "rejected stones."

If not before the campaign, then certainly during it, we came into human contact with more of those rejected stones. They are, in fact, the great majority of the American people—disenfranchised and alienated from a system that gives them *Dallas* and *Dynasty* instead of political participation, dope and prisons instead of jobs, and foreign "enemies" instead of a genuine education about our world.

The Jackson campaign gave us an unprecedented opportunity to get in touch with *the people,* that faceless creature the left is fond of invoking but about whom we really know so little. *The people* turned out to be a rich and wonderfully diverse array of folks who fed and housed us, provided us with lists and typewriters, staffed telephone banks, walked and knocked from door to door, and generally poured themselves out for a candidate they could finally believe in.

Among *the people* was Toni, a waitress in Portsmouth, New Hampshire, an ex-alcoholic and mental patient who, while recovering from surgery, put me up in her tiny two-room apartment beside her gerbils and her poster of Miss Piggy. Toni cooked marvelous pots of goulash for the Jackson volunteers, and if she had been offered the opportunity, would have gone on the road as the campaign cook. Then there was Michael, a slight, goateed Vietnam vet who ran a small typing service. Michael found himself the proud typist of the presidential candidate's speeches, dashing from one town to the next all over New Hampshire pounding them out on his little portable, sometimes with only half an hour to spare.

The people included Beverly, a Shaman Pee Mee of the Mother Earth Indian Church, and her husband, Win, an Ichabod Crane of a man, who spent almost every day volunteering in the Manchester, New Hampshire, campaign office, as well as Laura, a San Antonio delegate, whose high, honey-colored cheekbones reveal her Indian ancestry. A quiet but tough fighter for the rights of Central American refugees and a conductor on the modern "underground railroad," Laura knows what it is like to be a stranger in a strange land. As a child she had picked fruit and vegetables in the fields of southern California. *The people* also included Gwen, a Jackson delegate from Alabama, who was nurtured in the youth wing of the civil rights movement. At forty she has lost none of the fierce loyalty to the people as she knows them, the commitment to grassroots democracy, or the passion for political analysis that characterized the Student Nonviolent Coordinating Committee (SNCC) militants of the 1960s; and she is as hard on black political leaders who violate democratic principles as she was on the white sheriffs who confronted her with guns and firehoses in an earlier era.

The category embraced Arnette, a single mother living on disability, who understood the deep passion of the locked-out for a life of purpose and participation, and used the Jackson campaign as an opportunity to pass on the political skills and knowledge she had acquired in other campaigns. It included Steve, a young white construction worker who held the first political meeting he has ever held in his home for Jackson, because, as he put it,

"Jackson is the only one talking about human dignity and respect. That's what we don't have in this society, just plain respect!"

In spite of the trivialization our efforts met with from the mainstream press and political community—and even from parts of the left—those of us who worked in the Jackson campaign believe we were involved in an event of momentous significance. People poured their lives and resources into the campaign in a manner that can only be described as heroic. Some gave up jobs, lost jobs, were estranged or separated from families for months. For many, the campaign was a labor of love, a work of inestimable sympathy, undertaken to save a dying patient—American democracy, American idealism, even the American Constitution.

Having lived with the Jackson campaign for over two years, I am convinced that we were not in error. The Jackson campaign stands as a pivotal point in a longer term realignment of power that has the most profound consequences for the future, not only of American race relations, but of human survival. I have tried to shed some light on the nature of the contending forces that now vie for political power by using the Jackson campaign of 1984 as a kind of laser beam that gathers the inchoate streams of consciousness and experience of the last quarter century of American social history and concentrates them on the question: "What is to be done?"

Since this book is the outgrowth of twenty years of involvement in the movements for social change which it describes, the people who have contributed to it are legion, and I can name only a very few. I owe a very special debt of gratitude to Renny Golden, who has been a steady goad and inspiration over the years to our mutual struggle to wed reflection to action, poetry and spirituality to politics. Without her, this book could not have been written. Jim Dunn, Anne Braden, Ron Chisom, Arnett Lewis, Arthur Kinoy, and Dave Dellinger have been long-time political mentors. They have provided me with role models of courage and commitment to justice and truth, and their conversations have enabled me to think through many of the contradictions in the struggle to forge a progressive majority that this book seeks to describe.

Of the many individuals who assisted me in this particular project, I want to single out Colin Greer, Cornel West, Bill Tabb, and Tony Scott, who pointed me to valuable theoretical material and who provided me with constructive criticism of the entire manuscript. Enriqueta Vasquez critiqued parts of the sections on Chicanos and Native Americans, Suzanne Ross, Jay Bender, and Bill Howard provided me with many valuable insights into the black-Jewish controversy, and Abdeen Jabara with difficult-to-find information on the history and culture of Arab Americans. Lyle Wing opened doors in the Asian American and wider "rainbow" community in the San Francisco Bay area. The many conversations I have had with Merle Hansen, Darrell Ringer, and Carolyn Kazdin on the farm crisis have been invaluable in enabling me to understand the farm movement. In discussing the role of racism and the "white question," I have been helped tremendously by conversations with Anne Braden, Connie Hogarth, Art Kamell, Barry Weisberg, Arthur Kinoy, Ginger Rhodes, Mary Summers, Jim Dunn, Tom Deluca, Tony Watkins, Dave Dellinger, Barry Commoner, and Gwen Patton. Many conversations with Rev. Bill Howard and Rev. C. T. Vivian have been helpful in developing my understanding of Afro-American culture, the role of the black church, and the conflict between charismatic leadership and the need for organization. Stewart Meacham and Ellen David-Friedman were especially helpful in interpreting the Vermont story for me. Arnett Holloway gave me many hours of rich case study material on the situation in Seattle, and Gwen Patton was invaluable in opening doors in Alabama. Armando Gutierrez, Baldemar Valesquez, and Nellie and Robert Marrero were helpful with the sections on Latinos, as was Bill Means with material on Native American organizing, Steve Kirschbaum on labor, and Andy Humm on lesbians and gays.

Of the many "rainbow" people whom I met and interviewed in preparation for this book, I want to especially thank those who not only provided me with information and access to other interviewees but who housed, fed, and transported me. Since this book was written without large grants, I could not have done the work without the generosity of such people as Gwen Patton and Lynn and Scott Douglas in Alabama, Mary Dunn in Kentucky, Hugh White and Mary White in Detroit, Arnett Holloway and Mary Washington in Seattle, Dan Siegel in San Francisco, Mary Summers in Cleveland, Kit Andrews and Tom Smith in Vermont, Willie and Ann Ludlow in Oberlin, Ohio. A special thanks goes to the folks at Arrupe House, especially Father Bill Davis, who provided me with bed and board during the Jackson campaign and on my several subsequent jaunts to Washington, D.C.

Of the many wonderful folks with whom I worked on the Jackson campaign staff, I want to especially single out for their contribution to my understanding of the nature of the beast we were dealing with: Jack O'Dell, Acie Byrd, Rev. C. T. Vivian, Carolyn Kazdin, Anna Gyorgy, Mary Summers, John Saxton, Barbara Williams-Skinner, Lisa Levine, Maxine Greene, Albert Mokhiber, Armando Gutierrez, Jim Zogby, Rev. Willie Barrow, Donna Brazile, Lisa Levine, Felipe Braudy, Anita Bonds, Frank Watkins, Judy Howell, and Thomas Atkins. To Mary Summers and Peter Rider, who got me started in New Hampshire, and from whom I learned how to appeal to "the people," a special thanks.

Several people not only talked to me about their involvement in the Jackson campaign, but provided me with extensive oral histories that I had hoped to use in the book. Regrettably, I had too much material, and those stories had to be left out. However, the rich detail and insights they provided were critical to my ability to place the Jackson campaign in its historical context. To Laura Sanchez, Gwen Patton, Rev. Herbert Daughtry, Terry Williams, Jay Bender, Eddie Wong, Abdeen Jabara, and Anne Braden, go thanks for sharing their exemplary lives and for such luminous material on what life is like in the "Other America."

Several people provided me with the physical help so necessary to undertake a major writing project. Foremost among these are my husband, John, and daughters Jennifer and Megan, who put up with my long absences from home both during the campaign itself and while I was interviewing for and writing the book. My mother, Freda Dreany, provided me with a quiet place to work on the manuscript. Without her loving attention to my daily needs— including the need to get away from the material at intervals—the book would never have been written.

The Staffs of the Joint Center for Political Studies and the Southwest Voter Education Project provided me with much useful material on black and Hispanic voting and demographic patterns.

Karen Judd, my editor at Monthly Review Press, was a supportive and perceptive critic who saw the possibilities in what was at first a jumble of raw impressions and who worked patiently with me through several different drafts. To the other folks at Monthly

Review who allowed me to work on revisions amid the clutter of their own workspaces, and to Lenore Hogan and my niece, Elisa Shokoff, who helped with the early transcription of tapes, go much gratitude.

Carol and Ping Ferry, Karen Judd, Lee Hochberg, Consuelo Urquiza, Joyce Hamlin, Betty Thompson, and Tyrone Pitts were variously involved in helping me to secure the small grants needed to get this project off the ground.

To Jesse Jackson, who dared to call the Rainbow Coalition into existence, and who provided many people such as myself with the opportunity to be involved in one of life's great political dramas, goes the final accolade.

Introduction

1984. It was the best of times; it was the worst of times. It was the age of soaring black truth; it was the age of great white lies. It was the season of multicolored quilts and rainbows; it was the season of white male arrogance. It was the epoch of revolutionary hope; it was the belligerence of dying empires. It was Simpson-Mazzoli; it was sanctuary. We were heading for Armageddon; we were building a just society in a peaceful world. In short, the period was so like the present period, that some of its noisiest authorities insisted on its being received, for good or evil, in the superlative degree of comparison only.

—after Charles Dickens

In 1984 Jesse Jackson electrified the nation by becoming the first black person to make it to the run-off in the Democratic presidential primary sweepstakes. Theodore White, chronicler of traditional presidential races, asserted: "Winds are blowing . . . that have not stirred American politics in just this way in a half-century."[1] Another mainstream political analyst, Walter Dean Burnham, suggested that "Jesse Jackson represents something quite new in mainstream politics—something that seems in all probability to reflect an irreversible change with imponderable consequences for the future."[2]

In fact, there were really only two campaigns for the presidency in 1984—the Reagan campaign and the Jackson campaign, each representing distinctly oppositional constituencies, values, and political programs. The Hart and Mondale campaigns were attempts to shore up a liberalism that had become dysfunctional to American capitalism and the continued dominance of the world by the United States. Neither of these candidates had either a program or a vision that could seriously challenge Reagan's. The Jackson campaign, on the other hand, represented the emergence of a new vision of American national identity and purpose arising from sectors of the population that had hardly been represented in national politics in previous eras.

The Jackson campaign brought together into the debate over national policy several underground streams in American political life. Some of these had only recently come to political subjectivity, a dynamic his campaign consolidated. Others had had long histories of activism—but until 1984 they had to operate largely outside the arena of electoral politics, contending for power in street demonstrations, through intermittent civil disobedience campaigns and community organizing tactics, in solidarity work with third world liberation movements, and in single-issue lobbying for legislative change. Occasionally some of these voices surfaced in third-party electoral campaigns, but rarely after the decline of the Socialist party following World War I were these campaigns able to project a platform to a mass audience.

Until the Jackson campaign, political activity conducted by the groups that make up the Rainbow Coalition took place, for the most part, in separate ethnocultural, geographic, and class groupings. With Jackson's call for the locked-out to come together, these barriers were transcended and a remarkable consensus developed around a coherent set of policy objectives that, if met, could have drastically altered the course of history.

That the Jackson campaign did not alter history in the space of eight months is testimony not to the futility of its effort but to the newness of its task, the inexperience of its organizers, the contradictions that exist within and between the movements he attempted to unite, and to the enormously powerful interests it was up against.

Jackson's genius lay in linking nonelectoral forms of political mobilization and protest with traditional electoral politics, and in sensing those areas of convergence that could unite the interests of disparate groups around a common program. Although embryonic and fragile, the Rainbow Coalition represents the construction of a new kind of politics appropriate to the history, cultural realities, and changing socioeconomic context of late twentieth-century America.

Jack O'Dell, one of the strategists of the Rainbow Coalition, sees the Jackson campaign of 1984 as a pivotal point in a longer term transference of power from the military-industrial complex to the majority of the people, whose needs and desires are not now represented in the national government. He predicts the eventual replacement of the current Democratic party by the "progressive trend" represented in the Rainbow Coalition.

To understand the potential and the limitations of such a scenario, it is necessary to place the Jackson campaign in its immediate historical context. Chapter 1 locates the fountainhead of the Rainbow Coalition's ideology in the eruption of black self-organization during the late 1950s and early 1960s. The civil rights and black power movements exploded several dominant assumptions about the nature of American society, thus challenging the cultural hegemony of the white ruling elite and causing everyone else in the society to redefine their relationship to the centers of power, creating a groundswell of support for radical democratic participation in every area of institutional life.

However, the movements of the 1960s were not able to make the transition from cultural critique to political power. They had neither a body of organic leaders with experience in governing nor the kind of mutual working relationship that would have enabled them to overcome the racism and mistrust that have always diverted those who have attempted to organize for power from below.

As a result, the white ruling elite was able to crush this incipient revolutionary movement, and to coopt and manipulate the themes of race and ethnicity it elicited. Chapter 2 traces the reassertion of cultural and political control inaugurated by the neoconservative intellectuals, and its effect on the social movements of the 1970s. This history is important not only because it helps to explain the difficulty Jackson had in appealing to whites, but because it sheds light on the reaction of the Republican and Democratic establishments to the Jackson campaign of 1984, and is predictive of what can happen to subsequent attempts to carry the policy objectives of that campaign into the future.

By 1984, blacks had partially overcome one of the impediments to political power—the lack of leaders with experience in governing—but the racial and class cleavages that dominated the politics of the 1970s would continue to haunt the attempt to forge a multiracial coalition that could contend for power on behalf of the majority of the American people. Chapter 3 traces the emergence of the "rainbow" concept as a progressive response to the reactionary uses of race and ethnicity by the right. This chapter examines the dynamics within the black political community, within broad left forces, and in local electoral politics that enabled the black community to take the leadership in a bold new move to bring together the disparate elements of a potential progressive electoral bloc.

Starting late in the primary race, with no money for major media advertisements, with a staff inexperienced in running a national presidential campaign, and with no endorsements from any major white politician, the Jackson campaign registered some 2 million new voters, beat out four competitors, garnered between 3.5 and 4 million votes, won sixty-one congressional districts, three states, and the District of Columbia, and nearly every major urban center in the South, Northeast, and Midwest. Chapter 4 tells the story of the remarkable voter mobilization that was patched together, and the organization that made it work. It describes the source of its success and weaknesses and the lessons to be learned for future campaigns.

The greatest contribution of the Jackson campaign was the cultural coherence and unity it forged between differing sectors of the disenfranchised. Chapter 5 traces the process through which this happened. It locates its motive force in the "black perspective" from which the campaign was waged—a perspective derived from the particular experience of African Americans as they have struggled for human dignity in a country that has consistently denied them recognition and power. This chapter demonstrates that although it is a black perspective, more and more of the American people are coming to similar insights.

The process of soliciting the votes of the disenfranchised from a position of powerlessness—a situation in which there was nothing concrete to offer them, except hope—was a complicated one, requiring an enormous amount of cultural sensitivity, a good sense of timing, and just plain nerve. Chapters 6 and 7 examine the experience of campaign leaders who attempted to appeal to and mobilize the various "bows" in the Rainbow Coalition. The problems organizers encountered raise new issues for political activists, and an analysis of their experiences—their successes and failures—provides a valuable laboratory from which to assess future organizing.

The Jackson candidacy started out as a campaign to gain greater influence for blacks and other disenfranchised groups within the Democratic party, but as it evolved it found it had to challenge the very premises on which that party was based: white supremacy and upper-class control. The Jackson campaign became, then, not a movement to get into the "system," but a movement to change the system, to alter the fundamental assumptions on which the two-party system is based. Chapters 7 and 8 examine the Jackson campaign's challenge not only to the racially exclusionary mechanisms of the two-party system, but to the mechanisms that preserve it as a tool of the most powerful financial interests in the country. Chapter 7 looks at the campaign's challenge to the mostly unstated rules of political discourse that govern the issues the American public will be allowed to debate and vote on. It demonstrates that Jackson was able to penetrate those rules to the extent of presenting an alternative policy framework to the American public, but it also demonstrates the limitations on the ability of the campaign to penetrate the final system of controls and thus to be a real choice for American voters. Chapter 9 analyzes the Jackson campaign's challenge to the rules that guard against mass participation in the electoral process: party rules and voting impediments. It demonstrates that Jackson's call for the implementation of one person, one vote is a constitutional right that is violated time and time again—in fact, it may be implicit in the very structure of the two-party system.

In being black-led, the Jackson campaign exposed more fully than any movement in recent years the function of cultural and institutional racism in preserving class rule. Chapter 10 looks at the uses of racism by the mass media to divert and confuse the white electorate and thus, in this case, to limit their vote for the

Jackson campaign, as well as the response of the white Democratic party elite to the Jackson phenomenon. The result is further de-alignment from the old New Deal coalition and a search on the part of both party elites and the rank and file for other alternatives. This chapter also gives critical examination to the prevalent assumption among media and political elites that the Jackson phenomenon is responsible for a "white backlash" against the Democratic party. It examines the actual responses of the white electorate to the Jackson campaign as they were encountered by white organizers, and argues that although racism is a continuing problem with deep roots in American culture, it need not be an insurmountable one in the forging of a new multiracial electoral bloc.

Other attempts in American history to present an electoral challenge to racial and class dominance have met with only partial success, and in most cases with failure. Is the Rainbow Coalition of 1984 only a passing phenomenon? Or does it signal a new opening in American political life that was not present in earlier periods of our history? Chapter 11 examines the prospects for building an organized rainbow coalition that can continue to contend for power at the local, state, and national levels. It traces the faltering attempts to capitalize on the Jackson campaign's momentum between 1984 and April 1986, when the first national convention of the Rainbow Coalition was convened, and looks at three successful state organizing efforts—In Alabama, Vermont, and Washington State—that shed light on where rainbow politics are going and at the obstacles to the achievement of its goals. As of this writing, the National Rainbow Coalition as a functioning electoral bloc that can achieve real power for a platform of jobs, peace, and justice remains a dream in the minds of fools, saints and prophets. But as prophets of an earlier age put it, "without a vision, the people perish."

From Melting Pot to Boiling Cauldron: The 1960s Revisited

> There is a war going on and a transformation taking place. That war is not simply the contest between the socialist camp and the capitalist camp over which political/economic/social arrangement will enjoy hegemony in the world, nor is it simply the battle over turf and resources. Truth is one of the issues in this war. The truth, for example, about inherent human nature, about our potential, our agenda as earth people, our destiny.[1]
> —Toni Cade Bambara

The Jackson campaign had its roots in the social movements of the 1960s, which, more than any previous reform movements, began collectively to expose the undergirding institutions and myths through which the American ruling class maintains its power. Like Jesse Jackson himself, who came up in the civil rights movement, almost all of the top leadership of the Jackson campaign received their political education either in that or one of the other movements generated by it—the black power movement, the feminist movement, the anti-Vietnam war movement, the Chicano movement, the Native American movement, and various others. Through these movements, new interpretations of both the class stratification of American society and its racial, gender, and cultural arrangements were given a public platform and began to gain popular legitimacy.

In addition, the social movements of the 1960s raised fundamental questions about the role and legitimacy of government, the structure and function of the two-party system, and the relationship of the United States to the rest of the world. They provided new lenses through which to assess U.S. history, particularly the assumption that the United States had become a fairly effective "melting pot" through which diverse national groups were assimilated into the mainstream and individuals were allowed to rise to their potential.

The social movements of the 1960s were what the Italian Marxist Antonio Gramsci has called "organic" phenomena, which revealed the incurable contradictions of the U. S. political economy in a way never quite seen before on such a mass scale. In Gramsci's theory of social change, organic phenomena are events or movements of submerged classes that begin to break down the dominant world view—the system of values, attitudes, ideas, beliefs, and norms through which the majority are socialized to give their consent to the current political/economic system. Organic movements and events occur "underneath the surface" of formal institutions—in this case, outside the formal institutions of liberal capitalism; and they occur in a very uneven way, suffering setbacks as the bourgeois state moves to thwart the loss of its hegemony and then emerging again in a new form.[2]

Earlier labor struggles had revealed the essential class relations of U.S. society, but socialist and communist movements tended to focus exclusively on the capital-labor relation, somewhat obscuring the ways in which the system uses racism and sexism at home, and the manipulation of uneven levels of development abroad, to keep the working class divided against itself and the majority of whites allied with the governing classes. Class conflict, the engine of earlier social insurgencies, had by the 1960s somewhat lost its political currency. The prosperity made possible by the emergence of the United States from World War II as the dominant world power, coupled with the racial and sexual division of labor, served to obscure from the consciousness of the white male working class its essential subservience to capital. In 1968 historian John Lukacs observed that not only had "class" as a historical category become problematic, but that "we may be moving into an era of a certain classlessness, at least in the traditional sense of the word."[3] Following Weber, Lukacs saw status rather than contract as the emerging category of social discrimination. The consciously appropriated social status accorded to race, ethnicity, and gender, he argued, was the relevant identity through which various sectors of the American population began to reevaluate their relationship to the dominant institutions and mythologies.

The Jackson campaign updated the critiques of American society and the suggestions for its reorganization that had emerged during the 1960s and attempted to translate them into a coherent political platform and electoral strategy that could mobilize the majority of the potential American electorate—those who had never before engaged in electoral politics or who had become steadily alienated from the political process throughout the 1960s and 1970s. To understand the nature of the Jackson campaign's bid for power, it is necessary to review the history of the social movements of the 1960s in terms of the ideology they critiqued and the alternative world views they began to articulate.

This chapter does not pretend to be a definitive history of the 1960s. It surveys the broad changes in consciousness initiated by the black insurgency, which, when internalized and adapted by other groups, added up to a loosening of the hegemony exercised by the dominant ideology over the hearts and minds of the American public. The impact of this ideological break is far more serious than most historians—even those of the left—have credited it with being. The ruling elite, however, understood its implications clearly and in the 1970s moved to curtail its potential for radically overturning the existing system.

The Ideological Context for Insurgency

The movements of the 1960s were reflections of a worldwide phenomenon, called by Latin American liberation theologians the era of the "eruption of the poor" into history. Population strata that had been submerged by the colonial and neocolonial policies of the various European empires were becoming political subjects. Everywhere in the decaying colonial world the oppressed and exploited classes were throwing off the yoke of centuries of submission or were rebelling against the new forms of neocolonialism imposed on their societies by late monopoly capitalism. The rebellions were characterized not only by class factors, but by racial and cultural ones as well.

The social revolution that occurred in the United States during the 1960s was spearheaded by sectors of the population that had been politically submerged and economically marginalized—treated, that is, as nonsubjects within the great liberal myth of American identity and progress that had served as official ideology ever since the founding of the country. Although the revolt in the United States was sparked by groups that had been historically oppressed on the basis of race, class, and culture, it was eventually taken up by other groups—white women, white college students—who could not be characterized as "poor," but who sensed that their political subjectivity had been suppressed by the ruling myths and institutional arrangements of American society.

The social movements of the 1960s challenged three dominant and interlocking mythologies that had grown up to define America's origins and its destiny: the myth of America as the Promised Land, the myth of the melting pot, and the myth of government as the mediator among equally competing interests.

From the time of the first colonies, this country has been guided by a myth of origin that derives its symbolic power from the biblical story of Israel's Exodus from Egypt and its entry into the promised land of Canaan. In the Puritan translation of this story, Anglo-Saxons, fleeing the repression of Europe (Egypt), became the "New Israel," a people "chosen by God" bearing a "manifest destiny" to populate and civilize the New World. America itself is a "city set upon a hill," a demonstration model of the power of freedom and democracy, which is to be emulated by others. In his inauguration address of 1980, Ronald Reagan evoked the still useful power of this imagery, first enunciated by Governor John Winthrop of the Massachusetts Bay Colony three hundred years earlier.

Of course, the promised land "discovered" by the European settlers was already inhabited by peoples who had to be killed in order to make room for the "chosen people"; and the shining city on a hill created by American industrialism could be built only on the backs of Africans who served as chattel labor in the initial accumulation of capital. From the very beginning, the ideology rested on a gigantic lie, but as long as the real history of the settling of the Americas could be kept submerged and witnesses to its atrocities silenced through political disempowerment, every succeeding generation of Americans would continue to believe in the mythology. As William Appleman Williams put it, empire had become a way of life.[4]

To be sure, the governing class was always more candid within its own circles than it was with the public. Sam Houston, one of the founders of Texas, admitted that he and his cronies were nothing more than pirates when they staged a phony "declaration of independence" from Mexico in order to provoke a confrontation that resulted in taking the territory for the United States.[5] In 1948, George Kennan, then head of the State Department's Policy Planning Staff and considered by some one of the liberals in government, wrote in an internal memorandum:

> We have about 50 percent of the world's wealth, but only 6.3 percent of its population. In this situation, we cannot fail to be the object of envy and resentment. Our real test in the coming period is to devise a pattern of relationships which will permit us to maintain this position of disparity. We need not deceive ourselves that we can afford today the luxury of altruism and world benefaction . . . unreal objectives such as human rights, the raising of living standards and democratization. The day is not far off when we are going to have to deal in straight power concepts. The less we are hampered by idealistic slogans, the better.[6]

Such a cynical power-politics approach to both domestic and foreign policy has always characterized the American establishment, but it would be several decades (the 1980s, to be exact) before Kennan's prescription for abandoning any pretense to a belief in human rights would become operative on the public level.

Corollary to America as the guardian of liberty and democracy in the dominant mythology was the image of America as the land of opportunity, a place where anyone can make it if he or she only works hard enough, and of America as a "great melting pot," in which all the cultures melted down and came out—at least within a generation or two—as the typical American: white, usually male, Anglo-Saxon, Protestant.

From around 1910 until the 1960s, melting-pot theorists posited that each new ethnic group to enter the United States went through a cycle of "contact," "accommodation," and eventually "assimilation" into the mainstream of Anglo-American culture. Sociologists of the melting-pot school never meant that immigrant groups were totally assimilated, but there was at least a superficial uniformity that made differences in opinion, sentiment, and belief of secondary importance.[7] Nevertheless, it was assumed that each of the groups to enter American society, by dint of hard work and ethnic solidarity, had moved up out of the ghetto in which it had begun. Although there was class stratification, it could be argued that it was permeable. Such an analysis could not deal with the contradiction that blacks, who had been in the country longer than most of the other immigrant groups, had not assimilated, while Italians, Poles, Jews, Slavs, Irish, and Germans apparently had. So the liberal sociologists of the melting-pot school attempted to explain this anomaly by saying that it was the backwardness of southern attitudes toward blacks—the continuing legacy of slavery—that kept them inferior in the South, coupled with the rather late migration of blacks to northern cities that caused them to fall so far behind the European immigrants. Given time, such attitudes would soften and blacks would then be able to lift themselves up by their own bootstraps, as every other immigrant group had done. Oscar Handlin, one of the most prominent liberal historians of ethnicity, illustrates this tendency. He wrote in 1957:

> The United States has by no means realized the utopia of total equality. Evidence of discrimination still forms blemishes upon its life. But the pattern has been irreparably shattered. . . . The Negroes offer the most instructive example. North and South, they still suffer from injustices and still have legitimate grievances. But the integrity of the patterns of segregation has decisively been broken, and it is a matter of time before equality of status and opportunity is within reach.[8]

In the discipline of political science, the corollary to the melting-pot theory of social assimilation is the pluralist model of institutionalized political power. The central tenet of pluralist politics is that political power in the United States is more or less evenly allocated among blocs of competing voluntary associations or interest groups. The implication is that while groups may vary in the amount of power they wield, no one group exercises sufficient power to bar others from entrance into the political arena.[9]

The government's role is to mediate these competing centers of power, which work out their differences in a rational way through negotiation, compromise, and coalition-building, thus averting the need to resort to extra-parliamentary, violent, or disruptive means of making one's voice heard. Interest groups are mediators between the individual citizen and the government, translating the individual's concerns into a consensus, which then becomes part of the raw material from which political parties manufacture their policies.

Interest-group pluralism was an elite rationale for the political situation that arose with the emergence of corporate power and its ability to use channels other than the political parties to influence government on its behalf. Interest-group pluralism, which began to achieve salience in the 1930s and accelerated during the 1960s as an elite response to the insurgencies from below, was an admission that the structuring of citizen power through political parties had already become obsolete. It served, and still serves, to obscure the real influence of economic power over the U.S. political system by pretending that ordinary people are free to enter into associations that can actually wield power through a kind of self-correcting political "invisible hand," which mediates conflicting interests to everyone's benefit. Pluralist theory is comparable to laissez-faire economics (on which it appears to be modeled) in the extent to which it mystifies the reality of imperfect competition in the political marketplace.[10]

The Liberal Consensus

The dominant liberal consensus to which the social insurgencies of the 1960s reacted held that American society was becoming progressively more tolerant and that its institutional arrangements were basically benign. If some groups remained locked-out or disenfranchised, discriminated against, or economically inferior, it was because of lingering (individual) racial bias in the American population or friction between ethnic groups that was assumed to be "natural" when more than one group was competing for power within the same locality. Such disagreements could be worked out through compromise and negotiation. Women's inferior economic and political status was entirely overlooked, since women, by virtue of their biology, were not supposed to compete in the political or economic arena.

The melting-pot theory effectively masked the racial, gender, and class stratifications that were endemic to American capitalism, even hiding the evidence that white immigrant groups had not fared as well as the prevailing mythology had led them to believe. Researchers for the Kerner Commission (the President's National Advisory Commission on Civil Disorders) discovered this fact for themselves as they attempted to find some explanation for the apparent anomaly of the outbreak of urban rebellions in hundreds of cities across the country in 1967.[11]

While blacks, in melting-pot theory, were sometimes treated as another, if late-maturing, "immigrant group," for the most part the sociology of ethnicity presented the demographic history of the white immigrant groups that had come to the country before immigration restrictions were imposed in about 1920.[12] Native Americans were an invisible minority in American cities and a special category on hidden-away reservations to be dealt with through a peculiar arm of the government known as the Bureau of Indian Affairs. Mexican Americans and Puerto Ricans were rarely, if ever, noticed before the 1960s, and if so, were handled as if they were foreigners, even though Mexican Americans had been living on U.S. soil long before the first European settlers—the supposedly "real Americans"—came to the continent.

The pluralist model of democratic government ignored the legalized disenfranchisement of southern blacks, Mexican Americans, and American Indians as well as the condition of women as an economically dependent (on individual men) and politically marginalized caste. As long as women themselves failed to assert a politicized group identity, the pluralist model could continue to ignore the ways in which the biology-as-destiny theory of women's "place" served to ameliorate and contain the inevitable contradictions of capitalist economic crisis.

The Black Liberation Movement

Given the essential role of chattel slavery in the initial accumulation of capital in the Western world, and the pivotal role played by the color line in keeping the American working class historically divided and politically impotent, any political insurgency among the black masses was likely, if carried to its logical conclusion, to call into question the fundamental premises of the

American enterprise. Political journalist Andrew Kopkind has observed:

> Black power is an engine that drives the great vehicles of social change in America. The Civil War and the civil rights movement, slave revolts and student sit-ins, Marcus Garvey's separatism and Malcolm X's nationalism; black people's epic struggle for equality and quest for identity create both the pretext and the context for national upheaval and transformation. It is a radical dynamic that pertains to America's peculiar racial history, and in each generation it produces unique politics and unexpected leaders.[13]

The emergence of African Americans as political subjects during the late 1950s and early 1960s set into motion the greatest social upheaval since the demonstrations by unemployed workers and the industrial strikes of the Great Depression. Initially focused on getting rid of Jim Crow segregation, the civil rights movement, by the end of the 1960s, had generated a massive disaffection with the ruling institutions and guiding mythologies of the U.S. state, not only among black people, but among the majority of middle-class whites.

The civil rights movement began to tear away the view that had hidden America's systemic racism behind the facade of legality, the "peculiarities of the South," or the alleged innate inferiority and underdevelopment of the African-American people. In contrast to the elite assumption that the civil rights movement was simply an attempt to integrate blacks into the mainstream, C. T. Vivian, one of its leaders and later the religious coordinator for the Jesse Jackson presidential campaign, offers a different view:

> We could see that the condition of the Black masses had to be changed, that the values of the Black middle class had to be changed, and that *the direction of the entire nation had to be changed*. And we could see that in order to finally accomplish these things we would have to find a new method of social action—a method that would cement our people together and generate the force to make them effective.[14]

In provoking confrontation between violent, hate-filled representatives of southern state authority and nonviolent blacks demonstrating for rights already guaranteed by the Constitution, the civil rights movement did more than any other movement in recent history to expose the gap between America's image of itself and the reality. The impact of this cognitive dissonance on the black community was profound. As Vivian explained, civil rights leaders began with the same assumptions about the basic nature of American society that most whites had:

> We assumed that integration was the model for our success. We assumed that the barriers of segregation would be broken when enough good men saw the justice of our cause. We assumed that we were dealing with an open, democratic, and Christian nation, a nation which *had*, and would, implement the solutions to our condition. . . . But in our action we proved each of these pronouncements false.[15]

What civil rights workers learned was that every institution in America is permeated by racism, that those who hold most of the power in this society want it that way, and that no power is ever given up on the basis of mere moral appeals to the goodwill of the nation's leaders, but must be wrested from them through organized concentrations of counter-power.

The mythology surrounding the nation's formal commitment to representative democracy was especially exposed by those who participated in the attempt by the Mississippi Freedom Democratic party (MFDP) to unseat the all-white Mississippi regular delegation at the Democratic National Convention in 1964. The MFDP delegates thought they were acting on the very best principles embodied in the Constitution and in the Democratic party's rules. They had followed all the rules, had selected a biracial delegation, and were pledged to support the Democratic party's nominees and platform, which the all-white regulars refused to do. This should have guaranteed the seating of their delegation. The morality and justice of their cause was clear; many of them had been beaten and jailed and knew others who had died to exercise the right of franchise. They learned, however, that justice and representation were not what the Democratic party system was all about. Confronted by the intransigence of the party regulars, their liberal and moderate civil rights allies failed to defend their own rules and instead negotiated a compromise, which offered the MFDP two seats. The MFDP delegation voted it down and left the convention hall.

Cleveland Sellers of the Student Nonviolent Coordinating Committee (SNCC) (who was later to be a southern field organizer for the Jackson campaign) recalled the MFDP struggle:

> Never again were we lulled into believing that our task was exposing injustices so that the "good" people of America could eliminate them. We left Atlantic City with the knowledge that the movement had turned into something else. After Atlantic City, our struggle was not for civil rights, but for liberation.

After quoting Sellers, historian Harvard Sitkoff observes that the treatment of the MFDP delegation "snapped the frayed ties that bound SNCC to liberal values, to integration and non-violence and to seeking solutions through the political process."[16]

As the civil rights movement went north, into the Polish and Italian ghettos of the urban working class, African Americans learned another crucial lesson: The melting pot was in fact a boiling cauldron. Vivian observed, "America is in fact a collection of lonely ethnic islands, and other exclusive divisions; the seeming unity as a nation is really the precarious balance of power through which each body protects its own hard-won privileges." In Chicago's Gage Park, Vivian recalls, "we learned how little the melting pot has really melted, even with whites."

> After one march, two priests from the area and several laymen joined some of us to discuss what had happened. One of the priests said that he had known there were problems but that he had not had any idea the problems were so bad. A layman smiled and said, "We knew it, Father." This man went on to explain that everyone in the area hated each other—Poles hated Letts, Serbs hated Italians, Germans hated Irish. . . . What happened in Gage Park is that all the hatred whites had for each other was redirected when Blacks showed up. . . . This kind of thing happened so often in the North that we learned to stop listening to what the politicians told us about brotherhood just before election time each year. We had found out what they told each other in those smoke-filled rooms. There, the question was posed without rhetorical dress. And the question was simple: how to get the Irish vote, how to get the Jewish vote, how to get the Italian vote.[17]

Vivian articulates the painful lessons civil rights leaders were learning about American society:

> Nothing seems harder for most Americans to grasp than the idea that all men are somehow created equal. Democracy in this sense has never fully penetrated the American conscience. And, in fact, a

nation which was largely built upon the institution of holding human beings as property could not be expected to come to this concept readily. . . . White America for the most part does not even seek democracy for itself.[18]

African Americans came to such conclusions only after taking the American Constitution at its word, a process the majority of whites did not have to engage in, since the relative privileges granted them by the racial caste system masked an understanding of their own lack of power within it. As blacks got the franchise in the South, but were then fired from their jobs, cut off from welfare, or had their mortgages foreclosed; as they won the right to eat in restaurants but could not afford to do so; as they were elected to office but were then gerrymandered out, played by the rules only to find that the rules were changed, won affirmative action but were the first fired when the recession hit, they learned that "democracy, like justice, was a privilege rather than a right."[19]

Most of the younger members of the civil rights movement— those who got their training through the Student Nonviolent Coordinating Committee or the Black Panthers—were even more outspoken in the denunciations of the race-biased capitalist system. Many, in their conception of themselves, had moved from being reformers to being "revolutionaries." James Forman, one of the leaders of SNCC, had by 1967 come to see that "racism, capitalism, and imperialism" were the "three enemies of black people." Forman's account of his movement years in *The Making of Black Revolutionaries* moves back and forth, at the end, between vituperative, impassioned visions of revolutionary justice being enacted by the black masses and his acknowledgment that revolution in the United States was not at all imminent, and that the struggle for basic justice and liberation would be a protracted one, involving much preliminary work in building disciplined organizations and disciplined minds.

> Armed with a correct ideology, pursuing all efforts to make sure that the black working class has power and gives direction to the revolutionary struggle, working to develop all forms of popular struggle as well as a network of unknown revolutionaries, preparing for the long-range armed struggle inside the United States, uniting all into a disciplined, centralized, mass party or organization—thus we will surely advance our struggle in the seventies. We will be carrying on the work of all the black sons and daughters who have died in every

corner of Africa and the Americas under the whiplash of racism, colonialism, capitalism, and imperialism. And we shall win without a doubt.[20]

At the end of their lives, both Martin Luther King and Malcolm X had come to an analysis of the root causes of black oppression in America that was little different from that of the younger militants in SNCC and the Black Panthers. King was raising basic questions about the economic and political system that governed the United States that were not lost on the guardians of that system. There is a widespread assumption throughout the black community and among many in the white left that it was precisely because King and Malcolm were moving toward a more radical critique of American capitalism and imperialism—King from the posture of nonviolent democratic reform and Malcolm from the posture of black nationalist separatism—that they were killed.

In an address to the Southern Christian Leadership Conference, King suggested the direction in which he was moving in 1967.

> I want to say to you . . . as we talk about "Where do we go from here" that we must honestly face the fact that the Movement must address itself to the question of restructuring the whole of American society. There are 40 million poor people here. And one day we must ask the question, "Why are there 40 million poor people in America?" And when you begin to ask that question you are raising questions about the economic system, about a broader distribution of wealth. When you ask that question, you begin to question the capitalistic economy. And I'm simply saying that more and more, we've got to begin to ask questions about the whole society. We are called upon to help the discouraged beggars in life's marketplace. But one day we must come to see that an edifice which produces beggars needs restructuring. It means that questions must be raised. You see, my friends, when you deal with this, you begin to ask the question, "Who owns the oil?" You begin to ask the question, "Who owns the iron ore?" You begin to ask the question, "Why is it that people have to pay water bills in a world that is two-thirds water?"[21]

From an early, admitted ignorance of economics, King was moving toward a radical critique of capitalism.[22] Many African-American leaders who jumped on the black power bandwagon when it looked as if militant nonviolence had run its course toward the end of the 1960s, viewed Martin Luther King as hopelessly outdated. In fact, as black liberation theologian James Cone has since observed, "Martin King was miles ahead of us . . . and it is ironic that many of us thought he was too conservative! The fact is that he was in many ways too radical, because he was moving toward an economic analysis, and some say even Marxism."[23]

King was also moving toward an anti-imperialist critique. In a 1967 book entitled *Where Do We Go from Here?* he wrote:

> In the days ahead we must not consider it unpatriotic to raise certain basic questions about our national character. We must begin to ask . . . "Why has our nation placed itself in the position of being God's military agent on earth, and intervened recklessly in Vietnam and the Dominican Republic? Why have we substituted the arrogant undertaking of policing the whole world for the high task of putting our own house in order?"[24]

In a speech delivered to a gathering of Clergy and Laymen Concerned About Vietnam at Riverside Church in New York City that same year, he asserted:

> These are revolutionary times. All over the globe men are revolting against old systems of exploitation and oppression, and out of the wombs of a frail world new systems of justice and equality are being born. The shirtless and barefoot people of the earth are rising up as never before. . . . We in the West must support these revolutions.[25]

The effect of the civil rights and black power movements on African Americans was to remove the ideological blinders, the emotional and physical restraints that had functioned collectively something like the character armor described by the psychoanalyst Wilhelm Reich. Such armor had enabled African Americans to adapt to a racist society, but at the cost of an integration of the individual and collective self.

The civil rights movement—in both its southern and northern manifestations—called people forth from the niches in which they were weathering life in a racist culture, investing them with a courage and determination they did not know they possessed. Middle-class college students gave up school and the promise of upward mobility to work in life-threatening situations in the Deep South, and in conditions that third world revolutionaries would easily recognize. Working-class church people in the Deep South literally walked out of church and into confrontations with state authorities. One story recalled by Vivian is of a woman who marched out of church one day in her Sunday best and walked until her high heels gave out on her. She then kicked off her shoes and continued marching for freedom in her stocking feet.[26] Bernice Reagon, one of the members of the Freedom Singers, recalled that the movement gave people a sense of power that they never had before: "There was a sense of confronting things that terrified you, like jail, police, walking in the street—you know, a whole lot of Black folks couldn't even walk in the street in those places in the south. So you were saying in some basic way, 'I will never again stay inside these boundaries.' "[27]

Reggie Schell, a participant in the Black Panther party, described the change that began to occur among ordinary workers and street blacks as they joined the party.

> I'm talking about a man who's been on the job for eight years. He's not satisfied with the wage scale. He's not satisfied with the relationship that the boss has with him and other people around him. But he just takes it and takes it and takes it, because it is essential that he bring home the bread and butter. Now these men . . . are in a constant state of turmoil with themselves; and the Black Panther Party, when it came out, existed as something that was totally opposed to that—kind of "you won't take advantage of us any more.". . . What I'm saying . . . is that people live in a dual world until they find something that they can really believe in. . . . I found a lot of people, young people, just breaking with their parents for the same thing, for the same reasons . . . coming in and just wanting to be a part of what they figured was a tremendous force that was going to change American society. . . . People just wanted a fundamental change. I don't know if it was so much at that point to change or revolutionize the whole society or just to begin to revolutionize their own self over, to make them free mentally.[28]

The breaking of such constraints unleashed a floodtide of cultural expression and redefinition, of historical recovery and social critique unprecedented in American history, except, perhaps, for the period preceding and just after the Civil War. All of this exposed the self-serving rationale of the arguments put forth by elite sociologists that black people were "culturally deprived." For the first time, African-American culture began to penetrate beyond the black ghetto in a way that was truly transformative of dominant white values and perspectives. Before, African-American culture had either been confined to the black community or coopted by the white entertainment industry as a kind of exotic fare; now the image of masses of black people on nightly television protesting nobly for constitutional rights, standing up to state authorities, negotiating with the highest authorities in the land, and soaring with an eloquence unknown in white culture began to change not only the black community's perception of itself, but white America's perception of blacks.

No longer could the ordinary black person be portrayed in the movies as a smiling mammy or a shuffling Steppin Fetchit. No longer could school texts ignore the contributions of the African-American people to the building of the nation. Moreover, the skeleton in America's closet—the brutal history of its "peculiar institution"—was brought out to be reevaluated by historians and represented in flesh and blood on the stage. I personally recall being electrified by the staging of Martin Duberman's play *In White America*. I realized that I had never been exposed to this kind of history before, and that recognition was a revelation that there might be other things that had been hidden from me by the very institutions that had taught me all there was to know about the world.

Black history courses began to assess not only the reality of slavery and the complex mythology that had kept the full internalization of this American holocaust from reaching the consciousness of the majority of Americans, but also the record of courage, of resistance, and of alternative visions of human community that had lain hidden within the culture of the enslaved ones. Historian Vincent Harding has pointed out that one of the most profound and significant uses of such history is "its services as an entrance to the non-white, non-Western world," a world that white America would sooner or later have to deal with, not only internally, but in its international relations.

> A nation that combines the American predilection towards violence, the American stockpile of weapons and the American lack of empathy for the earth's humiliated peoples is a dangerous nation. Perhaps it can begin another life by introducing itself to the invisible men in its midst, by seeking to know the quality of suffering and hurt and the rebellion they spawn. Such an introduction must include—if not begin with—the past.[29]

Like so many of the historic myths broken open by black history to reveal their essential function as legitimation for a cruel system of class rule and racial apartheid, the black cultural and black power movements overturned contemporary norms of sickness and health, beauty and ugliness, justice and injustice. People who had straightened their hair to look more like white people now began going "natural." "Negro"—a badge of shame—became "black and beautiful." The "dark continent" was discovered to be a source of rich cultures and colorful, competent peoples. As Frantz Fanon's *The Wretched of the Earth* was read by young militants and as the ghettos exploded in open rebellion, black rage stepped forth from behind smiling faces as a form of collective psychic healing. Toward the end of his life even Martin Luther King saw rage as a "constructive and creative force." He sought to harness this rage in his plans for a massive poor people's civil disobedience campaign, which would engage in ongoing, organized disruption of business-as-usual in Washington, D.C., and in other major cities across the country until the government moved aggressively to resolve poverty and unemployment, deteriorating housing conditions and poor education.[30]

The civil rights and black power movements broke down the mystique surrounding leadership, class, and established authority. Bernice Reagon recalled:

> There was something about the Civil Rights Movement where leaders where defined by their activism. Not by their age or their class, so within the Black community people began to look up to students, to ask students what they should do about x, y, and z, and follow the leadership of all sorts of different people based on what they perceived to be an integrity and commitment to struggle and stick with that particular struggle.[31]

The discovery that students could be community and national leaders would have a profound effect on young white people a little later in the decade.

One of the most important effects of the civil rights and black power movements on the black community was the new esteem the black movement and black leadership began to receive in the international community. With the emergence of new independent black-ruled states in Africa and the rise of Islamic nationalism in the Middle East, the international constellation of power began to change. In this new context, African Americans had an independent mirror with which to assess their place in the United States, their own heritage, achievements, and visions for the future. In this mirror they began to recognize themselves as an internal colony of the United States, having some of the same characteristics as the European colonies found in Africa, Asia, and the Pacific. As Western imperialism's colonies began to liberate themselves, African Americans came to a new sense of their own revolutionary potential and in turn were recognized as allies by the leaders of third world liberation movements and newly independent governments.

Although Martin Luther King was imprisoned, beaten, spied on, and threatened with physical harm in his own country, he became a hero in many other parts of the world. In 1957 he received an invitation from prime minister-elect Kwame Nkrumah to attend Ghana's national independence festivities. It was the first of several trips King would make abroad, honored in country after country as a visiting statesman, and finally receiving one of the most prestigious of all international honors, the Nobel Peace Prize.

Malcolm X had argued that black people should identify with the majority of the world's oppressed peoples and elevate the black freedom struggle to an international struggle for human rights. On his last trip to Africa, in July 1964, Malcolm began marshaling support for a plan to bring the American racial problem before the United Nations under the human rights provision of its charter.[32] Three years later, SNCC declared itself not a "civil rights" organization, but a "Human Rights Organization interested not only in human rights in the United States, but throughout the world."[33]

SNCC and the Black Panthers established relationships with liberation movements and leaders in many parts of the third world and began receiving invitations to speak at international forums. James Forman recalls the effect such meetings and invitations had on the self-image of these young revolutionaries. In the summer of 1967 he and another SNCC leader traveled to a UN-sponsored seminar on apartheid, racism and colonialism in Zambia.

There are moments in history when you realize you yourself are making it. Howard Moore and I felt that way as we stepped before the microphone to address the assembled delegates of the United Nations and the liberation fighters. We had no illusions about the United Nations, but at the same time, there were delegates and liberation fighters around the very large rectangular table who were going to hear and to transmit to their sisters and brothers some of the ideas we would present. Moreover, we were going to raise in this body some of the issues that had confronted us for so many years and we had a good chance of drawing more support to our cause.[34]

The impact of the civil rights and black power movements on the black community's international awareness can be measured in the difference between black attitudes about international issues before and after these movements. Surveys taken in 1953 showed only about 20 percent of blacks, as compared with 33 percent of whites, saying they regularly read articles on international affairs. In 1957, far fewer blacks than whites could name as many as five countries, territories, or colonies in Africa. By 1967, the Carnegie Endowment for International Peace concluded its survey on American attitudes toward South Africa with the observation that "compared to their white counterparts, blacks evidence a higher interest in world affairs [and] a particular interest in Africa."[35]

International contacts and awareness not only enhanced the self-esteem of black movement leaders and their sense that they were involved in a movement of worldwide historic importance, but also began to affect how they viewed the question of alliances. After Malcolm X's return from Mecca in 1964, where he confessed to having eaten from the same plate, drunk from the same glass, slept in the same bed, and prayed to the same God as blue-eyed, blonde Moslems, Malcolm concluded that the animosity toward blacks in the United States was not an inherently racial condition but something induced by the historical relationship between whites and blacks.[36] Thereafter, his analysis was more anti-imperialist than racialist. There is speculation that Malcolm may have been moving to heal the rift that had developed between the interracial southern civil rights movement and the northern black nationalist movement he led when he made a visit to Selma, Alabama, two weeks before his death.[37] In September 1970, the Black Panther party called together the Revolutionary People's Constitutional Convention which drew not only blacks but Indians, Asians, Puerto Ricans, and white people.[38]

While the international networks the black movement leaders were developing would be important in the long run, the new sense of power that accrued to many of the younger militants as a result of these contacts caused them to misjudge not only the revolutionary ripeness of conditions within the United States as a whole, but the level of readiness of the black community itself for any large-scale insurrection. Reggie Schell's comments shown about the Black Panther party are indicative of the expanded self-importance the movement leadership derived from its international contacts:

> I believe that the Black Panther Party . . . was close to flipping this society over. We had established international relationships with other countries; this probably was the first time that it was done on this scale by any black revolutionary movement since this country existed. In the Party we had made contact with people in Hanoi and we were supposed to begin making deals with the U.S. government to exchange pilots for political prisoners here. We were in Algiers, we were in Cuba, and we had better relations with those people than the head of IBM.[39]

Nevertheless, this experience played an important role in the development of a new generation of leaders for the black community. The enhanced self-esteem, international reputation, and political sophistication that resulted would lead in the later 1970s to more concrete ties between leaders of the African-American movement and the leaders of emerging nations and national liberation movements. Jesse Jackson's ability to trade on these ties and experience in both his approach to issues and his political strategy in 1984 is due to the groundwork laid by movement leaders in the 1960s.

Toward the end of the 1960s, the focus of the black movement shifted from civil rights to economic power. Martin Luther King was in Memphis to support striking garbage workers when he was killed. In Detroit, black industrial workers and black-owned newspapers attempted to harness the power demonstrated in the 1967 Detroit rebellion to put forward a series of programs and revolutionary visions that amounted to a direct ideological, cultural, political, and economic challenge to the capitalist hegemony of the city.[40] These workers and journalists combined the experience of the black liberation struggle with the radical tradition within the labor movement and international experiences gained by some of their leaders to speak of a society in which the interests of workers and their families would become the foundation of all social organization. There were at the time over a quarter of a million black industrial workers in the greater Detroit area.

More than anywhere else in the United States, this movement

led by black workers defined its goal in terms of real power—the power to control the economy at the point of production; so observed Dan Georgakas and Marvin Surkin, who chronicled the story of Detroit's revolutionary experiment.

> The Detroil revolutionaries did not get sidetracked into a narrow struggle against the police per se or with one aspect of power such as control of education. The movement attempted to integrate within itself all the dissident threads of the rebellious sixties in order to create a network of insurgent power comparable to the network of established power. This movement . . . generated an amazing sequence of separate but interlocked confrontations in the factories, in the polling booths, in the courts, in the streets, in the media, in the schools, and in the union halls. What clearly differentiated the Detroit experience from other major social movements of the sixties and early seventies was its thoroughly working class character.[41]

By the early 1970s, the black movement, which had started out to overturn Jim Crow so that blacks could find a place in the mainstream society, had overturned just about every traditional assumption about American life. It exploded the myth of the melting pot, and disproved the notion that white racism would disappear and class stratification was permeable. It exposed the hypocrisy of so-called representative democracy, proved that black capitalism would not lift up the majority of blacks, revealed white America's sordid record of slavery, brutality, and genocide, exposed the myth that the American justice system was just, and gave lie to the assumption that America's foreign policy was intent on preserving peace.

Though never a unified movement, the black movement of the 1960s employed just about every means of organization and communication available to it, including mass rallies and marches, civil disobedience campaigns, the power of the vote, lobbying, consumer, and producer strikes, and, finally, mass urban insurrection. It made use of underground media, black-owned media, and establishment media, the networks and organizations of the churches, of black-owned businesses, of workers, farmers, and students, and through the welfare rights movement it even organized those considered too hard to organize—the nonworking poor.

The black movement generated a new culture—drawing on elements of black slave culture, Western Christianity, American liberalism, Islamic culture, Western African culture, and Marxism, in varying combinations. It broke down the old distinctions between religion and politics, between formal political institutions and extraparliamentary actions. The black movement was both reformist and revolutionary, or rather, it was aimed at making real the articulated but never fulfilled commitments to democracy, justice, and freedom embodied in the American Constitution.

The "Borning Struggle's" Offspring

In challenging the racial myths that had served to mystify for the majority of people the actual operations of power in capitalist society, the civil rights and black power movements challenged every other sector of American society to redefine its relationship to the systems of power. As Bernice Reagon explained, the civil rights movement was the "borning struggle" for all the other movements that characterized the political landscape of the 1960s:

> The exciting thing about the Civil Rights Movement is the extent to which it gave participants a glaring analysis of who and where they were in society. You began to see all sorts of things from that. People who were Spanish-speaking in the Civil Rights Movement, who had been white, when they got back turned Brown. . . . Some of the leaders of the anti-war movement were politicized by their work in the Civil Rights Movement. . . . For many Civil Rights Movement organizers and supporters, leaving a specific project or struggle didn't mean the end of political activity. These people came away from their Civil Rights Movement experience with a greater facility for seeing a wide range of questions. For many there was no end, nor rest. The Civil Rights Movement was only the beginning.[42]

To the critiques of American society offered by the black movement, the Chicano and Native American movements of the late 1960s and early 1970s added their own unique angles. Both of these movements sprang from peoples who had maintained through the centuries their own identities, separate from and against the dominant Anglo-Saxon myths of national identity and purpose. Both had histories of continuous resistance to the U.S. government and to the economic and cultural institutions of white bourgeois rule.

The black awakening did not so much generate movement among Chicanos and Indians as it gave their movements a national focus. What had previously been separate, isolated, and sporadic instances of resistance among separated communities and individual nations (as in the case of Indians) now became the "Chicano movement," and the "American Indian movement." In other words, separate nationalist struggles were welded into a pan-Indian and pan-Mexican American movement in much the same way that South African apartheid had driven separate tribes into a common identity and engendered resistance which took the form of a black African nationalist movement. The coalescence of separate identities into national movements brought recognition from at least parts of white America of the boiling caudron that lay beneath the surface of the melting pot myth.

The Chicano Movement

Though the Chicano movement was limited primarily to the Southwest, it was as profound in its questioning of traditional American values and institutions and in its assertion of a different sociopolitical culture as the black movement. Before 1945, Mexican Americans were of little political significance to white America. Although they could claim an ancestry in America that predated that of Anglos, they were generally viewed as "foreigners," and disparaged as "lazy," "stupid," and unproductive by Anglo society. Anglo law had set up borders with armed guards to prevent so-called illegal aliens from entering a country their ancestors had traversed for hundreds of years. The Chicano movement began to change all this. The movement took several different forms, depending on the social location and historical experience of various sectors of the Mexican American population.[43]

In the vineyards and lettuce fields of southern California and Texas, armies of newly proletarianized peasants revitalized and transformed the union movement, turning the struggle for wages and safe working conditions into a broad social, cultural and religious movement. The farmworkers' movement linked migrant workers with revolutionary symbols drawn from Mexican culture, and elevated the concept of the "poor" (a term of humiliation in Anglo culture) into a legitimate category of class struggle.

In the rural counties of northern New Mexico an armed peasant revolt with nationalist overtones, led by a fiery evangelical preacher named Reies Tijerina, occurred. In the barrios of East Los Angeles (the third largest Mexican city in the world) and other large urban centers, groups of young people evolved from anti-social youth gangs to self-defense organizations and then into educational and cultural revitalization movements. The best known group was the Brown Berets, which modeled itself loosely on the Black Panthers. On the campuses, middle-class Chicanos fought for Chicano studies, for an accurate appreciation of Chicano history, and for bilingual education. Chicanos began to challenge the Anglo-dominated Roman Catholic church and to form their own organizations within it, remaking the content and style of the religious socialization process. Still other Chicanos formed their own political party—La Raza Unida—and began to run people for office under its banner, challenging the two-party system and its control by Anglos.

All of these movements, diverse in origin as well as in tactics and strategy, were held together by a shared definition of the Mexican American that was forged during this time. Mexican Americans began to refer to themselves as Chicanos (a derivative of the term "Mexicano"), thus repudiating the idea of assimilation into the American melting pot. They also referred to themselves as members of a "new breed," of "La Raza," meaning "the people" or "the race." The term "Chicano" expressed a specific ideology. First, it was a refusal to accept the Anglo contempt for the Indian half of the Mexican-American identity and heritage. Rather, it celebrated that heritage and its life-giving insights. Second, to be Chicano meant to embrace biculturalism, to reject the Anglo demand to assimilate into the white world. To be *mestizo* (a mixed breed), formerly a mark of inferiority, was now elevated into a badge of pride. To be Chicano meant that one engaged in a quest for self-determination—politically, culturally, economically.

The Chicano movement marked a period of intense cultural flowering, during which new poetry, new music, new art, new dance, and new theater were created. To be Chicano also meant embracing an international understanding of human oppression, seeing the need for solidarity across racial and national lines. To be Chicano meant recognizing the unjust class stratification structured into the American economy and committing oneself to lift those at the bottom. Chicano heroes were those who did not forget their humble origins or the community of support that existed in the barrios. Individuals were entreated to achieve, not for individual enhancement, but for the sake of the Chicano people.

The American Indian Movement

More than any other movement, the American Indian insurgency of the late 1960s and early 1970s called into question the very legitimacy of the idea of the American republic and its right to the land it had conquered. As Vine Deloria has pointed out, American Indians "are unique in the world in that they represent the only aboriginal peoples still practicing a form of self-government in the midst of a wholly new and modern civilization that has been transported to their lands."[44] Because they can lay claim to an unbroken cultural tradition (in spite of overwhelming attempts by white authorities to obliterate Indian culture) and to lands guaranteed to them by U.S. treaties, Native Americans represent the quintessential "other" that stands against the major American myths of historical identity and purpose.

Of all the social movements of the 1960s, the American Indian movement presented theoretically the most profound challenge to the entire paradigm on which Western civilization rests. Our notions of time and space, linear history, the sharp demarcation between "sacred" and "secular," between "human life" and "animal life," the idea of individualism, the distinction between "religion" and "politics," our instrumental use of the natural world, all are challenged by the world view of the American Indian. The Indian understanding of human beings as just one part of the great web of sentient being raises the most fundamental questions about the "truth" of human nature itself—a truth that could help us to resolve some of the seemingly irresolvable impasses to which Western civilization, in both its capitalist and socialist manifestations, has brought us.

Though the American Indian movement was severely repressed by the U.S. government, the world view it embodied began to penetrate some sectors of white America. In the modern peace, ecology, wholistic healing, feminist, alternative technology, and new consciousness movements of the later 1970s one could detect the translation of pieces of that world view into language that was becoming more and more prescient.

Effect on Whites

The movements of colored peoples, in exposing the American myths that had served to hide the true history of the United States from its protagonists, had a profound effect on whites during the later 1960s and early 1970s. White Appalachians during this time discovered that they were an "internal colony" of the large energy companies and that their indigenous cultural heritage had been denied them by the dominant myths of American identity. White women discovered their wholesale exclusion from so-called representative democracy; and white high school and college students discovered that they were being groomed to become pegs in a vast educational and war machine in which they had neither voice nor rights. Even white elites associated with the Democratic party discovered their exclusion from a party system that had become corrupt, secretive, and moribund. Such elites inaugurated the most sweeping reforms ever in party rules and regulations, making possible Jesse Jackson's historic bid for the presidency in 1984.[45] White blue-collar workers also began to experience their own class victimization, though their class anger was easily deflected by racist demagogues such as George Wallace into anger against black militants and their "Eastern pointy-headed liberal supporters." The labor movement, which could have given white workers a positive source of identity and a heritage that was critical of the dominant institutions, had long since abdicated that responsibility, thus making it easier for racism to replace a legitimate sense of betrayal by America's dominant institutions.

Conclusion

By 1968, what had started out as separate social movements arising from very different social-class origins and cultural histories had become "the Movement"—an amorphous collection of people and organizations that represented in its totality an incipient revolutionary culture. It had generated the most thoroughgoing critique of the U.S. political and economic system in history. Though never structurally unified, the Movement consisted of the sons and daughters of the elite, black sharecroppers, working-class and professional people, GI's, older radicals, lesbians and gay activists, disabled people, high school students, women's liberation activists, Latino and Filipino farmworkers, Native Americans, Asian Americans, college professors, business executives, senior citizens, clergymen, nuns, show business personalities, musicians, Puerto Rican activists, old-time labor organizers, and lower-class dropouts from society.

By the early 1970s, however, most Movement activists felt as if they had been, like Sisyphus, pushing a boulder up a steep hill only to have it roll down again. Their critiques of American society and their visions of what the country could and should be went further than the concrete reforms they had been able to achieve. Because their ultimate visions had not been realized, they tended to underestimate their own power and to devalue the changes they had in fact wrought in American political and civil society.[46]

The Movement had ended McCarthyism and Jim Crow segregation; brought into being an unprecedented body of civil rights legislation; redefined the scope of federal responsibility for providing for the general welfare; developed alternative analyses of the American past; extended and deepened the conception of democracy, human rights, freedom, and representative government; opened up the Democratic party to the participation of ethnic minorities, women, and young people; opened up new career opportunities for women; passed legislation that stopped back-alley abortions; caused the government to bring into the light what had always been done in secret; brought down one president; hastened the U.S. withdrawal from Vietnam; and through enlarging the so-called social wage (primarily government benefits), initiated the most massive redistribution of wealth since the New Deal legislation of the 1930s.

It was black self-organizations that had generated the momentum for this great social ferment, established the pace, and provided the models. It is doubtful that the largest antiwar movement in the nation's history would have emerged as it did or been as militant as it was had it not been for the cultural dissonance provided by the black awakening.

In the radical democratic possibilities it announced, the ferment of the 1960s and early 1970s has often been compared to the period of Reconstruction after the Civil War, when, for the first time in the South, a system of public education was established, innovations in the care of the mentally ill and indigent were undertaken, people who were once slaves began to govern themselves, and social equality between the races began to flourish. The first period of Reconstruction was crushed, just ten years after it had begun, through collusion between northern industrialists and southern planters.

By the mid-1970s, the demands for reform and redistribution

being raised by the Movement had gone beyond the bounds of what was acceptable to the corporate establishment. Black insurgency during the civil rights phase could be met with legislation that overturned Jim Crow laws because vulgar apartheid had become dysfunctional for American capitalism. The South was a growing area for business expansion, and the Bull Connors and Jim Clarks were getting in the way of providing a suitable "investment climate." But when the insurgency moved from "equal rights" to anti-imperialism and distributional demands, like the first Reconstruction it had to be crushed.

The FBI's Cointelpro program, which included heavy surveillance, "dirty tricks," political frame-ups, and finally assassination of movement leaders, was only part of the story. So were massive demonstrations of military force (at the universities of Jackson State and Kent State, at the Democratic Convention in 1968, and in every city in which urban rebellion broke out in 1967), as well as the withdrawal of funds by foundations from every civil rights organization but the National Association for the Advancement of Colored People (NAACP) and massive infusions of drugs, which began to flow into the nation's ghettos.[47]

Even as the Movement was being physically crushed, the ideological apparatus of the state was moving to redefine the meaning of black empowerment within the national debate over public policy alternatives. Policymakers understood better than anyone else how pivotal the black insurgency had been to the awakening of every other sector of the American public to the enormous gap between America's ideals and its reality.

If the 1960s and early 1970s had been a time of popular democratic insurgency amounting to a Second Reconstruction, the latter part of the 1970s would be the era in which national "elites" retook control through both ideological and economic restructuring.

2

The New Right Assault on the Second Reconstruction

Throughout its history White America adjusts its expression of racism to accord with its economic imperatives and modifies its myths of racism to take into account the shifting economic circumstances. That is to say, racism remains a persistent value expression depending on economic opportunities; White America generates a new ideology to sanction any fundamental alterations in race relations growing out of basic economic modifications. It has been the fate of ideologues, for the most part, to compose analyses in keeping with the myths of racism rather than to expose White America's racial motivation.[1]

—Sidney M. Willhelm

Sidney Willhelm's observation is based on the recognition that throughout American history racism has served as one of the major tools of the ruling elite to maintain the class relations of capitalist society. Racist myths, thoroughly internalized by the white working class, have kept the entire class divided and therefore politically impotent, while the racial stratification of the workforce has served to restrain wages and democratic participation for the entire working class.[2]

51

The social protest movements of the 1960s occurred during a time of relative economic prosperity, so that some of their demands could be channeled into reforms that fit the pluralist interest-group framework of the ruling ideology. Black and feminist demands to be finally included in the American Dream could be translated into legislation that guaranteed voting rights, equal pay for equal work, and a bigger slice of the federal welfare dollar when the economy looked as if it were going to keep on expanding.

By 1970, however, the economic boom that had carried the United States out of World War II as the preeminent world power was over. In the climate of austerity that would follow, national politicians and their allies in the ideological institutions—the universities and think tanks—instituted an ideological counter-reformation to accommodate and justify the changing economic imperatives of their rule. Though the counter-reformation had as its target all of the countercultural movements of the 1960s, it was the African-American insurgency and the understanding of racism that had emerged from that movement that became the first target.

The full political and cultural import of the 1984 Jackson presidential campaign can only be understood against the backdrop of this attack. This chapter thus traces the ideological adjustments wrought in the dominant mythology concerning race, class, and ethnicity, which sounded the death knell of liberalism and laid the groundwork for the conservative bipartisan consensus of the late 1970s and the 1980s.

The Crisis of Legitimation

By 1970 American capitalism was in deep trouble. Europe and Japan had risen from the ashes of World War II to compete effectively with American corporations. The Vietnam war, which had given a temporary boost to the economy, was at the same time generating increasingly dangerous strains; and more newly independent third world nations were talking of breaking out of their dependence on the West, thus threatening unlimited U.S. access to new markets and cheap resources. Unemployment and inflation were growing together—a conjunction that mainstream economists had said was not supposed to happen; productivity was stagnating, as was investment, and the debt crisis was beginning to threaten the stability of the international banking system.[3]

American financial managers were just beginning to realize that the indicators they were watching were not registering the usually brief cyclical ups and downs, but a longer and deeper crisis— what Marxists call a "structural crisis." Keynesianism, which had seemed to solve the earlier structural crisis manifested in the Great Depression, was no longer keeping the crisis at bay. In 1977 Henry Kaufman, a partner in the prestigious New York Salomon Brothers investment banking firm, expressed the crisis nature of the period in these terms:

> The . . . crises . . . were of increasing intensity. During their most intensive moments, they contained all the ingredients that had fueled the financial debacles of old. How close we came to disaster in 1970, and then again in 1974 and early 1975, no one will ever accurately record. It was a frightening period with rapidly rising interest rates, some spectacular business failures, spiralling preferences for high credit quality liquidity, and doubts about the strength of some of the largest and most prominent financial institutions.[4]

The crisis in the economy was accompanied and exacerbated by the increasingly incessant voices of the poor, the oppressed, and the marginalized that the American pie be recut to include them. Calls for the democratization of the political machinery through which public decisions are made, demands for sovereignty for American Indians—on whose lands corporations had recently discovered vast new mineral resources, calls for the independence of Puerto Rico, the organizing of farmworkers, attempts by Mexican Americans and others to take over public space, and the flirtation of affluent white youth with Marxist and socialist theories of change began to frighten the politicians and policymakers whose job it was to manage the state in accordance with the continued accumulation of the private appropriation of capital.

Few on the left, then or since, have understood that they had helped to create a genuine crisis of legitimation within ruling-class circles, yet it is clear in a brief survey of the literature that that is exactly what was occurring. A *crisis of legitimation* is said to occur when the institutions through which the public is socialized to accept a given socioeconomic order no longer work to ensure mass loyalty to that system.[5]

In legitimation crisis theory, the state in capitalist democracies must act to support the production process, but in such a way as to conceal the unfairness of class rule, if it is to keep the loyalty of the public.[6] The insurgencies of the 1960s, along with the revelations of government corruption and duplicity that emerged in the *Pentagon Papers*, in the Watergate scandal, and in revelations of CIA infiltration of domestic groups had exposed the racist, sexist, and antidemocratic character of the system.

In forcing the state to intervene on their behalf, civil rights, welfare rights, and women's movements drew further attention to issues of choice, planning, and control, so that more and more areas of life began to be seen as legitimate arenas for public participation and decision making.

Ideas take on material reality when they move masses of people to take political action. Some of these ideas—namely those relating to civil rights for minorities, poor people, and women; electoral reform; the right of the people to know what their government is doing—were translated into law. Still other ideas, expressed in the insurgent movements of the 1960s—such as workplace democracy, or a foreign policy that supported, instead of crushed, third world aspirations to self-determination—remained unrealized. Although such ideas had not yet found a politically effective vehicle for their transmission into public policy, more and more of the public was beginning to adopt them.

Public opinion surveys taken at the end of the 1960s indicate that the public was indeed beginning to question its acceptance of the dominant ideology. Between 1958 and 1972, for example, the percentage of those who thought that government was run for the benefit of a "few big interests" rose from 17.6 percent to 53.3 percent.[7] In 1960, 18 percent of the people polled thought the government was spending too much on defense. By 1969 that figure had climbed to 52 percent, and by 1970, 58 percent in a Harris poll thought that defense spending should be cut.[8] In 1966, a Harris poll showed 41 percent of the public expressing "a great deal of confidence" in the federal executive branch and 43 percent in Congress. By 1973, only 29 and 21 percent respectively expressed confidence in these two institutions of government. In 1966, 55 percent expressed "a great deal of confidence" in business leaders; by 1973 only 27 percent had any confidence in business leaders. In 1966, 61 percent of the public expressed confidence in educators; by 1973 it had dropped to 33 percent. And in 1966, 62 percent had expressed confidence in the military; by 1973 only 35 percent expressed "a great deal of confidence" in the military. Pollster Louis Harris commented that these polls indicated a "massive failure of leadership," the "target of alienation" being the "heart of the entrenched establishment itself."[9]

This lack of confidence in the establishment was reflected in an apparent disillusionment with the two-party system, as demonstrated by increasing voter apathy, the popularity of "outsiders" like George Wallace and George McGovern, and the rise in crossover voting, indicating that the parties no longer commanded the kind of loyalty they once had.[10]

Other polls, moreover, indicated that a majority of the American public was open to "radical" solutions to the country's economic ills.[11] A Hart poll showed that 66 percent of the American public favored employee ownership and control of large corporations, while a plurality—44 percent—favored direct public ownership of natural resources.[12] Ninety percent of the public polled by Harris in 1970–1972 favored a federal program to give jobs to the unemployed, 83 percent favored more federal funds for pollution control, and 76 percent favored more federal funds for education.[13]

These attitudinal changes were occurring not so much among the lower classes as among the more affluent, a finding that startled Louis Harris. "The old New Deal assumption that the low-income people would put a floor under the status of the less fortunate just didn't hold water any longer. It would have been hard to believe in 1933 that by 1973 the upper 20 percent of the population income-wise would favor, by 73 percent, tax reform designed to soak the rich."[14]

Members of the governing and business elites responded to these findings with alarm. The old nostrums of liberal capitalism were no longer able to rationalize the changes they had concluded were necessary if the system was to avoid collapse. These changes amounted to a major restructuring of the process of accumulation by imposing a new level of austerity on the majority of working people, curbing trade unions, cutting back on social welfare, and lifting taxes and regulations on big business.

Political analyst Samuel Lubell, a consultant to Nelson Rockefeller, expressed the panic gripping establishment circles in 1970:

Always in the past, I have been optimistic about this country's political system. But as my research and interviewing went from one conflict to another, I became alarmed. These first findings suggested that a too rapid and uncontrolled rate of change was being injected into our society for the people and our political institutions to stand, and that this was beginning to tear the nation apart. . . . The compulsive force twisting our political insides and restructuring both parties is that rapid change has become the prime political disturber of our time. . . . These conflicts on the run have plunged us into zealous combat to remake American thinking, pressed with an intensity not known in the nation since the pre-civil war period. . . . This battling has been targeted largely at our institutions, with the public schools, universities, the draft, the police, churches, the welfare system, perhaps in the future whole cities serving as successive staging areas.[15]

Lubell's alarm is echoed in the report of the President's Commission on Campus Unrest, published in the wake of the Jackson State and Kent State killings:

The crisis on American campuses has no parallel in the history of the nation. This crisis has its roots in divisions of American society as deep as any since the Civil War. The divisions are reflected in violent acts and harsh rhetoric, and in the enmity of those Americans who see themselves as occupying opposing camps. Campus unrest reflects and increases a more profound crisis in the nation as a whole.[16]

By 1974, the business community was chafing that it was being engulfed by a "rising tide of entitlement." Financial analysts Leonard Silk and David Vogel reported after attending meetings of the Conference Board, a major corporate forum, that there is "concern in the nation's . . . boardrooms that Democracy in America is working all too well."[17] This theme was echoed by Samuel Huntington, a Harvard political scientist, in an analysis of the crisis delivered to members of the Trilateral Commission in 1975. The Trilateral Commission was founded in 1973 by David Rockefeller to bring together the governing elites from the three major capitalist centers (the United States and Canada, Western Europe, and Japan) in an attempt to coordinate responses to the developing economic and legitimation crises. Huntington spoke of "threats to the governability of democracy" brought about by "previously passive or unorganized groups in the population [which were] now embarked on concerted efforts to establish their claims to opportunities, positions, rewards, and privileges which they had not considered themselves entitled to before."[18]

According to Huntington, the pressure by blacks, Latinos, and women for equality of results, the vast questioning of authority, the expansion of participation in electoral politics, the proliferation of "cause" organizations, marches, and demonstrations, had resulted in an increase in governmental activity but a decrease in "governmental authority." A government lacking authority, he said, "will have little ability, short of cataclysmic crisis, to impose on its people the sacrifices which may be necessary to deal with foreign policy problems and defense." The obvious solution to this breakdown in authority, therefore, is "a greater degree of moderation in democracy."[19]

According to such elite thinking, democracies were never meant to provide for the full participation of all groups. In fact, they could function only if some part of the population (e.g., blacks and women) did not participate. Huntington was frank to admit that such an assumption was inherently "undemocratic," but that it also helped democracy to function more effectively. Huntington's idea of a time when democracy did function effectively was when "Truman had been able to govern the country with the cooperation of a relatively small number of Wall Street lawyers and bankers."[20]

Among the policymakers there was also concern that the explosions of democracy in the United States were having an effect overseas. Nathan Glazer and Daniel Moynihan, two of the key architects of the establishment's revisionist ideology, expressed a note of alarm at the domino effect the black movement was having on other countries:

> The black movement had as surprising a resonance abroad as at home. A "black power" movement developed in the West Indies, a "civil rights" movement in northern Ireland, "black panthers" formed in Israel (among oriental Jews) and some French Canadians explained they were "white niggers."[21]

By the mid-1970s there was talk in the boardrooms and business journals of the possible collapse of the capitalist system. A poll of eighteen hundred leading business people released by the Harvard Business Review in 1976 indicated that the U.S. business community believed that the American public favored an ideology in which "property rights are less important than rights to income, health and education."[22] A *New York Times* headline in 1976 asked: "Will the Bicentennial See the Death of Free Enterprise?"[23]

By the end of the decade leading business figures were calling for a conscious ideological assault against those who were challenging the system. D. J. Kirchhoff, president of Castle and Cooke, speaking before the Merchants and Manufacturers Association, put it this way:

> Until the mid-1950s we had a good image. Capitalism could rest on its own merits. We were effective and efficient. No one quarreled with that thesis. . . . What concerns me today is a more direct assault on our economic system. This siege is spearheaded by what can only be called a "movement"—an amorphous group of people who believe as an act of faith that capitalism is inefficient, wasteful, unjust, inhumane, exploitative, monopolistic and profit-oriented at the expense of the worker. . . . I am convinced that affirming our values in competition with the movement's tactics to erode our national economy is central to our survival.[24]

Both establishment and left analysts have seen the growth of the New Right during the 1970s as a kind of inevitable "popular reaction" to the excessive liberalism and social turmoil of the 1960s. Americans have come to believe that the "public" has become tired of chaos and is growing more conservative. As part of this reaction, a "white backlash" against black gains—a kind of spontaneous rebellion—was inevitable.[25] A more careful analysis, however, suggests that the reaction was not spontaneous or "natural" at all, but was a consciously orchestrated response by the governing class to the legitimation crisis they were experiencing.

In 1973, surveying a decade of taking the nation's pulse on a wide range of issues, Louis Harris concluded that the public was ready for the kind of change indicated by the polls cited earlier; a change from Cold War to coexistence, from inequality to a redistribution of wealth, *"even at the risk of shaking up the economic well-being of some of the nation's most powerful and affluent people,"* from polluting the environment to conserving and protecting it, even *"at the risk of outmoding many established and conventional ways of obtaining energy."* After Watergate, he concluded, "we must find leadership which can act resolutely in a crisis, but not leadership which will subtract the basic liberties of the country to consolidate its power."[26] Harris noted, however, that while the public was ready for such leadership, the leadership of the country was not.

> The facts . . . have pointed up just how badly the leadership of the country has read the temper, mood, and serious intent of the American people. Taken together, the record is a serious indictment of the political, social, and economic leadership of this country over the past decade. There is little doubt in this writer's mind that the public, although far from correct in many areas, nonetheless is far more sophisticated, far more concerned, and far more advanced than the leadership believed.[27]

The crisis of legitimation, which lasted through the 1970s spawned a multifaceted New Right movement that, by the time of Reagan's election in 1980, had succeeded in turning the parameters of public discourse 180 degrees. Gone from public debate was concern over racism, sexism, poverty, pollution, military spending, third world intervention, civil liberties, human rights, and a host of other concerns exhibited by the public in the earlier part of the decade. Instead the issues were school prayer, crime, the "communist threat," "reverse discrimination," the economy, pornography, and taxes.

The process by which this great reversal took place began with an attack on the effort of blacks and other ethnic minorities to achieve racial equality and self-determination. National sympathies for people of color, which had been growing throughout the 1960s, had to be redirected; for if the persistence and pervasiveness of racial oppression continued to be held before the American public, the essential character of the system would be increasingly exposed. There was no way demands for full equality could be met within the existing structures of capitalist society.

The Role of Neoconservative Intellectuals

The views of a small group of disillusioned liberal intellectuals, later dubbed "neoconservatives," played a pivotal role in reshaping the parameters of public debate over issues of racism, poverty, ethnicity and role of government in making up for past injustices. Neoconservative intellectuals parlayed their way to power during the 1960s and early 1970s by giving legitimacy to a policy of meanness, characterized by a reversal of the egalitarian and democratic values embodied in the social movements of the 1960s.

The neoconservatives are the focus of this analysis because they planted the ideological seeds that legitimated the emergence of a more overt New Right movement in the later 1970s. Virtually their entire repertoire of arguments has since been adopted by the Reagan administration.

As intellectuals associated with some of the most prestigious schools—Harvard, Yale—the neoconservatives have had extraordinary access to the top decision makers and mainstream media. They have served as advisors and behind-the-scenes policymakers for both Republican and Democratic presidents and members of Congress (Daniel Moynihan served in the Kennedy, Johnson, and Nixon administrations and is currently a New York State senator). In addition to having their own publications through which their views are promulgated (*Commentary, The Public Interest*), their work has appeared in virtually all of the mainstream liberal press and television networks, and their books have been published by the most prestigious publishing houses.

The neoconservative intellectuals are the *legitimators*, and the program they enunciated was exactly what the doctor ordered for an ailing capitalist system that was losing its public assent. Peter Steinfels describes the process through which neoconservative ideas become public reality.

> Daniel Bell writes a book, and a syndicated columnist appropriates its thesis for his Bicentennial musings. Irving Kristol derides "a new class" of liberal intellectuals for its snobbish attitude toward a business civilization and Mobil Oil incorporates this idea in its public relations advertising. Alexander Bickel, Yale Law School professor, writes an article on the failure of school integration in the north, and a White House aide refers to it twice in a 1970 memo to Nixon arguing that "the second era of Re-Construction is over; the ship of integration is going down; it is not our ship . . . and we ought not to be aboard."[28]

The first target of the neoconservatives was the nation's still new commitment to its racial minorities. By the end of the 1970s, the neoconservatives had convinced not only liberal policymakers, but even most progressives, that a "white backlash" had, in fact, occurred, which made it impossible to meet the demands of blacks and other groups for equity; that poverty programs had failed to achieve positive results, and thus taxpayers were pouring their money down a sinkhole; and that self-help was the only way

African Americans were going to be able to lift themselves out of poverty.

The Discovery of the Ethnic Factor

The seeds of the intellectual rebellion against black demands can be found in the publication of *Beyond the Melting Pot* by sociologists Nathan Glazer and Daniel Moynihan in 1963. The authors, in what was obviously an attempt to trivialize the uniqueness of the black experience in America, purported to discover an overlooked facet of American life—the persistence of the ethnic factor. Blacks were to be viewed as one of many ethnic groups, most of whom had overcome ethnic discrimination by exploiting the opportunities that were available to each group, while at the same time retaining distinctive values, mores, and sensibilities. Glazer and Moynihan neatly diverted the cause of social division in American society from institutionally structured racism and class conflict to conflicts over life-styles and values, which they asserted were more fundamental causes of division than race or class.[29] In the introduction to their collection of essays on ethnicity published in 1975, Glazer and Moynihan made more explicit the organizing principle, and therefore the politics, behind their work on ethnicity.

> One of the difficulties of social class as an organizing principle surely is that there is just not that much conflict of *norm* between social classes. In the West intellectuals and others at the top of the social stratification will fantasize about the differences between the values of those at the bottom and those in the middle . . . but it usually turns out that those at the bottom pretty much share notions of desirable and undesirable with those in the middle. Ethnic differences, however, *are* differences, or at least are seen as such. Marxists thought they would disappear.[30]

Diverting attention from structural inequities based on class and race to differences supposedly engendered by differing ethnic norms does not relieve Glazer and Moynihan of the necessity of explaining the disproportionate collection of people of color at the bottom of the socioeconomic ladder. They acknowledge that blacks as a group have suffered from racial prejudice and discrimination, but view such discrimination as largely a residue of past injustices. Blacks' continuing failure to achieve upward mobility is explained by the "culturally deprived" condition under which they allegedly emerged from slavery. Unlike other ethnic groups, whose close cohesion and self-help efforts, according to Moynihan and Glazer, are what enabled them to overcome poverty and discrimination, African Americans did not have the same kind of clannishness, the same close family ties. "Without a special language and culture, and without the historical experiences that create an elan and morale, what is there to lead them to build their own life, to patronize their own?" they ask. The one exception, they admit, is the black church, but they pass over this exception with barely a nod to its existence.[31]

The Discovery of the Black "Savage"

It is a short step from cultural-deprivation theories to blaming the victims for their own poverty, and that is finally where Glazer and Moynihan come down. Why have blacks not made use of the educational ladder to success as other ethnic groups have done?

> There is little question where the major part of the answer must be found: in the home and family and community—not in its overt values . . . but in its conditions and circumstances. It is there that the heritage of two hundred years of slavery and a hundred years of discrimination is concentrated; and it is there that we find the serious obstacles to the ability to make use of a free educational system to advance into higher occupations and to eliminate the massive social problems that affect colored Americans and the city.[32]

Glazer and Moynihan contend that the black underclass remains behind not because the economic system as presently structured is incapable of integrating them, but because of a self-perpetuating cycle of pathology inherent in the conditions of black family life. As numerous critics have pointed out, Moynihan's thesis was based on faulty logic. He attributed the welfare explosion in the 1960s to a rise in female-headed families and a general deterioration in social control within the black family, which allegedly increased the pool of those eligible for welfare. Yet black female-headed families increased by only 4.3 percent between 1960 and 1970. As Cloward and Piven have demonstrated, the families who got onto the welfare rolls after 1964 (the year when rolls dramatically increased) were just as much in need before the welfare explosion as after it. Thus, factors other than a deterioration in family life, such as the mechanization of agriculture in the South, which drove more blacks into the cities, and increased political action on the part of welfare recipients are more helpful in explaining the welfare explosion. Moreover, Moynihan ignored studies which showed that blacks had the same ideals regarding the family as whites, studies which showed that blacks and whites were practically identical in their control of the family, statistics which showed an increase in "broken" families among whites during this period, studies which indicated a greater rate of child neglect and abuse among white welfare families than among black welfare families, and the high mortality rate among black men that accounted for approximately half of the "broken" families in the black community. In addition, he ignored one of the most obvious facts about the black family, even the urban black lower class family, and that is the strength of extended family ties.[33] The pathology theme was later repeated in the controversial "Moynihan Report," *The Negro Family: The Case for National Action,* made public in 1965, in which the black matriarchal family is made the scapegoat for the ills of the black lower class.[34] If the cause of economic backwardness is found in an inherited condition due to *past* discrimination, not to *ongoing systemic exclusion,* then the solution becomes not public programs to reverse the systemic causes of racial discrimination, but black self-help.

Black self-help could not, however, be the total solution. As black groups continued to press state and federal governments for economic relief, particularly through the Welfare Rights Organization, a solution to the welfare mess had to be found. Moynihan came up with the Family Assistance Plan, "as part of an overriding short-term strategy to bring down the level of internal violence."[35] On the surface, the Family Assistance Plan sounded like an intelligent response to the plight of the urban poor, and its most progressive features were picked up by the media, thereby attracting liberal support. But according to political scientists Frances Piven and Richard Cloward, its longer term implications were regressive. The plan would have wiped out the procedural rights welfare recipients had won through protest and litigation, cut welfare allotments below those offered in the most liberal states, and imposed a workfare program on those deemed able to work, a program that would have amounted to a kind of slave labor.

While the Family Assistance Plan was never put into effect (the workfare program became public policy under Reagan), it fed into Nixon's strategy of turning popular opinion against welfare and its beneficiaries and encouraging states and countries to reduce welfare rolls. Discussions of the social pathology of the black poor and the ways in which the welfare system reinforced such pathology dominated congressional deliberations and national media for a period of several years. The *Moynihan Report* had a tremendous impact on public discussion about blacks in America. Its frightening statistics purporting to link broken black families with antisocial behavior encouraged a new form of subtle racism, which William Ryan termed the "savage discovery."[36] The focus of public concern was shifted from systemic racism and discrimination to the discovery of new forms of the age-old "savage" in the northern ghettos. "The all-time favorite 'savage' is the promiscuous mother who produces a litter of illegitimate brats in order to profit from AFDC."[37]

Linking alleged black pathology with a welfare crisis that by the end of the 1960s was straining state and municipal budgets served to build a political bond between entrepreneurs worried about taxes, state and local officials worried about revenues, blue-collar workers worried about inflation, and die-hard racists who did not want to see blacks get ahead as a matter of principle. It deflected attention from the systemic causes of inflation, mounting unemployment, and budget deficits by blaming middle-class and working-class economic anxieties on a self-perpetuating tangle of pathology in the urban "black underclass"—a term that began to appear with regularity and carried suggestions of the Nazi-era *untermenschen*.

The writings of Glazer and Moynihan were often filled with their own barely disguised racial prejudices. In a curious case of historical amnesia for men who claimed to be scholars, they erase from memory the entire history of black lynchings, the Ku Klux Klan, urban race riots, and other forms of antiblack violence, blaming militant blacks in the 1960s for disturbing the delicate fabric of ethnic relations that had allegedly existed for one hundred years. "It became possible—even from the point of view of the attackers desirable—for blacks to attack and vilify whites in a manner no ethnic group had ever really done since the period of anti-Irish feeling of the 1840s and 1850s."[38]

In the work of such writers, black groups agitating for change were viewed as "divisive" and "violent"; they insisted on "armed revolution, on the killing of whites, on violence toward every moderate black element." Their rhetoric was "anti-white" and "peculiarly virulent," and their actions were often "outrageous."[39] The "black underclass," Moynihan wrote, is a "disorganized, angry, hurt group of persons easily given to self-destructive violence." Another group of "radical nihilistic" black youth, not of the underclass themselves, he added, is "determined to use them [the black underclass] as an instrument of violent, apocalyptic confrontation with a white society they have declared is irredeemably militaristic and racist."[40]

For these former liberals becoming neoconservatives, blacks who in any way assert their right to equality and self-determination come close to being the "horde" or the "rabble"—long the dark underside of ruling-class consciousness, a projection of this class's own rationalized violence onto the victims of that violence.

To project such a view of the black poor was tricky for the neoconservatives in the late 1960s, for many more middle-class whites had come to understand the righteousness of black protest, had come to see the victims as having a just claim on the American conscience and cornucopia—as the many staff reports to the Kerner Commission, as well as the opinion polls cited earlier, attested to. Such white middle-class sympathies were thus a key target of neoconservative attack.

Weaning White Sympathy from Black Claims on the Conscience

From the late 1960s neoconservative intellectuals specifically set out to wean white liberals away from sympathy for (and in some cases solidarity with) the black poor, and from the welfare state as the solution to their plight. They did this, first, by attacking a "new class" of liberals for their misplaced sympathies. Speaking as "one of them," Moynihan told an audience of Americans for Democratic Action that "liberals must somehow overcome the curious condescension that takes the form of defending and explaining away anything, however outrageous, which Negroes, individually or collectively might do."

For liberals, this poses a special kind of problem that derives from our own decencies. Trying to be kind, trying to be helpful, we have got into the habit of denying the realities of the life-circumstances of the lower class, and this has curiously paralyzed our ability to do anything to change these realities. Typically, we have blamed ourselves for the shortcomings of the poor—and left it at that.[41]

From white responsibility Moynihan moved to the "shortcomings of the poor," a sleight of hand that led directly to his proposal to the Nixon administration that he institute a policy of "benign neglect" toward the black underclass.

Disparagement of liberal sympathies for the poor, as well as of white responsibility for structural injustice, was extended by other neoconservatives to the whole range of questions around the definition and implementation of equality, not only internally but internationally. Aaron Wildavsky, another neoconservative, was even more explicit about liberal guilt. "There is too much guilt engendered by the rhetoric of equality," he said; and Robert Moss, a British conservative writing in the *New York Times Magazine*, put the issue even more crudely: "We are hectored [by those] who appeal to the guilty conscience of the well-fed with images of starving millions [and] lecture us on our moral obligation for the supposed crimes of colonialism and capitalist exploitation."[42]

Since the minds of the "black nihilists" alleged to be directing and fomenting the disorganized black underclass were not to be changed, the solution Moynihan proposed to the problem of increasing black violence (and hence, ungovernability) was to deprive this group of "the Negro underclass which is the source of their present strength."[43] He proposed to do this by disengaging the federal government from the business of servicing the poor, turning that task over to state and municipal governments and private businesses, the assumption being that the black nihilists were feeding at the trough of federal poverty programs. Moynihan's proposal, in effect, laid the groundwork for revenue sharing, which was to become operative five years later.

In moving to roll back the Great Society programs, the policy makers were tacitly admitting that the real purpose for these programs had been to cool off the ghetto. Once this was accomplished, the programs were no longer needed. As one former education official later told me. "We all knew we were simply there to keep a lid on the explosions. The programs were never meant to provide real upward mobility for black people." Before the federal government could disengage itself from the welfare business, however, the programs of the Great Society and the War on Poverty had to appear ineffective in accomplishing the goals for which they were established, and a new constituency groomed that would call for their repeal, or at least not protest too loudly against it.

Beginning with the so-called Coleman Report, on equality of educational opportunity, in 1966, a series of studies, endlessly analyzed and commented on by neoconservative intellectuals, purported to show that the Great Society programs had been a failure. Although progressives and minorities had their own criticisms of such programs (they were never funded to the extent of the need; they were never meant to give the poor real power over their lives but to provide upward mobility for new minority elites), the neoconservatives had different criticisms. In highly publicized debates, they used what were at best ambiguous data to conclude that no amount of public intervention in the lives of the poor could turn around a situation of endemic and self-perpetuating poverty and underachievement. Since these programs had been tried and had obviously failed—except to provoke the underclass to make even more unreasonable demands on an already overloaded system—the government should get out of the business of trying to do what it could not do, and focus on what it could do best—the making of foreign policy. The program of the neoconservatives enunciated in the late 1960s became fully operative with Ronald Reagan's election in 1980.[44]

Creating the "White Backlash"

To bolster their rather weak polemic against federal programs, the neoconservative intellectuals postulated the existence of a rising tide of conservatism—to justify their own desire to curtail the social programs they saw as provoking the dissent they so feared. In part, the so-called white backlash that began to make headlines was a fabrication of the neoconservatives.[45] In time, it became a self-fulfilling prophecy as the New Right coalition came to power. This coalition represented die-hard segregationist sentiments of some George Wallace supporters, and the nouveau riche of the Sun Belt, and midwestern and border state white working-class populations whose instinctive class biases were encouraged by the neoconservatives, who continually elevated for criticism a group of white "liberals" and "intellectuals" who were soft on black militancy and welfare spending.

To say that the white backlash was a fabrication is not to deny that a certain percentage of the white population continued to hold to a rather virulent racist ideology. Most of these had voted for Wallace in 1968 and for the Dixiecrats twenty years earlier.[46]

Contrary to the proponents of the backlash theory, however, whites throughout the 1960s and early 1970s (even at the height of the ghetto rebellions in 1967) were becoming more sympathetic to the idea of full racial integration. Surveys conducted by the National Opinion Research Center of Chicago showed that there was a steady upward approval rate among whites of racial integration in schools, public institutions, and even residential settings. In 1942, only 35 percent of whites surveyed indicated they did not object to racial integration. By 1968, 65 percent approved of residential integration, and even more approved of integration in other areas.[47] In the South, the changes were dramatic, causing sociologist Paul Sheatsley to comment that southern attitudes were undergoing "revolutionary change" during the sixties.[48] A national Harris survey taken in 1972 showed a similar steadily upward acceptance, at least of the concept of equality for blacks. Among whites, 89 percent indicated that they "earnestly wanted to see equality for blacks," three out of four felt discrimination against blacks was morally wrong, and 52 percent believed that blacks would achieve equality.[49]

While whites and blacks continued to disagree about the *rate* at which change should occur, and while surveys showed that a majority of whites still resisted integration when it came to having to bus *their* children out of the neighborhood, most public opinion analysts (including those at the National Public Opinion Research Center, Louis Harris, and the authors of a report on racial attitudes to the Kerner Commission) held a cautiously optimistic view of the measures being taken to bring about racial equality. Citing surveys indicating that clear majorities of whites supported federal programs to tear down the ghettos and give jobs to all the unemployed, even when a 10 percent rise in personal taxes would be required, the authors of a report to the Kerner Commission questioned the source and intention of the backlash theory. Their conclusions deserve to be quoted at length:

Apparently the level of public support for proposals such as those recommended by the Kerner Commission has been underestimated by congressmen and others in political office. Perhaps the press has oversold the notion of a white backlash and has placed too little emphasis upon public approval for massive federal spending to overcome racial inequities. Perhaps, although a minority of white Americans who have received a disproportionate amount of attention from the press, oppose such programs the preponderance of American public opinion would support a war on poverty that goes far beyond any of the measures seriously considered by recent congresses. Thus, on the issue of public spending, the more important gap appears to be between public willingness and congressional unwillingness to initiate and support Federal programs in jobs, housing and education. . . . Each group [blacks and whites] would apparently support a strong effort at the Federal level to reduce intergroup hostility and neither views the remedy primarily in terms of establishing "law and order." The popularly reported—but misnamed "white backlash" phenomenon has served to rationalize our timidity in making bold and imaginative inputs toward the solution of our urban problems.[50]

Sociologists Andrew Greeley and Paul Sheatsley, who had studied racial attitudes for close to three decades, came to a separate but similar conclusion. "There is no persuasive evidence thus far," wrote Sheatsley in 1969, "that either demonstrations and other forms of direct action, or legal sanctions applied by government create a backlash effect and foster segregationist sentiment. On the contrary, they may simply demonstrate, even more conclusively, that it is more costly to oppose integration than to bring it about."[51] "The political leader who adjusts his style to an anti-integration backlash is adjusting to something that does not exist."[52]

Since most public opinion surveys taken at the end of the 1960s indicated that the majority of white Americans were in favor of more progressive public policies, the assertion of a white backlash by neoconservatives indicates an ideology in search of an audience, seeking to become reality through its repetition by people in high places and through the electoral alienation of the majority.

Moynihan's assertion, for example, that "as the black masses for whatever reasons became more violent, white resistance became more stubborn," was made in the same year Kerner Commission researchers found that whites overwhelmingly wanted the government to continue programs to reduce urban poverty and racial discrimination.[53] Moynihan's statement that there is "now a conservative majority" of Americans who have been brought into the system and now identify their interests with "one or more institutions that are manifestly part of the established order" was a rationalization for the neoconservative policies he was promoting rather than a statement about the actual disposition of the American people.[54] We see the same denial of reality in a statement made by Norman Podhoretz in 1973 that "it would be hard to find anyone who believes, or at least professes to believe in equality of condition as a desirable goal."[55]

With the publication of Richard Scammon and Ben Wattenberg's *The Real Majority* in 1970, the establishment of a conservative majority was allegedly anchored in fact. By manipulating census data, Scammon and Wattenberg argued that the "real majority" in the nation was increasingly unyoung, unpoor, unblack, and conservative. For this real majority, they argued, the combined social changes that brought crime, integration, undisciplined children, dissent, and new values were a threat; their response was to move to the "moderate center." Scammon and Wattenberg's moderate center had shifted considerably to the right.

Discovering the "White Ethnics"

Positioning themselves as conservators of traditional American values and of a politics of stability, the neoconservative intellectuals did not want to appear to be inimically opposed to basic rights for blacks and other minorities. Overt racism was a product of the "backward" South, or of the extreme right. The neoconservatives, however, were conserving the moderate "middle." How, then, were they to distance themselves from the public support for racial equality without appearing to feed racism? In addition, how, being members of the intellectual elite, were they to distinguish themselves from that same intelligentsia they excoriated for giving in to black militants and excessive welfare spending?

The "discovery" of a new class of "white ethnics" with which the neoconservatives identified solved both problems. The white ethnics were the descendants of southern and eastern European immigrants who were suddenly discovered to have been suffering from the same disease that afflicted racial minorities. In 1971, *The*

Rise of the Unmeltable Ethnics, by Michael Novak, presented this new group. "When the children of southern and eastern Europe survey their position in American society," says Novak, "they find two forms of bigotry arrayed against them. The first derives from Nordic racism—the second from intellectuals: traditional New England WASP intellectuals and Jewish intellectuals."[56] In defining white ethnics as people who themselves suffered from ethnic discrimination, Novak was able to avoid responsibility for the systemic racism that he was a party to as a member of the rising New Right elite.

> Racists? Our ancestors owned no slaves. Most of us ceased being serfs only in the last 200 years—the Russians in 1896. . . . It must be said that ethnics think they are better people than the blacks. Smarter, tougher, harder working, stronger in their families. But maybe many are not sure. . . . Racism is not our invention; we did not bring it with us; we had prejudices enough and would gladly have been spared new ones.[57]

Novak's definition of the white ethnic social group is slippery. Though bound by its southern and eastern European ancestry, the cultural attachment of white ethnics to their native countries had become highly attenuated by the time Novak discovered them.[58] What Novak describes—feelings of inferiority, alienation from the intellectual elite—are not ethnic traits but the injuries of class. In fact, taking into account only ethnicity (religion/nationality), sociologist Andrew Greeley found that the vast majority of white ethnics seemed to be quite successful in American society and anything but alienated.[59]

Novak cannot admit the endemic class stratification in the U.S. economic system that he so heartily embraces, so he must attribute the suffering he sees among certain groups of whites to ethnicity.

In confusing ethnicity with class, Novak reveals his own class prejudices. While claiming to love the white Catholic ethnics from whom he came, he describes them as socially and politically "backward," as believing that life is cruel and that survival is the first morality.[60] White ethnics are said to love their families and to want to protect them. But the same could be said of any other group of people. Concern for neighborhood and family is not a cultural trait peculiar to southern and eastern Europeans. The subtle assumption in the writings of these white ethnic spokesmen, however, is that white ethnics' love of family and neighborhood makes them different from low-income blacks who, according to neoconservative lore, have little attachment to family or neighborhood. The result is the promulgation of a false enmity between blacks and white ethnics.

The new "ethnic politics" that Novak asserts was arising from the white ethnic resurgence would have blacks bartering with white ethnic groups for pieces of a contended turf in a city or workplace. Novak's ethnic politics assumes that blacks and white ethnics come into conflict over cultural values rather than over the respective class positions they occupy in a restricted market. He envisions fair trading between whites identified vaguely on the basis of "historial memory, real or imaginary," "instincts, feelings, intimacies," and blacks who have been systemically excluded from American society because of their color.

In the early 1970s, when Novak wrote his book, some blacks were just beginning to move into the middle class, largely because of the government programs the neoconservatives wanted to eliminate. The ethnic Catholics with whom Novak identified, however, were no longer disproportionately blue collar, but middle class, as were the Jews.[61] Were middle-class Catholics and Jews to be placed in an equivalent bargaining position to blacks, who still faced widespread racial discrimination and disproportionate poverty?

Reading between the lines, Novak's call for a politics of family and neighborhood based on small-unit bargaining between groups is a call to abandon a politics of federal remediation for past group discrimination. By equating white ethnicity with the black condition, Novak laid the intellectual groundwork for the Bakke and Weber cases, which began the next phase of the neoconservative assault on the liberatory claims of the Second Reconstruction.

The so-called white ethnic movement, if it ever existed (its popular manifestation was largely the production of bumper stickers and other decals proclaiming the merits of being Irish or Italian), disappeared as quickly as it had arisen. Michael Novak, who in 1971 could speak passionately about the politics of neighborhood and family, would devote two books in the 1980s to the achievements of monopoly capitalism and the modern bureaucratic corporation—the very institutions that were destroying neighborhoods and families.[62]

Redefining the Black Middle Class

Along with the discovery of the white ethnics, the New Right also "discovered" a new social trend: Blacks were becoming affluent. In a controversial article published in 1973, neoconservatives Richard Scammon and Ben Wattenberg contended, on the basis of census data, that the majority of blacks had made it into the middle class.[63] Moynihan had earlier hinted at this in a polemic against the "new racialism": "Remember," he told graduating seniors at the New School for Social Research in 1968, that "the Negro middle class is on the move. . . . If there is an ethnic balance 'against' Negroes in many municipal bureaucracies today, there is likely to be one 'for' them in the not distant future."[64]

In a 1972 essay laced with statistics, Moynihan pointed out that a new group of blacks—husband/wife teams under thirty-five outside the South—was achieving parity with whites. "The trend lines are consistent and powerful," he said. "If they persist, that is to say, if the present income equality of these young black/white families holds up as they grow older, one of the fundamental correlates of race in the United States—inferior earning power—will disappear."[65] Moynihan castigated "radical ideologists" for "insisting that almost everything is getting worse, and denying that anything is getting better," though he admitted that a parallel trend was driving blacks at the lower end of the spectrum into deepening poverty and unemployment. His explanation for the existence of the black underclass, however, remained consistent: pathology of the poor black family structure.

While Moynihan, Scammon, and Wattenberg were correct that a significant group of blacks had made important strides in the 1960s, their conclusions about the end of racial correlates were clearly contradicted by some of their own findings, as well as those of others.

Even as Scammon and Wattenberg's article was published, the gap between black and white income, which had been closing during the 1960s, was widening.[66] At the same time that college-educated blacks were moving into the middle class, the number of female-headed families was growing, and correlatively, black poverty. Although blacks had increased their percentage share of professional, technical, managerial, entrepreneurial, and clerical positions, the percentage of black males concentrated in relatively poorly paid positions remained the same between 1950 and 1970—about two-thirds.[67] A detailed study of the occupations into which blacks moved in the 1960s (published in 1975) revealed that in "most categories the greatest gains were made in the least prestigious and least paid occupations."[68] The percentage of white males in 1970 occupying professional, technical, and managerial positions was more than double that of blacks.[69] Moreover, blacks, being the last hired, were becoming the first fired in the much-praised restructuring process.

Critics pointed out that Scammon and Wattenberg's conclusion that the majority of blacks had reached middle-class status was based on a faulty lumping together of job categories that, while classified as "white collar"—for instance, clerical jobs and security personnel—were actually low-paying, low-status jobs that often left workers at or below the poverty level. Scammon and Wattenberg relied too heavily on occupational status rather than income in their definition of what constituted the middle class.

The redefinition of the meaning of middle class for blacks was a key aspect of the broader New Right redefinition of the ideal of social equality. In the neoconservative literature of the 1970s one sees a preoccupation with the "dangers" and "excesses" of equality. Irving Kristol warns against those who "prize equality more than liberty." "The kind of liberal egalitarianism so casually popular today will, if it is permitted to gather momentum, surely destroy a liberal society." Moynihan bewails, "Everywhere, equality is the cry." Nathan Glazer warns that the demand for equality in political rights and power "also represents a demand for equality in economic power, in social status, in authority in every sphere. . . . There is no point at which the equality revolution can come to an end."[70]

According to the new logic, if the majority of blacks are entering the middle class, then continuing catch-up remedies such as affirmative action or open admissions are no longer needed, and the continuing demand for them by civil rights advocates represents simply the vested interests of a class that has come to depend on government programs for status and livelihood. Besides, according to the New Right, the black underclass is not served by government programs. Wrote Moynihan, "The social science of the 1960s had pretty much demolished the notion that much comes of 'enriched' service programs, excepting the enrichment of the service dispensing classes."[71]

What in effect the neoconservative intellectuals set out to do was to convince congressional and local policymakers that blacks had effectively exploited the democratic process to achieve their place as one of many equally competing "interest groups" in the American pluralist system. Continuing cries of pain from the black community they labeled "special interests" in a zero-sum conception of power that assumes that meeting black demands means withdrawing power from other sectors of the population, namely white males. These efforts were crucial in shifting the terms of the national debate over policy with regard to poor people and racial minorities. The intellectuals of the New Right successfully disarmed their liberal critics and helped to legitimize the structural changes demanded by capital during the 1970s.

Forging a New Electoral Constituency

While neoconservative intellectuals laid the ideological foundation for a right-wing shift, they could not ensure that the public would conform to the platform they laid out. Partly, that public was molded by the waning of militant minority movements (the victims of assassinations, government "dirty tricks", and continuous harassment), so that minorities' own interpretation of life in America's internal colonies could not be heard. Partly, the molding of a new activist conservative electorate was the work of New Right strategists, who aggressively wooed the most reactionary elements in American society—southern racists, fundamentalist preachers, and the racially biased class frustrations of white blue-collar workers—in the service of a long-term Republican realignment.

The strategy that lay behind the creation of an alleged "real majority" can be found in Kevin Phillips' book, *The Emerging Republican Majority*, published in 1969.[72] Phillips, an aide to Nixon's attorney general, John Mitchell, foresaw a long-term Republican realignment through the manipulation of campaign themes that would appeal to southern racists, long identified with the Democratic party, traditionally Democratic blue-collar Catholics in border states who were worried about inflation and antagonistic to the "eastern establishment," and the new entrepreneurs of the Sun Belt.

Phillips saw the 1968 vote for George Wallace as a way to capture some of these voters for the Republicans. He was sure that the "principal force which broke up the Democratic Coalition [was] Negro socioeconomic revolution and liberal Democratic ideological inability to cope with it."[73]

Nixon's adoption of Phillips' "southern strategy" in 1972 represented an explicit deal with southern conservatives such as Strom Thurmond. According to the editors of the Atlanta Constitution, the Nixon deal was this: "If I'm president of the United States I'll find a way to ease up on the federal pressures forcing social desegregation—or any other kind of desegregation."[74]

In preparation for his electoral victory in 1972, Nixon played to southern racists by urging Congress to impose a moratorium on court-ordered school busing, nominating conservative "strict constructionists" to the Supreme Court, pleading with the court for postponement in the Mississippi desegregation plan, and lobbying Congress to defeat the fair-housing enforcement program and the extension of the Voting Rights Act of 1965. He also vetoed bills and impounded funds designed to assist blacks, fired government officials who tried to implement integration guidelines, and weakened the offices for civil rights in the Justice and Health, Education, and Welfare departments.

The media played its part in producing a backlash effect by highlighting only the most violent and sensational moments of the continuing black struggle, and by running stories on alleged "welfare chiselers," thus giving visual substance to the neoconservatives' fears of black nihilists and the disorganized and unruly black underclass.[75]

Neither Ford nor Carter did anything to stop the systematic assault on the programs and concepts of equality and justice that had been articulated by the African-American and other social movements of the 1960s. President Carter, elected by the margin of the black electorate, appointed a number of blacks to federal judgeships, cabinet posts, and ambassadorships, but he also presided over the highest black unemployment rate in over a decade, the Bakke and Weber decisions undercutting affirmative action, and cutbacks in school lunch programs, financial assistance to black students, and health care for the poor, at the same time that he was raising the military budget. In effect, the ruling elite had made a deal to end the Second Reconstruction as they had the first.

The Winter of the Civil Rights Movement

As the 1970s came to a close, the New Right assault on the social movements of the 1960s appeared to have been successful. It had not killed the people's movements, for it was during the 1970s that the citizens' action, ecology, and antinuclear movements flourished, but the insurgent right had succeeded in keeping the movements fragmented, in reversing momentum in several areas, and in creating a stalemate in others.

The 1970s was a particularly low period for those who had hoped that the black liberation movement would change the direction of the country. Had both Martin Luther King and Malcolm X lived to effect a rapprochement between the civil rights and black power movements—as it appeared might be ready to happen when Malcolm made a visit to Selma, Alabama, two weeks before his death—the history of the 1970s might have been different. But in the bitter aftermath of the assassinations and multiple assaults on black insurgency, the black movement itself remained divided between competing factions and ideologies. Although black activists recognized the need for unity, there seemed no leader or organization capable of pulling it off. It was the movement's "winter," wrote historian Vincent Harding, a period in which there was a "dangerous loss of hope among black people, hope in ourselves, hope in the possibility of any real change, hope in any moral, creative force beyond the flatness of our lives."[76] "The realization of failure and political uncertainty cut across virtually every tendency of the black movement by the mid-and late 1970s," said Manning Marable.[77]

In the leadership vaccum that was left, the African-American movement split into two camps. On the one hand, northern, largely urban community organizers and academics turned increasingly to black nationalist or Marxist-Leninist prescriptions for change. On the other hand, a growing body of black elected officials and professionals, who owed their political fortunes to the Democratic party and other institutions of the white ruling class but their offices to black constituencies, sought power through traditional ethnic interest-group politics.

Given the lack of finance capital available in the black community, the steady deterioration of life in the urban ghettos, and the absence of a unified militant black social movement, black politicians, with their access to the patronage and social services so badly needed by the black community, began to assume an influence out of all proportion to their numbers.[78] (In the early 1970s black politicians constituted less than 1 percent of all elected officials.)

The media, including the black press, the Democratic party, and numerous academics made much of the power of the "new black vote." The alleged emergence of a black political and professional class enabled the white elite to proclaim that blacks were indeed making it in the system and that it was time to put the civil rights era (i.e., the era of agitation) behind us. In 1975, William Julius Wilson's book *The Declining Significance of Race* appeared to critical acclaim.[79] Wilson purported to demonstrate through an analysis of socioeconomic trends that race was no longer the barrier it once was to black achievement.

But even as Wilson was proclaiming the end of the salience of racism, his predictions were being undermined by the restructuring of the economy, the greatest since the Great Depression. This resulted in the loss not only of the secondary (unskilled) labor markets African Americans had always depended on to sustain their families, but of the skilled and professional jobs into which upwardly mobile blacks had hoped to move with the help of affirmative action. The cutbacks in social welfare spending hurt not only the poor, but the black working class and professionals, for whom the government had become the chief employer. Between 1972 and 1976, the proportion of black families earning more than $24,000 declined from 12 percent to 9 percent. Between 1974 and 1977, there was no net increase of black men in private industry.[80] Black college enrollment (which had been steadily increasing since the 1960s) peaked in 1976; thereafter, it started a downhill slide. The number of black female-headed families increased tremendously, producing a generation of children destined to be permanently locked out of the economy.[81]

The reversal of black expectations—experienced on a daily basis but not fully understood or critically analyzed—led to increasing racial hostility not only at the lower levels of the economic ladder (as conflict broke out in declining industries over maintaining seniority for whites versus affirmative action for blacks), but at the middle-income levels, as blacks and whites contested for diminishing access to higher education and professional jobs.

As a result of declining black opportunities and the eclipse of black insurgency, black political rhetoric and activity during this period were focused internally. The need for racial solidarity to achieve black economic, political, and cultural self-determination was stressed over transforming the larger society. As Manning Marable concludes, nationalism has historically characterized those periods when hope for changing white America seemed dim.[82]

Paradoxically, black politicians could broker for programs, jobs, and development investment with the white establishment while using black nationalist rhetoric in the black community that was well to the left of what would be acceptable among those from whom they sought favors.[83] As long as such rhetoric was encapsulated within a dependent black community, and as long as black power brokers accepted the limits of pluralist, interest-group bargaining, they were safe.

The Black-White Divide

While black politicians learned to parlay their leadership role in the black community into limited benefits from the white bourgeoisie, they had almost no contact with any other sector of the white community. Having direct contact neither with black leadership, nor with a black insurgent movement that could project its message beyond the ghetto, white organizers of social movements were forced to rely on their own racially limited perception of American social reality. It is in the nature of the psychosocial dynamic of racism that it blinds even well-meaning white people to the actual operations of institutionalized racism.[84] Bereft of contact with progressive black leadership or of direct knowledge of conditions within black America, white liberals and social activists were ill-equipped to understand either the ideological revolution initiated by neoconservative intellectuals or the effects of the economic restructuring on the black community.[85]

Whites saw African Americans being elected to office, becoming corporate officers, appointed judges, and appearing in television sit-coms and they assumed that the civil rights revolution had been won. They did not see the virulent underside of the New Right counter-revolution in the alarming rise in police killings of young black men, the growing gap between the black middle class and the black poor, the soaring black unemployment figures, the deterioration of black education, or the "economic draft," which sent young black men into the military as the only way out of the poverty cycle—a program which had been promoted by Moynihan as perhaps the best way to achieve black manhood.

White antinuclear activists often bemoaned the lack of black involvement in their movement and with their "issues," assuming that blacks were uninterested in "peace" or environmental pollution. They forgot that the black community sustained disproportionate casualties during the Vietnam war, that black G.I.s had led the so-called fragging movement (mutinies in which recruits turned against their officers) within the military that hastened the war's end, and that blacks worked in the "dirtiest" jobs and lived in the most polluted sections of town.

As a result of the black-white divide, both blacks and whites were seriously hampered in their ability to make even reformist demands on the system. During the civil rights movement the mobilization of white liberal support (as indicated by the opinion polls) acted to enhance the bargaining position of black militants by increasing the political consequences for the white political establishment of opposing "acceptable" black demands.[86] The end of this support weakened the black movement.

One indication of this weakness is the Full Employment and Balanced Growth Act that the Congressional Black Caucus (CBC) succeeded in getting passed in the late 1970s. In its final form, it was so stripped of its original intent that it was virtually meaningless.[87] Though the CBC had made some attempt to get support from white liberals beyond the Congress, their outreach was limited to the leadership of the traditional liberal civil rights and labor bureaucracies. Support for the bill had not been taken up by the white social movements that were organizing street demonstrations and civil disobedience campaigns at the grassroots level.

Cut off from the black experience, which might have broadened and deepened their understanding of the forces at work in American society, the white-led movements of the 1970s organized around either limited local "winnable victories," such as stopping redlining in particular neighborhoods or reducing utility rates, or broad, national, but somewhat abstract ("common denominator") issues such as stopping particular weapons systems or passing the Equal Rights Amendment. A broadly endorsed national movement that focused on the struggle for full employment might have raised some of the fundamental economic issues that would have exposed the restructuring of the economy then taking place.

Conclusion

The utopianism and cultural vitality that had characterized the mass movements of the 1960s was in eclipse by the end of the 1970s. Liberalism, as the dominant ideology of the governing elite, had given way to neoconservatism, and on its right, to a virulent form of Cold War and political manichaeanism. In such a climate, the black movement was demoralized, defensive, and splintered along class and ideological lines, while the white left, also fragmented, was either increasingly narrowly based or had settled for a kind of least-common-denominator pragmatism.

By the end of the decade, much of the country's industrial base had been transferred to the third world. Jobs were increasingly found in the low-wage, nonunionized financial, sales, and service sectors. The shrinking of the middle class, the growing gap between rich and poor, and the creation of a new class (the professional-managerial elite or "yuppies") through the high-tech industries had profound implications for the future of social movements.

One consequence was the restratification of the workforce, so as to make obsolete the old definitions and subjective experiences of "working class," "middle class," "blue collar," "white collar," "professional," technical," and even "managerial." Was an unemployed steelworker living on welfare still blue-collar? Was a secretary who worked in an office as one of a pool of computer operators considered white-collar? Was a college teacher who worked part-time at three different schools as an adjunct making a subsistence-level wage to be considered professional? Or was the black businessman who ran a mom-and-pop store with no employees and netting less than $20,000 a year to be considered managerial?

The difficulty each single-issue or single-constituency movement had in both formulating an ideological response to the crisis and in developing effective change strategies is reflective of the chaos engendered by the restratification of the workforce. Neither race, nor class, nor gender categories alone could now describe the experiences of most people who benefitted or suffered from the restratification, yet the movements were stratified along those old lines. The result was to confuse and fragment an already fragmented constituency for radical social change.

This confusion at the level of everyday experience explains the popularity of the simplistic, individualistic message of the religious right for so many lower-middle-class and working-class whites in the late 1970s, and Ronald Reagan's election in 1980 by a minority of the potential electorate. The Jackson presidential campaign of 1984 offered itself as a response to the demoralization and fragmentation of the social-change constituency and as an antidote to a politics of narrowed self-interest and crude disdain for human suffering. But such a movement, in turn, would have led its participants to see that only through a radical restructuring of the system could full employment goals be met. It was just such an insight that the system's managers were determined to keep the public from grasping. Racism—both in the white left and as deliberately fostered by those in power, was the prime mechanism.

3

The Emergence
of the Rainbow Coalition

My commitment as a presidential candidate is to focus on and lift those boats stuck on the bottom full of unpolished pearls. For if the boats on the bottom rise, all boats above will rise—my views in this regard are the exact opposite of the "trickle *down*" views of President Reagan. The way I propose to do this is to build a new functional "Rainbow Coalition of the Rejected" spanning lines of color, sex, age, religion, race, region and national origin. The old minorities—Blacks, Hispanics, women, peace activists, environmentalists, youth, the elderly, small farmers, small businesspersons, poor people, gays and lesbians—if we remain apart, will continue to be a minority. But, if we come together, the *old minorities* constitute a *new majority*. That is how I propose to be nominated and elected President.[1]

—Jesse Jackson

The concept of building a rainbow coalition to capture state power represents something new in American political life. In its commitment to "lift those boats stuck on the bottom" it makes a claim for overturning the class system represented by Reagan's "trickledown" economics; but in describing the constituency for such a program, Jackson utilizes categories of people who are defined, not in the classical Marxian sense solely by their relationship to the means of production, but as "rejected" because of race, national origin, gender or sexual orientation, age, or ideology.

The language of the Jackson campaign was not rigorously scientific, but rather figurative and biblical, yet it reflects an intuition that the currents of frustration and alienation surfaced by the social movements of the 1960s and 1970s were leading inexorably in the 1980s to the potential for the development of a mass class consciousness. That is, if the separate sectoral movements could see past the artificial barriers that kept them apart, and come to respect the specificities of each others' sense of betrayal by the dominant system, they would discover that they had become a "class for itself" with the power—at least in numbers—to change the system that was oppressing all of them.

This insight grew out of the actual realignment of economic and political power that was taking place throughout the 1970s—a realignment that the election of Ronald Reagan in 1980 both reflected and accelerated. The changes described at the end of Chapter 2, were the result of the political ascendancy of a new coalition of right-wing politicians and finance capital that had overturned the assumptions on which the liberal welfare state of the last forty years had been built.[2] New Deal liberalism had actually prevented the potential of the class consciousness produced by the Great Depression from gaining political hegemony. It had done this by shifting the conception of the polity as aggregates of contending classes based on power and wealth to that of a pluralism of separate but equally competing "interests," which it was the business of the party to mediate.

Now, however, with the demise of the liberal spending and taxation systems that had characterized federal policy since the New Deal and its replacement with a more rigorously class-skewed system of rewards, more and more of the American people—including the small business people and farmers cited by Jackson, as well as white skilled labor—were being cast into the category of the "rejected." The new pattern of accumulation and distribution, based on corporate deregulation and a militarized economy, was affecting the sensibilities and threatening the life-styles of even the white middle class. More and more white middle-class peace activists and environmentalists now had a personal stake in aligning themselves with lower-income strata in a new political configuration to overturn such regressive policies.

Until the Jackson campaign, however, no movement or leader had been able to draw the perspectives of these separate sectoral movements into a unified political program. The 1960s had demonstrated that African Americans had the potential to lead the struggle for long-term social change, but to do so, they would have to build a movement that could sustain itself for the long haul. Before his death, Martin Luther King recognized the need to transform the civil rights movement into a broad-based, multifaceted, organized, and sustained movement for progressive change.[3] Because blacks were not numerically strong enough to enforce the civil rights reforms they had achieved, let alone to carry out a more radical process of political transformation, King foresaw the need for long-term alliances with nonblack groups. He recognized that the coalition that had backed civil rights legislation would not necessarily back the kind of "human rights" agenda he came to see was necessary, requiring structural economic change.

King's proposed Poor People's Campaign, which was to have been a massive civil disobedience campaign calling for a $12 billion economic bill of rights, might have been the vehicle for uniting progressive and liberal middle-class whites with a multiracial legion of poor and working people, but his untimely assassination cut down the only person who could have provided the moral and organizational leadership for such an undertaking. Though in conception the Poor People's Campaign was a kind of prefiguring of the Rainbow Coalition of 1984, the campaign that took place after King's assassination sank in the mire of official sabotage, internal dissension, scarce resources, anarchy, and police repression.[4] Those who committed themselves to pulling it off (more as a memorial to King than anything else) were unable to develop its potential.

Why did not black leadership in the 1970s move in the direction envisaged by King? Class interests and a lack of political vision have usually been the reasons cited, but that is only a partial explanation.[5] The other part lies in the fact that the assassinations and the violent repression the black movement met with at the end of the 1960s, along with the misperceived "white backlash" against black gains, had a profound effect on the black psyche. Every black person in the country was convinced that whoever emerged in the future to lead a movement that challenged the fundamental premises of the American corporate economy and state would become a target for assassination, and there was nothing that white people were going to do to prevent that from happening.[6] Leftists who decry the "sellout" of black leaders to "bourgeois" politics fail to appreciate this reality.

Such a conviction may lie behind the failure of the 1972 National Black Political Convention (which brought together eight thousand politically active blacks to Gary, Indiana) to act on the radical political agenda it set forth. The convention called for the disciplined organizing of an independent black political formation, which would take the black community "beyond the decadent white politics of American life" and of a society "built on the twin foundations of white racism and white capitalism."[7] Shortly after the Gary convention, however, a number of the most prominent leaders of the conference (including Jesse Jackson) returned to the fold of the Democratic party, some working for the election of Hubert Humphrey and others for George McGovern. Thereafter, the National Black Political Assembly, and the National Black Independent Political party that it spawned, were unable to secure the kind of leadership that was necessary to sustain such a radical project.[8]

Seen against this backdrop, the emergence of the Jackson campaign in 1984 as a progressive, black-led, multiracial, anticorporate, and anti-imperialist movement that took an electoral form must be appreciated as a daring and visionary innovation—all the more so when we consider that it occurred during the administration of one of the most reactionary presidents in history, at a time of resurgent racist violence and public retrenchment.

Several conditions were necessary before blacks were willing (and able) to reach out beyond their own community to lead a national movement for progressive social change. First was the failure of interest-group politics to overcome the systemic powerlessness and poverty experienced by black Americans. Second was a resurgence of extra-electoral "movement" activity—mass demonstrations, and so forth—which convinced the black community that it might find allies for a challenge to the rightward drift of the national political climate. Third was the emergence of a new kind of black-led multiracial "progressive" politics that went beyond the parameters set by interest-group pluralism and began to elect candidates at the local level. Finally, there was the work of certain bridge-building networks, which laid the interracial groundwork for the emergence of the Rainbow Coalition. This chapter surveys the preconditions for the emergence of the "rainbow" as a political bloc in the Jackson campaign. It views that campaign as a logical outcome of the political pressures from below and above that drove the black elite to search for new strategies of political empowerment.

The Failure of Black Interest-Group Politics

The Jackson campaign confounded conventional political wisdom. If the campaign—waged by a black man who had never held elective office before—was an attempt to win the presidency, then it could only be explained as the delusion of a fool or a madman. If, on the other hand, it was a bid for *black influence* within the Democratic party, then, according to many traditional black politicians, Jackson was going about it in the wrong way. The traditional interest-group assumptions about political power held by most black politicians formed the basis on which many of them refused to endorse Jackson, fearing he would split the black vote and thus weaken blacks' influence with the white front-runner. Others, who operated from the same assumptions, felt that a black "leverage" candidate running in the primaries could win enough delegates to bargain with a white candidate at the convention for such black concerns as jobs, fair housing, and civil rights laws. Most of the black politicians who supported Jackson thought that greater black participation in the Democratic party through the use of a black candidate who could generate excitement in the black community would force the party to respond to black needs. Washington, D.C., mayor Marion Barry commented, "We need to strengthen electoral politics as it relates to blacks and Jesse offers a new course. Complacency has set in, in the Democratic Party. We lost to President Reagan, not because he was better organized, or better. We lost because Democrats stayed at home. . . . They just weren't excited about the Democratic agenda."9

In his own pre-announcement campaigning, and indeed at many points throughout the campaign itself, Jackson seemed to accept the assumptions of interest-group politics. At a rally in August 1983 in Fayette County, Mississippi, he told blacks, "We are looking for our piece of the power," and throughout the campaign to black audiences, Jackson reiterated the refrain, "Our time has come."[10]

However, while incorporating appeals to ethnic solidarity and interest-group leverage as specific tactics, the Jackson campaign went beyond the boundaries of this paradigm. The campaign was a kind of hybrid of the social-movement politics of the 1960s and the black interest-group politics of the 1970s, moving toward a new synthesis whose outlines are only beginning to be perceived.

To understand the Jackson campaign as a social movement operating within the framework of traditional interest-group politics, one has to examine the hopes invested in black electoral politics in the 1970s and the obstacles such politics encountered.

Historically there have been three ways in which the black community has sought to overcome its structured powerlessness and poverty in white America. The first, represented in the slave rebellions of the eighteenth and nineteenth centuries and the urban ghetto rebellions of the 1960s, was the way of desperation—mass insurrection against an overwhelmingly powerful enemy. Various black nationalist self-help movements, including the clientage politics of Booker T. Washington, Marcus Garvey's Universal Negro Improvement Association, and the Nation of Islam, as well as numerous short-lived attempts to form black parties, represent the second approach. Essentially, black separatism leaves intact the racial caste system, attempting to generate power from within the socially devalued group. Still a third approach is found in the attempts of broad, interracial organizations (the National Association for the Advancement of Colored People; the Urban League) and black-led social movements (the civil rights movement) to force concessions from the white business class and state through the use of either constitutionally recognized remedies or civil disobedience campaigns. This approach depends for its success on the manipulation of sectors of the white community into siding with the minority against corporate elites or the state.

Prior to the passage of the Voting Rights Act of 1965, black involvement in electoral politics as a means of remedying black powerlessness and poverty was negligible, especially at the national level. In 1952 about 60 percent of all African Americans and 75 percent of southern blacks had never voted for president.[11]

Because of their underrepresentation in the electorate, blacks who were involved in electoral politics had to settle for inclusion in the white patronage system. In large cities, black ward bosses served as brokers between the white machine and their constituents. Once elected, they tended to remain in office, kept there by the patronage they were able to dispense to an otherwise powerless constituency, and, often, by their forced complicity in a system of corruption that was the way of life in large city machines. Manning Marable has observed that in racist societies "racists have historically used corruption as a means to co-opt Black leaders and to minimize dissatisfaction among the oppressed masses. A Black man or woman who refused to steal, who rejected petty graft, was not to be trusted."[12]

The passage of the Voting Rights Act opened a new era in black politics. With this tool, blacks hoped that they could overcome their dependence on clientage politics and begin to assume their place within the pluralist, interest-group tradition that had appeared to work for other groups, such as the Jews, with whom comparisons were often made. Since blacks, as a racially stigmatized group, lacked access to economic power (i.e., property, control over the means of production, wealth), they hoped that by gaining political control of geographic enclaves they could begin to affect the mechanisms of distribution that denied blacks a fair share of the social surplus. What was not fully appreciated was that by the time blacks entered electoral politics as a significant national voting bloc, the rules of power had changed. It was not the ability to deliver votes to a candidate that counted, but the ability to deliver money, in which the black community was sorely lacking.

The history of black electoral activity since passage of the Voting Rights Act illustrates the difficulties this approach met with in effecting any real change either in the calculus of black power or in the life conditions of the majority of the black population.

Though blacks began to be elected to office in record numbers after the passage of the Voting Rights Act (between 1965 and 1982 black officeholders increased tenfold), by 1984 they still constituted only 1.2 percent of the total number of elected officials nationwide. The rate of increase was heaviest in the 1960s and in the South, the result of both the rising expectations generated by the civil rights movement and the concentration of blacks in rural Black Belt counties and small towns.[13] Even in the South, however, the region with the highest concentration of black elected officials, their numbers nowhere approximate black representation in the total population. Blacks in the seven southern states covered by the Voting Rights Act make up 26 percent of the population, yet hold only 6 percent of the elective offices. The white power structure has found numerous ways to circumvent the Voting Rights Act, including economic intimidation, at-large voting, dual primaries, redistricting to dilute black voting strength, the manipulation of the absentee-ballot process, and numerous impediments to registering, such as limiting the hours during which registration can take place.

Even more indicative of the lack of real power than the small percentage of black politicians is the sectoral distribution of black officeholders. Fifty-three percent of the black officeholders in the South are mayors of small (less than 1,000 population) black-majority towns, dependent on white-controlled county systems and white-dominated state legislatures. In rural southern areas, county governments play a particularly influential role in the allocation of goods and services and state legislatures can often override the prerogatives of local elected officials. In 1977, blacks held less than 2 percent of the elective county offices in the South.[14]

Black mayors in the rural South are thus without any effective control over the jurisdictions they serve. This was clearly seen in the case of Eddie James Carthan, the young black mayor of the tiny Mississippi Delta town of Tchula, who, in the waning years of the Carter administration, sought to change the economic and political calculus of his desperately impoverished town through an infusion of federal and foundation grants and loans. When Carthan refused to accept a bribe from the white planters to be as he called it, their "good little boy," their representatives on the board of aldermen, the county commission, the state legislature, and the judiciary made his administration virtually ungovernable. The state legislature passed a law applicable only to the town of Tchula rescinding some of the mayor's prerogatives. Numerous lawsuits were brought against Carthan, so that he began to spend more time in court than in city hall. When this failed to deter him from carrying out a redevelopment plan for the area, the white power structure resorted to a series of criminal frame-ups designed to drive him from office and to discredit him in the eyes of other black aspirants to political office. If it had not been for a defense campaign that called national and international attention to this case, Carthan might have been sent to the gas chamber. (The last indictment brought against him was for capital murder.)[15]

Ostensibly more impressive than the number of small-town mayors in the South is the number of blacks who have been elected to head the nation's largest cities. In 1984 there were nineteen black mayors serving cities with populations of 100,000 or more. Four of the nation's six largest—Chicago, Los Angeles, Philadelphia, and Detroit—have black mayors.

Black mayors have been able to make some difference for the black middle class. A new stratum of black professionals has been employed under their aegis, more blacks have been hired in the police forces, and more black businessmen have gotten city contracts. At the same time, black mayors have had to preside over the steady deterioration of inner-city neighborhoods. The irony of black political ascendancy in the cities is that it was made possible only by white flight, which robbed the metropolitan center of its tax base. In order to get revenue for basic services, black mayors have had to collaborate with white financial interests, which have turned once ethnically vibrant central cities into glass and steel recreational and business centers for the rich. Coming to power in the midst of the national and international economic crisis, black mayors have had to cut welfare benefits and break strikes of municipal employee unions. Thus, as blacks gained control of the city machinery, they found the power had fled elsewhere. Their administrations have been characterized by sometimes militant rhetoric, but in performance they have not been terribly different from their white predecessors, at least in regard to increasing life chances for the majority of the black population.[16]

As it turned out, the growth of a class of black urban politicians presiding over majority-black districts and cities was useful to the corporate elite and their consensus-seeking organizations. Black mayors have been placed in a quasi-neocolonial position according to Marable.[17] Ever conscious of their beleaguered status within white America, African Americans have been reluctant to challenge the mayors and city councils they have only recently elected and on whom they now depend to deliver city services. Knowing this, white finance capital can be assured that its downtown interests will be protected and that political unrest in the black ghettos will be contained.[18]

The ability of the Congressional Black Caucus (CBC), formed in 1971, to effect changes in federal legislation that would materially benefit the black masses has been even less successful than the efforts of black mayors. Although the CBC has taken strong, progressive positions over the years on a number of issues from the need for increased social welfare spending to cuts in the defense budget, it has been a voice crying in the wilderness. The legislation black congresspersons would need to pass in order to demonstrate that there was real hope for the majority of black Americans (such as a full-employment bill with teeth in it) suggests changes the U.S. political system is incapable of making.[19] As a result, the Congressional Black Caucus and other black leadership forums have increasingly functioned to enhance the individual careers of the black middle class—those who can profit from the incremental benefits the system is capable of granting, rather than the distributive justice it will not concede.

The Search for New Political Strategies

As the trajectory of black hopes plummeted toward the end of the 1970s, black leaders began to search for new mechanisms of empowerment. The search was intensified after the election in 1980 of Ronald Reagan. Reagan had initiated his candidacy in Mississippi, coding his announcement in the language of "state's rights," a symbolism that was not lost on the black leadership of the nation or on such white racist groups as the Klan, who were emboldened by Reagan's election to a new level of activism, even involving themselves in electoral politics. Reagan's immediate cuts in programs affecting the poor and working classes and his intention to roll back the civil rights legislation of the last twenty years drove deep fear into even the more affluent sections of the black community.[20] Black politicians, whose constituencies were poor and getting poorer (even though the bulk of their vote came from the more affluent and educated sectors of the African-American community), could no longer afford to ignore conditions in the ghettos. Neither could black businessmen, who still depended on a predominantly black clientele. By 1982 these conditions had reached epidemic proportions. One out of five black adults and one out of two teenagers was unemployed; one out of every three black Americans was living below the poverty level, and the "official" unemployment rate for blacks (not counting discouraged and underemployed workers) was three times that of whites.

Not only were conditions worsening for the black poor and working classes, but the newly created black middle class was beginning to experience a loss of income and status—a phenomenon confirmed in a report issued in 1984 by the Urban Institute, which shows that between 1980 and 1984, *every* sector of the black community experienced declines in incomes and standards of living. Hardest hit was the median-income family (the base of the black politician's power), whose income between 1980 and 1983 fell by 5.3 percent. This was in contrast to the findings for the white population, which showed that the top 60 percent of the white population experienced income gains.[21]

Deteriorating conditions of life within black America spurred renewed efforts to develop unity between conflicting sections of the black intellectual and political strata. In 1981, the National Black United Front (NBUF) was formed by a wide variety of militant urban-based nationalists, promising that ideological and personality differences that had inhibited the black nationalist movement throughout the 1970s had finally been overcome.[22] NBUF, headed by Brooklyn, New York-based pentecostal minister Herbert Daughtry (who would later play a prominent role in the Jackson campaign), established chapters in some twenty-two cities and attempted to channel the seething anger and alienation of ghetto blacks into campaigns against police brutality, and for the reformation of the criminal justice system, as well as into negotiations for increased municipal and corporate investment in the inner city, support work for the dramatically escalating South African liberation movement, and other efforts to educate and improve the quality of life in the black ghettos.

In another strand of the black nationalist movement, the National Black Political Assembly, which had been meeting since 1972 but had failed to develop the independent political party outlined in its original "Black Agenda," announced in August 1980 that the new party had been formed. The party, reported Marable:

> would not be a Black version of the Democratic and Republican parties, but a progressive black institution that would work for Black liberation and social transformation. It would include all major political, religious and social currents, tendencies and organizations within the national Black community. The party would not advocate an exclusively electoral political program; rather, it would concentrate on mobilizing the Black community for political and economic empowerment.[23]

Delegates to the National Black Political Assembly voted to encourage blacks to work for progressive local and state candidates, but to vote against Carter, Reagan, and John Anderson, either by refusing to vote for president, or by selecting a progressive third-party candidate instead.[24]

Growing out of the efforts of the Congressional Black Caucus to develop a more effective response to the deepening crisis in Black America, the black leadership, aligned with the Democratic party, traditional civil rights organizations, and black churches and businesses, formed the "Black Leadership Family," and in 1982 issued its *Black Leadership Family Plan for the Unity, Survival and Progress of Black People.*[25] It was hoped that this plan would be widely circulated throughout the traditional institutions of the black community and that it would form the basis of a shared perception of current realities and act as a call to greater unity of action.

The plan is significant in that it reflects the black leadership's heightened awareness of group insecurity. In an open letter to black institutions included in the plan, Washington, D.C., representative Walter Fauntroy stated: "As Black Americans we are confronted today with the most serious challenge that we have faced in this century to our rights to full participation in the economic, political and social life of this nation."[26] The *Black Leadership Family Plan* warns of "black economic re-enslavement in the 80s," of "political hit lists" of elected officials who support black interests, of the official harassment and disruption of black self-defense organizations, of congressional efforts to dismantle key civil rights legislation, of the increase in police brutality, of the media's systematic exclusion of positive black role models, and of a range of attacks on black business, which will destroy the potential for black economic development.

The Black Leadership Family Plan, while calling on blacks to "reach out in coalition with Whites, Hispanics and other minorities whose interests coincide with ours," also warns that blacks must be wary in choosing their allies. While listing the usual enemies of black progress, the plan warns that opposing forces "will be more subtle and insidious" than the obvious ones such as the Ku Klux Klan and will include government officials, corporations, the media, foundations, and university and other research groups.[27]

Black civil rights and political leaders were not only worried about the increasing racism and repression symbolized by the Reagan administration, but about their own ability to manage the deepening alienation and despair of poor blacks. The drug epidemic was wreaking havoc on black institutional life and on families, destroying the cultural glue that had historically held black communities together. A growing lumpen class with no allegiance to traditional black values threatened the ability of the black leadership to hold it all together. This was dramatically illustrated in the Miami rebellion of May 1980, which broke out over the police killing of Arthur McDuffie, a black insurance executive. Economically, the rebellion was the most devastating social uprising in American history. Commented Manning Marable, "White and black liberals were shocked and even bewildered by the rebellious rage that came from the depths of the black community."[28] Although church and civil rights leaders, including Jesse Jackson, were quickly dispatched to the scene to try to mediate the situation, they were summarily ignored by the black community of Dade County.

Growing out of this heightened awareness of insecurity—both from Reagan's America and from the black lower classes—traditional civil rights and political leaders initiated between 1982 and 1983 a series of voter education and registration drives that soon took on the frenzy of a new crusade, as a *New York Times* editor observed: "Some sections of many urban areas look and feel almost as they did during the civil rights movement two decades ago. Indeed, some people even refer to the new political activity as a crusade; others use the term, 'the movement'."[29]

By bringing more blacks into the Democratic party, these leaders hoped not only to avert a second Reagan victory, but to regain their status as mediators and brokers for the black community. They were buoyed by studies in the 1980 vote demonstrating that Reagan's margins of victory in New York, Mississippi, Alabama, Louisiana, Tennessee, South Carolina, North Carolina, Arkansas, Massachusetts, Kentucky, and Virginia were less than the number of unregistered blacks in those states. Black leaders hoped that if they could get blacks to register and vote in large enough numbers, they could defeat Reagan and possibly even turn the Senate back to the Democrats. For many, however, there was a question of motivation. Could millions of alienated blacks be motivated to register and vote for a traditional white politician? Black leaders were aware that their credit as brokers with the Democratic party was running out. Stung by Jimmy Carter's betrayal of black hopes during his last years in the White House, black Democrats were not at all sure they could deliver black voters to the white frontrunner. Thus, the idea of running a black presidential candidate in certain localities as a way of galvanizing the black vote began to gain credibility. Chicago congressman Gus Savage gave expression to this point of view in his syndicated column early in 1983:

> It seems unless we speak for ourselves we will be ignored or taken for granted in another national political campaign. . . . We should be about raising our own issues, mobilizing ourselves and strategizing to maximize our influence. Otherwise, most so-called Black spokespersons will become available to the highest bidder, trying to broker without a base, which amounts to begging as always, supposedly advising from behind some campaign trailer. Why not a serious Black presidential candidate?[30]

Quick to seize a political opportunity he had been contemplating for years, Jesse Jackson launched his own "Southern Crusade" in the summer of 1983 to register 2 million new voters throughout the South with the slogan "Hands that once picked cotton can now pick the president." Jackson was testing the waters for his own candidacy, which would be announced later that fall.[31]

As the 1984 presidential election primaries approached, the leadership that had grouped around the *Black Leadership Family Plan* held a series of hearings around the country to develop a comprehensive black political agenda that could serve as the black community's criteria for evaluating the presidential candidates.

The People's Platform, issued somewhat belatedly in March 1984, goes beyond the defensive rhetoric of the *Black Leadership Family Plan* in calling for a "new covenant for America."[32] *The People's Platform* recognizes four major shifts in the social, economic, and political reality of America, which it claims to address: the shift from a predominant white population to one that is nearly 25 percent nonwhite; the shift from a labor intensive industrial economy to a high-tech, service-oriented economy; and the growth of a critical mass of blacks, other minorities, and women who have matured politically to the point of demanding political equity, parity, and reciprocity.

On the basis of these shifts, the black leadership group that issued *The People's Platform* felt it was ready to issue a new call to all Americans to join in redirecting the priorities of the nation. *The People's Platform* was the most comprehensive policy statement to emerge from the stratum of the black establishment to date and the most politically "left" of any of its proclamations. It sharply critiqued the fundamental value and policy orientation of the Reagan administration and in certain areas—particularly foreign policy—also represented a repudiation of the positions of the Democratic party. For example, *The People's Platform* calls for the rejection of the East-West framework for international relations and its replacement by a North-South framework; it calls for normalizing relations with Cuba, the removal of U.S. troops from Honduras, the end of efforts to destabilize Nicaragua, and recognition of the Palestinians' right to a sovereign state. It calls for an immediate reduction in the military budget and a pledge of no "first use" of nuclear weapons; condemns the invasion of Grenada; and calls for sanctions against South Africa.

In its domestic proposals, *The People's Platform* is mildly social democratic. It demands that "the nation commit itself anew to a reordering of national priorities that place human needs and investment in human capital ahead of development of frightening weapons of mass destruction." It calls for comprehensive new industrial and urban policy, government planning, progressive tax reform, a commitment to full employment, and the lowering of interest rates. The platform falls short of the radical critique of capitalism offered by the National Black Political Assembly of 1972 and of the redistributive principles enunciated by the People's Convention held in the South Bronx in 1980. In short, it was the response of a black leadership stratum caught between their class interests in the maintenance of the now tenuous welfare state and more radical policy thrusts from below.

The Resurgence of Mass Mobilization

The Black Leadership Coalition, which issued *The People's Platform*, was pushed to move from a defensive to a more aggressive posture not only by signals such as that sent by the Miami rebellion, but also by the renewal of mass street demonstration, which indicated a general level of economic frustration and political alienation that went far beyond the black community.

The Carter administration and the rightward drift of the political climate had betrayed the hopes not only of blacks, but of all poor people, peace activists, environmentalists, labor, women, and family farmers. Carter's own Council of Economic Advisors had gone along with the business community's call for recession and played a major role in gutting the Humphrey-Hawkins Full Employment and Balanced Growth Act. In 1979 Carter reversed a campaign pledge and announced the decontrol of oil prices. Supported by the federal government, energy companies moved aggressively to exploit coal and uranium reserves, sending shock waves through the Native American and environmentalist communities.[33] In the spring of 1980, Carter announced sweeping budget cuts in social welfare spending. The prolonged holding of U.S. hostages in Iran had unleashed a new jingoism and calls from conservatives and prominent members of the business community for increased military spending and a tougher U.S. stance toward the third world. In his 1980 campaign speeches, Carter boasted that he had deregulated the airlines, trucking, and financial institutions and that he was working on deregulating the railroads.[34]

Faced with the Democratic party's betrayal of its New Deal tradition, left-liberal constituencies that had worked in separate issue or ethnic movements throughout most of the 1970s began to see the need to mount a national, unified movement to counter the policies of both the Republican and Democratic establishments. To do so, however, meant overcoming almost a decade of movement fragmentation.

In retrospect one can see three mass mobilizations that were crucial to building the Rainbow Coalition in the early 1980s.

South Bronx: The People's Convention

One of the first signs of a new militancy and the beginning of a public demonstration of interracial solidarity was the "People's Convention" held in August 1980 at the time of the Democratic National Convention in a devastated area of the South Bronx, New York. It was an area the Carter administration, with much public fanfare, had promised, but failed, to rehabilitate. Several miles downtown, amid the glittering skyscrapers of New York's rebuilt midtown, the Democratic party was renominating Jimmy Carter for the presidency.

In the South Bronx, over three thousand people—black, white, Latino, Asian, Native American—representing hundreds of community organizations, peace groups, political organizations, labor groups, tenants' groups, environmental groups, women's organizations, and so forth—met to adopt the "Declaration of Charlotte Street," which was both a declaration of political intent and a "people's platform" for peace and justice that prefigured—and in some instances went beyond—the platform enunciated by Jesse Jackson four years later. The three thousand delegates then led a march of fifteen thousand people downtown to the Democratic Convention, under the banner: "Too Many Broken Promises: Now We Will Be Heard!"

The "Declaration of Charlotte Street" began: "We have gathered together in this election year of 1980 because the Democratic and Republican parties have completely failed to respond to the needs of our communities and our peoples." Written in popular language, the "Declaration of Charlotte Street" is one of the most remarkable statements of unity to have emerged from any of the people's movements of this century.

In its description of the environment in which it was born and the people for whom it spoke, the declaration eloquently summed up the changes that had occurred over the last quarter century that were slowly, if fitfully, bringing more and more people to discover their common destiny. Among the conditions described were the massive gentrification programs that were displacing poor and working people in city after city across the nation, the rising rate of farm foreclosures, the crisis of health care, the wave of plant closings throughout the industrial Northeast and Midwest, the drug epidemic in the nation's ghettos, the diminishing hopes for gender equality, and turmoil throughout the third world.

Though the People's Convention did not result in an ongoing political program, it did present a comprehensive set of political principles—the People's Agenda—upon which public policy could be based. In this respect it represents an advance over earlier attempts to bring about broad popular unity around a common program.[35]

The People's Agenda included strict controls on profits, prices, interest rates, and rents; a cut in the military budget with funds transferred to needed social services; a progressive restructuring of the tax system; protection of the right of labor to organize and strike; a national health service; massive direct funding for housing, to be controlled by the affected communities; the financing of education through general funds rather than property taxes; radical welfare reform; the shutdown of nuclear power plants and the pursuit of safe, renewable energy sources; laws to prohibit multinational corporations with large nonfarm investments from purchasing land for food production; public funds to create farm cooperatives; unconditional amnesty for undocumented workers; an end to all forms of discrimination based on sexual orientation, age disability, and religious or ethnic background; an end to drug experimentation and sterilization abuse; a foreign policy based on respect for the freedom and independence of all nations; full recognition of the sovereignty of the Native American nations within the borders of the United States; the right of Puerto Rico and the Palestinians to independence and self-determination; the lifting of the blockade against Cuba; an end to all support for South Africa, the Duvalier regime in Haiti, Marcos in the Philippines, and dictatorial regimes; an end to the attempt to develop a "first-strike" nuclear capacity and the dismantling of all nuclear weapons; an end to draft registration.

In addition to its enunciation of a common set of political principles, a number of things set the declaration apart from previous popular left proclamations: the articulation of the need to work at both the inner and outer forms of oppression, and a commitment to take those principles into the arena of local electoral work. It was the experience gained by organizers working within a progressive ideological framework in several local electoral campaigns that gave impetus to the Jackson campaign of 1984.

June 12 Disarmament Rally

The second important mass mobilization was the rally held in New York City, 12 June 1982, at the time of the Second Special United Nations Session on Disarmament. The rally is critical to this history not only because it was the largest gathering of its kind in U.S. history, but because of the political battles that were fought and the lessons that were learned during the course of organizing for it.

The rally was initiated by the predominantly white peace organizations, which, throughout the 1970s, had worked in isolation from black and third world community struggles. Peace leaders saw the rally as an opportunity to demonstrate to the president and Congress that there was broad national support for an end to the nuclear arms race.

In order to get a massive turnout, peace leaders thought they had to limit the demands made by the demonstration. However, as rally plans got underway, representatives of black, Latino, Native American, and Asian-American organizations—most considerably to the political left of the rally's initiators—demanded representation on the planning committee. They also insisted that the march call for an end to U.S. intervention in the third world, a redirecting of the nation's priorities from military spending to human needs, and an end to racism and other issues of concern to people of color.

Bitter fights broke out in the planning committee over the attempts by people of color to be represented. The inclusion of the National Black United Front and its chairman, Rev. Herbert Daughtry, was a special bone of contention. Failing to understand that conditions within minority communities were driving their leaders toward a more radical political posture, white peace leaders charged the people of color with left sectarianism, while the people of color charged that this accusation was merely a smokescreen for the racism of the white peace activists. This was the first time since the anti-Vietnam war movement that black and other minority activists had made a serious bid to shape the direction of a movement that white activists saw as "theirs," and it very nearly exploded.

Explosion was prevented by many compromises. While some of

the third world groups seeking representation on the executive committee were given a place, other more politically "moderate" black leaders acceptable to the white peace movement were also added. The march's demands were expanded from a single call to freeze and reduce nuclear weapons to include a demand that money for military spending be transferred to meet human needs. Anti-intervention speeches and slogans were to be allowed at the rally.

Contrary to the white peace leaders' fears that expanding the focus would alienate middle-class white people, the march was a tremendous success, drawing almost a million people to New York in the first really integrated antiwar mobilization since the 1960s. In retrospect, the rally represents some maturing of the left-liberal movement in the fact that racial tensions were fought through and their power to disrupt kept within limits.

After the June 12 rally, attempts were made to overcome historical racial divisions and to keep the fragile coalition alive. A number of white activists who would later play a prominent role in the Jackson campaign were convinced that they had to look more seriously to black leadership and to working with black movements than they had in the past. One of these was Barry Commoner, a leading environmentalist who had run as the presidential candidate of the Citizens' party in 1980. Commoner broke with the party in 1984 to support the Jackson campaign, explaining that he thought that white leadership was not capable of advancing the kind of politics that was likely to make a difference in the country.

1983 March on Washington

The third significant mass mobilization during the early 1980s was the 1983 March on Washington. Conceived by civil rights leaders Dr. Joseph Lowery of the Southern Christian Leadership Conference (SCLC) and Martin Luther King's widow, Coretta Scott King, as a commemoration of the 1963 March on Washington, the 1983 march soon turned into a generalized proclamation of the people's demand for redirected national priorities. By 1983, the civil rights agenda had become the demand for "Jobs, Peace, and Freedom."

Though there were attempts from some quarters of the old-guard civil rights establishment, right-wing Jewish groups, and top AFL-CIO officers to keep the march within safe political boundaries that would not alienate the Democratic party leadership or finance capital, the groundswell of anger and alienation among a wide variety of the march's natural constituencies forced its leaders to adopt a more radical posture and to move to the left in their choice of allies.[36] "Throughout the country," said Manning Marable, "centrist forces expressed a willingness to work with the left as never before"; and during the march itself the left, from Democratic Socialists to Marxist-Leninists, was an "open and unambiguous current."[37]

For the first time since the 1960s, the institutional force of the trade union movement came together with civil rights and black political leadership, and for the first time, labor leaders who in the 1960s would have been cold warriors stood on the podium with leaders of third world revolutionary struggles. Again, for the first time since the 1960s, the black churches utilized their institutions and their intra- and interdenominational networks to mobilize their members for a massive display of solidarity and protest. The turnout was greater than it had been in 1963.

A new ingredient in the march not visible in the earlier 1963 March on Washington were contingents of family farmers. The backbone of American conservatism since the end of World War II, farmers were now a constituency in a state of political transition. Due to deliberate government policies (influenced by big business), farmers had been steadily overextending themselves. When land values and commodity prices collapsed, farmers found themselves in a situation comparable to that of the Great Depression. By 1982 farmers' net interest payments on their debt exceeded net income. Two thousand farmers a week were losing their farms to foreclosure, and many of these farmers were beginning to see themselves as the new "niggers."

The People's Convention of 1980 had recognized the growing crisis in the farm belt, but it was the 1983 March on Washington that brought significant delegations into contact with the black and peace movements. The farmers would be one of the most important "bows" in the Jackson Rainbow Coalition of 1984.

As Marable has noted, the march was nearly marred by the still unresolved conflicts between the march's more moderate black leadership and representatives of militant black nationalist and lesbian and gay groups, but in the alliances it built and the issues it addressed, it represented a clear advance in expressing the growing unity of a new "rainbow" political bloc, a unity that would be further consolidated, though not totally or easily, by the Jackson campaign of 1984.

Many who had organized for the March on Washington had hoped that the "coalitions of conscience," organized in hundreds of cities in preparation for the march, would continue as institutionalized expressions of this growing alliance. But the black political/civil rights leaders under whose auspices the march had been organized and who had the public authority to call for its institutionalization seemed incapable of taking on the role or unwilling to do so.[38] They feared their legitimacy as brokers for the black community with white political and corporate elites might be jeopardized by unleashing a multiracial insurgency from below. The same kind of foot-dragging would be apparent in the aftermath of the Jackson campaign. The inability of the black leadership to move from intermittent mass mobilization to organization is a dilemma that continues to confound the building of a progressive movement adequate to the political tasks of the 1980s.

In retrospect, however, the March on Washington was a significant catalyst for the electoral campaigns that were to follow. In addition to spurring black voter registration, the march gave Jesse Jackson a national platform from which to project his as yet unannounced candidacy and to receive the acclaim (there were shouts of "Run, Jesse, Run" from the crowd) that would help to cement his image as the preeminent leader of the black masses.

The Convergence of Social Movements and Electoral Politics

Frances Fox Piven and Richard Cloward have pointed out that social movements, in moments of electoral instability, can break the grip on ruling class hegemony and open up new political visions and policies from below; without the ability to translate those visions and policies into voting blocs and money to support candidates, however, social movements remain vulnerable to repression and demoralization.[39]

The failure of black interest-group politics to stem the tide of the right-wing assault on the gains of the civil rights era, as well as the failure of the extra-electoral social movements of the 1970s (i.e., the peace and environmental movements, the so-called citizen action organizations) to achieve the legislative victories for which they marched and demonstrated, can be laid to the separation of the social movements from electoral politics. The election of Ronald Reagan in 1980 shocked many left activists into discovering the dialectical relationship between social movements and electoral institutions. As leaders of social movements saw their demonstrations ignored by an increasingly conservative Congress, and as blacks discovered that the black mayors they had elected were unable to advance their interests, discussions of the need for a new wedding between movement-building and electoral politics assumed a fresh urgency.

Such discussions were not new, of course. The Student Nonviolent Coordinating Committee (SNCC) had attempted to build an independent political party—the Lowndes County Freedom party—in Lowndes County, Alabama, in the late 1960s. The Mississippi Freedom Democratic party and La Raza Unida party in the Southwest had attempted to channel the unrepresented needs of African Americans and Chicanos into electoral vehicles that could contend for real power. The Black Panther party in California had even entered the electoral arena in Oakland, California; and throughout the late 1960s and 1970s there had been several attempts to field independent presidential candidates on third-party tickets. The momentum of these earlier efforts had always faltered, however, for lack of a broad electoral base and the institutional and financial resources to build such a base.[40]

By 1979, three major ways of approaching the interrelationship of movement-building and electoral work could be distinguished among left-liberal forces outside the black community and the left sectarian parties. The Democratic Socialists of America (DSA), a merger of two formerly separate social-democratic formations (the Democratic Socialist Organizing Committee and the New American Movement) held that working within the Democratic party to enlarge its left wing and promote socialist values and ideas was the best hope of creating the kind of electoral vehicle that could eventually deliver a social-democratic program. DSA was composed of predominently white left-wing intellectuals and trade unionists. A second approach was taken by a group of philanthropists with ties to the environmental, peace, and women's movements. They decided in 1979 to form the Citizens' Party, and to run environmentalist Barry Commoner for president in the 1980 election. Though the Citizens' party attempted to attract blacks and other minorities, its top-down initiation and decision to run a national candidate in 1980, rather than to build slowly and organically the base for such a party in black and low-income communities, quickly lost it the support of a few black organizers who had initially been attracted to it.

Still a third alternative was proposed by a loose multiracial coalition of movement veterans and community organizers known as the People's Alliance.[41] In an internal working paper written in anticipation of the 1980 elections, the People's Alliance proposed a dialectical process of working toward the eventual formation of an independent People's party, by using an inside-outside approach to the Democratic party. The People's Alliance saw the need to develop a "people's platform," which could be used in local campaigns to evaluate candidates, and to build unity between the fragmented sections of the people's movement. The creation of local independent political movements open to all popular forces regardless of party affiliation and the building of support for candidates who adhered to the People's Platform (regardless of their party affiliation) would, they thought, sharpen the contradictions within the Democratic party and create unity between popular elements within the party and people's organizations and movements outside the party. By this means, they hoped eventually to contribute to the conditions for a mass breakaway from the Democratic party, but they were not sanguine that such a breakaway was on the immediate horizon.

Organizers affiliated with the People's Alliance differed from those in DSA and the Citizens' party in their recognition of the centrality of African Americans to the building of a progressive political bloc. They understood that at this stage in history most African Americans were still tied to the Democratic party through the patronage it dispensed and the positions held by the black community's organic leaders, but they also recognized the ambivalence of those positions for the people who occupied them—especially as the Democratic party became more and more a mirror image of the Republican party.

Based on this analysis, the People's Alliance initiated the People's Convention of 1980 in the South Bronx as a way of drafting its People's Platform, which could become the basis for a new independent politics. Organizers allied with this tendency—which was subsequently renamed the Coalition for a People's Alternative (CPA)—worked in a number of local electoral campaigns for progressive, usually black, candidates from 1980 through 1983. Through its newsletter, occasional conferences, and national network, the CPA circulated news and analyses of such campaigns.

The experience gained by these organizers and the success of a number of the races they were involved in strengthened a commitment to independent political action among a broader cross-section of the left-liberal social movements and encouraged movement activists to see electoral politics as a necessary if insufficient arena for the projection of their interests and the building of a progressive power bloc.

In February 1984 the Coalition for a People's Alternative convened a national meeting to discuss strategies for the presidential races that year. Participants decided to actively support the primary campaign of Jesse Jackson, seeing it as an opportunity to enlarge the constituency for a progressive people's platform and as the best way, given historical circumstances, to forward the building of an independent political movement on a national level. The conference established the National Committee for Independent Political Action as the vehicle that would coordinate work on the Jackson campaign and carry forward the work of building an independent political movement beyond the campaign.

Progressive Electoral Politics: A New Political Paradigm

The movement activists of the 1960s who had moved into electoral politics in the 1970s—people such as SNCC's Marion Barry, mayor of Washington, D.C.; John Lewis, elected to the Atlanta City Council; and Students for a Democratic Society (SDS) leader Tom Hayden, who was elected to the California state assembly—tended to emphasize the electoral arena to the neglect of movement-building. In the 1980s, however, the movement of left-liberal activists into electoral politics was beginning to take on a different gestalt. Electoral politics was no longer seen as a substitute for movement-building, but as a necessary complement. Although it was difficult to do both simultaneously, there was a growing realization that the two forms of political activity were dialectically related.

By registering people who had never participated in electoral activity before and educating them on the issues, movement activists, who knew how to mobilize people, could enhance the power of voting blocs. They could take advantage of the fact that the parties did little or no recruiting or educating of nonvoting constituencies, most of whom were low-income and uneducated. The momentum generated by electoral campaigns, they found, could be used as a vehicle through which to reach a larger public with progressive ideas and values.

A number of local campaigns in the early 1980s began to dramatize the success of this wedding of social movements with electoral institutions. Mostly black-led, but multiracial in character, these campaigns had a value orientation decidedly to the left of previous black campaigns. The difference between politics in this new "progressive" framework and politics in the traditional pluralist interest-group tradition can be illustrated in six areas.

First, traditional politics, while giving lip-service to the Democratic ideals of equality, representation, democracy, and legality, often violates these values in practice, through the "deals" that competing interest groups are compelled to make with each other. Progressive politics, on the other hand, tries to make these ideals practical. It seeks to open up the electoral process to the greatest number of people, to create an educated electorate, to change the rules through which representatives are selected to ensure that each person's vote counts, and to ensure that the weaker or underrepresented sectors of the population have adequate access to the system.

Second, politics waged within a progressive framework sees black nationalism as a means to an end, not as an end in itself. It recognizes that nationalism is the most effective mobilizer of black and other racially and culturally oppressed peoples, but it rejects the zero-sum assumptions of the white racist state in which black nationalism has usually operated. In the use of black nationalism by both integrationist and separatist politicians, the given structure of power and privilege is not challenged. Blacks are simply encouraged to seek a "piece of the power." As James Jennings has pointed out, "Black nationalism as 'integrationist' or 'separatist' may begin as a healthy reaction to the history of black oppression in this country, but eventually it becomes decisive and 'exploitable' by wealthy and powerful interests."[42] As an end, black nationalism fails to challenge the racial caste system built into the distribution of wealth, status, and power in the United States, causing the apparent anomaly of a Marcus Garvey embracing the Ku Klux Klan or the Klan providing protection for Louis Farrakhan.

Black nationalism within a progressive framework pursues the mobilization of black pride as a way to challenge racist structures and to encourage people to question the distribution of wealth and power in American society. It can be an opening to a progressive pluralism, not a pluralism of competing interests within a limited framework of power.

Third, progressive electoral politics seeks to mobilize the masses not simply to seek a few concessions from the powerful for representatives of racial or gender groups, but to overturn the systems of power and privilege. Gaining token positions for individual blacks or women while ignoring the systemic conditions that perpetuate black poverty and female powerlessness is the result of traditional interest-group politics. Electing representatives of such groups who are held *accountable* to the poor and working classes is an example of politics waged within a progressive framework.

A fourth distinction between traditional and progressive politics lies in their conceptions of community and national development. Progressive politicians place people's needs for food, clothing, and shelter above investment profits, downtown convention centers, and luxury housing. Progressive politicians pursue redistributive tax policies, and use their leverage with corporations to force concessions to meet the basic needs of citizens. The values of mutuality and reciprocity, rather than a Hobbesian view of the world as the war of all against all, dominate the foreign policy perspective of the progressive politician.

Fifth, progressive politicians aggressively seek to educate their electoral constituencies and use this aroused citizenry as leverage against the entrenched interests of the corporations and the state. This means not only educating the citizenry about local issues, but helping them to understand how local needs are related to larger regional, national, and international systems of power.

Finally, progressive politics understands the necessity of finding ways to create solidarity among blacks, Latinos, other minorities, and poor, working-class, and progressive elements of the white middle class. It understands that the greatest barrier to meeting the needs of its citizens is the racism that can be so easily exploited by those in power to demoralize those attempting to work for structural change.

"Progressive Politics" in Municipal Elections

In varying ways a number of local campaigns during the early 1980s began to exhibit the characteristics of this new progressive politics. In 1979, in Philadelphia, a multiracial coalition of left political cadres, community organizers, leaders of rank-and-file union groups, and the National Black United Front succeeded in preventing the third-term election of Philadelphia's racist mayor, Frank Rizzo. The Stop Rizzo Coalition combined direct action, agitation, and electoral organization, registering over fifty-thousand new, mostly black, voters and building active ward committees in half the city's wards. On election day, the city's black population voted twenty to one against a charter change that would have allowed Rizzo to run for a third term, thus turning the city's racist climate around.

Buoyed by this victory, movement activists ran Lucien Blackwell, a city councilman and former trade unionist, for mayor on a strong populist platform, stressing relief for the city's have-nots and working people, quality integrated education, and an end to violence against women, among other issues. Though Blackwell lost to a white opponent with a far larger campaign chest, the movement behind his candidacy paved the way for the election of a black moderate, Wilson Goode, the next time around. Though in retrospect Wilson Goode's administration has been a distinct disappointment for progressives—some would even say a disaster—progressive politics must be seen in a dialectical context.[43] That a black moderate followed a white racist is progress. As I seek to demonstrate, it takes the failure of traditional black politics to deliver for the black majority to push the electorate to adopt a more progressive politics. This was demonstrated in 1984 when the black electorate defied Wilson Goode, who had endorsed Mondale, to win the city for Jesse Jackson.

In 1979, a multiracial progressive coalition of community activists in Berkeley, California, known as the Berkeley Citizen's Alliance (BCA), succeeded in electing one of their members, Gus Newport, mayor and winning four out of nine seats on the city council (by 1984 they had won eight out of nine). BCA, an umbrella group for all of the movements that had come out of the 1960s, had learned from experience that just electing a black to office did not significantly change the value orientation of the politics practiced. The black man they had elected in 1971, Warren Widener, had reneged on most of the issues BCA members held dear.

Newport, whose activist roots go back to the civil rights movement, won the election in 1979 through an aggressive grassroots campaign to get out the vote in working-class and student neighborhoods, after the BCA won an initiative changing the time of elections from April to November, when there is a higher turnout. Financially outspent by the incumbent the BCA used one thousand volunteers to run a grassroots, issue-oriented campaign based on strong rent control and antigentrification policies, opposition to nuclear power, a labor-intensive jobs program, opposition to the national military budget, environmental protection, and South African divestment.

Unlike black mayors who had capitulated to powerful financial interests, Newport saw the city government as a platform from which to defend the interests of working people and minorities from state, national, and international policies and ran his campaign on this basis.[44]

In 1981, self-identified socialist Bernie Sanders was elected mayor of Burlington, Vermont, the largest city in a state that had always voted heavily Republican. Low-income and tenant organizing by activists who had been politicized in the movements of the 1960s catapulted Sanders into office. His highly issue-oriented platform broke the back of the do-nothing Democratic machine and has enabled him to increase his margin of victory in each subsequent election. Sanders's election demonstrated that an appeal to class interests among poor and working-class whites through effective door-to-door work was capable of producing a victory for progressive politics. Sanders's electoral success also demonstrated that working-class whites, who usually supported reactionary foreign policies could be turned around on these issues when their relationship to domestic class concerns was clearly demonstrated. The Sanders administration sent the largest shipment of material aid to Nicaragua that has ever been sent from this country.

The two electoral campaigns of most significance to the Jackson campaign were the 1983 mayoral campaigns of Harold Washington in Chicago and Mel King in Boston. In 1973, shock waves reverberated throughout black America at the news that Harold Washington had become Chicago's first black mayor. It was not so much the fact that Washington was black that was significant as that he had beaten the Chicago machine, a prerequisite for moving toward any real distribution of resources that might benefit the majority of Chicago's black population. Washington's candidacy thus represented a break with the traditional black clientage politics of the past and opened up the possibility of a new politics based on a different value orientation—one committed to honesty, the well-being of the poor and the working class, and the healing of the city's racial wounds.

Washington's election in one of the most racially polarized cities in the nation was the result of the unique opening created by the death of Mayor Richard Daley in 1976, creating a period of electoral instability that black activists could then exploit. Daley's death was followed by a period of unprecedented black protest activity, which was eventually channeled into mass voter registration campaigns, "the most extensive mass electoral mobilization in the history of Chicago politics."[45] Washington, who grew up in the machine but who, as a U.S. congressman, carved out an independent niche, was *drafted* from this mass movement, not handpicked by party regulars as every other mayoral candidate had been. "The selection of Harold Washington as the candidate of Blacks for mayor was unique in the respect that neither big business nor the machine wanted him to run," commented Alkalimat and Gills.[46]

As in the Jackson campaign to follow, Washington had no money for major media advertisements, but depended on armies of volunteers to get the word out in the city's wards. Washington's dynamic presence in the debates was also an important way of his reaching a wider audience. Like that of Jackson, Washington's campaign organization was composed of a combination of professional pols and movement activists. While heavily black, his campaign staff, particularly its field organization, included a cross-section of organizers from the major ethnic groups represented in the city's population. Indeed, it was support from sectors of the Latino, white-poor, and working- and middle-class communities that, along with a heavy black turnout, guaranteed Washington's victory in a city that was 40 percent black. In the general election, the Latino vote was particularly significant (it jumped from 25 percent in the primary to 74 percent in the general election), enabling Washington to defy a racial backlash among the white electorate, who bolted their traditional Democratic party allegiance to vote for a white Republican.

The energy and élan created by the black poor and working class in Chicago around the campaign brought national and international attention to it. It caused the Democratic party to view Washington's campaign as a peg in its strategy to defeat the Republicans in 1984 and sent positive signals to movement activists throughout the country that indeed it was possible to elect a progressive to office in one of the most racially divided cities in the country. If it could be done in Chicago, it could be done anywhere.

Alkalimat and Gills sum up the lessons of the Washington campaign, which were to reverberate widely throughout the following year:

> First, Black adults demonstrated that under specific conditions they will defy all expectations and mobilize at unprecedented levels. These conditions are unity of Black leadership, public attacks from white racism, and a legitimate form of mobilization such as voting. Second, Black movements to solve problems in society can be the basis for a multinational united front under certain conditions. These conditions are unity of a community-based multinational leadership, a build-up of community-based struggles around concrete economic and symbolic issues, and political ideology that is inclusive—not exclusive—of diverse communities and social groups. Third, when (reactionary) white power is confronted successfully by (progressive) Black power—especially if it is allied with a "rainbow coalition" in working-class and poor communities—the struggle will be of worldwide importance.[47]

If Harold Washington's victory demonstrated the power of an aroused black electorate, with some help from other nationalities, to beat one of the most powerful machines in the country, Mel

King's race for mayor of Boston that same year demonstrated that a black progressive running in a nonblack majority city could build a rainbow coalition of blacks, whites, Latinos, and Asians that could challenge class rule and come close to winning.

King, a black maverick state assemblyman with a long background as a community activist in struggles around education and housing, first ran for mayor in 1979, winning 15 percent of the vote. His goal was to challenge the distribution of wealth and power at the local level by stimulating increased black electoral activity, running an issue-oriented campaign, using campaign leadership that was grassroots oriented, and building a rainbow coalition. As James Jennings has pointed out, it is hard enough for blacks running for office within the traditional framework to get elected; it is even more difficult for a progressive black to win.[48]

King not only came close to winning the preliminary election in 1983 (he lost to Ray Flynn, who eventually became mayor, by only 400 votes), but it was King who raised the major issues of the campaign—the linkage of downtown development to the support of neighborhood housing, and racism. In his use of the "linkage" theme, King demonstrated how the traditional racism of Boston's white working class could be subverted through a platform that spoke to their class interests in better housing and neighborhood revitalization. As a result of King's race, all of the candidates were forced to repudiate the use of racism in their campaigns and to summon the once racially troubled city to a higher calling.

Unlike other black mayoral candidates in predominantly white cities, King did not appeal to the class interests of the white middle class, but to the various social issues that sectors of this class were concerned about: women's issues, lesbian and gay rights, crime, peace. His class orientation was to poor and working-class people. In this way he cut across traditional racial and class divisions and brought about the kind of unity that has eluded so many other black politicians. King's emphasis on issues—even if in traditional wisdom they might be seen as detrimental to his image or might lose him votes with certain constituencies (such as his support of gay rights)—set him apart from other candidates as a person of principle rather than an opportunist.

Next to demonstrating that a progressive challenge to status quo politics, both in terms of class and social issues, could attract voters, King's races also demonstrated that an electoral campaign can be used to bring about greater interracial unity. His 1979 race helped to create and propel multiethnic networks and coalitions that continued to work on common concerns after the election was over. It was this greater interracial unity that enabled the second King race to do as well as it did. Out of both races came the institutionalized Rainbow Coalition of Boston, which set the pace for future political work in the city and gave hope and impetus to the formation of a rainbow coalition as the cornerstone of Jackson's presidential campaign.

Bridge-Builders

The most potentially radical feature of the Jackson campaign was not the fact that a black person was running for the presidency—the system has always been able to accommodate tokens—but the idea of asserting that one could build a rainbow coalition that spanned lines of race, class, gender, age, and religion. Such unity has rarely been achieved in American history, and as long as it has not, the development of a viable American left has been critically undermined.

Without the work of certain bridge-building individuals and networks during the late 1970s, Jackson's Rainbow Coalition would never have gotten off the ground. Bridge-building between the races and across class lines goes against the grain of the entire political history of the United States. Bridge-builders must not only buck the structural arrangements designed to isolate racial/ethnic communities from one another, but the internal defensive mechanisms built into each oppressed community that make it hard for it to enter into power-sharing arrangements with others.

Bridge-building organizations or networks are begun by people who understand the necessity of interracial cooperation to any progressive project in the United States and who work tirelessly, and often with little tangible support, to bring people together so that mutual understanding and trust can develop. Individual bridge-builders are genuinely rooted in their own racial/ethnic/gender/class communities but are culturally bi- or trilingual. Because they operate against the grain, bridge-building networks and institutions are generally underfunded, understaffed, and largely unappreciated for the vital role they play in keeping a progressive option for change available.

Five bridge-building networks throughout the latter half of the 1970s and early 1980s played significant roles in helping to create the climate that made the announcement of the Rainbow Coalition possible.

The first of these was the People's Alliance, a national multiracial network of social movement activists, community organizers, and some representatives of left parties that had worked together to organize alternative bicentennial celebrations in 1975. People associated with the alliance were veterans of the civil rights and antiwar movements of the 1960s, who recognized that to build a base for independent, progressive political action multiracial networks would have to be built in local areas. With little money and but one staff person, the People's Alliance could do little more than provide a loose network for an expanding group of the country's best organizers—from the labor, peace, environmental, community-based, and third world solidarity movements. Through face-to-face exchanges at national conferences, the "white" bias of the antinuclear and peace movements was critiqued and individuals who had key roles in those movements were encouraged to wean them from their white, middle-class orientation.

The People's Alliance—and its subsequent metamorphoses as the Coalition for a People's Alternative and, later, the National Committee for Independent Political Action—was primarily responsible for disseminating information and analyses on the new progressive politics that began to emerge at the local level in the early 1980s. Organizers affiliated with the alliance played a critical role in both the Harold Washington and Mel King mayoral races and would play significant roles in building the rainbow component of the Jackson presidential campaign.

Another important bridge-builder during this period was Theology in the Americas (TIA), a religious network of progressive Roman Catholics, Protestants, and traditionalist Native Americans.[49] Begun in 1975 by an exiled Chilean priest who saw the need for Christians in the United States to develop a "liberation theology" that grew out of reflection on the experience of its own marginated and oppressed groups, Theology in the Americas became a forum for the exchange of experiences, analysis, and theological reflection among African Americans, white feminists, Chicanos, Puerto Ricans, Asian-Pacific Americans, and Native Americans. TIA provided the space and time necessary for a variety of progressive intellectuals and religious leaders, leaders of national peace and justice organizations, and grassroots activists to learn from each other in a way that is rare in American society. During this process, stereotypes were shed and new paradigms for understanding the nature of the American past and current reality were adopted.

TIA was especially significant in providing a forum for an exploration of the relationship between broad Christian norms and progressive political action. Its Black Theology Project developed and circulated among a broad spectrum of black church leaders a revolutionary "black theology," which drew on African tradition, historic black Christian political praxis, and a class analysis of U.S. imperialism. It thus gave legitimacy to the black church's involvement in social protest and progressive electoral politics. This context is important for understanding the centrality of the black churches to the Jackson campaign.

Through the voluminous books, articles, and conferences produced by Theology in the Americas between 1975 and 1984, a Christian left was gradually forged, paralleling the growth of the Christian right, but of course without the financial or political backing enjoyed by the right. As the crises in Central American, the Philippines, and black America deepened at the end of the 1970s, this Christian left moved from critique and dialogue to active resistance to American racism, capitalism, and imperialism. An international conference convened in 1980 by Theology in the Americas in Detroit was one of the most remarkable events of this century. The conference brought Christians who had been actively involved as leaders in a number of third world revolutionary movements, including those in El Salvador, Nicaragua, the Philippines, and Puerto Rico together with North Americans who were involved in their own communities' struggles for justice, liberation, and peace to discuss the role of religion in the building of progressive political movements around the world.

Theology in the Americas provided a forum for the development of a religion-based pluralistic understanding of American national identity that would be tested in the political realm during the 1984 elections. Indeed, as the Jackson campaign was announced, many of those associated with Theology in the Americas immediately joined the campaign, seeing the Rainbow Coalition as the logical expression of the bridge-building they had been engaged in for the last nine years. Theology in the Americas was particularly helpful in the early stages of the Jackson campaign in locating people who could mobilize the Asian community for the Rainbow Coalition and in providing the Asian-Pacific policy perspective for the campaign.

A third type of bridge-building network is illustrated by the Southern Organizing Committee for Racial and Economic Justice (SOC), begun in 1975 by black and white veterans of the southern civil rights movement, who saw the need to continue the kind of bridge-building function the Southern Conference Educational Fund had provided during the civil rights era.[50]

A southwide network of individual organizers and some one hundred grassroots organizations (including peace, tenant, unemployed, and labor groups). SOC saw its purpose as helping to build a southern movement that could revitalize the continuing struggle against racism, economic injustice, and militarism. Using these themes, it linked local organizations together through occasional conferences, workshops, training sessions, and a newsletter.

SOC newsletters and conferences kept a sense of the "movement" alive across the South throughout the bleak period of the late 1970's contributing to a belief that southern blacks and their white allies could once again play a pivotal role in turning the country around. SOC leaders such as Rev. C. T. Vivian and Anne Braden played key roles in founding the National Anti-Klan Network, which mounted an effective national resistance to the growing influence of the Klan and other groups that had received a green light from the Reagan administration. Vivian eventually became Jesse Jackson's religious coordinator, while Anne Braden played a crucial role in organizing southern whites for the campaign. SOC's annual workshop in January 1984, which was described by Braden as an "electrifying event," became a recruiting ground for some of the best Jackson campaign organizers across the South.

Equally significant, but largely overlooked, roles were played by two national training institutes. The Center for Third World Organizing brought black, Latino, Native American, and Asian-American community leaders together for training, particularly in linking local to international issues. The People's Institute for Survival and Beyond provided multiethnic leadership training to low-income groups and social movement leaders in undoing racism, in understanding the threat militarism posed to effective community organization, in seeing culture as the "life-blood" of any community, and in learning from the history of people's movements. Organizers associated with the People's Institute were instrumental in founding the national defense campaign that saved Tchula, Mississippi, Mayor Eddie Carthan's life, and educated people around the country on the new threats to black political empowerment. As a result of this campaign, many whites across the country learned about the new face of racism in America.

Though Jesse Jackson became the symbol of the new black electoral insurgency in 1984 and the spokesperson for the Rainbow Coalition, he was, like any great leader, thrust up by the people's movements already in motion. In the campaign of 1984, Jackson would as much be shaped by the "old minorities" who were struggling to become the "new majority" as he would shape that movement through the force of his own unique charisma.

4

The Voter Mobilization: Part Spiritual Crusade, Part Political Campaign

This day we gather strangely exuberant and hopeful amidst so much chaos, confusion, despair and pain. We sense that we are part of a special moment in history, pregnant with possibility. We courageously press forward for we dare not abort this moment. We are destined to redirect the course of this nation and we shall. . . . We are here to heed the call of this nation's highest and noblest principles that we might fulfill our mission to defend the poor, make welcome the outcast, deliver the needy and be the source of hope for people yearning to be free everywhere[1]

—Jesse Jackson

On November 3, 1983, at the Washington, D.C., Convention Center, Jesse Jackson announced his candidacy for the presidency of the United States. To many observers, the announcement was a bit quixotic. Not only was the campaign late in getting started (most presidential candidates began their campaigns two years before the vote), but traditional wisdom maintained that in order to run for the presidency, a candidate would have to begin with a campaign chest of at least $1 million in seed money.[2] Moreover, Jackson had never run for political office before, and, of course, every "serious" presidential candidate had had substantial prior political experience—either as a member of Congress or as a governor, which also meant the ability to command a cadre of experienced political operatives. Wide name recognition and the promise of backing from key figures in the business and political establishment were also prerequisites for such an office. In addition to these assets, it was estimated that a black candidate would have to be able to mount a substantial voter registration drive, since he or she could not count on the votes of too many whites.

Except for the voter registration drive (which had been initiated by Operation PUSH, the national civil rights organization he headed) and name recognition in the black community (he was known by only 50 percent of the whites polled), Jackson had none of these assets. "When we started out," said Percy Sutton, chair of Jackson's finance committee, "some of our friends thought we should take a trip to the nearest psychiatrist." This chapter examines the remarkable organization that unfolded between November 3, 1983, and July 19, 1984, when the gavel came down on the Democratic National Convention. It was an organization built against the skepticism of friends and enemies, against all external odds, and in spite of many internal impediments.

As Marx observed, people do not make history under circumstances of their own choosing, but under conditions inherited and transmitted from the past.[3] Such conditions are both objectively dictated and subjectively experienced. In 1984 they included the systemic racism fed by the mass media and political power brokers; the absence of a history of cooperation and trust among the various groups that made up the potential rainbow coalition; the inexperience of campaign organizers in running a national presidential campaign; the lack of financial and institutional resources; and the very real threat that such a candidacy posed to the guardians of the class system. Subjectively, the campaign was inhibited by the ethnocentricity of much of its black base, the sexism that existed in large segments of the black male leadership, personal jealousies and rivalries, and the insecurity and fear of people who had been politically disenfranchised for so long. That the campaign succeeded in spite of these factors is a tribute to the enormous capacity for hope resident in the African-American community, and in the vitality and creativity of a people who, because they have been shut out of the centers of power and decision making, have had to develop collective resources of spiritual sustenance and physical survival that may yet be the source of this nation's own salvation. The campaign taxed and tested the ingenuity of its organizers, producing some disasters and many missed opportunities, but one of the most vibrant and creative electoral campaigns this country has ever seen.

Turning Organizational Deficits into Assets

The campaign began in November 1983 with only about $50,000, and most of that already spent. When Jackson aides began looking for an experienced black campaign manager, they discovered that while some blacks had held titles in previous presidential campaigns (e.g., "National Deputy Campaign Director"), none had been a part of the inner circles where the critical strategic decisions are made. Preston Love, Jackson's campaign aide who began pulling a team together, had managed Andrew Young's successful mayoral race in Atlanta, but he had had virtually no political experience in a national presidential campaign. Arnold Pinkney, the Cleveland businessman whom the campaign finally hired as manager, had worked for Hubert Humphrey in 1972, but had retired from poliltics in 1978 to run his businesses. Jackson's legal team, which he brought with him from Operation PUSH, had to become versed in a matter of weeks in an arena of law with which it was entirely unfamiliar. The campaign never had any polling experts. Toward the end of the campaign, when it was decided it would be useful to have an analysis of the Jackson vote, three social scientists volunteered their time to do the data collection and computer analysis.

Jackson began and ended the campaign without financial backing from a single large Political Action Committee (PAC), without money for major media advertising (the only paid television commercials were in California at the end of the campaign), without the endorsement of a single prominent white politician or newspaper, and without the support of most of the moderate civil rights and black political leadership.

The press and political experts interpreted these liabilities as weaknesses that would quickly force Jackson to drop out of the race. Even by most blacks, he was viewed as a purely "symbolic" candidate. As of February 1, the *Washington Post* reported that "some workers are just now being hired and trained to canvass and state coordinators are still being chosen, money is scarce and the paid campaign staff is sparse."[4] But by May 7, *Time* was compelled to observe that "Jackson has overcome a lack of funds. . . . and a campaign organization that does not deserve the name."[5]

What the press and mainstream political analysts interpreted as liabilities for the most part turned out to be the campaign's greatest assets. Lacking large financial backers, the campaign was forced to rely on contributions (mostly in small checks of from $10 to $25) from hundreds of thousands of working-class people across the country. The process of generating such funds—through churches, sororities and fraternities, fish-fries, bake sales and fashion shows, luncheons and cocktail parties, and through the sales of parapher-nalia—thus involved in the political process hundreds of thou-sands of people who had never been involved before and gave them a stake in its outcome.

Lack of funds also forced campaign workers to be more creative and ingenious in gathering and employing resources than they might otherwise have been, and this, in turn, involved more peo-ple in the political process. For example, when I arrived in New Hampshire to mobilize peace activists and religious leaders, I found a state campaign office with only three telephone lines and no other equipment. Since I needed a typewriter immediately to get out a mailing, I was forced to look for one in the community. The typing was done in the home of a retired United Church of Christ minister, who became one of the campaign's key supporters. His lists of clergy were just what we needed to bring together a successful statewide rally at a Rochester church. He and his wife also housed two of us from the campaign staff, thus saving money on hotel bills. This story was multiplied everywhere the campaign went. Local radio stations donated equipment and air time, small business persons turned their shops and offices into unofficial campaign headquarters, local restaurants donated food to cam-paign volunteers, local button-makers and graphic artists pro-duced some of the most visually rich political propaganda that has been seen since the days of the Wobblies, fashion designers cre-ated special "rainbow" couture, which they donated to the cam-paign to be used for fundraising purposes, and in New Hampshire, a local carpenter built a collapsible wooden rainbow that stretched from one end of the stage to the other over Jesse Jackson's head. In short, it was a "people's campaign" existing in the midst of a culture that had totally divorced the electoral process from the everyday lives of ordinary citizens.

Of course, such bottom-up involvement also produced some headaches for the national staff. During the first half of the campaign many local people, unfamiliar with election laws and having to "make do" without material or financial resources from the national office, failed to keep the right kinds of records. Halfway through the campaign a team of accountants had to work furiously to reconstruct the paper record in order to be in compliance with the Federal Election Commission. The numbers of small checks that came into the national office also meant a tremendous record-keeping burden for the comptroller and her staff. The financial accounting department turned out to be the largest department in the campaign.

But the absence of control by white business interests allowed the campaign to take the kinds of political risks that no other Democratic or Republican presidential campaign dared take, and enabled Jackson to remain relatively independent of the enormous pressures to concede to traditional interest-group politics. As a result, the campaign challenged not only the racism in the American electoral system, but its class function as well, taking the movement beyond where Martin Luther King had left it at the time of his death.

The absence of political operatives trained in previous presidential campaigns also proved to be an asset, for it meant that a whole new cadre of people received on-the-job training in running a presidential campaign. Many of them were left-liberal organizers from social movements that have usually operated outside of or on the periphery of political campaigns. The Jackson campaign gave them training at the very highest level of political operation without requiring that they compromise their ideological integrity. The campaign thus developed a new generation of political leaders who, in the future, would be able to wed a progressive idealogy to the skills and tools needed to achieve political power. If the campaign had done nothing else, this would have been sufficient.

The Jackson campaign was the first in which a variety of civil rights activists, Marxists, social democrats (in and out of the Democratic party), black nationalists, and even some disaffected

Republicans worked together and came to an ideological convergence. What is even more remarkable is that the campaign, in the midst of a resurgent anticommunism led by the White House, escaped the kind of red-baiting that had done in the Henry Wallace campaign of 1948—the last major presidential campaign that, in addition to including avowed Marxists, challenged the class and racial assumptions undergirding the dominant parties.

Both traditional politicians and the national media continuously misjudged the capacity of the campaign both to mobilize the electorate and to sustain itself throughout the primary season principally because they failed to appreciate the indigenous networks in the black community that Jackson was able to exploit. The same mistakes were made by white analysts who saw the civil rights movement as a purely spontaneous uprising and were continuously skeptical of the black community's capacity for self-organization.[6]

The indigenous resources that enabled the black community to be the base for the most effective challenge to ruling-class electoral power since 1948 included the charismatic tradition within black culture, independent black institutions such as Operation PUSH, the churches, and networks of small businesses, social clubs, and independent radio networks. Of these, the role of the charismatic leader and the institution and network of the black churches were perhaps the most important.

The Charismatic Tradition

The charismatic leader has had a long tradition in the black community. Its origins can be traced to the medicine men in African culture, who, in the slave culture of the New World, were often those who interpreted the meanings of events and called their people to a sense of solidarity, pride, and the first stirrings of resentment against their oppressors.[7] From Nat Turner through Marcus Garvey, to Martin Luther King and Malcolm X to Jesse Jackson, the history of black political awakening against oppression has been led by charismatic "holy men," who discern the signs of the times and call their people forth to do battle against oppression.

Almost all black political analysts are in agreement that the Jackson campaign could not have gotten off the ground without the charismatic personality of Jesse Jackson. Jackson's own sense of the politically possible, which often ran against the judgment of his closest advisers, not only enabled the campaign to get started, but was the single most important factor in the campaign's ability to sustain itself through the primary season and to emerge as a movement with the potential for changing the political alignment of the nation.

In addition to the gift of political judgment, the charismatic person must be possessed of enormous—almost superhuman— energy and drive, for he or she must overcome not only the structural barriers poised to prevent any insurgency among the masses, but the internalized fear, insecurity, and mistrustfulness of a people who have seen their hopes rise and then be extinguished all too often. Alone of all the black figures discussed as potential presidential candidates in 1983, Jesse Jackson possessed these gifts. Rev. Bill Howard, one of Jackson's advisers and coordinator of Jackson's 1983 mission to Syria, observed that "Jesse doesn't think small. I've been constantly impressed with his inability to be contained by ordinary limits. When things have been well contained, well-prescribed, he has been known to break down walls to attempt the impossible."

This enormous physical and emotional drive was necessary not only for the reasons cited, but for another critical reason: the lack of sufficient financial resources to command television time meant that Jackson, more than any other candidate, had to be in direct touch with the public. Campaign days, therefore, usually started at 6:45 A.M. and ended at 2:00 A.M. While campaign workers were eating meals, Jackson was preparing himself for the next public event. In contrast to the other candidates, who scheduled three and sometimes four campaign stops a day with breaks in between, Jackson raced from one rally to the next, sometimes covering as many as twelve events in one day. The campaign entourage was known for arriving late at its destinations, and crowds were often kept waiting for two and three hours for the candidate's arrival. At one large rally in downtown Detroit, a crowd of several thousand waited outside an auditorium for two hours in below-freezing weather. When Jackson finally arrived, it was 11:00 P.M. and the crowd, which at one point had swelled to about nine thousand, had dwindled to about two thousand. As a result of the need for people to meet the candidate in person, some

campaign stops were missed entirely, and not a few local organizers were embarrassed by Jackson's failure to show up. "It's
amazing that Jackson could do even half of what he did, much less
be alive after it," C. T. Vivian commented to me.

Many of the black politicians who did not support the campaign, some black leftists, and most white journalists disparaged
Jackson's drive, attributing it to an enormous ego and a personal
need for publicity.[8] Another point of view, however, was offered
by Vivian, who has known Jackson since he was in seminary.
"Jesse's growth has been phenomenal in the last ten years," said
Vivian. "He's at another level. He's in another league. . . . He's got
more on the ball, understands more things, moves in ways not
only that other people can't move, but don't even understand. He's
our best chance." While not denying the role that ego plays ("What
person who runs for president doesn't have an ego?" quipped
Jackson on several occasions), his ambition during the campaign
and after had the aura of a kind of "divine madness." At several
points during the campaign, Jackson expressed the conviction that
he was being "led" by a "divine mission" to turn the country in a
new direction, admitting that many of his decisions came to him
in the form of "intuitions," rather than as carefully calculated and
collectively reached decisions.

This form of political instrumentalilty was foreign to most of
those who were paid to observe and analyze it. One *Washington
Post* reporter, groping for words to capture the essence of the
emotional message Jackson conveyed, described it in these terms:
"Passion: Extreme compelling emotion of burning intensity; great
anger, fury, hate, grief, love, fear, joy. To travel with Jesse Jackson is
to witness the sudden awakening of the locked out."[9]

It is interesting to note that this reporter places negative emotions first: "anger," "fury," "hate." One suspects that her own fear
of the kind of emotionalism aroused by the black charismatic
preacher/politician colored the choice of her words. A similar
reaction was found among several potential white supporters who
likened the frenzy Jackson was able to whip up in a crowd to the
emotionalism stirred by Hitler. Some refused to support the campaign, even though they claimed to like its message, for just this
reason. White feminists were particularly alienated by the black
male charismatic style, equating it with the kind of male dominance they were struggling against.

Such responses indicate the cultural gulf that lay between the black base and the white majority the campaign sought to reach. Those familiar with black church worship could better understand the cultural and historical context out of which the charismatic tradition arises. In Jackson's speeches were the familiar biblical allusions, cadences, and intonations of the black Baptist preacher. In the black church tradition, the preacher is part showman, part exorciser/healer of the internalized social demons of racism and political subjugation, part molder of social solidarity. The fervent emotionalism displayed by black worshipers is ritualistically modulated, and it has, according to Gayraud Wilmore, "only partly been in response to social, and political deprivation. Shouting and 'getting happy' are also residual expressions of a spontaneous and liberative African spiritual inheritance."[10] In its essentially generous attitude toward the world and in its implicit antiracism, the emotionalism generated by the black charismatic preacher is at the opposite end of the spectrum from the kind of emotion aroused by Hitler.

While most of those who supported Jackson believed that a charismatic leader was necessary to arouse the black base, some also saw Jackson's charisma as a potential problem. Bill Howard expressed the fear that the campaign might have raised people's expectations to a potentially dangerous level, particularly if there were no movement or competent leadership to translate it into winnable programmatic goals. "The charismatic leader," he told me, "cannot ask his followers to take too many extrarational leaps, because then we have a cult," rather than a political movement. Howard feared that if nothing tangible resulted for the black community from raising their expectations, their "spirituality" would drop to a lower ebb than it was before.

Jackson's charisma also presented problems for those who saw the need to begin immediately after the campaign to build a long-term political organization that could translate the energy he aroused into a movement that could win real power; during the campaign itself, Jackson's spontaneous intuitions often conflicted with the plans campaign organizers had made for his schedule. Bill Howard told me about a meeting of church leaders he had been asked to call that was to be used as a training session in how to involve the churches in the political campaign. "That meeting was sabotaged by Jackson's sudden announcement that I was leading a trip to Syria!" "But when Jackson says, 'Go,' you usually go," explained Howard, "because you know something important is going to happen."

As it turned out, the trip to Syria to release captured American airman Lieutenant Robert Goodman proved to be a turning point for the campaign, giving it an international prestige and importance it might not otherwise have had. Since Jackson's intuitions were usually not only ideologically but politically correct, it was often hard for campaign organizers to argue against following his direction. On one of the occasions when Jackson was persuaded by his advisers to take the politically cautious route—postponing a much-discussed trip to Central America in favor of spending more campaign time in New Hampshire—the advisers turned out to be wrong. It was at the time that Jackson was polling 16 percent in New Hampshire that the press released a story about his having referred to Jews as "Hymies" and New York as "Hymietown" in a private conversation with black reporters. That month-old story hounded Jackson throughout the New Hampshire primaries and beyond, cutting into his votes from Jews and white liberals. After his mission to Syria, Jackson was received in New Hampshire (Lieutenant Goodman's home state) like a conquering hero returned home. He was drawing large, enthusiastic white crowds three times the size of his opponents when the "Hymie" remark broke in the press. It is conceivable that had he been in Central America when the story broke, the press would not have been able to use the remark to obscure the wider import of his message. The story would have been his role as a potential peacemaker in Central America, and the 16 percent he was polling might have turned into a vote of similar proportions. If Jackson had won 16 percent in this white-majority state, the campaign would have been catapulted to a new level of significance with white America, and could possibly have changed the course of history.

The tension between the need for charismatic leadership that tends to follow its own inner voice and the need for careful, systematic organization building also meant that there would be some opportunities missed. Wayne Barrett of New York's liberal weekly *The Village Voice* hinted that Jackson might have been able to win at least his paper's endorsement had the Jackson campaign responded to entreaties from the *Voice's* editor for an interview.[11] Frequent changes in the campaign schedule meant the inability to plan as strategically as one might have wanted to.

The risk that charismatic leaders run of being targeted not only verbally, but physically, by the opposition was another factor that affected the campaign. Everyone who worked for the Jackson campaign was aware of the constant danger to which he exposed himself. According to the Secret Service, Jackson received 311 death threats during the campaign, more than any other candidate. Jackson himself was only too aware of the danger that broadcasting his schedule ahead of time posed. Having been with Martin Luther King at the time of his death, he knew that the FBI through a phony letter sent to King by an allegedly black group had deliberately pressured King into changing his accommodations in Memphis from a white-owned to the black-owned motel where he was shot. What appeared to campaign workers, the press, and even the Secret Service as chaotic scheduling may, therefore, have been a deliberate strategy to keep his enemies confused. Jackson hinted at this in a talk to campaign workers. "Our campaign has been called chaotic. They say, 'you go here, you go there,' but all good quarterbacks do that. We can't reveal our schedule to give our enemy advance warning. The fact is, we've been creative." Secret Service men joked during the campaign that even they did not know where Jackson was going to be until shortly before the event.

For campaign workers, the inability to plan well in advance of events meant having to pull things together at the last minute. While this did not seem to be a problem in attracting black crowds to campaign rallies, it was a problem in organizing whites, Latinos, and other nonblack constituencies, for whom the campaign lacked the automatic racial attraction and whose communities lacked the indigenous communications networks such as those provided by the black churches. To organize Chicanos, Puerto Ricans, white workers, and white "conscience" constituencies demanded a great deal more advance planning and cultivation than the campaign was able to offer. Still, miracles did happen. On the morning of the worst blizzard of the season in New York City, more than 350 peace activists of all colors turned out to hear Jackson give a major address on Central America with only three days warning. On the platform were such notables as Ramsey Clark and Pete Seeger.

The tension between charismatic leadership and the need for organization-building also meant that there were really two campaigns: one on the road with Jackson, and the other in the national office. Although policy papers were produced in the national office, it was on the road that policy was shaped, as Jackson encountered the various constituencies in his Rainbow Coalition and was compelled to respond to them. Jackson's decision to call for a 20 to 25 percent cut in the military budget, for example, was made in New Hampshire as he encountered the peace community. His decision to oppose the Simpson-Mazzoli immigration bill was a response to the strong feelings in the Hispanic community against this bill. His farm policy was shaped as he encountered hundreds of farmers protesting foreclosures and their inability to get loans from the Farmers Home Administration. Thus, policy as well as several strategic decisions were made as the campaign went along, with the result that staff in the national office were always having to "catch up" with the latest decision the candidate had made on the road. This tension between the demands of a political campaign for advance planning and strategies targeted at achieving quantifiable results, and the movement character of so much of the Jackson campaign, was something campaign workers learned to live with, however uncomfortably. Given the nature of the U.S. social reality, with its lack of a major left party and the importance of the black base to any future political challenge to the political system, it is a tension that is likely to be with us for some time.

Operation PUSH and the Jackson Campaign

Without the backing of major sectors of the black political leadership or of the white-dominated Democratic party, a progressive candidate would not have had the institutional resources necessary to mount a national presidential campaign on the scale of the Jackson campaign. It was just such institutional resources that Shirley Chisholm lacked when she attempted to run for the presidency in 1972. For this reason, the organizational apparatus provided by Operation PUSH became indispensable to the Jackson campaign.

Operation PUSH had extensions into the black community base across the country, and supplied Jackson with an immediate administrative infrastructure that allowed the campaign to get off the ground quickly, once the announcement was made. Operation PUSH supplied the campaign with many of its seasoned, behind-the-scenes operators. Among those in important positions in the campaign were Sylvia Branch, Jackson's executive assistant, who moved her home from Chicago to Washington to become the campaign's scheduler; Frank Watkins, a long-time Jackson aide who traveled with the candidate, at times alternating as political strategist, speech writer, and press aide; Rev. Willie Barrow, a woman with an energy almost as enormous as Jackson's, a wit as volatile, and a tongue as golden, who took a leave of absence from PUSH to become the campaign's national deputy campaign manager for field operations; Jack O'Dell, who had worked with Martin Luther King and later as PUSH's international affairs director, handled Jackson's correspondence, and continued to advise him on international affairs; and Lamond Godwin, another Jackson aide who did initial advance work for the campaign.

About half the viable state operations were either chaired or coordinated by people—usually ministers—associated with local affiliates of Operation PUSH. In several instances, such persons turned out not to be the best campaign organizers, either because they lacked experience in running electoral campaigns or because their existing ties to the local Democratic party establishment interfered with their ability to run a campaign that fundamentally challenged that establishment. In addition, most had had little experience in mobilizing nonblack constituencies. Nevertheless, without the ability to tap into a national network of trusted colleagues such as that provided by Operation PUSH, the campaign would never have gotten off the ground.

The campaign taxed the human and financial resources of PUSH to such an extent that there was a question as to whether the organization could continue after the campaign was over. A decision was eventually made that it would, with some of the Jackson staff returning to pick up the organizational pieces and the others remaining to keep alive the skeletal framework of an emerging national Rainbow Coalition.

The Role of the Black Churches

As one of the few wholly indigenous and independent institutions in the black community, with a presence in every black neighborhood across the nation, with a grassroots fundraising capacity almost unequaled by any other institution, with national and regional communications networks, and as the spawning ground for black leadership, the black denominations were indispensable to the Jackson campaign.

Because of his experience in the Southern Christian Leadership Conference (SCLC), Jackson understood better than most of the black political leadership that the black churches were the only means through which an independent black political campaign could be generated.[12] Just as the SCLC became the unofficial social action ministry of the black churches, so the Jackson campaign became the unofficial political action ministry of the black churches.

Jackson's national deputy campaign manager for the religious community was C. T. Vivian, with whom he had worked in the Southern Christian Leadership Conference. A minister who had begun his career on the national staff of the all-black National Baptist Convention, "C. T.," as he is affectionately called, was a veteran of many of the civil rights movement's most dramatic confrontations with authority. After leaving the SCLC, he had gone to Chicago to head the Urban Training Institute, which trained ministers from all over the country to develop socially conscious ministries for the inner city. Vivian had also worked for a time for the predominantly white National Council of Churches, had been dean of a theology school, and was a founder of the National Anti-Klan Network, one of several educational and social change projects he has started over the years.

Thus, with wide contacts throughout both black and white churches across the country (nine of the ministers trained by Vivian at the Urban Training Institute became bishops of their denominations), Vivian was well situated to lead the churches into a remarkable mobilization.

Working under a tremendous handicap—no office space, no telephone, and little money—Vivian immediately set up a number of statewide and citywide training sessions for local clergy and lay leaders shortly after Jackson's candidacy was announced. "The idea," he explained, "was to make certain that the churches understood themselves as an organizing unit." The strategy was to have the voter registration and education, fundraising, and get-out-the vote operations all in the same institution. To do that, Vivian had to train ministers to be spokespersons for Jackson and his program to offset the deficits Jackson had built up in certain communities. He also had to train church leaders in the complicated laws regulating campaign contributions and bookkeeping, and to educate them in the byzantine rules of Democratic party procedure. Vivian concentrated on the caucus states; that was where detailed instructions in party rules and political maneuvering would pay the most dividends and where the churches' ability to organize people and get them to the polls or caucus sites (often in church buses) might pay off.

The vast majority of the black churches responded to the campaign's appeal, and competed for a place on Jackson's itinerary. Well over 90 percent of the black clergy endorsed the campaign within two months of Jackson's announcement speech. They were helped by the endorsement of such nationally known figures as T. J. Jemison, president of the National Baptist Convention, with a membership estimated at 6.5 million. It was no doubt Jemison's endorsement and active participation in the campaign that turned out the large Louisiana vote for Jackson, enabling him to win that state. Jemison's predecessor had not supported Martin Luther King nor endorsed the civil rights movement, but Jemison belonged to a new generation. He was the beneficiary of changes that had occurred in black theological thinking between the black power movement and the 1980s—changes that were equipping the black church to reassert the role it had played at an earlier time in its history as the nurturer not only of the spiritual hopes of the black masses, but of their political hopes as well. The support of the pentecostal churches—especially the Church of God in Christ (the fastest-growing black denomination)—also marked this period as different from the civil rights era. Few pentecostal churches in the 1960s countenanced political action as a form of Christian spirituality. As Wilmore has explained:

> Before the recent development of a black theology the church never seriously considered a worldview and value system that sought to transform the collective consciousness of black Americans rather than permit them to be satisfied with manipulating political structures which change every four years only to remain the same.[13]

The black churches were important not only because they provided a means of reaching large numbers of parishioners, but because of their outreach into the larger black community. Most black churches are situated in the ghetto or have constituencies that live in large public housing projects. The black church has always been the center of innumerable activities, which sustain not only the congregation, but also the nonchurch population. Many of them have sponsored housing projects for the poor and the elderly; most have day care, Head Start, and after-school programs for children of neighborhood residents; and many of them own radio stations from which they broadcast to the wider public. It was a network of radio stations owned by Bishop Willis in the Tidewater section of Virginia that broadcast information about how to work the Virginia caucus system. These stations ran continuous information about the campaign in the weeks preceding the caucus vote. As a result, blacks flooded the caucuses and Jackson won the popular vote in the state. According to Jackson aide Rev. Bill Howard, in every one of the twenty states in which Jackson won federal matching funds, his ability to do so came from the churches.[14].

The black churches not only gave the campaign its troops and its initial fund-raising capacity, but provided it with its unique flavor. The campaign was as much a spiritual crusade as a political contest. Gospel choirs usually sang at campaign rallies, prayers were prayed, and people would "get happy" over Jackson's speeches as they would over a rousing sermon in the black church tradition. One campaign supporter was led to observe that the campaign was "one long sermon." Campaign rallies gave participants a chance to show off their musical talents and their oratorical gifts to one another in the long waits before Jackson's arrival. Ministers practiced the chants: "Run, Jesse, Run!" so that by the time Jackson arrived, the audience had been primed to a fever pitch.

The church setting, with its hymns and prayers, reinforced the black community's sense that it was in the vanguard of a historic mission to bring justice and healing to the country. It was this sense of mission that Martin Luther King evoked in supporters of the civil rights movement and that Jackson took to a different level.

The National Campaign Structure

What *Time* called a "campaign organization that does not deserve the name" was a combination of official bureaucratic organization and movement organization—a hybrid that few traditional political pundits understood. On paper, the campaign had all the trappings of a bureaucratic organization: a campaign manager and deputy campaign managers, a treasurer, a comptroller, a national committee, and so on. The reality beneath the appearance was sometimes a bit more fluid. Roles and emphases changed depending on the amount of money available and very often on the spur-of-the-moment decisions of the candidate to be in a different place at a different time. For instance, when Jackson announced that he was leading a march on the Mexican border to protest the proposed Simpson-Mazzoli immigration bill, the farm/rural affairs coordinator (who spoke Spanish) was dispatched to the border—not to mobilize the vote, but to organize a protest rally. Many of the national staff literally worked their way into the campaign—volunteering until there was enough money to hire them officially.

The lack of up-front money hampered the ability of staff to do the kind of job necessary to mobilize the greatest numbers of voters, especially among the nonblack constituencies. Local campaign organizations were often without the materials they needed to take Jackson's program to the people. This forced them to produce a lot of the campaign material by themselves with money that came out of people's back pockets. Most of the time, this resulted in creative popular expressions, but sometimes it backfired. When national staff members came into Detroit a few days before the vote, they discovered that a brochure produced by local activists contained essentially ethnic language that would have the effect of turning off potential white voters.

Financial difficulties, on the other hand, meant that campaign staff and volunteers were often forced to be jacks-of-all-trades, which was the best possible training they could have received. When I went to volunteer in New Hampshire, having had no previous electoral experience (although I had had extensive organizing experience), I found myself not only mobilizing those I had come to mobilize, but doing press releases, gathering information for input into the candidate's speeches, editing some of the speeches, preparing specialized brochures and fliers, doing advance work, introducing the candidate from the podium, and organizing volunteers.

The campaign's ability to transform the latent gifts that people brought to it into potent political skills is illustrated in the case of

Mary Summers, a physician's assistant from Cleveland who had come to New Hampshire to be the state's deputy campaign manager and ended up becoming Jackson's major speechwriter and later a senior policy analyst for the Rainbow Coalition in its transition period. Summers began writing Jackson's speeches when she noticed that he was tending to repeat himself at every campaign stop. The daughter of an English professor and the granddaughter of five generations of (white) Southern Baptist preachers, Summers had been a member of Students for a Democratic Society while in college at Radcliffe. Her trip to join the Selma to Montgomery march as a high school student and her antiwar experiences as a college student were formative in her political development and led to her involvement in electoral politics in Cleveland, where issues of race and class were paramount. Summers developed an ability to enter into the spirit of Jackson's political and spiritual mission, translating his politics from the "black perspective" into an idiom that was universally appealing. As a result, the campaign produced a body of the most remarkable campaign speeches in the history of American politics.

The lack of money also meant that young people were given an opportunity to prove themselves in a presidential campaign they would otherwise not have had access to. A Ramapo College student from New Jersey was the campaign's press coordinator in New Hampshire, a Howard University journalism student became the campaign's national press coordinator, and a twenty-five-year-old and a college student were the campaign's youth coordinators. Donna Brazile, who had organized the 1983 March on Washington, was just two years out of college when she served as national rainbow coordinator for the first half of the campaign and as coordinator of special projects during the second half.

While the top positions in the campaign were held by people with long experience in electoral politics (though not in presidential campaigns), the "rainbow department" was staffed chiefly by people who had come out of the social movements of the 1960s and 1970s. Anna Gyorgy, who had worked on Ralph Nader's staff and was the author of a major compendium on the nuclear industry, *No Nukes*, headed the environmental desk; John Saxton, who headed the peace desk, had come from the Mobilization for Survival; Carolyn Kazdin, the farm and rural coordinator, had formerly been executive director of Rural American Women; Bill Means was one of the leaders of the American Indian movement; Maxine Greene, who organized low-income housing tenants, was executive director of the National Tenants' Organization. The Arab-American desk was staffed by a young lawyer, Albert Mokhiber, in consultation with Jim Zogby, who was then executive director of the Arab-American Anti-Discrimination League. The Hispanic desk was filled by Felipe Braudy, who had come from the League of United Latin American Citizens (LULAC). Volunteers from the lesbian and gay community provided sporadic coverage of the lesbian and gay desk. A national campaign committee filled in other gaps that were missing in the staff configuration.

Though the organized white feminist movement held itself aloof from the Jackson campaign, claiming that Jackson could not be trusted with feminists' interests, the structure of the Jackson campaign—at least at the national level—defied all of the other campaigns in the opportunities it gave to women. Women made up half the deputy campaign managers. The first press secretary was female, as were the treasurer and comptroller, slots usually reserved for men. Four of the campaign's seven departments were headed by women. These included the field operations and convention operations department; the rainbow department, special projects, and fundraising and finance. Women made up more than 50 percent of the campaign's entire staff. Though sexism operated in more subtle ways, structurally the campaign could hardly be faulted.

The national campaign staff was about 75 percent black, reflecting both its base and its priorities. Those who were assigned to mobilize the nonblack constituencies at times felt like the campaign's stepchildren. This was due both to the lack of adequate funds—which meant that money was used first to mobilize the black base and only secondarily for outreach into other communities—and to the lack of confidence among several members of the senior campaign staff that nonblack sectors of the population would rally to a black candidate. Indeed, it was the internalized mistrust that a rainbow coalition could be forged that inhibited the campaign's ability to reach out beyond its black core. Such mistrust was natural, given the history of race relations in this country, but unfortunate; and it was very often Jackson himself who pressed both black and nonblack staff to reach out beyond what they thought politically feasible.

As a result of the internalized ethnocentricism of the black leadership, the campaign had no comprehensive "rainbow" strategy that would have enabled its staff to make the best use of demographic variables other than the black variable as it entered each state race. Campaign managers also downplayed the class variable within the black community. Maxine Greene, director of a national, primarily black network of low-income public housing tenants, for example, was continually frustrated by the second-class treatment she felt she and her constituency received. Since there was no structural link between the field operations department (staffed by blacks) and the rainbow department (staffed by the mostly nonblack ethnic and issue-oriented staff), the concept of building a rainbow coalition was not thoroughly integrated into relations with local organizers. This often resulted in Jackson and his traveling entourage having to quickly assemble the appearance of a rainbow at various events. In one unfortunate case, a large multiracial event had actually been planned by local Ohio organizers only to be canceled by Dayton's black city coordinator when Jackson's schedule was shortened. When Jackson came to the area and saw that there was no multiracial presence on the stage, he called out to a white woman who was sitting in the audience with her baby to come forward to represent the rainbow. The (black) organizer of the canceled rainbow event, who was present, saw this as an embarrassment for the campaign.

Just a week before the Philadelphia primary, national rainbow department staff who went into the city found that there had been almost no organizing among whites, even though the city was known for being the home of several national peace organizations. By the time the national staff arrived, it was too late to organize a get-out-the-vote campaign in white neighborhoods and the best that could be done was to organize a press conference in which most of the leading white peace activists from the city endorsed the campaign. It was such incidents that led many in the press to question Jackson's assertion that he was building a rainbow coalition.

Even where attempts to visually represent the rainbow were built into the schedule, the aura surrounding Jackson and the need for blacks—especially black clergy and politicians—to be seen with him often overwhelmed the best-laid plans of the campaign staff. At one rather amusing occasion in Philadelphia, a multiracial entourage was carefully planned to appear with Jackson as he gave his victory speech. The people representing the various "bows" in the rainbow met with Jackson in his hotel suite, which was several floors below the room in which the victory celebration was to be held. When the elevator doors opened to take people to where the press was waiting, all of the men shoved on and the doors closed. When the dust settled, the women looked around and discovered that they had been left behind!

Another difficulty in the campaign's structure that prevented the utilization of an effective rainbow strategy was the lack of structural liaison between the rainbow department and the operations of the issues policy department, which was headed by Dr. Ronald Walters, a Howard University political scientist. In this case, academic elitism prevented those in charge of "policy" from understanding that the rainbow staff were experts in their respective fields. Not only were the rainbow staff well versed on a theoretical level, but they had worked with issues "on the street," where issues take on material reality and are tested against public response. Though rainbow department staff were eventually able to have some influence on the final policy platform, the lack of effective liaison between these two departments created some blunders and missed opportunities.

In spite of these impediments, the Rainbow Coalition did grow. In local areas—in places like Seattle; Cincinnati; New York; Louisville and Lexington, Kentucky; Nashville; Atlanta; Lincoln and Omaha, Nebraska; Portland and Eugene, Oregon; San Francisco and Los Angeles; Salt Lake City; and the entire state of New Mexico, the campaign had a decidedly multiracial caste. The campaign gave people an opportunity to work together in a way that had never been possible before, and in so doing, began to break down the centuries of hostility and mistrust that has prevented the emergence of a progressive movement that could make a difference in American politics.

Voter Mobilization Strategy

Faced with little money and a "front-loaded" primary season, the campaign managers' strategy was to target selected states and cities where there were large, concentrated black populations that the campaign was reasonably sure, given the commitment of the churches, could be mobilized quickly. When the national campaign began, not a single state organization was in place. "No one envisioned that we could run a *national* campaign," recalled Arnold Pinkney. But by January 10, the campaign had filed in thirty-two states.

The South was to be the primary area of concentration. Carolyn Kazdin, who was the first white staff member hired (other than Frank Watkins, Jackson's long-time aide), argued that Jackson should run in the Iowa caucuses, which was the first state test of the candidates' viability. Kazdin had a number of farm contacts in Iowa and felt certain that Jackson could get a reasonable showing, especially since no one but McGovern was speaking to the emerging Midwest farm crisis. At this point in the campaign, however, there was little optimism among Jackson's advisers that he could do well in a white-majority state. Thus, the campaign sat out a televised debate on the farm crisis and had only a skeletal network of volunteers to work the caucuses. Most of Kazdin's contacts went with McGovern.

On the basis of the reception of an early Jackson speech in New Hampshire on acid rain, the campaign decided to enter the primary there, running chiefly on the issues of peace and the environment. Few of Jackson's campaign managers, however, expected to see the large and enthusiastic crowds he drew in this traditionally conservative and almost totally white state. Their amazement at this scene convinced them of the viability of mounting serious campaigns in other states without large black constituencies.

As predicted, the big wins came on "Super-Tuesday"—March 13—when twelve states held primaries and caucuses, among them the Deep South states of Florida, Alabama, and Georgia. Prior to this time, Jackson and Mondale had been running about evenly in attracting the black vote, but Jackson's large black turnout in these states began to turn the tide in his favor. The next big surge came almost immediately, on March 17, with Jackson winning the entire popular vote in Mississippi and South Carolina and coming within four hundred votes of winning in Arkansas. From then on, Jackson's viability with the black community was assured and a multiracial strategy began to get more attention.

By the end of the season, the Jackson campaign had registered 2 million new voters, and had won nearly 4 million votes, about 21 percent of the total votes cast.

While analysts continued to belittle Jackson's boast to be building a Rainbow Coalition, the beginnings of that coalition could be discerned. Twenty-two percent of Jackson's vote nationwide—an estimated 788,000 votes—came from whites, with relatively little systematic organizing having been done at the grassroots level. Jackson received about 33 percent of the national Hispanic vote, and 40 percent of the Asians in San Francisco's Chinatown, 20 percent in California, and 23 percent in New Jersey voted for him. Jackson decisively won the 18-29-year-old vote in the Northeast.

Perhaps more impressive than the raw vote totals was the organization that actually came together from such inauspicious beginnings. Starting with a handful of staff and $50,000, the campaign had organizations in thirty-eight states by July, although not all were on the same level of sophistication. Close to $4 million had been raised. Even more remarkable is the fact that the average donation was only $27. Every vote of Mondale's cost him over $3; Jackson's votes came in at $.99 apiece. The Jackson campaign was the first to pay off its campaign debt, with a margin of error of only 1.5 percent—a record. It had been the most cost-effective of any of the campaigns of the 1984 season. No newspaper articles gave this side of the story.

More important than all these figures, however, were the qualitative changes the Jackson campaign was beginning to make in the political life of the nation. In South Carolina, for example, members of the state Democratic Party Executive Committee—about half of them white—voted to make Jesse Jackson their "favorite son" candidate. In Mississippi, Jackson forces took over the party machinery in most of the state's twenty-one black-majority counties and in some of the white-majority ones by winning controlling seats on county executive committees. In Alabama, Jackson insurgents overthrew the two-decades long rule of the black Alabama Democratic Conference, which had accommodated itself to the racial caste system of the white-controlled Democratic party. Said civil rights activist Anne Braden, there was now at least a chance that in some places in the South some whites could begin to form *honest* coalitions with black leadership based on a new conception of power sharing.[15]

And in Vermont, Massachusetts, New Jersey, Oregon, Washington, and in numerous smaller units across the country, new progressive multiracial political organizations were spawned that would begin to elect people to office, not on the basis of "image" or popularity, or even on the basis of color or gender, but on the basis of their commitment to the shared ideals of the Rainbow Coalition.

5

Politics from the Black Perspective: The Ideology of the Jackson Campaign

The extraordinary level of contradiction and potential social change that exists in this society is continually frustrated by the process of fragmentation and decentralization of conflicts. To recognize this differential starting point of the contradictions, to unify them progressively in agreement with the structural determinants through a *practice* of increasing political and ideological convergence, seems to be the major challenge for any movement of social change in the United States.[1]

—Manuel Castells

At the beginning of 1984, the Jackson campaign faced the challenge of taking the fragmented and decentralized potential-social-change constituency in the United States and welding it into a unified political vehicle that could contend for state power. The campaign was an effort to create, out of the collapse of post-World War II liberalism, a majoritarian American left, reconstituted, as Jackson said of his campaign, "through the eyes of the Black perspective—which is the perspective of the rejected." In this attempt, the Jackson campaign was plowing new ground. No other movement with majoritarian aspirations had ever been so thoroughly black-led and controlled.[2] This meant that the campaign "saw" the institutions of power and the constellation of national and international forces from a unique perspective—that of the hidden "third world" within the heart of the white, capitalist empire. Such a perspective implied both a class and a cultural critique of American institutions, but also a fundamental commitment to certain enduring American ideals, such as political democracy, equality under the law, due process, and the idea of America as a refuge for the "tired and the poor."

In *The Souls of Black Folk*, W. E. B. DuBois had described the black perspective as a conflictual one:

> One ever feels his twoness—an American, a Negro; two souls, two thoughts, two unreconciled strivings; two warring ideals in one dark body, whose dogged strength alone keeps it from being torn asunder. The history of the American Negro is the history of this strife,—this longing to attain self-conscious manhood, to merge his double self into a better and truer self. In this merging he wishes neither of his older selves to be lost.[3]

On one level, the Jackson campaign can be interpreted as the black community's effort to work out, on the plane of national politics, the merger of its two warring selves. The campaign functioned, therefore, as a psychosocial therapeutic process for the African-American community. But it was more than just a cathartic experience, as some have caustically commented.[4] Precisely because it attempted to merge a critique of American society from the perspective of the African-American experience with the seldom-fulfilled ideals embodied in core American political institutions, the Jackson campaign offered the American people a unique opportunity to turn the nation in the direction of peace, justice, and true internationalism. Some rose to the challenge, others misunderstood it, and still others were thoroughly threatened by it and sought to destroy its potential.

This chapter looks at the ideology of the campaign, observing how Jackson reinterpreted the political landscape of 1984 from the African-American perspective, and articulated a political project whose time had come.

Jacksonism versus Reaganism: A Prologue

Interviewing Jackson in January 1984, Robert Scheer observed:

> Both Jackson and Reagan are clearly in the political arena to do serious battle over the social direction of the country, no matter what

other material and psychological rewards may be provided by the exercise. . . . What is perhaps most interesting about Jackson is that he has risen to challenge the assumptions of Reaganism as a political philosophy more directly and energetically than has any of the other candidates.[5]

Scheer's observations reflect the central fact of the 1984 election period. Jackson's candidacy forced the debate outside of the stale one between Republicans and Democrats, offering a choice between polar opposite philosophies of life and government, made salient by the political and economic events of the last twenty years. To the philosophy that justified the rule of the rich and powerful, he asserted a claim from the underside of history for a more equitable distribution of wealth and power. "The black base from which we start," said Jackson, "is not a color, but a point of view; it's a way of looking at things from the bottom up, not the top down."[6] From the top down, America's dominance of the world at any cost had become the overriding moral imperative. From the bottom up, the possibility of America as a healer, reconciler, and peacemaker was raised.

As spokespersons for these two philosophies, Ronald Reagan and Jesse Jackson were the only true protagonists in the drama of 1984. The historical significance of the Jackson campaign was its ability to bring into the center of our national political discourse those challenges to traditional political assumptions and beliefs raised by the social movements of the 1960s, that, as long as they remained on the periphery of American political life, greatly restricted the goals that appeared to be politically achievable. Simply by raising the issues, the Jackson campaign redefined the political possibilities, not only for 1984, but for subsequent political campaigns.

In relation to Jackson and Reagan, the platforms and rhetoric of Gary Hart and Walter Mondale suggest efforts by one sector of the ruling class to maintain class rule while attempting to appease constituencies traditionally associated with the Democratic party with symbolic gestures because their class interests could no longer be accommodated by that party. In spite of attempts to manufacture an "image" for these candidates—Mondale as "experienced," "competent," and Hart as young, "future-oriented," the man of "new ideas"—both appeared inconsistent, weak and without a coherent philosophy of government, not because of a failure in "packaging," but because they had no place to stand, no clear position to defend. Their petty bickering on television was symptomatic of their lack of moral consistency, allowing Jackson to appear as the true statesman.

Both men attempted to give a human face to the increasingly inhumane policies mandated by capital's new accumulation process. This was evident in the gap between their images and the actual policies they espoused. While ostensibly representing the interests of organized labor and hailed by the National Organization for Women as the man "who has demonstrated that he understands that women's issues will be winning issues in 1984," Mondale supported union concessions in the interest of a reindustrialization policy that gave incentives to industry, while it pursued the dual labor market so injurious to women and minorities. Although he claimed to represent the old New Deal coalition, Mondale would have accepted at least half of Reagan's cuts in the welfare state, reinstituting only those most beneficial to the white middle class.[7]

Hart's neo-liberal high-tech proposals at least had the virtue of appealing rather directly to the class interests of the young professionals he was courting, yet his ostensible sympathy for their concern about war and Central America had a hollow ring to it. Hart had consistently proposed expanding the arms budget, and "modernizing" warfare. Neither Hart nor Mondale would commit themselves to "no first-use" of nuclear weapons, and both placed deficit reduction over meeting human needs. After the Democratic Convention, Mondale's position on the nuclear freeze and the party's commitment to nonintervention in Central America were pushed into the background of the foreign policy debate, as Mondale strove to out-macho Reagan as a preserver of America's military superiority around the world.

The key to Jackson's policy orientation, as well as to the tactics employed by his campaign, lay in the two major influences on his life: his blackness, and the prophetic tradition of the Judeo-Christian heritage as reinterpreted by the black Christian church. This chapter explores the effect of the "black experience" on the character and policy orientation of the Jackson campaign.

The Politics of Black Consciousness: Hope in a Different Future

Black theologian John David Maguire has outlined some of the major elements in what he calls "black consciousness," that body of unassimilated perceptions, values, and modes of interaction that is the legacy of the black experience in America.[8] These include the hope for a new kind of future, the need for self-affirmation, a sense of solidarity with all the oppressed, a double consciousness that sharpens the power to perceive injustice, and the drive to recover the truth of the past. An additional attribute of black consciousness is its emphasis on the quality of personal relationships and personal example in the conduct of public life. African-American historian Lerone Bennett has elsewhere described some of the characteristics of black consciousness:

> By the grace of God and the whip of history, black people, in the main, have not completely assimilated those values that are driving Western man to social and spiritual suicide: acquisitiveness, for example, numbness of heart and machine idolatry. . . . To the extent these things are foreign to the black *experience*, to that extent the black man is uniquely qualified to take the lead in recasting the human values of our civilization.[9]

All of the great African-American leaders in varying degrees have been the symbolic bearers of black consciousness for their race. Thus, when Jesse Jackson announced that his campaign, while not "for blacks only," would be a campaign growing out of the "black experience and seen through the eyes of a black perspective," he was placing himself within a historic tradition—accepting the mantle and the risks of those who had gone before him: Nat Turner, Frederick Douglass, W. E. B. DuBois, Marcus Garvey, Malcolm X, Martin Luther King.

Since one of the primary characteristics of black consciousness is the "unquenchable expectation for the birth of a new community," it was inevitable that the engine of social change in Reagan's America would be the black community. Black consciousness, says Maguire, "develops a vision of a society unlike those at present because it is not built on a moral-geological fault, the unbridgeable chasm between rich and poor, privileged and oppressed. It denies that these gaps have to be.[10]

Jackson's announcement speech spoke directly to that dream of a new society based on a different moral framework:

> Running for the presidency gives me the opportunity to serve this nation at a level where I can help to restore a high moral tone, reestablish a sense of idealism and common decency in the national

discussion of public policy issues, offer a redemptive spirit to the nation and rekindle a sensitivity to the poor and dispossessed in our country. I want America to again become the hope and beacon of a free world, jealously guarding human rights for all human beings and the right to self-determination. . . . There must be a new litmus test for measuring the nation's greatness. It must not be measured by economics, political and military might alone. Our nation's greatness must be measured by our ideals and principles—and how closely we approximate them.[11]

Such hope in a different future lies latent in black culture most of the time. It is reinforced through black music, through the black church tradition, and in the ability of African Americans to laugh and celebrate in the midst of trouble. But it has been the singular task of the great African-American leaders to tap into that fount of hope at certain historical junctures, arousing the black community to a level of social and political commitment that outward circumstances could not have predicted.

Alone of all the black leaders in 1984, Jackson perceived in the events of the Harold Washington and Mel King campaigns that the historical juncture had arrived.[12] A plausible explanation for Jackson's ability to seize the moment—even against the judgment of most black political and civil rights leaders—was that he was in touch with the currents of frustration and hope across the country to a greater extent than any of the others. Few at the time recognized the conditions making possible the rainbow electoral rebellion of 1984. Through Operation PUSH, Jackson had crisscrossed the country, speaking to black audiences at the grassroots level and sensing their readiness in the responses he got to his messages. As a clergyman, Jackson was also continuously in touch with the cultural matrix that nourishes black hope and keeps it alive. Traditional black politicians, who must spend most of their time in meetings with their white colleagues, lose touch with the cultural sources of black protest. The extent to which Jackson was able to call the black community to a level of political commitment unknown since the 1960s, and in violation of the conservative political climate that reigned in 1984, is testament to his instinctual awareness of the historic psychosocial currents of black hope.

Jackson's language suggests that he perceived his candidacy not in the framework of interest-group politics but as a historic mission with a moral, almost messianic, purpose: to save the soul of America. "We sense that we are part of a special moment in history, pregnant with possibility," he stated in his announcement speech. To a women's rally in New Hampshire, he explained:

There is a tremendous cynicism in this nation about our ability to heal the fractures in our coalition. Our coming together will send a message that will inspire people all over this nation and all over the world. A relative handful of people can determine the climate of American politics. You have a tremendous opportunity, disproportionate to your numbers, because of timing and other circumstances, to help set the climate for this nation. We should not miss this moment.[13]

In answering a *New York Times* reporter as to what was the most important problem facing the country over the next decade, Jackson pointed to the social costs of the Reagan entrepreneurial revolution, which had driven him to lead an electoral protest.

There's within this country a growing sense of insecurity, the American people feeling unprotected. Many people are feeling unprotected by law, that the Justice Department is not committed to justice. There's been a cut-back in this Administration on the enforcement of laws vital to the civil rights of American citizens. Women did not get an equal rights amendment passed. For blacks and Hispanics the Voting Rights Act has not been vigorously enforced. Workers are victims of plant closings without notice. Slave labor markets abroad undercut the American worker and there is the feeling that the American worker can't do anything about it, that when you're violated you can't go to the Justice Department.[14]

The deep hope resident in African-American culture—a hope annealed through trial by fire—enabled Jackson to see what many of those he sought to bring into his Rainbow Coalition could not see in 1984: the fact that America's racism, classism, sexism, and imperialism had finally come home to roost. The contempt for human life bred by an oppressive system, but heretofore inflicted mostly on silent minorities, the poor, and the third world, was finally being experienced by large sections of the white working and middle classes. Jackson's campaign for the presidency was waged on the premise that more and more of the American public—if given the option—could be brought to see the world through the eyes of the black perspective. The black perspective meant hope, healing, justice, peace. The alternative was unthinkable: nuclear war, ecological destruction, possibly an American style of fascism.

Jackson's mission to use his campaign to begin the building of a rainbow coalition was thus born of the hope that white America had a residue of decency left that could be appealed to. In answer to a journalist's question as to why he believed white America would support a black, Jackson replied with an optimism that was to characterize his perception of reality throughout the campaign:

> Well, since Reagan took office, the nation has undergone a devastating period of racial and class polarization and a kind of willful perpetuation of the gender gap. Most Americans find that distasteful. The sense of selfishness and greed of the present Administration has set a climate in this country that most Americans don't identify with in their heart of hearts. So there is a search now by people to go another way, to seek a new course. When I walked through the plant of *The Boston Globe* recently, you could hear workers, many of whom had Archie Bunker as a frame of reference, cheering me, telling me, "I'm glad you brought the boy [Lieutenant Goodman who had been imprisoned in Syria] back home!" We are growing up as a nation. Those guys probably didn't want Sam Jethroe to play baseball for the Boston Braves, probably heckled Sam Jones and K. C. Jones when they played for the Celtics. And though Boston went through a period of Louise Day Hicks-type polarization, the city obviously prefers the image of Mel King and the Rainbow Coalition to that of Hicks and the rocks and the buses.[15]

The Politics of Double Consciousness

Nurtured in the black experience, Jackson was conscious of the fact that hope and pessimism are material forces that have political effects. The historical project of every ruling class has been to inculcate in the populace the conviction that the particular sociopolitical calculus of forces is "the way things are and will always be." Because of their particular dehumanization in white America, African Americans have been forced to develop internal sociopsychological mechanisms that allow them to hold in tension a realistic understanding of the depths of their oppression and, at the same time, the possibility of their overcoming it. Maguire calls this double consciousness the "phenomenological realism" of black consciousness.

In our national history from the Br'er Rabbit tales through the solos of John Coltrane, black consciousness has marked Afro-American arts by a distinct lack of sentimentality, by the insistence that life has to be peeled down to its real pains before it can be made honestly liveable. The sense of simultaneously operating at two levels, this split-level consciousness, has always been there.[16]

Phenomenological realism was demonstrated in the Jackson campaign in two ways. First, Jackson consciously used mechanisms—stories, language, visual imagery, and the very audacity of his running in the first place—to fill his audiences with hope and a sense of the self-affirmation needed to overcome the political pessimism that was continuously fed to the American public by the Reagan administration, the media, the Democratic party regulars, and conditions within the black community itself. Second, Jackson was relentless in his efforts at getting Americans to face the stark reality of what their government was doing in their name, often using comparisons to develop moral clarity in his audiences. For example, in a press interview he compared U.S. intervention in Nicaragua with the Watergate affair:

We must all realize the seriousness of a situation that makes Watergate look benign. Watergate was stealing; Central American action is killing, maiming and destroying. . . . It is not enough for Walter Mondale to call mining the harbors a clumsy and ill-concealed act. It is not enough to imply that the main problem was not informing Congress adequately. Our foreign policy in Central America is wrong.[17]

Jackson was also frank about the internal problems—drugs, family instability, poor education, the adoption of destructive values—that plague the black community. In some respects, he sounded like the neoconservatives on this issue. Unlike them, however, he did not suggest that the solution to black pathology was to be found solely in the black community, but in a conversion of the entire society to a different value system. Both internal black discipline and external public supports would be necessary to alleviate the misery of the black underclass. The Jackson campaign thus offered a level of social criticism that was unique in the history of major party politics, equaled only by the third-party campaigns of Eugene Debs and Henry Wallace.

The internalized legacy of self-hatred suffered by African Americans due to centuries of slavery and segregation has led black leaders to an acute awareness of the need to instill attitudes of self-affirmation in their followers. Without a sense of their own dignity and power, people cannot hope to change the unjust conditions in which they suffer. Through biblical allusions, Martin Luther King fostered in southern blacks a sense of their moral authority as the conscience of the nation; Malcolm X appealed to the nobility of his followers' African roots in a similar fashion; and as the civil rights and black power movements gained potency, blacks' involvement in political activity reinforced their conviction that, indeed, they were capable of overcoming.

One of the mechanisms Jackson used to instill hope in his audiences—to fire them up for the political struggle—was his use of ritual-like slogans. To some white observers, Jackson's chants, such as "Repeat after me, 'I Am Somebody!' " "Down with Dope, Up With Hope," or "Red, Yellow, Black, White, All Are Precious in God's Sight," sounded gimmicky and manipulative—even smacking of demagoguery. Yet his use of such appeals was neither gimmicky nor manipulative. They served an important political function, one rooted in the experience of black suffering, but designed to turn that suffering into a source of healing for the nation. Jackson is a master of mass psychology. In an interview with Robert Scheer, he recalled the origin of his use of these slogans during the Poor People's Campaign of 1968:

> On that particular morning, it was raining, Dr. King was dead, Robert Kennedy was dead, we were really in despair. I looked down from that truck [on which he was standing] and saw black women, white women, Indian women, most of them with babies, very few men— one boy died—some of them catching hepatitis, the Government had turned its back on us; just us, nobodies! And I told those people, "Don't let them break your spirit! Repeat after me: 'I am somebody!' Say, 'I may be poor, but I am somebody. I may be on welfare, I may be unskilled, but I am somebody. Respect me!' Say, I am more than what you see. The me that makes me me, my essence is important; I am God's child, I am somebody!' "And it became a battle cry. People began to gain strength. Now, around the world, people have chanted that battle cry.[18]

Jackson understood that the psychic scars carried by white workers, farmers, Latinos, Native Americans, disabled people, and others with whom he used these chants were as damaging to our national well-being as the scars carried by African Americans. The hidden injuries of class, of sexism, the tyranny of heterosexual norms and the corrosive effects of racism on whites, make it easier for the ruling class to project reality as a Hobbesian war of all against all—to convince the public that their only means of survival is to "look out for number one." The values of competition and individualism, the distrust of others instilled in most Americans from an early age, allow the ruling class to maintain its political and economic hegemony without the use of overt force.

The Jackson campaign, then, functioned as a kind of social therapy, exorcising the demons of hopelessness and powerlessness from those who flocked to it. The ritual-like repetition of self-affirming slogans acted as a kind of mantra, driving self-doubt from those who experienced the greatest powerlessness: blacks, poor people, farmers who were losing their land, unemployed workers, American Indians, and so on, infusing them with a new sense of historical destiny and purpose.

Jackson also used a kind of teaching parable to illustrate the necessity of overcoming negative thinking. He would often say, "You can look at a slum and see the seamy side: boarded up windows, boarded up minds, dope, unemployment, no hope. But I look at a slum and see the sunny side: windows to be fixed, buildings to be repaired, jobs to be created; children to be educated."

By bringing the campaign into communities where no other presidential candidate had ever gone before, Jackson was also practicing a politics of affirmation. Rallies were held in the Chinatowns of New York and San Francisco, in Arab mosques, on Indian reservations, in centers for the disabled, and in lesbian and gay centers. Camera and microphones followed Jackson into the homes of a single Chicana mother in San Antonio; a West Virginia miner suffering from black lung disease; an unemployed steelworker's family in Homestead, Pennsylvania; a working-class Irish family in New York; Puerto Rican residents of a low-income housing project in Connecticut; and a farm family in Nebraska that was about to lose its farm to foreclosure. Jackson spent the night with such people, listening to their stories and then retelling them to audiences at subsequent campaign stops. It was symbolic action, designed not only to expose the systemic injustice and consequent suffering that lay beneath the surface of the fantasy woven by the Reagan administration, but to affirm the humanity, dignity, and legitimacy of the "locked-out and forgotten," as well as the legitimacy of their social hurts and special needs.

The Politics of Solidarity

Each of Jackson's speeches began with an acknowledgment of the particular character, history, and contribution to American life of the audience to which he was speaking. Read together, the speeches reflect a pattern: affirmation, acknowledgment of the suffering experienced by a variety of Americans, and a call to move through that suffering to a higher collective solidarity. The black community's historical need for self-affirmation, thus, through the vehicle of the Jackson campaign, served a larger sociopolitical purpose: that of creating a sense of solidarity with the oppressed everywhere. One of the characteristics of black consciousness is that it leads to an identification with the underdogs of history. W. E. B. DuBois wrote about this sense of kinship in *The Souls of Black Folk:*

> As I face Africa I ask myself: What is it between us that constitutes a tie that I can feel better than I can explain? The real essence of this kinship is the social heritage of slavery; the discrimination and insult that binds together not simply the children of Africa, but extends through yellow Asia and into the South Seas, wherever people are oppressed.[19]

It was this sense of kinship with the oppressed, more than any utilitarian calculation of interests, that determined both the Jackson campaign's outreach to specific constituencies and its stance on foreign policy. Jackson's much-publicized trips to Syria, Central America, and Cuba, his call for the recognition of Palestinian rights, for nonintervention in Central America, for divestment from South Africa, and a withdrawal of support from the Duvalier and Marcos regimes in Haiti and the Philipines, came out of the black community's innate identification with the victims of U.S. imperialism. Those trips were also symbolic, meant to convey the need to get beyond "enemy thinking" and to see human beings everywhere as potential allies who occupy the same planet.

Guided by the black perspective, the Jackson campaign was continuously drawing connections between population groups and issues that the American public had been socialized to see as unconnected. In doing this, it was challenging the electorate to overcome its long-standing reliance on the hegemonic value of individualism, which viewed collectivities and nations as atoms in a ruthless universe of competition for status and control. The Jackson campaign was also challenging the American public to see patterns and systemic relationships between seemingly isolated issues and events.

In his last book, *The Trumpet of Conscience*, Martin Luther King had expressed the black community's instinctual knowledge of the web of interconnectedness that bound the American people together and linked them, inexorably, to the fate of seemingly distant events:

> It really boils down to this: that all life is interrelated. We are caught in an inescapable network of mutuality, tied into a single garment of destiny. Whatever affects one directly, affects all indirectly. We are made to live together because of the interrelated structure of reality.[20]

Now, through the vehicle of an electoral campaign, with its access to mass audiences and to the mass media, Jackson was able to get this message out to a far larger public.

In a *New York Times* interview, Jackson linked women's rights, children's health and safety, and workers' rights to the fate of the Voting Rights Act—typically thought of as an issue affecting only black voters in the South.

> If the Voting Rights Act is enforced . . . and you end second primaries which keep black people, Hispanics, women and poor people from a securer justice, you'll get 12 to 20 black, Hispanic and female congresspersons by next November. If that happens, we'll get our share of legislators and judges and other officials, that will trigger the passage of the ERA. Women will all be protected in the South if the Voting Rights Act is enforced, and they are our natural allies. Since 70 percent of all poor children live in a house headed by a woman where there is no man, to enfranchise women is to protect the children. The women who go out into the workforce will end right-to-work laws because you have the power to do so. Thus workers will get paid for their work.[21]

In a speech in Youngstown, Ohio, in May, Jackson linked the devastation wrought by steel plant closings in the Mahoning Valley not only to the decision of the parent company (Lykes) to diversify rather than upgrade its aging steel facilities, but also to deliberate government decisions made as far back as the Nixon administration to support corporate profits over the welfare of the people who built the steel industry.

In Omaha, a Jackson rally brought farmers together with blacks at an urban poverty center where the farmers gave away beef to poor inner-city residents. Jackson reminded his listeners that beef prices had risen for the urban consumer from fourteen cents a pound in 1965 to over a dollar a pound in 1984, while farmers were being driven from the land, meatpackers' wages were being cut, and more and more inner-city residents were falling into poverty. "Here we are today," Jackson proclaimed, "the fruits of our Rainbow Coalition coming to bear with farmers offering the beef to Nebraska's hungry. This is the true meaning of our Rainbow Coalition: the locked-out coming together to support each other."[22]

In New Hampshire, Jackson turned what had been, until then, a white middle-class concern over environmental pollution into a working-class issue by reminding his listeners that "It is the poor, the elderly, the minorities, whose drinking water is the most polluted, whose air is the most dangerous to breathe, whose food is the least nutritious, whose jobs are the most hazardous."[23]

In speech after speech, Jackson lectured, sermonized, and cajoled his audiences—with the wit and verbal virtuosity characteristic of black culture—to see past the artificial barriers of race, class, sex, nationality, and age to the links that bind one group to another, as when he asked rhetorically of delegates to the National Hispanic Leadership Conference: "What do we have in common?" and then answered:

> First, both of us learned about foreign policy in America and got our foreign policy experience in essentially the same way. Blacks were brought to America as slaves against our will, and Hispanics were annexed to America against their will. Slavery, annexation and economic exploitation form our common foreign policy experience and perspective. We view national life from the perspective of the rejected, the downtrodden, the exploited and the colonized.
>
> Secondly, we are enslaved and are rejected and are exploited because of our skin color. Hispanics were annexed and are rejected and exploited because of caste, culture, and language.
>
> Lastly, what has benefited one group has benefited the other and together our progress has benefited the nation. Blacks took the ini-

tiative to end segregated education in 1954, but blacks, Hispanics, and whites have benefited from multicultural and bi-lingual education. . . . Ceasar Chavez and the farm workers suffered and struggled for worker's rights, but the entire labor movement and the nation benefited.[24]

In a speech to a white women's audience in Portsmouth, New Hampshire, Jackson expanded the conceptual framework in which issues like the Equal Rights Amendment (ERA) were to be understood.

The ERA is a family movement, not just a woman's movement. Seventy percent of all poor children live in a house headed by a woman. . . . ERA is a children's movement. For men who have a conscience, it is their movement. We make a fundamental mistake to let civil rights just be a black movement, or ERA just be a women's movement, or for the peace movement just to be for some college students and some professors on campus. We must see the interrelationship of all these things. That's what makes us mature. We cannot be just one-issue people.

Elaborating on this altered framework for understanding social issues and political alignments, Jackson then spelled out its implications for politics:

This generation must not judge the ball-game by a given homerun, or by a given error in a certain inning. We must look at the box score and the bottom line. . . . We are trying to bridge gaps. We are trying to heal brokenness. . . . We are going to redefine politics in this nation. Because we are going to begin the judging based upon character and content and not upon color. We are going to rise above race and sex and the measurement of what makes sense in this country. That's what makes us significant. There's a new movement in this country; its about healing.[25]

In this passage one detects echoes of Dr. King's famous phrase that "a man is not judged by the color of his skin, but by the content of his character." Jesse Jackson had now elevated that dictum to the level of an international norm of political behavior.

In a speech to the Foreign Affairs Council in Philadelphia, Jackson drew connections between our foreign and domestic policies that the white peace movement had consistently failed to make:

Our nation's leaders must not be allowed to hold a dove in one hand, a missile in another. . . . The peace movement cannot allow candidates to claim to have a program for meeting human needs if they are not willing to take the money out of the arms race and put it into feeding the people . . . for every $10 billion we spend on defense, we lose 40,000 jobs in more labor intensive industries. An endless cycle of pain, unemployment, oppression, depression for the people of this country, for the people of other lands. Injustice at home breeds injustice abroad. Injustice abroad breeds war; and war breeds injustice at home.[26]

Black consciousness holds both reality and hope in tension. Thus, in the same speech, Jackson moves from critique to hope:

I see a great source of hope in the troubled relationship between our domestic policy and our foreign policy. My hope is that when we decide as a nation to break this cycle of pain, we can establish a new harmony between the nations and peoples of the earth. We need no longer believe that the interests of the people of this country are opposed to the interests of the people of other lands.

The Politics of Historical Memory

Jackson used the theme of ethnic pluralism, not to proclaim the virtues of America as a land of opportunity for anyone who was willing to work hard—as Mondale had done in his acceptance speech at the Democratic Convention—but to call his audiences to a higher human solidarity, by looking at the themes in each ethnic group's experience through which it could discover its ties to others. Those themes were sometimes painful and ugly, not always examplary as in the model offered by the melting-pot school. A speech delivered to Arab Americans in Worcester, Massachusetts, exemplifies this approach:

As you know, the rainbow is the symbol of our campaign. The rainbow, for us, represents the coming together of many groups, discovering together that what unites us is more important than what divides us. . . . I have come to you this morning after having addressed the B'nai B'rith in Framingham and the Emanuel Baptist Church here in Worcester. With each community there was a sharing. . . .

As I know of the sufferings of blacks, and Jews, I also know of your pain. Anti-Arab sentiments, so prevalent in Western culture, are but another form of anti-Semitism. . . . And even today, killings and occupations are legitimated by anti-Arab racism. . . . There is, in the Middle East today, a cycle of pain and dehumanization and violence. Tragically, Arabs and Jews, both victims of others, have today become victims of one another.

Each of us knows our own pain. Sometimes we draw a circle around our pain and see nothing but it.

I come before you, as I came before blacks and Jews earlier today, to invite you to join me in going another way. We should go out from our own circles and see each other's suffering. We should trialogue together, and become reconciled with one another. . . . I have long felt that it is a tragedy to see the lack of talk in the Middle East, but it is even worse to see it here. . . . For all of the Middle East, dialogue and not violence can open the road to peace. We can help to begin that process right here. The peace we establish between ourselves can be exported to the Middle East. Our peace can be as contagious as their war.[27]

In San Francisco, Jackson appeared before a Chinese-American audience with the mother of Vincent Chin, a young Chinese man who had been senselessly murdered in a bar in Detroit by two white unemployed auto workers, who assumed he was one of the Japanese they had been led to believe were taking away their jobs. Jackson used the occasion to recite the painful odyssey of the Chinese in America, connecting the injustice of the Chinese Exclusion Act of 1882 to the proposed Simpson-Mazzoli immigration bill, which, if passed, would similarly exclude and harass immigrant Latino workers, and then to the entire history of racial exploitation in this country.

We must tell the world that we have had enough of immigration law based on race and racial bias. We must tell the world the truth—the truth that racial divisions are used by those who would exploit the labor of the peoples of the earth for their own benefit. The story has been repeated over and over again, with Chinese people brought to this country in gangs to build the railways, with slaves from Africa brought to work in the cotton fields, with Japanese and Chicano agricultural workers imported and exploited for their labor in the fields. The labor of the Chinese and the Japanese and the Chicanos and the black people of this country has made handsome profits—not for us, but for those who ran the railways and owned the cotton fields, the vineyards and American agribusiness. They have used us and they have used our labor. . . . Cleverest of all, they have used the terrible conditions under which we live and work—conditions which they have established—to turn American working people against us whenever it suits their purpose. "They are stealing your jobs" is the message. Don't organize unions for better working conditions, organize the Ku Klux Klan to protect your community.[28]

In these speeches, Jackson was demonstrating two other characteristics of black consciousness: its concern for history, and its relentlessness in speaking truth to power. "Black consciousness," says Maguire, "implies a special openness to and urgent searching for the past, animated by the conviction that what one is depends profoundly on what one was."

Black consciousness implied . . . an openness to the whole story, to whatever the search discloses, even if it be a new vision of epic convulsions and stark suffering; even if the histories we've formerly been taught are shown to be a compound of falsehood, half-truths, omissions and rationalizations.[29]

Black consciousness uncovers not only a history that is shameful, but also one that reveals a "fantastically strong subterranean life of self-affirmation and strength" at the heart of suffering and pain.

Over and over again, Jackson's addresses played on this phenomenological realism about history—exposing to the light what no other major presidential candidate had ever dared expose, such as the entire deceitful history of the nuclear industry, which he laid out to an audience in Exeter, New Hampshire, in the shadow of the Seabrook nuclear plant. But at the same time as he exposed the lies and omissions of official American history, he committed his listeners to draw strength and insight from the past, for buried within it were also the dreams of countless Americans who had the vision of a different future that was still waiting to be fulfilled. In a speech to the Wisconsin state legislature, Jackson recalled a piece of that history.

The people of Wisconsin have played a great role in the history of this nation. Many leaders of the great progressive movements that have shaped our past came from this state. Farmers and populists joined together to preserve their land and their farms, to set a new agenda for this state and the nation. They had a dream of a nation in which the people—the hard working people of the land and of the cities—would set this nation's priorities, not the bankers on Wall Street. Their dream lives on.

Many of the leaders of the anti-war movement came from this state in the 1960s. They had a dream of a nation that would not demonstrate its power in the world by bombing and napalming the people of a small third world nation, fighting for self-determination. They had a dream of a nation that would seek peace and justice among the peoples of the world. Their dream lives on. . . .

The oldest struggle of all. The fight of the Great Indian nations for justice for their people, for ancient treaties to be honored, for the land, its waters and its people to be treated with respect. The American Indians were the first great environmentalists. Their dream—their vision—of men and women living in harmony with nature becomes more critical to our future as a nation every day.[30]

Jackson's responses to Reagan's policy on Central America reveal the way in which American leaders have been able to get away with a policy of world domination to the extent to which they have kept the American public mystified about its own past. In two interviews, Jackson demonstrated the influence a correct understanding of the American past could have on our foreign policy assessments.

We ought to be more patient with the Third World nations in their transitions for development. After all, there was a ten or twelve year difference between General George Washington and President George Washington. We ourselves had to evolve into a more mature democracy. A substantial number of people got the right to vote 100 years after that. So for us to try to make them [Nicaragua] do in three years what we didn't do in 12 years is unfair.[31]

When this government embraces the landed gentry in El Salvador, we're misreading [our own] history.[32]

Jackson's speeches and media appearances served an educational function for the American public, correcting the miseducation of that public in ways that would begin to bear political fruit only after the campaign had run its course. During the campaign, one continually ran into evidence of its educational effects in the comments of people who said, over and over again: "Jackson is the only one who is making any sense; the only person speaking the truth."

The Politics of Personal Diplomacy: Telling Truth to Power

Black culture shares with certain other cultures an emphasis on personal relationships and personal example in the conduct of public life.[33] This contrasts with the utilitarian individualism and technical rationality that characterize the white middle class values that have become hegemonic in American society.

Jackson continuously emphasized the role of the leader as one who "leads," who sets the pace for the nation, who teaches the public and calls it to commit itself to fulfill the national ideals. His insistence on the effectiveness of personal diplomacy and face-to-face negotiations to solve international disputes was reiterated throughout the campaign and dramatically illustrated in his successful release of Lieutenant Goodman from a Syria prison, as well as his negotiation for the release of prisoners from Cuba.

Jackson's people-to-people crusades, based on his belief in the efficacy of personal action and example, baffled media commentators and infuriated political scientists who were used to assuming a technical-rationalist framework where abstract rules and behavior coded to roles and status were assumed to dictate foreign policy. His forays to Syria, Central America, and Cuba were seen, not as flowing from a deeply rooted cultural understanding of political action, but as the naive maneuverings of a political opportunist.[34] Journalists questioned his "credentials" to deal with substantive foreign policy matters. Characteristic of the knee-jerk anticommunism that had overtaken the mainstream media, the *New York Times* characterized Jackson's successful negotiations with Fidel Castro for the release of forty-eight Cuban and American prisoners as "a collaboration with the enemies of democracy."[35] *Newsweek*, while admitting that Jackson had scored an incredible coup in his successful mission to Syria to free Lieutenant Goodman, trivialized the event as a "political coup composed of one part divine inspiration, one part pure chutzpah, and a truckload of plain, old-fashioned luck."[36] This characterization contrasted sharply with the meaning the event held for Jackson and every other member of his delegation, who saw the trip as a humanitarian pilgrimage for world peace, with deeply religious resonances, one that proved the efficacy of the black community's brand of personal and moral intervention in world affairs.[37]

Some political scientists were not even so flattering as *Newsweek*. Typical is political scientist Henry Plotkin's assertion that Jackson's visits to the third world "raised questions about his foreign policy." Plotkin saw the sinister spectres of "black separatism, anti-Semitism, [and] prototalitarianism" haunting the campaign.[38]

Beneath the fear expressed by people like Plotkin and the reductionism inherent in the characterization of Jackson's diplomacy as opportunism lies the unadmitted consciousness that much of what passes for rational foreign policy is, indeed, motivated by the personal fears, prejudices, and lust for power of those in the foreign policy establishment. By openly acknowledging what others have admitted only in political memoirs written after the fact, Jackson was calling attention to the emperor's nakedness in a way that made political pundits squirm.

> Everybody knows that the personal relationship between Kennedy and Khrushchev was crucial in that period [the Cuban missile crisis]. All of life really *does* boil down to personal relationships. . . . If Andropov and Reagan had met each other and communicated and expressed their common desire to avoid mutual annihilation, with a real desire to do it, those two men could have relieved tension in this world, but they didn't know each other. So they talked *at* each other rather than relate *to* each other, and that violent noncommunication has us on the brink of disaster.[39]

The Jackson Campaign as Education for Citizenship

The American public is perhaps one of the most politically illiterate in the world. When it votes—and it has the lowest voting record of any Western democracy—it is likely to be on the basis of either party habit or, more likely today, on the candidate's "image," which is carefully fashioned by an industry of political packaging experts. Few voters are ideologically oriented—that is, they do not see or make connections between issues on the basis of any coherent philosophy of government. All of this is evidenced by a public that elects Ronald Reagan president while disagreeing with almost all of the policy issues he espouses.[40] Perhaps even more alarming than this is evidence that voters in a 1986 Illinois Democratic primary election may have voted for candidates representing the neofascist Lyndon LaRouche because their Anglo-

Saxon names, while unknown, were pitted against the "foreign-sounding" names of the regular Democratic Party candidates.[41]

The Jackson campaign began in November 1983 with little more than a black perspective, with a general commitment to the as yet unfulfilled ideals of American democracy, and with the still general and untried concept of building a national Rainbow Coalition of the locked-out and rejected. That perspective directed its choice of audience and constituency and it was the audience and constituency that supplied the Jackson campaign with the specific policy issues that became a part of the campaign's final program.

In every community into which the campaign went, Jackson's speechwriters would gather all of the relevant material on that community's "misery index," on the history of people's struggles for justice and democracy in that area, and on current issues of concern around which community struggles were being waged. They wove this material into speeches and campaign strategies designed to reflect back to these communities the power and grandeur contained in their efforts. Jackson took the prepared speeches, inserting his own insights and anecdotes into them.

Because the Jackson campaign was publicly committed to the locked-out and rejected, campaign organizers traveling with the candidate, as well as those in the national office, were flooded with every conceivable request from every disinherited group in the country for Jackson to speak publicly to their issue: Vietnam veterans seeking compensation for Agent Orange poisoning; American Indians seeking land claims; farmworkers seeking justice from the Campbell Soup Company; opponents of the death penalty trying to avert an execution; victims of police violence seeking justice; sanctuary workers trying to stop the deportation of Central American refugees; farmers who were trying to stop the foreclosure of their farms; peace activists attempting to prevent the stationing of nuclear warships in New York harbor; Latinos trying to save bilingual education and halt the Simpson-Mazzoli immigration bill; families of political prisoners seeking release of their loved ones. Given the limitations on people's time and energy, the lack of financial resources available to the campaign, the swiftness with which events had to move, and the lack of prior organizational planning, the campaign managed to be a remarkably open and democratic one—to a large extent truly shaped by the locked-out and rejected. In style and substance it more clearly resembled the third-party campaigns of Eugene Debs and Henry Wallace than any of the campaigns of major party candidates.

The task of responding to the tremendous needs of the locked-out, as well as preparing the candidate to respond to those needs, was monumental for the small Jackson staff, especially when the candidate had to make five and six campaign appearances a day, often in more than one city. The campaign was an experiment in public education comparable only to the efforts of the soapbox orators who traveled across the country in an earlier day, agitating for workers' rights or woman suffrage—only this time, the issues were expanded exponentially.

Jackson attempted to educate not only the public but those who shaped the public's views. "Part of my mission," he said, "is to challenge the media of this nation to move away from the diversion of Hart's age or where Mondale has been, because Hart's age and Mondale's past do not constitute national emergencies. But 34 million people in legal poverty is an emergency."[42]

If the candidate was continually educating the public, the public was also educating the candidate. Though Jackson's instincts were usually right, he too had to be educated on issues and ethnic perspectives of which he was ignorant. In several of his early speeches, for example, Jackson called for Europe and Japan to begin shouldering the burden of their own defense, which the United States had borne since World War II. A Japanese activist had to inform him that the Japanese Constitution prohibits the country's rearmament and that the Japanese, because of the experience of Hiroshima and Nagasaki, are extremely sensitive to the question of militarization. Jackson's positions on abortion and lesbian and gay rights went through a similar overhauling as he was forced to deal with women and homosexuals as part of his locked-out. He was quick to learn. By April, Theodore White was moved to comment that "no man has grown more in the past two months in poise, in passionate eloquence, and political smarts as Mr. Jackson."[43] It was a somewhat patronizing comment, as if Jackson were starting as a neophyte. Nevertheless, there was truth to the observation.

The Jackson campaign was thus a dialectical interaction between candidate and audience, both growing and expanding their vision as they pursued the elusive prey of political power. The effect on the black community was particularly striking. Blacks were heard conversing on street corners about foreign policy issues that just months before would have been entirely beyond the range of their frame of reference. Those who heard Jackson in person responded to his message with unparallelled enthusiasm. Even in white New Hampshire, Jackson drew crowds that were three times the size of those of the other candidates, and crowds that were far more enthusiastic.

Most of the nation, however, did not hear the candidate directly, until his final speech at the Democratic Convention, and the media rarely reported the substance of his speeches. They preferred to focus on the Jewish-black controversy and to fuel the sensation caused by Muslim Minister Louis Farrakhan's intemperate remarks.

In spite of such impediments, by the end of June, those who had worked on the campaign around the country had come to a clear consensus on a set of platform issues representing the "ideology" of the Rainbow Coalition. They had also come to a sense of their own role in a historic mission to restore the values of peace, justice, and democracy to an ailing nation. Speaking for thousands of others, Rose Sanders, youth coordinator for the Jackson campaign in Alabama, remarked: "He [Jackson] has imbued us with a new sense of history."[44]

On 29 June 1984, hundreds of Jackson organizers from across the country—black, Latino, white, Native American, and Asian American—gathered at the McCormick Inn in Chicago for the National Rainbow Leadership Conference in preparation for the Democratic National Convention just a few weeks away. Conference participants had seen almost every one of the Jackson campaign's platform planks go down to defeat in the Democratic party platform hearings held prior to their meeting. The campaign had managed to win enough votes for four minority reports—on affirmative action, no first use of nuclear weapons, cutting the military budget, and voting rights—that would be taken to the convention floor; but the efforts of party regulars to steer the party to the right had finally won out.

The effort to save America's soul would be a protracted one, in which the Jackson campaign was only a first skirmish. Delegates to the National Rainbow Leadership Conference expressed their resolve and their hope in the future, in this way:

We, the members of the Rainbow Coalition declare our resolve to become a permanent presence in the fight for a more humane, equitable and progressive America in both its domestic and foreign affairs. In making this declaration, we are at first consciously distinct from conservative forces standing for the status quo, and liberal forces seeking minor reforms. We are a progressive movement for major changes in the substance and structure of American life. . . . We now know that many of the issues we have raised in the forum of the Platform and Rules Committees of the Party were rejected because they were too progressive and were either defeated or relegated to the status of Minority Reports. We are not discouraged but rather encouraged that even in the face of superior numbers we stood on principle rather than compromise our integrity.[45]

6

Beyond the Melting Pot: Building the Rainbow Coalition

America is not like a blanket, one unbroken piece of cloth, one color, one character, one texture, one religion. It is more like a quilt of many patches, many pieces, many colors, many textures, many religions, many sizes. And yet everybody fits somewhere, everybody is somebody.[1]

—Jesse Jackson

The Rainbow Coalition Jesse Jackson attempted to forge was to be based on a recognition not only of the multiracial character of American society, but also of its multidimensionality. Like any symbol the rainbow could be gimmicky; but as the embodiment of a new conception of the body politic, the Rainbow Coalition is extraordinarily politically creative.

In contrast to the image of the melting pot, the rainbow affirms diversity as a positive political value. To enter the "national" ethos, it suggests, individual groups—whether defined by culture, class, gender, age, religion, or region—do not have to give up their distinctiveness.

The assimilation process associated with the melting-pot theory required that European Americans give up their ties to homeland, culture, and language in order to be considered American. In replacing these with an ersatz national culture that demanded they identify with the dominant symbols of power and righteousness without giving them the means to achieve real power, the acculturation experience of European Americans was virtually destined to breed racism.[2] The frustrations working-class people encountered in the marketplace could easily be displaced onto others who by virtue of their darker skins, structural economic marginalization, or more recent immigrant status were seen as outside the pale—as "un-American."

Jackson specifically differentiated the bonding of the various constituent elements in the rainbow from the integrationist goals of the earlier civil rights movement, which had been based on the paradigm of the melting pot. Integration, he recognized, had always raised deep-seated fears among whites—fears deeply imbedded in American culture as a result of slavery and based on sexual myths related to miscegenation. With the Rainbow Coalition, he said, "there are no psychological or sexual hangups. . . . The Rainbow Coalition is made up of independent groups."[3]

The concept of a nation built on independently organized, self-determining groups was certain to have profound implications for how the country conceived of "national identity" or national loyalty, versus group loyalty, and how it adjudicated inequalities between groups. The melting-pot paradigm accepted ethnic differences so long as they were kept in the private sphere, while demanding that everyone conform to a single national political culture.

Theodore White began to grasp the dimensions of the new definition of the polis that the Rainbow Coalition implied when he observed: "In effect, Jackson is demanding that the Democrats propose to the nation a coalition government, not just of interests and regions, but of race and of ethnics—the famous 'rainbow coalition' which, if accepted, could remold the contours of classic politics."[4] But White grasped only part of the rainbow's complexity, for Jackson had also said that the rainbow was a "point of view"—a view "from the bottom up"; a "destiny"—to "change the direction of the nation"; and a "school of thought"—the "progressive school."

In effect, the concept of the rainbow demonstrates how the ethnic and gender consciousness of the 1960s, the class consciousness of the 1930s, and the survival consciousness of the 1970s and 1980s were converging into a new conception of national identity and purpose, and into a totally untried political praxis. The Jackson campaign sought to mobilize different sectors of the electorate with appeals based on each sector's consciousness of its own particularity. This consciousness was a combination of factors intrinsic to each group's historical origins as well as a product of the way in which it had been treated by the society's dominant institutions.

This made for an extremely complex method of organization and demanded special sensitivities on the part of organizers that were not always present. The groups that were mobilized into the Rainbow Coalition could be defined by five broad typologies. First, there were groups defined by their minority ethnic or national/cultural origin status: African Americans, Hispanic Americans, Asian Americans, Native Americans, Arab Americans, and Jewish Americans. Second were the groups defined by gender or sexual orientation: women, lesbians and gays; third were those defined by their relationship to the processes of production: farmers and labor. Fourth were those that might be called "conscience" or "ideological" constituencies: generally white middle-class peace and environmental activists. Finally, there were groups that had come into political focus as entitlement groups: disabled people and public housing tenants.

Yet even this typology obscures the complexity of the consciousness the Jackson campaign embraced, for most individuals fit into more than one of those categories. The categories of women and disabled, for example, cut across all racial/ethnic groups and classes. Farmers, labor, and public housing tenants are multiracial categories. Lesbians can either identify with the gay rights movement or with the women's movement. Arab Americans can be found in all classes. Indeed, many Arab Americans who supported the Jackson campaign were wealthy Republican businessmen. Even within each racial/ethnic group there are distinctions that the American system of rights and privileges often obscures. Most Native Americans, for example, do not think of themselves as an "ethnic group," but as members of distinct nations. Their particular struggle for sovereignty, therefore, has a different meaning and profoundly different implications for the future of the American polity than does the struggle of African

Americans for dignity and equality. The terms "Hispanics" and "Asian Americans" obscure the differences among the many nationality groups that these terms attempt to cover. Moreover, the white majority was not approached by the Jackson campaign as a racial/ethnic group, but rather through the different sectoral movements with which various whites have identified—movements that have the potential of dissassociating certain whites from the dominant political ethos and uniting them with other strata in an oppositional political bloc. The question of white identity and racism as it affected the Jackson campaign is taken up in Chapter 10.

Few who flocked to the rainbow's banner in 1984 fully understood the radical dimensions of the political breakthrough to which Jackson was calling them. It is doubtful if even Jackson was fully cognizant of the dimensions of his project at the beginning of the campaign. Those dimensions would begin to come into focus only as he set off on the road and began to encounter the enormous complexity of the American social landscape. The Rainbow Coalition was a little like the elephant whom the blind men were trying to identify, each feeling a piece of the animal and taking it for the whole.

Blacks, for the most part, saw in the Jackson campaign a chance to register their frustration with the racism of the Democratic establishment and to flex their political muscle, even if it was only symbolic. Not a few black politicians and businessmen and some Hispanics supported the campaign for the increased influence they thought it would bring them within the Democratic party. Other Hispanics, along with peace activists, environmentalists, and lesbians and gays, rallied to the campaign because Jackson was the only one who was speaking to their issues. Arab Americans and Asian Americans supported the campaign because, for the first time, they had been offered a place in the political sun. Native Americans wanted to get a message about what was happening to their communities out to a wider audience and saw the Jackson campaign as a way to do that.

Thus the reasons for supporting the campaign were as diverse as the constituencies it drew; but in the process of getting involved, a wider dimension, a new synthesis began to be perceived. This chapter and the next look at the process of organizing each of the major rainbow constituencies—at their responses to the call issued by Jackson, at the internal contradictions within the campaign and within and between the groups, and at the campaign's successes and failures in attempting to build the Rainbow Coalition. In this chapter we consider three broad groups—blacks, Latinos, and women—that, due to their historical marginalization from the political process, are obvious members of the rainbow as envisioned by Jesse Jackson, and that in their numbers have the potential to make the Rainbow Coalition a majority electoral bloc. The Jackson campaign was successful with blacks, made impressive inroads with Latinos, in spite of tremendous obstacles, and was much less successful with white women, for reasons that will be explored.

The African-American Base

In defiance of all predictions (early polls showed that Jackson could take only 40 percent of the black vote), the Jackson campaign was for a brief moment the single most significant unifier of the African-American community since the days of Reconstruction. Under one banner, most of the salient strands of black ideological thought, black leadership styles, and black community activity came together, thus overcoming two decades or more of fragmentation. The only exception to this were blacks who for reasons either of personal ambition, personal rivalry, or the inability to discern the tides of history continued their allegiance to the old interest-group politics of the Democratic party regulars and a few radical black leftists and nationalists who viewed any kind of campaign waged within the two-party system as a sell-out.

The campaign employed a wide range of organizers and leaders in the black community. It included former Student Nonviolent Coordinating Committee (SNCC) activists and those who had been allied with the older generation in the Southern Christian Leadership Conference (SCLC); nationalists of both the Marxist and separatist stripes; democratic socialists both in and outside the Democratic party; left independent socialists; and center-left Democratic party officials.

In addition to the black churches, a variety of Islamic and African cultural sects supported the campaign. For the first time, the Nation of Islam involved itself in electoral politics. Sororities and fraternities, masonic lodges, women's networks and clubs, black businesses, indeed every manner of institution resident in the black community was caught up in the fervor of the campaign.

For the most part, the black leaders who did not support the campaign were those who were more heavily tied to white support, either as mayors of large cities—Wilson Goode of Philadelphia, Andrew Young of Atlanta, Tom Bradley of Los Angeles, Coleman Young of Detroit—or by virtue of their rank in the old civil rights establishment—Coretta Scott King, Benjamin Hooks. In exchange for a "place" in a racially stratified system, politicians who had endorsed Mondale fought hard to deliver for their candidate, but in the end, the masses went with Jackson, creating new contradictions within the black leadership stratum that only time would begin to sort out.

Wilson Goode's support of Mondale while his city went for Jackson presaged the beginning of Goode's decline; Andrew Young was disgraced at the convention when he tried to argue for Mondale's position on voting rights; Charlie Rangel, whose New York district went for Jackson, would later move to endorse the Rainbow Coalition. In Detroit, Jackson supporters accused Coleman Young of using the same "plantation politics" that had been used against blacks by whites in the South.

Class Struggle Within the Black Community

These cleavages are dramatically illustrated in Alabama. Here, Montgomery city councilman Joe Reed, the chairman of the all-black Alabama Democratic Conference (ADC, the "black caucus" of the white-controlled Democratic party), fought hard for Mondale to become the ADC's nominee, but Reed's manipulation of the nomination process and his vicious public denunciations of Jackson backfired. Jackson insurgents, who had been grumbling for years about Reed's dictatorial control of black political life in the state and angered by Reed's attacks on Jackson, used the enthusiasm generated by the Jackson campaign to dislodge the ADC machine from its more than twenty-year influence over the state's black political life. The Jackson insurgents' power base was in the five rural western Alabama Black Belt counties of Greene, Sumter, Lowndes, Perry, and Wilcox. The Alabama Black Belt, which covers ten rural counties, is so named for its rich black soil, but it is also the black majority area of the state. Over the years, civil rights activists had managed to overcome a century of racist intimidation to elect their own people to a majority of the elective offices, including the state senate and assembly. Jackson swept these counties by a margin of 2-1, as well as Tuscaloosa and Mobile counties, winning a majority of the state's black vote. It was only Birmingham mayor Richard Arrington's machine, which worked for Mondale, that allowed Mondale to win the black vote in that area.[5] Tuskegee professor Willy Fluker believes that Jackson's statewide popular vote may have been much higher than the official count of 19.6 percent. Jackson supporters cited numerous irregularities, which they asserted the ADC and the white Democratic party covered up. Based on his experience, Fluker believes that Jackson may have won the popular vote in the state, though he was unable to get state election commissioners to turn over district breakdowns.[6]

The split between Jackson and Mondale backers in Alabama reflects a split within the black leadership group along the lines of age, class, and ideology. Interviews with campaign activists revealed that leaders of the Jackson insurgency tended to be between thirty-five and forty-nine years old. Most were veterans of the original civil rights movement. Several had been active in SNCC, still others in SCLC, and some in more radical black nationalist groups. Over the years, their beliefs had changed, moving from civil rights and black power goals to a conception of economic and political empowerment based on a participatory conception of democracy, the accountability of elected officials to the base, a class analysis, and an internationalist perspective. In practice, this translated into outreach efforts to involve the largest number of grassroots people in the electoral process, using elective offices to progressively educate the electorate, and seeking political power as a means of redistributing economic power and benefits. Although interested in black economic and political power in black majority areas, the Jackson forces were clear that whites had to have fair representation, provided it did not mean white racist control of the power structure. The Jackson insurgents had welcomed representatives of the African National Congress and the Sandinistas to the Black Belt, indicating that they see themselves as part of a worldwide movement for justice and democracy.[7]

The old-guard leadership of the ADC, on the other hand, and the majority of those who backed Mondale, were older, generally petty bourgeois urban blacks associated with the teaching profession. Indeed, the ADC had been created out of the Alabama Education Association, the state affiliate of the National Education Association. These people had not been active in the civil rights movement, but had taken advantage of the restructuring of race relations brought about by the ending of Jim Crow segregation to insert themselves as brokers between the black base and the white controlled party, essentially maintaining the racial caste system while talking "black." Jackson supporter Gwen Patton called them "Toms of the new type."[8]

A similar but differently nuanced split occurred within the Jackson campaign itself. Not all of those who supported Jackson did so for the same reasons. Some, like Rev. Herbert Daughtry, chairman of the National Black United Front (NBUF), saw that the black masses were flocking to Jackson and felt that it was the responsibility of committed nationalist leaders to be where the people were, giving them guidance. "A lot of people in NBUF mistrusted Jackson," he explained to me:

> People felt he was part of the establishment, that he would betray us down the line. But I thought I had seen enough to convince me that people were going that way. . . . So if that's where the people are, you're either going to have to stand to the side and be run over, or stand on the side and hurl criticism. The best thing that could be done, irrespective of whatever you think about Jesse, is to try to get close enough to him to make him honest, to keep him honest. And to do that you needed to have input into what his thinking would be. . . . I thought that Jesse was going to articulate the issues; I thought that the things he had been saying all along he was going to say.

Other community leaders saw in the campaign an opportunity to generate a new grassroots movement from the enthusiasm and energy that Jackson aroused. James Livingston, a community activist with SCLC in New Orleans, told me:

> I've had problems with Jesse Jackson since 1972–1973, with some foul moves I think he's made. The reason I supported him was because I thought the campaign would be the impetus point for galvanizing masses of people and would create the impetus for building a movement beyond the election, knowing the election was not going to have a major impact on the fortunes of the people.

Many black politicians, particularly those from black majority districts and cities, on the other hand, were counting the newly registered voters who would be added to their districts. They dared not be in public opposition to their constituency, which was going with Jackson. "If black politicians thought they were on a pilgrimage or crusade," said Bill Howard, one of Jackson's advisers, "they wouldn't have joined us." Many continued to retain the same kinds of reservations about Jackson as their colleagues who endorsed Mondale (e.g., that he was opportunistic, egocentric, or that his campaign was only symbolic). At the same time, they feared the kind of insurgent grassroots movement that the campaign was stirring up. In black majority districts, their own power could be threatened by a new group of poor voters demanding benefits they could not deliver. Such politicians did not necessarily see themselves as part of the "progressive" school of thought announced by Jackson. As Gwen Patton explained:

> Black leaders, represented by ministers in the past and now usurped by politicians today, continue to stifle the movement of people below. Community and neighborhood associations, grassroots formations are discouraged, and if formed out of socio-political-economic conditions which give natural rise to such formations, the groups are undermined and attacked by Black politicians. The Black-on-Black interaction has an eerie god-father character, whereby Black citizens are not to take charge of their own lives in any collective way, but are non-verbally mandated individually to go to Black politicians to "fix" what was originally a legitimate social concern now transformed by blaming the victim into a personal problem.[9]

Some clergy who had ties to Jackson through Operation PUSH compromised their support of the campaign by their ties to the local Democratic party machine controlled by Mondale forces. Their churches depended on daycare funds and manpower money that came through the city machine, or in some cases their own prestige in the community may have rested on their ties to party officials. Assuming that Jackson was not going to win the election, some black politicians and clergymen played a double game, hedging their bets with both Jackson and Mondale forces. Some politicians supported Jackson publicly but made little effort to get out the vote for him beyond what their own machines controlled. Some clergy raised money for Jackson, held rallies in their churches, and even got themselves elected delegates to the Democratic National Convention, but they also made sure that Mondale got the majority of the delegates.

In many cases, however, militant community leaders who had joined the Jackson campaign because of its grassroots character and ostensibly progressive ideology saw through such games. Blacks in Philadelphia were outraged when they learned that black ward leaders who publicly supported Jackson had printed Jackson's name at the top of the ballots but the names of Mondale delegates beneath it, so that the public unwittingly voted for Mondale delegates when they thought they were voting for Jackson.[10]

In Louisiana, community organizers were similarly angered when they learned that their mayor, "Dutch" Morial, the head of the state campaign, would be out of the country in the crucial week before the election. They were also upset by the lack of grassroots outreach and involvement by the chairman and coordinator of the campaign and held a press conference to expose them. A long-time community activist and organizer, Ron Chisom, told me that he thought the "politicians were in it for their own mileage." In Louisiana, he said, there was no literature given out, never any door-to-door work done, and the low-income housing tenants with whom Chisom works were totally ignored. When the campaign leadership brought Jackson into the state for a whirlwind tour, said Chisom, they met only with the black bourgeoisie. "When Jesse came in for a big rally, it was one of the poorest representations I've ever seen. The place held 3,000 people, but there were only about 600 there." Chisom explained that he and other grassroots organizers saw the enthusiasm that was out there among poor people and got their own literature, which they began to give out in the food stamp lines, housing projects, and barrooms.

In many places criticisms of how the campaign was run and the class consciousness heightened by the campaign with its radical rhetoric about the locked-out redounded on Jackson himself. Barbara Major, director of the Louisiana Survival Coalition, an organization of welfare mothers, told me: "I appreciate Jesse having the nerve enough to run, but he should have had nerve enough to get up and say, 'not even my brothers who consider themselves leaders will in any way ignore my people.' " For Major, the failure to organize grassroots people was "like a slap in the face" to them.

Low-income housing tenants from across the South who had gathered in Atlanta for a conference during the campaign were, according to Major, "pissed" when Jackson sent his wife Jackie to meet with them while he was across town "hob-nobbing with the big-wig elected officials." Many others, such as Washington state coordinator and former SNCC activist Arnette Holloway, felt that while Jackson was good at articulating the issues, he still operated from a practice of elitism, choosing figureheads to head his state campaigns who had no grassroots experience or commitment. She told me, "It was just deltas [middle-class sororities and fraternities] and preachers." "You know what it looked like to me— people were more interested and excited around the country about his [Jackson's] campaign and what it meant for them than the leadership he surrounded himself with." Holloway concluded that although Jackson's candidacy brought it all together, at the same time it may have eliminated him—that is, the campaign may have generated an awareness that has grown beyond the "single leader syndrome."

In several places in the country, criticism by grassroots activists of the top-down management of the campaign by state and local coordinators led to the formation of insurgent grassroots coalitions that existed alongside the officially chartered campaign organization and in some cases blossomed into ongoing rainbow coalitions after the campaign.

In New Jersey, a rainbow coalition headed by community activists campaigned in wards the Gibson machine (Newark mayor Kenneth Gibson headed the state campaign) would not touch. A flier circulated during the campaign accused the Gibson machine of having failed to build a grassroots organization in the state or even a voter registration drive, and of having hand-picked the delegates running on Jackson's ticket. "They [Gibson and the Newark City Council] are using the momentum of the masses' support for Jesse Jackson so they can return to office on the backs of the people," the flier maintained. In Seattle, a multiracial coalition of low-income and working-class people who were working for the campaign were angered by what they saw as the sellout of their campaign by its state chairman, Rev. Sam McKinney. One of

McKinney's close associates, an aide to Congressman Lowery, who was appointed by McKinney to the Jackson state campaign committee, was seen in a televised documentary on the caucus process sitting in a session with Mondale strategists. After the campaign, the coalition of low-income activists formed the Rainbow Institute, which formalized itself as a separate entity from the Rainbow Coalition headed by McKinney.

Obstacles in the Democratic Party

Cleavages within the black leadership were heightened by the intransigence of the Democratic party regulars in refusing to grant concessions to Jackson's demands for a change in the party rules and the elimination of voting impediments. Some black journalists began to articulate publicly what many grassroots organizers were saying privately: that black Mondale supporters were traitors to their people.[11]

At the end of April, some high-level Jackson supporters began a series of meetings with Mondale delegates to try to deflect black in-fighting on the convention floor. Said Texas representative and Mondale endorser Mickey Leland after one of these meetings, "You're going to see black Mondale delegates . . . more aligned with Jackson principles on the convention floor."[12]

In early June Jackson met with members of the Congressional Black Caucus, many of whom had endorsed Mondale, and argued that their support for his fight for fair rules and proportional representation could heighten their stature in the party by forcing the white Democratic leaders to include blacks on key convention committees and party posts.[13] While agreeing in principle to help Jackson, the Mondale delegates were in fact unable to win any substantive concessions from the party bosses except for a "fairness commission" that would not meet until after the November election. Jackson's candidacy did, however, increase the visibility of Mondale blacks on the convention program. Forced to appear to be giving something to blacks, the white party establishment went through the motions of interviewing Mondale endorsers Tom Bradley and Wilson Goode for the vice president's spot, appointed several Mondale blacks to prominent convention positions, and showed a film on Martin Luther King as part of the convention program—a way of giving Coretta King a speaking role.

But when they used Andrew Young to speak against Jackson's minority plank on voting rights, in what journalist Ethel Payne called a "Greek tragedy of his own making," the appearance of unity evaporated. It was a moment of truth for many who were present. Here was Young, "a once proud Black symbol of courage and integrity . . . now reduced to a Charley McCarthy wooden puppet mouthing the instructions of his handlers."[14] Young was roundly booed and jeered, and not only by Jackson supporters, who saw him selling out their interests for a place at the white man's table. The next day Coretta King was booed as she tried to defend "my mayor, Andrew Young," whom she felt had been wrongly booed and deserved an apology. It was Jesse Jackson, who had alternately outwitted and outlasted his white and black detractors and stood up to the white party bosses, who was seen as embodying the historical "soul" of the black community. It was a similar irreverence for rules and procedures that endeared the flamboyant Harlem congressman Adam Clayton Powell to black America, and never more so than when he was under attack from his white colleagues in Congress.

After Young's embarrassing debacle and Jackson's brilliant convention speech—during which nearly every black and many whites on the convention floor wept—a unity meeting of black delegates was called, at which Jackson criticized his supporters for having booed Young and called for reconciliation. At a press conference following the meeting, nearly every black delegate, with the exception of Coretta King and Julian Bond, hailed Jackson as "our leader." A tumultuous reception for Jackson by delegates to the National Association for the Advancement of Colored People convention two weeks earlier had even brought Benjamin Hooks around.

But in the aftermath of Mondale's nomination, that unity appeared to come apart again, as black Mondale supporters complained that they were afraid they were being given short shrift in appointments to Mondale's campaign organization in favor of Jackson backers. Jackson's backers, however, felt they had been given nothing but crumbs from the party. Herbert Daughtry angrily told a meeting of Jackson supporters:

> We are prepared to stand four more years of Ronald Reagan, rather than Democratic party disrespect. . . . If we can't deliver an ultimatum to Mondale, then we're going to have to say, "If you won't

respond to the demands before you, go on and get your back-side whipped by Reagan."[15]

The incident revealed the continuing conflict within the black leadership between those who would still attach themselves to power and those who were seeking to create a different power base. Which way black politicians went in the future would depend on whether the Rainbow Coalition could actually deliver that new power base to the elected leadership or replace that elected leadership with new blood. In 1984, it was still too early to tell.

Lessons for the Future

The story of black political participation in the Jesse Jackson campaign illustrates at least three points about the political character of the black community as a whole. First, the campaign demonstrated that blacks will defy elite assumptions about voter apathy if given a real choice. The Jackson turnout was proportionately the largest black voter turnout in history. Everywhere the Jackson campaign carried its message—a message of hope and the promise of political *participation*—the black community responded with unprecedented enthusiasm and commitment, creativity and ingenuity. The enthusiasm generated by the campaign is illustrated by the comments of two campaign workers in New York's East Harlem, Nellie and Roberto Marrero, who told me that the young people were dancing in the streets of Harlem on election day. At one polling place in Harlem the line was so long that at 9:00 P.M. when the polls closed, there were still people lined up all the way down the street waiting to vote. In defying the majority of the elected black leadership as well as the black trade union leadership (over 80 percent of all black trade unionists voted for Jackson) the black community in voting for Jackson was demonstrating that it would no longer be bought off by either platitudes or patronage.

Second, the black vote for Jackson demonstrates that the black base is the only viable one from which to launch a social democratic program for the United States. Though it was true that for black voters the issues Jackson articulated were less important than the fact that "one of their own" was running for president, it is also true that because of their social class location, most African

Americans are naturally inclined toward progressive domestic and foreign policies, less susceptible to the manipulative uses of anticommunism and war hysteria.

Third, the Jackson campaign illustrates a growing disenchantment among black Democrats with the Democratic party and an increasing willingness to consider independent or third-party options. The Jackson campaign heightened class consciousness both within the black community and vis-à-vis the white power structure of the party to which blacks had been so faithful. Moreover, it gave black leaders a closer look at the maneuvering, skills, and weaknesses of the white power structure than they had ever had before. A poll taken during the campaign indicated that had Jackson run on an independent ticket in 1984, 59 percent of the black electorate would have voted for him. For blacks, at least, American politics would never be the same.[16]

The Hispanic Electorate: Natural Partners

The Hispanic population in the United States is a great reserve of cultural vitality and political power, yet it is only recently that its political potential has begun to be recognized. The media in the late 1960s and early 1970s did not focus on the Chicano movement as it did on the black movement; thus both its cultural insights and the awareness of the movement's repression by police and government agents went largely unnoticed by both black and white America. The farmworker movement, led by César Chávez, practiced a form of popular liberation theology well before that term had achieved currency in the United States. The movement was a source for the idea of the "poor" as a motive force in history—a concept that is central to Latin American liberation theology and one that was employed by the Rainbow Coalition in the idea of the locked-out and forgotten stones as the cornerstone of a new political majority.

Currently, only 59 percent of eligible Hispanics in the United States are registered to vote, and only 48 percent of those eligible to vote did so in the November 1984 election.[17] Yet if current immigration and birthrates continue, by the year 2000, Latinos will be the largest ethnic group in the United States. Since 85 percent of all Spanish-speaking people are concentrated in nine states and twenty cities that control 193 (or 71 percent) of the electoral votes needed to win the presidency, they constitute a critical swing vote in future elections.

The Latino population in the United States is, of course, composed of many separate nationality groups and thus has many separate political networks, distinct cultural sensitivities, and mores that have to be taken into consideration by political organizers. An indication of the polyglot nature of the Latino population is illustrated in the remarks of Chicago Democratic ward committeeman Jesus Garcia:

> You can tell where you are from the sounds and the smell of the cooking. In Mexican areas people are doing the taco thing with beans and rice; in Puerto Rican areas it's roast pork and fried rice. If you walk around Pilsen [a Mexican enclave] you'll hear mariachi music; in [Puerto Rican] Humboldt Park you'll hear salsa and conga drums.[18]

No one organization or leader speaks for all Spanish-speaking people, and there is no single national Latino-controlled institution—like the black church—that can be used to mobilize the masses. Moreover, most rank-and-file Latinos do not follow either established elected leadership or even those organizations that ostensibly speak for the Latino majority, such as the League of United Latin American Citizens (LULAC), or the Mexican American Political Association (MAPA). Most Latino elected leaders came to power as a class of "brokers" between the Latino population and the Anglo power structures. Rodolfo Acuna, Elizabeth Sutherland Martinez, and Enriqueta Longeaux y Vasquez, authors of two books on Chicano history, argue that these leaders serve the interests of the Anglo system since their own positions and upward mobility depend on it.[19] New York Puerto Rican activists Nellie and Roberto Marrero told me that elected Puerto Rican leaders act like feudal lords, building their own fiefdoms through the use of patronage, but enjoying little respect from the grassroots community and offering almost nothing to it in the way of substantive legislative reforms or real political power.

Together on the Issues

In spite of the apparent fragmentation in the Latino communities of the United States, the Latino population is surprisingly unified when it comes to positions on issues. With the exception of Cubans, whose anticommunism pulls them to the right on foreign affairs, all Latinos share similar values and tend to vote as a bloc for candidates who address those values. Latinos have voted overwhelmingly Democratic. They oppose cuts in social programs to reduce the deficit; are worried about unemployment and want more money put into jobs programs; oppose increases in the defense budget and U.S. intervention in Central America; and support a nuclear freeze. Education is a high priority for Latinos, and they have fought fiercely for bilingual education; they favor amnesty for undocumented workers and overwhelmingly support the Equal Rights Amendment.[20]

In terms of class, Latinos are overwhelmingly poor and working class. In a survey conducted by the San Antonio-based Southwest Voter Registration Education Project, two thirds of the Mexican-American electorate in 1982 had family incomes of less than $15,000.[21] A 1983 Congressional Research Service study on children in poverty reported that 38.2 percent of all Hispanic children were living in poverty, compared with 46.7 percent of black children and 17.3 percent of all children.[22] Latinos occupy a middle position between white and black, but in terms of median income are much closer to the black than to the white. Income figures are skewed, however, by the relatively high incomes enjoyed by Cubans—most of them middle-class refugees from Castro's Cuba. On the other hand, more than 40 percent of Puerto Ricans live below the poverty line.[23]

For Want of a Latino Strategy

Given the issue and class compatibility between the black and Latino populations, it was logical that Latinos would be a prime target for organizing into the Rainbow Coalition. It may be the most serious shortcoming of the Jackson campaign that its managers did not recognize the importance of the Latino vote to their undertaking. Jackson got about 33 percent of the Latino vote nationwide, but it was almost in spite of, not because of, the national campaign leadership. Armando Gutierrez, a former professor of Latin American studies who began working for the campaign in mid-April, told me that while black campaign leaders may have had a genuine desire to have a black-Latino coalition, they failed to operationalize that desire in terms of allocating resources and time to it. The Hispanic desk was filled by Felipe Braudy, a Puerto Rican who came to the campaign at the recommendation of LULAC leaders. Armando Gutierrez, a Chicano, was added midway through the campaign primarily as a speechwriter and on-the-road consultant on Hispanic affairs. Yet neither felt he had the ear of campaign leaders or much authority to shape overall policy. "There simply was no Hispanic strategy," said Gutierrez.

Part of the problem stemmed from the lack of effective contact between black and Latino leaders at either national or local levels since the late 1960s. Even then, there had been little interaction, except through the more militant younger groups such as SNCC and the Black Panthers. Thus black Jackson leaders made the mistake of assuming that titular leadership in the Latino community implied real leadership. If this was untrue of the black community, it was even less applicable in Latino communities. The campaign counted on Tony Bonilla, former president of LULAC, who was appointed to the campaign's national committee, to mobilize the Mexican American masses, but according to members of the community, everyone in the Chicano community knew that Bonilla had no history of grassroots organizing.[24]

Without a Latino strategy and with no knowledge of the authentic indigenous organizers, campaign managers made some terrible blunders. In California, local activists who presented themselves to Jackson managers and were hired as the state's Hispanic coordinators, had a long reputation in the Latino community of being divisive and sectarian.[25] Since no one had the ability to check them out, they inserted themselves in the campaign and probably made more enemies for it than friends. Knowledgeable sources said there were a lot of Chicanos in southern California who were attracted to the campaign but who were not willing to come out and be associated with the coordinators.

In San Antonio, which has a 45 percent Chicano population, virtually no organizing took place in the Mexican-American community, except what was put together by San Antonio's only Chicano delegate, community activist and sanctuary worker Laura Sanchez. As a result, the campaign missed the opportunity for Jackson to speak before a crowd of an estimated 30,000 Mexican Americans who turn out in the streets each year for the Cinco de Mayo festival. Even Sanchez had to fight the city's black campaign leadership for the resources needed to reach her people, as well as for a place on Jackson's itinerary. She felt that local black politicians and businessmen viewed her efforts to reach beyond their narrow machine base as a threat.

The one event that was to be held in a Catholic church in the Latino community on the theme of sanctuary for Central American refugees very nearly fell through because the black campaign manager wanted Jackson to appear instead at his shopping mall. Due to some fast work by staff in the national office, Jackson's traveling staff, and Sanchez's refusal to give up, the event was saved, but not before her reservation of the Catholic church and her commitment from a Catholic monsignor to appear with Jackson had fallen through. The rally was eventually held in a black Baptist church, but the campaign's ability to speak to the Chicano community in a cultural idiom they understood was lost forever.

Sanchez told me about the experience: "We salvaged some of it, but a lot of the spirit we had generated for the rainbow was lost, because people felt betrayed. I tried to encourage them and tell them, 'Look, we're dealing with something new.'" "It was really a big shame," she reflected later, "that the Latino population did not become educated about who Jesse Jackson is and what he represented, because if they had been educated beforehand, we would have carried many more votes than what we got out of the Hispanic population." Sanchez described the actions of black leaders as analogous to that of having been given a new doll they were not going to part with. "I don't blame them for wanting to maintain leadership," she added, "but I also feel that they have to leave a path open for others to come and stand beside them."

In New York State, where Jackson won his first Latino victory with 34 percent of the statewide vote, and in New York City, where he carried every Latino-majority district by margins as high as 2 to 1, the organizing was done by grassroots activists with little help from the national campaign office and no help from elected Hispanic leaders, none of whom endorsed Jackson. The campaign was spearheaded by people from the boroughs of Manhattan, the Bronx, and Brooklyn who had been active in community struggles around housing, education, and Puerto Rican independence. Their story is an example of the creativity and ingenuity of community organizers that often goes unnoticed by people trained in traditional political campaign work.

A husband and wife team, Roberto and Nellie Marrero, first

learned of the Jackson campaign through contacts in the National Black United Front. They then started to call their activist friends throughout the city and discovered a great deal of interest in the Jackson campaign. The black state coordinator, Brooklyn assemblyman Al Vann, was at first reluctant to go into turf belonging to elected Latino leadership, but the Marreros and their friends convinced him that none of these leaders were going to support Jackson and that they did not speak for the Latino community. On one of the coldest days of the year, in December 1983, about 175 Latino activists from around the city braved the weather to meet with Jackson in a building in East Harlem and there decided to form a city-wide "Latinos for Jackson" committee. They had come out to the meeting on the basis of a letter sent by the Marreros in which they outlined their reasons for supporting the Jackson candidacy:

1. It provides an opportunity to vigorously oppose the racist and anti-worker policies of Ronald Reagan which have resulted in social service cutbacks, massive unemployment, an insane arms race and military aggressions against countries all around the world.

2. It provides an opportunity to raise the level of political activism and participation of our community in defense of its own interests at a time when the level is pretty low.

3. The campaign, the candidate and his positions provide an opportunity to bring political debate into sectors of our community which are not usually involved in this type of activity but which will be receptive during this period, especially if we make it a door-to-door campaign.

4. Through the development of joint work in registration brigades, leafletting, postering, talks and fundraising activities we can begin to create the basis for mutual trust which hopefully can lead to future political activities in defense of the rights of our community, not only among political activists, but more importantly between activists and the community in general.

5. The campaign provides an opportunity to create a united front with the Afro-American community based on our common interests in a city where the so-called minorities are the majority.

Borough coordinators were immediately selected for the three boroughs in which the majority of Latinos reside. About $3,000 was raised for literature through a large cocktail party and several borough dances. Literature was printed in English and Spanish, geared to the Latino community's unique concerns, but also to the black community with whom Latinos share much turf.

According to the organizers, Latino politicians thought at first the campaign would roll over and die. When it appeared to catch momentum, they then used right-wing nationalist tactics to try to derail it. "How come you're supporting a black?" was the tactic. But the community organizers believed in the necessity of black-Latino unity and were not deterred by these ploys. On the ground level they knew that blacks and Latinos shared the same ghettos and faced the same problems and that it was the lack of unity and cooperation between the two groups that had kept them from having more power in the city.

The culmination of the campaign was a large festive parade from the southern end of East Harlem through the length of this half-black, half-Hispanic neighborhood to a rally at the New York State office building in the heart of all-black Harlem. That march, too, had to be fought for. City campaign leaders had originally planned to have it start on the predominantly white side and end in Harlem, but the symbolism of moving through Latino territory to black territory was important to the organizers. On the stand that day in Harlem with Jackson were a rainbow of figures representing New York's many ethnic communities. Jackson's large vote in New York placed the campaign on the map for the first time as having the potential of building a rainbow coalition.

Jackson Speaks to the Issues

As the primary season moved to the Southwest, pressure on all the candidates to carry the banner of the Latino electorate increased. The Jackson campaign's lack of a Hispanic strategy was saved by Jackson's own commitment to speak to the gut issues of concern to the Latino communities he encountered and by indigenous organizers such as Laura Sanchez and the Marreros, who plunged into the campaign and did the work in spite of the odds.

Jackson was the only one of the three final candidates who unequivocally opposed the hated Simpson-Mazzoli immigration bill, spoke vigorously for bilingual education at a time when the nation was retreating on this issue, dared to defend the practice of providing sanctuary for Central American refugees, refused to use the term "illegal alien," referring instead to "undocumented workers," went to Central America to focus attention on the need to bring about a negotiated solution to the conflict there, traveled to Mexico to demonstrate the need for the United States to treat Mexico as a respected neighbor, spoke out against the abuses to which farmworkers were subjected, and led a protest rally at the Mexico border against reactionary immigration policies.

As the campaign progressed these positions and actions began to bring him greater attention within the Latino community. In mid-April, press reports indicated growing disaffection with Mondale among Hispanic leaders after he failed to appear at a forum of the National Hispanic Leadership Conference. Conference leader Raoul Yzaguirre, president of the National Council of La Raza, reported that the members of the conference were most impressed with Jackson and promised to get the word out to voters in California and Texas that Jackson's campaign "gives us the opportunity to build an Hispanic-Black coalition."

The Farm Labor Organizing Committee (FLOC), headquartered in Toledo, Ohio, with affiliates in ten states, endorsed the Jackson campaign in late April, as Jackson took up their fight to win better wages and working conditions from Campbell's Soup. FLOC campaigned heavily for Jackson in Ohio, and sent their leader, Baldemar Valesquez, to the Rio Grande Valley in Texas to organize farmworkers there. Jackson won 17.5 percent of the Hispanic vote in Ohio and 43 percent in the Toledo area, where FLOC organizers went door-to-door. In Hidalgo County, south Texas, Jackson won 33 delegates to the state convention in an area in which his name had not even been known prior to FLOC's organizing. In New Mexico, the La Raza Unida party, an independent party founded during the Chicano movement of the late 1960s, disbanded so that its members could work for Jackson in the Democratic primary. Jackson lost the endorsement of the California-based Mexican American Political Association to Mondale in June by only four votes.

A Lost Opportunity

As the convention approached it was clear that there was a strong current of disgust with Mondale among the Hispanic delegates for his refusal to unequivocally oppose the Simpson-Mazzoli bill. Mario Obledo, president of LULAC, urged the delegates publicly to withold their first-ballot presidential votes to symbolize displeasure with voting rights impediments and House passage of the Simpson-Mazzoli bill. Since Mondale was supported by the majority of the almost three hundred Hispanic delegates, such a boycott would have thrown the nomination process into a whirlwind. It was the perfect opportunity for Jackson to pick up three hundred extra votes as an indication of the support for his positions on the convention floor. Mondale's key supporters were literally booed off the stage at the Hispanic caucus meetings. Of all the caucuses at the convention, the Hispanic caucus was the one most vulnerable to movement, observed Gutierrez.

Because of the lack of a central Latino strategy, however, those planning convention strategy in the national office had not had the foresight to recognize that they would need Latino supporters who could work the convention floor and the Hispanic caucus to lobby for this strategy. The Latino staff person, Felipe Braudy, had been dismissed before the campaign went to the convention on the assumption that his services would no longer be needed. Armando Gutierrez, who could have directed Latino strategy at the convention, was given no authority to do so. Those grassroots organizers who were at the convention tried desperately to get floor passes at the last moment, but were up against time and opportunity constraints. Complaints that their leadership was not taken seriously, that they were simply junior partners in the Rainbow Coalition, were voiced in an atmosphere of frustration. At the last minute, Mondale was forced to come out and make a public statement against the Simpson-Mazzoli bill, after which his delegates fell in line. Jackson did not get the Latino votes that could have turned the convention around. Next to the black base, the Latino population remains the Rainbow Coalition's most important potential area for growth, but that potential will be realized only to the extent that blacks and Latinos begin working together at both the leadership and grassroots levels.

Women: A Hard Choice

The Jackson campaign's experience of organizing women as a special constituency group within the rainbow reveals the deep racial and class cleavages that exist within the larger society and are mirrored in the approach to dealing with the special oppression of women.

Black and other third world women supported Jackson in equal numbers to their men. From deputy campaign manager and treasurer to door-to-door canvasser and telephone bank operator, they were active at every level and capacity of the campaign and raised thousands of dollars for the cause. African-American women supported the campaign not only because Jackson was the first black presidential candidate, but also because he was the first presidential candidate to articulate a position on women's issues in language that reflected their own experience.

Jackson spoke to the gut concerns of working women, single parents, and poor women on welfare: the concern among black and Hispanic women over the poor education their children were getting in the public schools; the need to strengthen and expand maternal health care and child nuturition programs; the lack of adequate child-care facilities; and the drug epidemic that was sweeping the nation's ghettos. He explained the onerous implications of Reagan's much-touted workfare program; and finally, he made one of his major priorities the need to preserve and reinforce affirmative action programs.

On the basis of Jackson's stand on women's issues, the feminist movement should have been the campaign's most important ally. Jackson not only had the most progressive position on all of the traditional "feminist" issues, such as the Equal Rights Amendment (ERA), freedom of reproductive choice, and legislation supporting equal pay for equal work and work of comparable worth, but he was the only candidate calling for the reinforcement of affirmative action programs with goals and timetables (quotas) that had served not only racial minorities, but white women in the workplace. Moreover, he was the only candidate to pledge that if nominated he would name a woman as his running mate.

Jackson had not always been so good on feminist issues. As Manning Marable has pointed out, like most African-American males, he frequently made sexist statements that "revealed a failure to comprehend the particularity of women's oppression," and he had once opposed the right to abortion.[26] Like even the most well-meaning males, Jackson could occasionally slip with a remark or anecdote that had a sexist ring to it. But in seeking to enlarge the black base from which he began, Jackson was compelled to change his position on a number of different issues, even breaking with his home base, the black Baptist church, on the abortion and gay rights issues; and in broadening that base, his own thinking inevitably changed.

Jackson was probably more aware than either his top male aides or the majority of white feminists that the black base and the organized feminist movement represented a potent political union. He pointed out that the racial and class skew of the women's movement undermined its own objectives, and offered his campaign as a way of enlarging the constituency for feminist legislative goals. A campaign position paper stated:

> As a matter of strategy and perception the struggle around ratification of the Equal (and Economic) Rights Amendment has been led by too narrow a constituency—upper middle class white females—and that is one of the reasons it has failed to gain passage. But if the women's movement is now willing to put forth an affirmative effort to involve the masses of women—Black, Latino, Native American, poor and basic working class women—then ratification has a realistic chance of passage. To that end, I will use my candidacy to help organize excluded women to involve themselves in the movement for passage of the ERA. Despite your efforts to include all women, it has not become reality yet.[27]

Tragically, that union did not emerge. The race and class privilege of white female Democratic party leaders and the Jackson campaign managers' ignorance of dynamics within the white feminist movement resulted in the campaign's failure to develop a white feminist caucus or lobby within the campaign.

White women's responses to the Jackson campaign in fact, followed the pattern of splits within the women's movement that had occurred over the past decade. At least three broad factions could be distinguished by their differing ideologies, constituencies, and organizing strategies: liberal feminists, radical feminists, and (broadly) socialist-feminists.

Of highest visibility was what has been called the "bureaucratic wing" of the women's movement or "liberal feminism." It is represented by such organizations as the National Organization for Women (NOW), the National Women's Political Caucus, and *Ms* magazine. Composed chiefly of white middle-class and professional women, this faction focused almost exclusively on issues of paramount concern to them: pay equity, passage of the Equal

Rights Amendment, sex discrimination in education, and reproductive rights. Though one political faction within NOW stated in its 1975 platform that it was not just interested in "getting women into the mainstream, but in changing the mainstream itself," the organization tended to support working for reform within mainstream institutions. While the benefits won by groups such as NOW were relevant to all women, in actuality they created a new elite of affluent white women who tended to ignore or downplay the survival needs of working-class and poor women, and racial minorities for adequate housing, health care, child care, and income maintenance.[28]

The media and corporations played up this narrow, organized, and well-funded stratum, creating the impression among women outside this stratum that this was *the* feminist movement. In truth, the women's movement was an amorphous, decentralized movement with many tendencies.

By 1984, after years of frustrating public advance and then retreat on women's legislation, liberal feminism was demoralized. NOW had fought an expensive and ultimately losing battle for the ERA. The National Abortion Rights Action League (a coalition of reproductive rights groups) had found itself out-organized by the religious right and in danger of losing the legislation that had been won over the last decade. Clearly, some new dramatic tactic was needed if legislation benefiting women were to be preserved and the liberal wing of the movement sustained.

Thus, in advance of the 1984 elections, the "gender gap" was suddenly discovered. Women, it was demonstrated, had voted by a margin of 8 percentage points for Carter over Reagan in 1980, reflecting their generally more liberal position on issues of social spending and war and peace. With the news that 6 million more women than men had voted in 1980, the gender gap became significant.[29]

A large voter education, registration, and turnout campaign was thus instituted by liberal feminist organizations in preparation for the 1984 elections, and prominent Democratic women were positioned in the campaigns of the two front-runners. For the first time in its history, NOW endorsed a presidential candidate—Walter Mondale—and put its organizational machinery to work for the person who was certain to be the Democratic nominee. In exchange for delivering the female vote, liberal feminists expected a reward.

Jackson's decision to enter the race threw a monkey-wrench into the best-laid plans of the liberal feminists, for it meant that women's loyalty would be split between the obvious front-runner and what they saw as a black "protest" vote. Instead of approaching the Jackson campaign to discuss how white women and blacks could ally politically to get their mutual needs met, the leaders of the predominantly white liberal wing of the movement distanced themselves from the Jackson campaign, apparently unable to recognize their own issues when advocated by a black man. Many expressed suspicion of Jackson's new-found feminism. Others, who were Jewish, participated in the Jewish community's general hostility toward the campaign as a result of Jackson's anti-Semitic remark. The icy relationship between leaders of the white liberal feminist movement and the Jackson campaign only confirmed black women's perception of the women's movement as deeply infected by racism and classism, especially when their candidate had the best position on women of any of the presidential contenders.

The second wing of the feminist movement, which has come to be known as "radical feminism," was shaped largely by the social alienation of lesbians and women who have been the victims of male violence and extreme male oppression. This wing of the movement has produced some of the most vibrant expressions of feminist culture and much-needed advocacy for and services to women in crisis, such as rape victims, battered women, women needing abortions, and homeless women and children. For this sector of the women's movement, however, racism and the injuries of class tend to be subsumed under the concept of "patriarchy," or male domination. Separatism, often linked with political lesbianism, is generally the operative political strategy.

While some lesbian feminists undoubtedly voted for Jackson, many radical feminists sat out the 1984 election or voted for Sonia Johnson, the woman who had been excommunicated from the Mormon Church for her work on the ERA. Johnson ran as the presidential candidate of the Citizens' party on a radical feminist/peace/ecological platform. Although there had been an attempt to persuade Johnson to support the Jackson campaign, Johnson thought that any cooperation with the male-dominated political establishment was tantamount to accepting a piece of power in an edifice that was "rotten" and "made of greed, violence and inequity." It was time, she said, for women to stake out their own terms and not follow those established by men.[30]

Most of the white feminists who gravitated to the Jackson campaign identified with an amorphous third wing of the women's movement. No single organization or set of institutions defined this sector. Early in the 1970s the term "socialist feminism" would have described many of these women. At that time, many were active in socialist-feminist unions that had sprung up in several cities across the country, but by the early 1980s these unions had dissolved, and the women could be found working in a variety of left party formations and peace and justice organizations, or active in community organizing efforts.

White women associated with this tendency view women's issues within the wider geopolitical context of capitalism and U.S. imperialism, holding that women's oppression is dialectically interwoven with racism and class exploitation. Such women gravitated toward the Rainbow Coalition not solely on the basis of Jackson's position on women's issues, but because of the campaign's generally progressive character on a variety of issues. Because they entered the Rainbow Coalition as "peace activists" or "environmentalists" or "Jews for Jackson," however, their feminist credentials were overlooked by the black campaign leadership in its assessment of women's participation in the campaign. There were many such women who could have given strong leadership to a women's desk in the campaign, and might even have mobilized rank-and-file members of organizations like NOW, but because they were unknown to the black leadership of the campaign, their skills went undetected.

When campaign managers looked for a white woman to head the women's desk, they thought in terms of mobilizing women who identified with the bureaucratic wing of the movement, since this was the only "women's movement" they knew. This proved to be a critical mistake. The person they chose, Barbara Honegger, was hired largely for her name recognition. A policy analyst with the Reagan White House, she had been fired in 1983 when she revealed Reagan's ERA alternative as a sham. As a whistle blower,

Honegger had been virtually persona non grata until the Jackson campaign picked her up.

During the early stages of the campaign, Honegger made good press copy, but she had neither the background in feminist organizing nor credibility within the feminist community to do the campaign much good. When her story became stale, she was transferred to the national office to do general policy analysis and by mid-April she had left the campaign. Thus, as the campaign approached the Democratic Convention and it became clear that the women's caucus was the largest constituency that might be persuaded to vote for the rainbow's platform, there was no one in the national office who had the sole responsibility of working with women. At the last minute, Barbara Williams Skinner, a deputy campaign manager, and myself as the rainbow coordinator were assigned to try to repair the damage, but it was too late. By that time the liberal Democratic party feminists had thrown themselves into the fight for a female vice president, virtually ignoring the substantive platform proposals put forward by the Jackson campaign on issues the women's movement should have supported.

Ironically, it was Jackson's early and consistent espousal of a female vice president that helped create the political opening for white feminists to struggle for Geraldine Ferraro's selection. Once they had achieved it, however, they ignored the politics that made it possible. The failure of white feminists to acknowledge their debt to Jackson further infuriated Jackson's female supporters. It was a brand of racial arrogance they had seen once too often.

As the Democratic Women's Caucus in San Francisco began to celebrate the selection of the first female vice presidential candidate, Mildred Kyles, a black Jackson delegate, took the microphone.

> It is good, perhaps, to have a woman on the ticket. However, I would hope this caucus would address itself to the fact that Mr. Mondale did not even allow a Black woman to be in the interviewing process, and I think that is a slap in the face to Black women. . . . I would hope that this caucus remembers the women of color because we are women too, we're fighting for all women, not just white women.[31]

After this, there were attempts by prominent Democratic women, notably Colorado representative Pat Schroeder and *Ms* editor Gloria Steinem, to acknowledge black women's grievances and their contributions to the struggle for women's rights. But the die was cast. The very fervor with which the white Mondale and Hart delegates celebrated Ferraro's triumph rang hollow for those who knew the price that had been paid for that Pyrrhic victory: the selling out of Jackson's substantive issues related to peace, justice, and democracy. Ferraro, after all, was the chairperson of the Democratic Platform Committee and had engineered the defeat of Jackson's platform planks on peace, affirmative action, and voting rights.

Knowing that the choice of Ferraro was a foregone conclusion, but wanting to register a protest against the process that had excluded black women, some Jackson delegates attempted to nominate Shirley Chisholm from the floor, but that move was squelched when a vote for acclamation for Ferraro was proposed and rapidly passed. This move angered black female delegates, including many committed to Hart and Mondale. They saw it as a further demonstration of the racism of the Democratic party establishment, male and female. Alabama delegate Gwen Patton expressed the mood of many others when she observed to me: "Apparently winning is not enough for the Mondale forces. Capitulation seems to be the cornerstone of their leadership."

Until the Democratic National Convention of 1984, black women active in politics had been junior partners in the generally male-dominated black political forums and silent partners in the National Women's Political Caucus. As a result of their experience at the Democratic Convention, they decided to form their own national political institution, a move that was encouraged by Jackson. Plans for the formation of the National Black Women's Political Conference were made at meetings of Jackson delegates immediately following events on the convention floor. In the future, the unique political voice of black women should begin to assert itself, posing a new equation for the relationship between white feminists and the black movement.

7

A Voice for the Locked Out:
Widening the Rainbow Coalition

The rainbow takes on many combinations. There are ideological rainbows; the rainbow has a color dimension. The rainbow makes room for the locked-out, the rejected stones. There's an age dimension to the rainbow. It makes room for the very young and the very old. There's another dimension. There are schools of thought. . . . The rainbow is a call to be progressive.[1]

—Jesse Jackson

Common to the black, Hispanic, and female populations that Jackson tried to mobilize for the rainbow was their ability to choose among various political options, according to their different race and class goals as well as their perceptions of success. This was also true of other, less obvious groups, traditionally loyal to the Democratic party but defecting in recent years: labor and Jewish Americans, and to a lesser extent, peace and environmental activists. To a number of other groups, by contrast, Jackson was not only the first but the only one to give them a voice. This was true of Asian Americans, Arab Americans, Native Americans, lesbians and gays, disabled Americans, and family farmers.

199

Asian Americans: Becoming Visible

Next to Hispanics, Asian Americans are the fastest growing ethnic minority group in the United States. Like the term "Hispanics" the term "Asian Americans" covers a wide diversity of national groups, with differing cultures, histories, and political orientations. Perhaps even more than Hispanics, it is hard to generalize about Asian Americans. The Vietnamese, among the most recent immigrants, are the products of U.S. imperialist acculturation and anticommunism in Indo-China; thus most enter the United States with a built-in bias toward the "American way of life." Many Japanese Americans, on the other hand, while generally economically secure, remember a time when they were herded into concentration camps by the U.S. government. Some Asian Americans, such as the Chinese, were driven here by economic deprivation and persecution; others, including the more recent Korean arrivals, come to better their relatively more advanced economic status.

Perhaps the one thing that could be said to unite Asian Americans in 1984 was the universal experience of being politically invisible for those who shape political policy. In San Francisco, where Asians make up one quarter of the population, only twenty thousand of a population of one hundred thousand were registered to vote in 1984, none of the elected supervisors were Asian, and only two Asian Americans held administrative positions in city government. One of the reasons for such political invisibility is the value that Eastern cultures place on low visibility and behind-the-scenes influence. Thomas Hsieh, a vice president of the California Democratic party, explained that there is an "attitude in our culture which says that the good, solid citizen should not be involved in politics. Politics is dirty."[2] The other reason for Asian-American invisibility, of course, is American nativism. In the early 1980s, an increase in racist violence directed at Asian people, as well as aggravated social problems faced by newly arrived immigrants as a result of Reagan's cutbacks and the administration's bellicose foreign policy, began to draw younger Asian Americans into the political arena. The Jackson campaign was the only one to recognize their political potential and to seek them out. Asian Americans who had begun to get their political feet wet through involvement in local government, community organizing, peace and solidarity movements, or the Asian Caucus of the National Democratic Committee, saw in the Jackson campaign an opportunity to put Asian Americans on the political map. Cindy Ng, of New York Asians for Jesse Jackson, summed up why she and her colleagues had decided to support the campaign:

> Things are critical in our community thanks to Reagan and Koch [mayor of New York City]. We are fighting gentrification and landlord arson. Budget cuts. Racist violence, which is on the rise. . . . A few weeks ago, a Chinese garment worker, Mrs. Cheng, was pushed in front of a subway and killed. The newspapers said her attacker was crazy. But do you know what his defense is? His lawyer says he is paranoid of Orientals. So he kills. These are issues that concern us. But we find that our concerns are ignored by the powers that be. Asians are grossly underrepresented; taken for granted by the politicians.[3]

In the Asian community the Jackson campaign was organized primarily by second- and third-generation Japanese and Chinese Americans and by anti-Marcos Filipinos in their early to mid thirties. The younger generation was not as inhibited by cultural prohibitions about involvement in public life as their elders. Most had been politicized in the student movements of the late 1960s and early 1970s. There they began to get in touch with how their own communities had suffered from racism in the United States and began to reclaim their ethnic heritages within a new, more politicized framework.

In New York, Asian Americans formed the New York Asians for Jesse Jackson Committee, which held a number of fundraisers featuring musicians, dancers, actors, and poets, and did door-to-door petitioning in Chinatown to get Jackson on the ballot. Their activity helped shape Jackson's Asian-American policy, which, among other things, called for redress and reparations for Japanese who were interned during World War II. The group hosted a rally in Chinatown at a senior citizens' center and took Jackson to tour a Chinese garment shop. It was the first visit by a presidential candidate to this section of the city. Jackson also spoke at rallies in Los Angeles' "Little Tokyo" and at a large rally in San Francisco's Chinatown.

Asian-American Committees for Jackson were also formed in San Francisco, Los Angeles, San Diego, Oregon, Seattle, New Jersey, and Honolulu. A national network of such groups raised

$15,000 for the campaign and ran eighteen Asian delegates in California. Jackson won 20 to 21 percent of the Asian vote in California, 25 percent in New Jersey, and 10 percent in New York.

For the Asian Americans who worked with the Jackson campaign, it was the chance of a lifetime to gain skills in electoral politics. Eddie Wong, a young Chinese-American filmmaker who had never been involved in electoral politics before, told me how he got involved in the campaign in San Francisco.

> When the state campaign organization started coalescing, they started hiring people, and I was hired as a part-time field organizer, basically to handle precinct operations. . . . At that point I decided to quit my full-time job and give it a try. It was an historical movement, and you knew it from the day you were in it. . . . Being half-time meant working ten to fifteen hours a day, easily. For myself, it meant getting real quick education—like having to know what the numbers really are, how many precincts there are, how we are going to target different areas. So I had to go out and talk to people who had done it before.

Wong moved from being precinct organizer to becoming part of the overall management team for the Bay Area operations. He found that he was so good at it that he went on from there to manage another campaign in the November election.

For many Asian Americans, the Jackson campaign shattered the myth of the "model minority"—a myth that had served to mystify the actual racial and class oppression suffered by these communities and had kept them from being recognized as a political bloc whose needs and perspectives must be addressed by those in power.

Arab Americans: Beyond the Stereotype

There are approximately 2 million Arab Americans currently in the United States. Most reside in a few large urban centers—Detroit (the largest group, with about 225,000), New York, Chicago, Los Angeles, Pittsburgh, and San Francisco. Included in such estimates are assimilated Arab Americans (most of them Christians from the Syrian province of the Ottoman empire) who migrated with the great waves of southern and eastern European immigrants around the turn of the century, and unassimilated Arabs (more likely to be Muslim) who came with a second immigration wave that began in 1948 and accelerated after the Arab defeat in the Arab-Israeli war of 1967.[4]

Of the early immigrants, 90 percent started out as peddlers, rising through family networks in which capital was rotated and family loyalty, the work ethic, and thrift were valued, to become prosperous businessmen. Others were drawn by Henry Ford's offer of $5 a day to every worker and ended up as unskilled laborers in the auto factories, alongside the first wave of southern blacks to migrate to the urban industrial centers. The more prosperous and assimilated Arabs tended to join the Rotary and Kiwanis clubs, since that was the "American" thing to do, and to vote Republican. Most were ideologically conservative.

Beginning in 1967, however, two sets of events began to change the political orientation and consciousness of most Arab Americans. One was the increase in Arab nationalism as a result of the "Six-Day War" in the Middle East and the anti-Arab racism that infected white America. Abdeen Jabara, a Detroit lawyer and vice-president of the Arab-American Anti-Discrimination Committee, told me:

> At that time the American press was trumpeting the tremendous victory that "our side" had won against the Arabs, and the anti-Arab racism that prevailed was overwhelming—in the press, the cartoons. So after a period of recovery from shock, we began to organize on a national and local level. . . . We began to organize Arab intelligentsia and professionals. But also on the local level we began organizing and agitation in the large Arab communities, with demonstrations, seminars, leafletting, and interacting with other groups on campus and off.

The most intense interaction was with the black community, for the second set of events to affect Arab Americans was the civil rights and black power movements, which provided a model of ethnic consciousness—particularly for younger Arabs living in large, black-dominated urban centers, such as Detroit. The Black Muslims were a particularly effective cultural force, explained Jabara:

> Malcolm X constitutes the making of my consciousness. . . . It is hard to underestimate the influence of the Black Muslims on the Arab and black communities in the inner cities. They were the only ones on the street corners day in and day out talking about international issues.

As early as the late 1960s, such radical black organizations as the Student Nonviolent Coordinating Committee (SNCC) and the Black Panthers began taking up the cause of the Arab and Palestinian struggle. The radical movement in the Detroit auto factories in the early 1970s involved both Arab and black workers and espoused the cause of Arab nationalism. John Watson, one of the leaders of that movement, traveled with Jabara to the Middle East, and black auto workers were involved in mass demonstrations against the United Automobile Workers (UAW) purchase of Israeli bonds in 1973. Although the black civil rights leadership was pro-Israel during this period, that posture began to change as more and more blacks in the urban ghettos were influenced by Muslim rhetoric and as Israel's links to South Africa began to be understood. In 1972 and again in 1976, the National Black Political Assembly issued powerful statements in support of Palestinian rights and condemned Israel's activity in Africa.[5]

In the late 1970s several leaders of the protest sector of the civil rights establishment—figures such as Southern Christian Leadership Conference (SCLC) president Joseph Lowery; Washington, D.C. representative Walter Fauntroy; Operation PUSH president Jesse Jackson; and Harlem minister Wyatt Tee Walker—went to the Middle East in order to acquaint themselves directly with the dynamics of that region, which were tending to affect dynamics within the black community at home. Following those trips, several black organizations, including SCLC, Operation PUSH, and the National Black United Front, along with white peace and justice organizations, the Palestine Human Rights Campaign, and the National Association of Arab Americans, formed the Middle East Peace Action Coalition to work at a more balanced approach to the Middle East crisis—one that affirmed the right of both Israelis and Palestinians to their own homelands and viewed the Palestine Liberation Organization (PLO) as a legitimate party to any negotiations.

The Abscam scandal of the early 1980s, when the federal government entrapped and indicted several members of Congress for taking bribes by sending FBI agents to pose as Arab sheiks, led to the further consolidation of Arab-American national identity and to the formation of the Arab-American Anti-Discrimination Committee. The cynical use of Arab stereotypes angered everyone and the response to the Arab-American Anti-Discrimination Committee was overwhelming. "We had rich and poor, Christian and Muslim Arabs who wanted to join us," Jabara said.

Jackson's trip to Syria to release Lieutenant Goodman had an electifying effect on the Arab-American community. Many Arab Americans switched their party affiliation to vote for Jackson and many registered to vote for the first time. "When we heard Jackson was coming to Detroit after Syria," said Jabara, "we raised $10,000–$15,000 within a couple of days with no trouble at all. About 2,000 people waited for two hours in a Shiite mosque in Dearborn, Michigan to hear Jackson speak." While not large in numbers, the Arab-American community, with its substantial business class, played a major role in Jackson's fund-raising effort during the second half of the campaign.[6]

Although no statistics are available, it is likely that the majority of the Arab-American vote went for Jackson. Arab support for the Jackson campaign may have increased Jewish hostility toward the campaign, but it began to help ease the tension between blacks and Arabs in at least two urban communities—Detroit and Syracuse.[7] More important, however, the participation of Arab Americans in the campaign broke the taboo that had previously excluded them from the political process. Their participation in electoral politics is now assured and their role in any future political realignment could be a major one—perhaps comparable to that played by Jews in the political realignment of the Democratic party during the New Deal.

Native Americans: Under Siege

Considered in traditional cost-benefit terms, Native Americans represent an insignificant voting bloc. They have neither the numbers, the money, nor the political will to become heavily involved in U.S. electoral politics. As members of coherent "nations," the most politically active among them are more interested in pursuing national sovereignty and land claims than in entering into the inevitable compromises and assimilation associated with involvement in the electoral process. The difference between black involvement in electoral politics and Indian involvement is the difference between ethnic and national struggles, as American Indian leader Ward Churchill explains:

> While we share a common oppression with our brothers and sisters of African, Latin and Asian origins within the U.S., the goals, objectives and many of the means of our struggle must be understood in terms necessarily different from theirs. We "the Indians" of the North and "indios" of the South—all the people of the Americas—struggle for the liberation of our homelands rather than for the liberation of land upon which to build our homes. We of all the people of the Americas, engage in our struggles from the basis of our cultures, our freely collective societies, born in, and long since integral to, this hemisphere rather than struggling to create liberatory cultures allowing the expression of human freedom.[8]

For the Jackson campaign, support of Native American sovereignty was a moral and ethical imperative. The campaign could scarcely afford to speak for the locked-out and rejected and for the right of self-determination overseas and ignore the national claims of American Indians. But for Native American traditionalists, the decision to become involved in the Jackson campaign was a bit harder to understand. American Indian Movement (AIM) leaders, who did the major organizing for the campaign, were interested in the visibility Jackson could bring to their struggle to resist the assimilationist policies of the federal government and the chance the campaign provided to educate the American public about the legitimacy of Indian land and religious claims. Ever since huge deposits of coal, uranium, and natural gas were discovered on formerly "barren" Indian reservations, assimilationist policies had accelerated. According to Interior Department estimates in 1977, tribes in the western half of the United States owned approximately 11 percent of all the national coal reserves; at least 30 percent of all low-sulphur coal west of the Mississippi capable of being strip-mined; between 40 and 50 percent of the nation's uranium; 4 percent of oil and natural gas reserves; and a large share of the nation's oil shale and geothermal resources.[9]

Since the early 1970s, Indian leaders had been caught in a terrible bind. The showdown at Wounded Knee had caused dozens of their best leaders to be lost to them through prison and assassination, and had cut off most of their support from non-Indian groups. The federal government was going full-speed ahead with a policy of either starving the Indians out if they chose to remain on the reservations (the Bureau of Indian Affairs [BIA] has a virtual stranglehold on all social welfare and employment programs that impact the reservations) or offering the tribes money to buy the land they already owned. Since the Indians' world view, including their languages, is intimately tied to the land, to sell or leave the land meant virtual death for the tribe.[10] While not wanting a Wounded Knee II, many Indians felt they were being driven to some final conflagration.

It was in this context that American Indian Movement leaders made the decision to become involved in the Jackson campaign. Vernon Bellecourt, who has been called the "organizational genius" of the American Indian Movement, was named to the Jackson's national campaign committee, and Bill Means, another AIM leader, was hired to organize Indians for the campaign.

Indians responded enthusiastically. Indian people in New York, North Carolina, Florida, Oklahoma, Mississippi, Wisconsin, Minnesota, Iowa, South Dakota, Texas, New Mexico, Arizona, and California participated in Rainbow Coalition rallies and organizing. In Arizona alone, every tribe formally endorsed the Rainbow Coalition, as did tribal councils representing one-third of all Indians nationally. At least 15,000 new Indian voters were registered through the campaign in seventeen states and a half dozen Indian delegates for Jackson went to the Democratic National Convention.

In Arizona, efforts to involve Indians in the campaign helped to expose their lack of access to the democratic process. For example, there was not one polling place for 35,000 registered voters on the Arizona side of the Navajo Nation. Some voters had had to drive as far as 80 miles to vote in previous elections. The Arizona Rainbow Coalition succeeded in securing several polling places on the reservation.

Jackson made a campaign visit to the Navajo and Hopi Nations, which no presidential candidate had ever visited. Indian leaders showed Jackson the devastation wrought by the energy companies in the vast Grants mineral belt region of New Mexico. They told him that some coal leases negotiated in perpetuity by the Bureau of Indian Affairs with U.S. transnational corporations paid the Navajo people 7 cents a ton, when the market value often exceeded $30 a ton. They explained that the Navajo Nation each day produces enough energy to light up Phoenix and Albuquerque for the next thirty years, yet 40 percent of Navajo households were without adequate electricity.

As a result of his exposure to Indian realities, Jackson called for the abolition of the BIA, for the creation of a cabinet-level agency to deal directly with the president in developing Indian policy based on treaty rights, and for the institution of a block-grant system for allocating services under U.S. treaty obligations. It was a radical posture for any presidential candidate to take, and one virtually ignored by the mainstream press; yet that position, if made an integral part of a future presidential campaign waged by the Rainbow Coalition, could revolutionize U.S. politics.

Lesbians and Gays: Out of the Political Closet

Jackson was the first presidential candidate to have a fully developed policy on lesbian and gay rights and to openly court this constituency. He was the only candidate to hold rallies in gay and lesbian centers and to mention gay issues in the context of the presidential debates. This was a considerable risk to his own reputation in the black community, since many blacks, for both religious and community survival reasons, were opposed to public support of the homosexual movement.

Early in the presidential campaign, many lesbian and gay activists supported the campaigns of Cranston and Hart, not realizing that Jackson had a much more progressive policy on gay rights. That began to change as they learned of Jackson's position. Speaking of candidates' responses to a gay/lesbian questionnaire gay activist and Jackson campaign worker Thomas Atkins said:

> It is clear that only one candidate has both an understanding of the problems facing our community and meaningful proposals to implement necessary changes. A careful reading and comparison of the responses of these presidential hopefuls clearly shows that it is Jesse Jackson who is the strongest advocate for gay rights.[11]

The proposals Atkins referred to were Jackson's support of a comprehensive bill that would add prohibitions against discrimination based on sexual orientation to the already existing categories of the 1964 Civil Rights Act, and the extension of that ban to the military and various national security agencies. Jackson also argued for the removal of a lesbian and gay exclusion to the provisions of the Immigration and Naturalization Service, endorsed the idea of an official executive liaison for the lesbian and gay community, and called for increased federal spending for AIDS research and treatment.

For New York gay activist Andy Humm, there were even broader reasons for supporting the Jackson candidacy:

> Along the way some of us . . . realized that we could no longer see our issue as separate from others, and that no one was going to give us anything from on high. That's when we turned to Jesse Jackson and the space he had prepared for us in the Rainbow Coalition of the Rejected. Jesse wasn't making promises to us, he was making plans with us. We were no longer a powerless minority scrapping for our piece of the pie, but one of many minorities which, together, constituted a new majority that worked with each other for each other's dignity and justice.[12]

In Washington State, the organized gay movement, most of whose members had endorsed Gary Hart, became the Rainbow Coalition's most useful ally. Campaign coordinators discovered that the gay movement was the most politically organized constituency group in the state. They had done their own voter survey and found the gay community tended to vote as a bloc. Although most were supporting Hart by the time they learned of Jackson's positions on gay rights, they were easily persuaded by Jackson campaign workers to vote for Jackson's entire platform. Some delegates even switched their allegiance to Jackson once they learned of his program, and many joined the Rainbow Coalition once the campaign was over. As a result of the collaboration between Jackson forces and Hart's gay delegates, the Washington Democratic party passed Jackson's entire fifteen-point platform. Though black forces in many other parts of the country failed to see the political potential of an alliance with the organized gay and lesbian movement, the experience in Washington State stands as a reminder of the new political alliances the campaign began to generate.

Disabled Americans

Disabled Americans make up approximately 12 percent of the American population. Inspired by other popular movements in the 1960s, they too began to organize for political and social empowerment. The disabled movement called that nation's attention to the discrimination that exists everywhere against people with handicapping conditions, and succeeded in getting certain legislation passed. Since Reagan took office, however, legislation affecting the disabled has been relegated to the status of "voluntary compliance," and to the effects of trickle-down economics.

According to Pete Anderson and Alan Loewenthal, who represented the California State Disabilities Caucus of the Democratic party (the first of its kind), Jackson was the only presidential candidate receptive to representing the disabled vote. In cooperation with this caucus, Jackson stayed in the home of a disabled resident, talked with members of the disabled community about their concerns, and addressed a rally at an Independent Living Center for disabled people in San Francisco. The following morning, he led a "wheelchair march" to the Independent Living Center, where he described the growing disability movement as "at its heart a civil rights movement" that all of us must share. "I see no difference," he said, "between being sent to separate schools because you're black or because you're disabled, . . . or between being given separate entrances to buildings because you're black or because you're disabled."[13] Jackson deplored the cutbacks that the Reagan administration had made in vital services to the disabled, and called for measures aimed at strengthening civil rights legislation for the disabled, restoration of federal programs, and a rational system of economic support for disabled workers so that those who want to work can do so. As a further symbol of his commitment to this constitutency, two disabled Americans appeared with him on the podium at the Democratic National Convention, representing the Rainbow Coalition. The response of the disabled community went largely unnoticed by the press, but at each of Jackson's rallies they were there, cheering the only candidate who had bothered to notice this locked-out constituency.

Family Farmers: Down but Not Yet Out

Perhaps the most unexpected group to heed Jackson's call to join the Rainbow Coalition were the normally conservative family farmers, primarily from the South and Midwest. It is not hard, however, to explain why they should have been driven to join a campaign that spoke for the locked-out and the rejected.

An extended crisis in farm country, driven by government policies that had deliberately encouraged farmers to overextend themselves and then called in the debt when land values plummeted in 1980–1981, was reaching a climax as the Jackson campaign swept through the Midwest.[14] A full-blown collapse of the financial structure of family farm agriculture was in the making. Between one-quarter and one-half of the remaining 2 million family farmers—people who had seen themselves as the bedrock of the American economy and most of whom had voted for Reagan in 1980—four years later were deeply in debt and losing their land to foreclosure. For the individual farmer, Doug Harsh from Wisconsin told me the crisis translated into a 500 percent increase in costs over a twenty-year period, while selling prices remained the same or went down. For black farmers, the crisis was suicidal. A study by the U.S. Civil Rights Commission in 1982 concluded that there would be no black-owned farms left by the year 2000.

For farmers, the crisis meant not only the loss of a job, but the loss of an entire way of life. The world view of rural America was coming apart. People who had not known anything else for generations, independent entrepreneurs who had bought all the American myths about the value of hard work, individualism, and "free enterprise," were now suddenly thrust into the ranks of the lumpen proletariat. Many were turning to alcohol, even committing suicide, and not a few marriages were breaking up under the stress.

Because of this, the farm population was perhaps the most volatile sector in the nation. The far right understood this: such groups as the Posse Comitatus, the Ku Klux Klan, and the Aryan Nation were organizing vigorously in farm country, pointing the finger at the legitimate culprits—the government and the banks—but lacing their accusations with a virulent dose of anti-Semitism, racism, and survivalist violence.

Since depressions are driven by the farm sector, farmers have been the backbone of most major challenges to corporate America and the pivot of a number of electoral realignments, beginning with Shays' Rebellion in the 1780s, moving through the Populist movement of the 1890s, the Socialist movement in the early part of the century, to the protests of the Southern Tenant Farmers Union in the 1930s and 1940s. It was a rural heartland protest movement that threw the Republicans out of power in 1932 and again in 1954, just after Eisenhower's landslide reelection, when the Republicans lost 47 seats in the House, most from rural constituencies.

However, with the exception of the Southern Tenant Farmers Union, which maintained biracial leadership and fought hard against the racist divide-and-conquer tactics of the Ku Klux Klan and southern planters, most farm movements have foundered on racism. This time, however, with their numbers greatly diminished and the prospect that family farming might be headed for complete extinction, progressives in the farm movement saw the necessity of uniting with other oppressed groups, which included blacks, Indians, and Latinos. Jackson's candidacy and the concept of the Rainbow Coalition was the vehicle that would make that possible.

The North American Farm Alliance (NAFA), a coalition of over fifty farm groups from twenty-three states and two Canadian provinces, had emerged to lead the progressive wing of the struggle. NAFA was headed by Merle Hansen, a white-haired Nebraska farmer whose mild appearance belied a biting wit and a capacity for sharp analyses. Hansen had grown up in the Depression and could remember when the left had been the leading force in farm country.

> When I was a kid there were all kinds of people that identified with the political left. The Non-partisan League, the Farmers Alliance and the Farmers Union were really started by left-wing people because, on the whole, people on the left are the organizers and they have a good analysis of the crisis.[15]

Hansen's farmer father had been a socialist, and the present farm crisis had driven Hansen to step into his shoes. More than most farmers, he saw clearly that the farm crisis was a national social justice crisis that was not going to be solved in isolation. Farmers, Hansen contended, must begin building alliances with other groups that share common goals: peace activists, inner-city residents who depend on farm food, minorities, labor, the unemployed, women:

> We have to educate the farmers about the causes of the crisis, and the participation of these other groups helps clarify those causes. When you're working side by side with these other groups, you gain an understanding that these issues are very much related, that they all

have a common origin, and only by working together can we make progress.[16]

To illustrate the connections, the North American Farm Alliance had organized food giveaway programs in the inner cities, declared farm country a nuclear-free zone, and even led a group of farmers to Nicaragua, where Nicaraguan farmers offered them land to grow crops.

Hansen had led a group of farmers to the 1983 March on Washington and there had dinner with Jesse Jackson. Thus, when the campaign was announced, Hansen was appointed to the national campaign committee as the farm representative and spoke at Jackson's announcement ceremony. With NAFA's network of farm leaders and organizers throughout the country, the campaign had a ready-made constituency.

Since family farmers represent only 3 percent of the national population, their importance to the Rainbow Coalition was obviously not in the number of votes they would bring, but in the pivotal role they play in the economy. Because American farmers are the raw-material producers for much of the world, their plight has implications for the political economy of the world—the availability and quality of food, the ability of the land to sustain human life, and so on.

Fortunately, the campaign had in Carolyn Kazdin, former director of Rural American Women, a person who understood the pivotal nature of the farm crisis and who worked to shape a farm policy that spoke directly to the farmers' plight, but linked it to wider foreign policy concerns and international economic structures. Kazdin also had a ready-made network of rural activists who could be plugged into the campaign quickly.

A Progressive Farm Policy

Because of the inability of the campaign's black leadership to understand the importance of the farm crisis for the future of their own movement (this was natural since few in the country really understood the farm crisis), Kazdin believes Jackson missed a golden opportunity to enter the Iowa caucuses with the most progressive farm policy of any of the presidential candidates. Coming up with that policy, she told me, was an educational process for everyone involved.

Jackson took this policy—which called, among other things, for a price-support system to achieve 90 percent of parity, an immediate moratorium on farm and home foreclosures, and long-term loans at low interest rates to recapitalize the farm debt—directly to the farmers in campaign rallies in Arkansas, Kansas, Missouri, Nebraska, and Wisconsin, and via radio programs broadcast to the farm community. In speaking about the farm crisis he also educated his audiences on the sources and history of the crisis, presenting them with an analysis many had never heard before. Kazdin told me: "The farmers needed direct contact with him in order to overcome the large cultural gulf between the white midwesterner and the southern black. But when they heard him, they just ate him up."

On one memorable occasion in Columbia, Missouri (which Jackson won), a group of about two hundred cheering farmers came out to a protest rally at the Farmers Home Administration with brown paper bags over their heads to demonstrate their fear of reprisals from their creditors. Jackson addressed the crowd from a tractor. Kazdin reported:

> The Secret Service gave us a hard time. They had sharpshooters on all the roofs. They were surprised Jackson was getting this kind of support and probably didn't believe it. So their own prejudices came out as to what kind of support they were going to give us. Jackson wanted to lead a tractor caravan of farmers to a rally that had been planned in a black church about a mile away. They woudn't let us out of the parking lot. As Jackson was driving around the lot on a tractor, a huge rainbow came out in the sky. The farmers, being religious, all shouted: "It's a sign! It's a sign!"

Several farmers did go with Jackson to the church, where they spoke from the podium. Most had never been in a black church before. Many decided then and there to run as Jackson delegates.

The Jackson campaign provided the occasion to bring groups of black and white farmers together for the first time, as well as to bring farmers into contact with city folk. In that encounter, many white farmers, like Darrell Ringer of Kansas, discovered that "what they've been doing to you [blacks] for hundreds of years, they're now doing to us." Ringer, a young farmer who had lost his farm to foreclosure, confessed to having voted for Reagan in 1980. In November 1984, he ran for the U.S. Congress from Bob Dole's home district as a "rainbow" candidate, garnering 23 percent of the vote in this heavily Republican district, having had no previous campaign experience and only $30,000 to work with.

Most Jackson farm delegates, unfamiliar with the rules and political process, lost out after the first or second round of delegate selection, but several took vans to San Francisco anyway. They wanted to be where the action was, and it was with the Jackson campaign.

Labor: The Rank and File Speaks

Labor was a different story, however. With the AFL-CIO's heavy investment in Walter Mondale, the Jackson campaign obviously could not count on the labor machinery to turn out the vote for Jackson. Toward the beginning of the campaign, therefore, labor support was written off and there was no labor desk established in the national office. As it became clear that labor was not following the direction of the AFL-CIO leadership (Hart took a good deal of labor support in New England and black union households went with Jackson), campaign leaders began to see the possibility of drawing rank-and-file votes through Jackson's ability to address issues of concern to workers who were being laid off, forced to accept concessions, and disgruntled with their union leadership.

Halfway through the campaign, Steve Kirschbaum, a steelworker from Massachusetts, was brought into the campaign to organize labor rallies to coincide with Jackson's itinerary in Massachusetts, Maryland, Ohio, Pennsylvania, New Jersey, and West Virginia. To highlight the plight of unemployed steelworkers in Homestead, Pennsylvania, Jackson visited the food bank of Local 1397 United Steelworkers of America, and stayed in the home of an unemployed steelworker. He walked the picket line with Local 61 Shipbuilders, who were in their ninth month of a strike against the Dravco Corporation, a multinational that wanted the workers to take a 38 percent wage and benefit cut, and he led a march of unemployed steelworkers and their families on the shutdown steel mill in Youngstown, Ohio.

In Rahway, New Jersey, where eight hundred Oil, Chemical, and Atomic Workers (Local 8-575) were locked out of their jobs at Merck Pharmaceutical Company, Jackson walked the picket line and helped build a solidarity rally of three thousand workers and supporters. He was the only presidential candidate who responded to their cries for help. At this rally he also highlighted the struggle of the White Lung Association and their efforts to get justice for the victims of asbestos-related disease.

In all-white Mud Fork, West Virginia, an area of high unemployment for members of the United Mine Workers, nearly two hundred miners and their families—black and white—welcomed Jackson, who stayed in the home of a white coal miner. The next day Jackson joined the miners in their demand for repeal of the Taft-Hartley Act, and the West Virginia Black Lung and Disabled Miners Association in their fight for compensation for the victims and their families.

In Arizona, Jackson supported the striking Phelps-Dodge workers; he spoke to enthusiastic rallies of furniture workers in Baltimore. In Jackson's calls for plant-closing legislation that would give workers the option of buying the plants, in his denunciation of corporations for taking their investments to "slave-labor markets" abroad, and in the connections he made between the high military budget and the lack of money for social services and employment, he appeared to strike a responsive chord with many workers. Open affiliation with Jackson was discouraged by the AFL-CIO leadership, but scores of local trade union officials and staff members said off the record that they supported Jackson.

The Jackson campaign seems to have fueled a growing revolt among union activists who were beginning to make their break with the union bureaucracy. In the Pittsburgh area, the Jackson campaign was led by the presidents of three local unions—one of them the largest steelworker local in the country—and by a dozen lower-level local officials. Darrell Becker, president of Shipbuilder's Local 61, told reporters that he supported Jesse Jackson because he is the only candidate willing to come out and attack the corporations for their greed. . . . He is the only one who speaks for us and our issues."[17] In addition to the Pittsburgh area, local Labor for Jackson committees were formed in New York City, Seattle, Boston, San Francisco, Detroit and Washington, D.C.

Where Jackson campaigned heavily for labor, he won their votes. Homestead Pennsylvania, 70 percent white and devastated by plant closings, voted for Jackson overwhelmingly. In New York State, Jackson won 30 percent of the union household vote, including 44 percent of trade unionists who were between eighteen and twenty-nine years old; the black trade union vote went for

Jackson in spite of the endorsement of Mondale by the Coalition of Black Trade Unionists. While the labor vote for Jackson was not significant enough to boost his overall rating with whites, it is likely that this would change in the future. If white workers perceive that there is no public figure speaking to their issues but Jackson, they will begin to gravitate toward the Rainbow Coalition.

Peace and Environmental Activists

One sector of the Rainbow Coalition whose political potential was far from realized was the peace and environmental movement. In many ways, this is surprising. For one thing, Jackson made nuclear disarmament and a noninterventionary foreign policy a keystone of his campaign in his attempt to woo this predominantly white middle-class constitutency. George McGovern's exit from the race left Jackson as the only candidate who could be said to have anything like a peace and environmental policy. After hearing a speech Jackson gave at a conference to stop acid rain in New Hampshire, David Brower, founder of one of the largest environmental lobby groups, Friends of the Earth, called the speech "the best environmental statement that any presidential candidate has ever made."[18]

Moreover, the leadership of the organized white peace and environmental movements played an active role in the Jackson campaign—formulating policy, organizing rallies, and in many localities getting out the vote. In virtually every city where there were significant peace and environmental movements, the groups organized campaign endorsement rallies. I estimated that most of the nation's leading peace leaders and a good number of its environmental leaders endorsed the campaign.

There were, however, two major exceptions to this support: the leadership of the nation's two largest mass-based peace organizations, the Nuclear Freeze movement and SANE, and a coalition of Central America solidarity groups (the Central America Peace Campaign), which was founded specifically to influence the positions of Hart and Mondale. Though a number of individuals on the boards of these organizations supported Jackson, the organizations themselves had made a decision to put their organizational machinery behind voter registration efforts. The Freeze movement ran delegates for both Hart and Mondale, and the Central American Peace Campaign attempted to organize delegates for both candidates to support their slogan of "Talks Not Troops." As it turned out, neither the peace nor anti-intervention movements made much headway in influencing Hart and Mondale, and both groups ended up, at the Democratic Convention, urging their delegates at the last minute to support the Jackson minority planks on peace. Karen Mulhauser, coordinator of a large peace coalition that was fronting for Mondale during the primaries, received a job as Mondale's "peace staff" for the general election. She told me afterward that she had had no access to Mondale or his top advisers during the course of the general election.

For those peace leaders who supported Jackson, the experience proved invaluable. Most had previously shunned electoral politics as distracting and compromising. Said John Saxton, Jackson's peace coordinator:

> Reverend Jesse Jackson's campaign . . . has been a tremendous catalyst for peace work all across America. For a peace movement historically skeptical of electoral politics and politicians of either of the two major parties, there has been a significant and vitally important shift in outlook and activism centered around Jesse Jackson's quest to reshape the Democratic Party. And there is now more experience in multiracial coalition-building that can serve as the basis for the transformation of a lasting political force for social change in the U.S.[19]

For white peace and environmental activists the Jackson campaign was the first chance since the disarmament rally on 12 June 1982 to work closely with black and other third world people around the peace issue. This time, however, the leadership was black. From this experience, white activists learned vital political lessons: first, that the issues of peace and the environment can be translated into language and campaign strategies that will speak to constituencies not traditionally associated with the predominantly white middle-class peace and environmental movements; second, that minority communities are the strongest base for the constitution of a peace and environmental movement that can win power; third, that the public forum offered by electoral politics provides access to sectors of the population that the peace and environmental movements would not ordinarily have, and thus can be used to educate and mobilize people for these movements' issues. Electoral politics need not take away from movement-building, but can be a vital adjunct to it.

Such lessons, however, were slow in coming, and not everyone fully grasped the implications of what they were involved in until after the campaign was over. While individual peace and environmental leaders played active campaign roles, in the final analysis they failed to organize the masses of whites who might have been motivated to support the campaign. Part of the problem lay in the inexperience of white peace and environmental "movement" leaders with the electoral process. Lacking the expertise to develop voter education and get-out-the-vote campaigns, they tended to focus on rallies and endorsement press conferences alone.

Many peace movement leaders who were not involved in the campaign tended to see their co-workers' involvement as taking time and energy away from the ongoing needs of their own organizations, rather than seeing the coalition-building made possible by the campaign as ultimately essential to the advancement of their peace and environmental goals.

The lack of voter mobilization by white peace and environmental activists was not solely the fault of these activists. The problem also lay with the black campaign leadership's failure to commit resources to mobilize these constituencies. For example, senior campaign staff did not provide the money or commitment to develop a brochure that would address white peace activists until the campaign was halfway over. Thus, local peace and environmental activists were left without a clear statement of Jackson's policies in these areas that could have been used to mobilize voters. Many local activists said that had they had such a resource, they would have been able to do more effective organizing at the grassroots level. The last-minute scheduling of the candidate also interfered with the ability of white activists to mobilize their communities. People who identified with either peace or environmental concerns needed to be cultivated and informed in advance, but rallies called two days ahead of time hardly allowed campaign organizers to do the kind of advance work necessary to get people out to hear Jackson.

Nevertheless, it was peace and environmental activsts who provided the basis for most of the white support Jackson received, and they would continue to be among the Rainbow Coalition's most important sectors. Their involvement for the first time held out the promise that a truly multiracial/multiclass peace movement could be built in the United States.

Jewish Americans: Outside the Rainbow?

A major question for the future, however, relates to Jewish voters. While Jews represent only 3 percent of the American electorate, they have played a significant role in the course of Democratic party politics for the past several decades. In previous eras that role was in the service of the left, providing the bedrock on which enlightened ideas about racial and ethnic equality and economic democracy could spread to the white population. In 1984, however, attempts by many Jewish leaders to derail the Jackson campaign functioned in the service of the right. This situation reflected changes in the overall class composition of American Jewry (Jews are now the most affluent ethnic group in the United States); the rise of a neoconservative right-wing lobby within the Jewish community, which receives enormous support from the Reagan administration; and increasing tensions between blacks and Jews over civil rights issues, notably affirmative action.

These were only some of the factors in the black-Jewish divide, derived from long-standing tensions between the groups as a result of their proximity to (but not knowledge of) one another in the fierce scramble for status and economic power in some key cities, as well as U.S. support for Israel, which dominates Jewish emotions and political policy and increasingly figures in African-American political perceptions. Just as blacks have absorbed the Jewish stereotypes available in the general culture, so American Jews participate in the racism of white society. Because of the two groups' particular histories of genocide and persecution, both are unusually sensitive to any indications of threats to the group and thus any such threat—real or perceived—is likely to carry a high emotional charge. All of these factors complicated the relationship of Jewish Americans to the Rainbow Coalition in 1984 and provided the campaign's enemies with their most effective weapon—divide and conquer.

The Jewish factor in the Jackson campaign began well before a racial slur that Jackson made in a private conversation with black reporters appeared in the press in February 1984. (Jackson referred to Jews as "Hymies" and to New York as "Hymietown.") Before Jackson announced his candidacy, but in anticipation that he would do so, a nineteen-page confidential memorandum sharply critical of Jackson's history of statements about the Jewish community, and particularly his positions on the Middle East, was circulated by the Anti-Defamation League (ADL) of B'nai B'rith throughout the Jewish community. Copies were leaked to reporters and other opinion-makers. The memorandum took many of Jackson's statements out of context and lumped them together in such a way as to characterize him as a person dangerous to the Jewish community. The memorandum was a vicious personal attack on Jackson, characterizing a whole series of his actions and utterances since 1973 as anti-Israel, anti-Semitic, pro-PLO, and pro-terrorist.

The memorandum served to keep Jackson from getting the support of any prominent members of the Jewish community and of liberal non-Jewish Democratic forces as well. By the time black leaders obtained the document, a great deal of damage had already been done. Thus, when the "Hymie" remark surfaced in the press in February—at least a month after it had been made in an "off-the-record" conversation with black journalists—Jewish leaders and many members of the press had already been primed to suspect the worst.

The public furor created by the "Hymie" remark and the press's constant hounding of Jackson on this theme served to obscure early attempts by Jackson to resolve the deepening schism between the two communities. An analysis of these incidents reveals the formidable currents that were at work to create enmity between blacks and Jews and to paint Jackson as responsible for the schism.

Early in January Jackson sought to arrange a private meeting between liberal and moderate Jewish leaders and his key black supporters in the Christian church to discuss relations between the two communities. A number of black leaders were lined up, but word came back from the Jewish leaders that they were unwilling to meet with him at that time. The reason given was that they needed "more time to touch base with their constituencies" and to prepare for the meeting. John Collins, who had tried to arrange the meeting, told me he believed it was the climate engendered by the ADL memo and the attitudes it symbolized that led the Jewish leaders to decline the invitation.

Jackson still wanted to meet, but before another meeting could be arranged, the "Hymie" remark broke, and the possibility of a calm exchange of views was lost in the inflammatory public climate created by the press. Later, in April, shortly before the New York primary, an invitation was extended to Jackson to appear before a meeting of the Conference of Presidents of the Major American Jewish Organizations, which had also invited Mondale and Hart. Jackson and his advisers, fearing that such a meeting could amount to another public grilling that could damage Jackson's chances in the New York primary, proposed a format in which he would be accompanied by a number of other black leaders in a kind of black-Jewish summit, with a press conference to follow the meeting. After much discussion, the protocol was finally worked out, but before it could be implemented, Jackson withdrew. He thought it was now too close to the primary and that if it backfired, it would hurt his prospects in New York.

Jackson's failure to apologize immediately for the "Hymie" remark was probably a crucial mistake. There is every reason to believe that he actually did not think the remark was anti-Semitic and that it had not been made in a racist spirit. However, Jackson's failure to realize the depth of feeling that such a remark engendered, even in the liberal Jewish community, probably cost him votes and much of the work of the New Jewish Agenda, a progressive force within the Jewish community that has worked to support the two-state Middle East position within American Jewry.

For Jay Bender, a member of New Jewish Agenda who did work with the campaign, but at considerable emotional cost, Jackson had the best position on the Middle East of any of the candidates. It was a matter, however, of separating remarks about the Middle East from remarks about Jews, which the ADL memo, the media, Jackson himself, many black leaders, and much of the left failed to do. Bender explained the dynamics to me from his perspective.

> Jackson set himself up as a moral force. And to a great extent he was, but there was this blind spot. The moral force collapsed from "Hymie" to the convention. . . . I think in some ways there has been more progress on anti-racism than on anti-Semitism. I think part of

that is because we can see blacks as oppressed people. To most people we deal with, Jews don't appear to be oppressed and so the question of anti-Semitism doesn't seem to be as burning in most people as the question of racism. Jews aren't being shot by American police all the time the way blacks are. But we have long memories. We're not talking about 2000 years ago, we're talking about the last generation.[20]

If the black community failed to understand the intense emotions that any perceived derogation of the Jewish people aroused in even the most liberal Jews, progressive Jews, for their part, failed to perceive the depth of anger and betrayal felt by the black community when "their" presidential candidate became the object of an intense political attack from powerful sectors of the Jewish community who intended the derailment of the campaign. Behind Jackson's apparent ambivalence on how to handle the "Hymie" remark was an intense controversy within the campaign fueled by anger over the revelation of the ADL memo and feelings that a double moral standard was being used to judge Jackson in comparison with other public figures.[21] Some in the campaign did not want Jackson to apologize at all. Angered by the almost monolithic hostility of the Jewish community toward a campaign that in every other respect was morally head and shoulders above the others, they recalled the withdrawal of organized Jewish support from civil rights organizations when the black community insisted on directing that movement, a withdrawal that had left the black movement and its leaders more vulnerable to the assaults of the political right.

Black resentment increased when Jackson's apology for the "Hymie" remark failed to satisfy Jewish leaders. Immediately after the apology at Temple Abath Yushurun in Manchester, New Hampshire, on February 26, for example (this was two weeks after the first press report of the "Hymie" remark), Howard I. Friedman, president of the American Jewish Committee, insisted that it was not enough. "While we welcome this particular acknowledgement," he said, "we call upon him now to re-examine other statements he has made in the past about Jews, about Israel, about the Holocaust, about so-called Jewish Power."[22]

Not even a second apology, made before the B'nai B'rith in Framingham, Massachusetts, on March 4—which Jackson gave against advice from campaign aides—could stem the attacks from the Jewish leadership. This time, in preparation, several members of New Jewish Agenda were asked to help shape the speech. Jay Bender eventually wrote the final draft. The speech was a beautifully crafted summation of the mutual suffering of blacks and Jews, of the many historic ties between the two communities both through their common use of the Hebrew bible and the instances in which their struggles for freedom and justice had merged, and a call to mutual understanding, forgiveness, and solidarity. Jackson had to brush past twenty pickets outside chanting "Jackson is a racist pig!" and overcome shouts of "Jew Hater" from a few in the audience in order to give the speech.[23] With so few public Jewish voices supporting the campaign, it was hard for black leaders to feel much charity toward the Jewish community, and there did appear to be an effort among powerful Jewish forces to sabotage the campaign.[24]

Nation of Islam head Louis Farrakhan did not help Jackson's case with the Jewish community. While people who have studied the Black Muslims argue that his rhetoric is largely metaphorical and a part of an apocalyptic religious tradition, it was nevertheless inflammatory, lending itself to distorted and alarmist headlines in the press. It kept the controversy brewing, obscuring the essential Jackson message, and prevented his platform from being understood[25]

Jackson eventually repudiated much of what Farrakhan said, and put distance between Farrakhan and the campaign; but he refused to repudiate the man. Not only would his understanding of Christian principles dictate his "separation of the sin from the sinner," but what few Jews or non-Jewish whites understood was the wide respect Farrakhan enjoyed in the black community, even among some of the most "respectable" elements of the black middle class. Farrakhan's core constituency numbered only about ten thousand but his charisma and uncompromising oratory served a cathartic function for the anger that simmers beneath the surface of black America. For blacks who understand the depth of alienation in the black ghettos of America, Farrakhan's rhetoric and economic proposals actually serve as a constructive channel for rage that could otherwise be physically destructive. C. T. Vivian told me:

> Farrakhan comes from those who completely divorce themselves from a real role in American life. They write the whole society off as

so totally racist that its not worth working with, talking about, being involved in, saying that we've got to search for another path.

Cornel West adds another insight:

> Needless to say this [Farrakhan's] rhetoric is shot through with anti-white, anti-Jewish, and homophobic xenophobia as well as support for a feeble black business nationalist strategy for black betterment. Yet it does reveal just how far removed white America, both left and right, is from black realities and sentiments when most believe that what attracts a cross-section of black America to Farrakhan's speeches is his anti-Semitism.[26]

The near universal condemnation of Jackson by the Jewish leadership made it almost impossible for Jews of any prominence to associate themselves with the campaign, and of course, the more Jackson and Farrakhan were maligned in the press, the greater was black support for them. Jewish and black anger propelled one another in a vicious spiral from which there seemed no way out. Fortunately, for the campaign and the nation, there were a number of courageous Jews who supported the campaign and worked hard for it, believing that, in the overall analysis, the campaign was the only one that was addressing the great moral and political crises of the nation.

Two Jews served on the national campaign staff and a number of others worked as coordinators of state and local campaigns. During the New York primary, Suzanne Ross, who had fled as a child from Nazi Germany with her family, spoke as a Jew before a large black audience in one of Brooklyn's largest black churches, and again at the Democratic National Convention. Jay Bender appeared with Jackson at the annual meeting of the Arab-American Anti-Discrimination Committee in an appearance for which he was called a "Nazi lover" by a Jewish newspaper. Lisa Levine, a member of Jackson's national staff, spoke to a number of Jewish groups and was interviewed by the Jewish press.

A group of forty Jews took out a full-page ad in the *Village Voice* during the New York primary to express their support for the Rainbow Coalition, as did a group of about one hundred in Los Angeles during the California primary. In the San Francisco Bay Area, a group calling themselves "Jews for Jackson" organized a public meeting that brought together over one hundred Jews and Arabs for an endorsement of the campaign. Sabina Virgo, a Los

Angeles Jew, spoke at a large outdoor campaign rally during the Democratic National Convention in July, and a group of New Jewish Agenda delegates worked with Jackson delegates to try to get a more even-handed Middle East policy through the Democratic platform committee. Also significant was the work done by Jewish and black voters in Berkeley, California, to support an initiative authorizing the mayor to petition President Reagan and other government officials to decrease aid to Israel in direct proportion to the amount Israel spent on West Bank settlements. This measure won 40 percent of the vote.

In the final analysis, the percentage of the Jewish vote for Jackson was about the same as that of the white vote. Jackson received about 5 percent of the Jewish vote in New York and 8 percent in California. What is more significant, however, is the 11 percent vote Jackson received from 18–24 year old Jewish voters in New York. It is likely that the black-Jewish controversy cut into Jackson's non-Jewish white liberal vote, but it is impossible to assess how much of a factor this was. Certainly, from anecdotes told by campaign workers around the country, the bad publicity appears to have poisoned Jackson's image in the minds of a certain sector of the white public as the candidate of integrity and moral purpose; whether such people would have voted for Jackson if the controversy had not arisen is a question that remains long after the counting.

The future of black-Jewish political relations remains questionable. Jackson's speech at the Democratic National Convention (heard by almost 50 million people across the country) was the first chance most Jews and the general public had had to hear an entire speech, rather than having certain statements lifted out of context. That speech, while similar to the entire body of the message he delivered during the campaign, seems to have redeemed him and the black community in the minds of many Jews. Jay Bender told me: "For [New Jewish] Agenda people I think the convention speech was very important. As soon as he finished, the phone rang and I got about five calls from people around the country saying, 'We apologize. You were right.'" A prominent Jewish member of the Democratic National Committee, who had earlier described herself as literally "sick" about what she perceived as the anti-Semitism in the campaign, told me after Jackson's convention speech that she felt he had "made it all right."

Whether such sentiments will translate into closer political cooperation in the future between liberal Jews and the Rainbow Coalition has yet to be tested. Certainly Jews, above all other white groups, continue to be the base for liberal political programs. Although the Jewish vote has become more conservative over the years, the majority violated their class interests and voted for Mondale in 1984 in spite of predictions by some neoconservatives that they would abandon the Democratic party. Prominent Jewish leaders also participated with black leaders in getting arrested outside the South African consulate for opposing apartheid. On every issue but the Middle East and affirmative action, Jews and blacks continue to agree. Yet these two along with the "Hymie" remark were enough to derail Jewish support for the black community's presidential candidate.

It may be that the much-touted Jewish-black civil rights alliance was always overdrawn—based on a paternalistic relationship common among whites in general that was bound to change when blacks came to political maturity. Whether Jews, who have never felt terribly secure in the United States in spite of their relative affluence, will see it as in their own best interest to side with the Rainbow Coalition or whether the more prosperous among them will follow their class interests and their allegiance to Israel and move to the right in violation of many of their traditional values remains to be seen. Much may depend on events in the Middle East and South Africa, on the state of repression in the United States, and on the ability of the Rainbow Coalition to attract to itself major constituencies beyond its black base.

8

The Poorest Campaign with the Richest Message: The Challenge to the Rules of Political Discourse

White America for the most part does not even seek democracy for itself. . . . A genuine, functioning democracy . . . would require many of the same inputs necessary to any vital people's movement. It would require the consent and regular participation of its members, supported by free access to information and open discussion. It would require lines of mutual responsibility and accountability between the representatives and the represented. It would require an ability for the body politic to design and obtain laws which served it and promoted its ends.[1]

—C. T. Vivian

If one part of the Jackson campaign's strategy was the use of the techniques of black consciousness to psychologically and intellectually prepare and to progressively unify a constituency for social change, another part lay in its attempt to penetrate one of the most carefully guarded preserves of U.S. class rule: the two party system. By running in the Democratic party primaries and caucuses, Jackson used the party machinery to challenge the underlying assumptions and expose the undemocratic effects of its operation. He did so as the agent of a constituency that had been consistently locked out, and on behalf of the ideal of democracy itself.

It is not at all clear that many of the black politicians who joined Jackson in this effort intended the campaign to be a clear challenge to the class rule for which the party is an instrument. For most, it was a way to increase their "influence" within this bastion of class rule.[2] But Jackson's own value commitments, and the social conditions experienced by the constituencies for which he spoke, determined that the campaign would push against the limits of interest-group pluralism. Jackson had made that clear at the beginning of the campaign. "Ultimately, the poor do not just want friends, they want to be *empowered*. And when you start speaking of empowering the poor, then you have to redistribute the power of those who already hold it."[3] Jackson's challenge to the class rule represented by the Democratic party was twofold: this chapter examines the broad challenge to the informal limitations on political discourse imposed by the party leadership, while Chapter 9 explores the narrower challenge to formal internal party rules and voting impediments. To understand the implications of these challenges, a brief history of the nature of the American "democratic system" is a necessary backdrop.

American Civics Revisited

Elite ideology has always maintained the illusion that participation in American democracy actually works through the electoral system—that is, by casting an individual vote, people are, in fact, exercising decision-making power. In reality, elites in control of the electoral process have sought to prevent the franchise from being widely available, and even where available, from being the means to the effective exercise of citizen power. Not only are the ideological choices offered the voting public limited to those acceptable to the ruling class and corporate power structure, but every reform that has opened up access to the electoral arena to more of the citizenry has been the result of mass popular struggle—the Civil War and the struggle for the fourteenth and fifteenth amendments, the Populist movement of the 1890s, which called for the popular election of presidents and the principle of "one man, one vote," the woman suffrage movement, and the civil rights movement.

Just as quickly as reforms have been won, those in power have created new barriers to the exercise of the vote. Within a handful of years after the passage of the fourteenth and fifteenth amendments, northern industrialists, in an exchange with southern planters for control of the national government, withdrew federal support for Reconstruction governments, thus unleashing a reign of terror across the South that effectively began the one-hundred-year disenfranchisement of southern blacks. With the crushing of the Populist movement's efforts to enter the electoral arena on behalf of the class interests of small farmers and urban laborers, northern and southern financial interests moved in the 1890s to "reform" state election laws so that another challenge from below could not be mounted. Such "reforms" as poll taxes, grandfather clauses, literacy tests, and the "white primary" not only completed the disenfranchisement of blacks, but excluded half the whites who were the base of the Populist party, while such institutions as the "run-off" or "dual primary" guaranteed that any black or insurgent candidate who happened to slip through the preliminary barriers would be defeated at the polls. By the onset of the Great Depression, registration restrictions had reduced voter turnout in national elections from 75 percent to a little over 50 percent.[4]

Again, after the next great wave of democratic reform, which culminated in the passage of the Voting Rights Act of 1965, whites in the power elite—particularly in the South but not only in that region—introduced new impediments to voting. These included gerrymandering districts to break up minority voting blocs; annexing white enclaves, and instituting at-large elections to dilute black voting strength; purging registration rolls and requiring re-registration; limiting the hours and places where registration was available; limiting those who could qualify as registrars; outlawing registration by mail; and requiring double registration—one for county elections and another for state and federal elections.

The effect of such barriers was dramatized in Mississippi—the state with the highest percentage of blacks—where gerrymandered districts had prevented the election of a single black member of Congress in one hundred years, and in the state capitol of Jackson, where at-large voting for city council seats meant no black representative for the city's 45 percent black population.

But it was not only southern blacks who had been disenfranchised. The United States is the only Western democracy that has no automatic registration. Even when people vote, the votes are not counted proportionately in allocations of political power, but are put into a pool of votes, which can mean they may not be counted at all. Democratic party rules in 1984, for example, mandated that a candidate had to get 20 percent of the vote—the "threshold rule"—in a given electoral district in order to get a delegate to the Democratic National Convention. In other states, a "winner-take-all" rule was in effect—that is, all of the delegates in a particular district were awarded to the top vote-getter. The electoral college represents a further delimitation of the power of the individual vote, making it possible for a presidential candidate to get the majority of the popular vote, but to lose the election.

The party system that governs U.S. democracy has itself kept the American public politically inert and illiterate. With few exceptions, parties have historically been closed clubs, neither seeking nor welcoming new members, and shielding their deliberations in the familiar "smoke-filled rooms." One study points out that the closed party organization ignores even the forms of participation: county, state, and national chairmen, who in theory are elected by and accountable to a representative party committee or broader party constituency, are usually named by other leaders in the organization, or by a single person—the governor, president, or party's candidate.[5] Though parties are supposed to be the instruments through which government is provided with competent political executives, they have no formal means of screening candidates for their ability to govern, no training programs for developing political executives or party professional staff, no systems for holding elected officials accountable to campaign promises or party platforms, and no regular means of gathering public opinion on issues for input into the formulation of party policy—except around the time of the platform hearings prior to the party's presidential nominating conventions.

Because the major parties must represent the interests of *both* the ruling class and the working class, they have not been interested in staking out clear positions on issues anyway, preferring to keep the ideological waters muddy in the interest of ruling-class control.

The laws and regulations governing delegate selection to the presidential nominating conventions are a confusing and arcane amalgam of state laws and party procedures that vary widely from state to state. State legislatures have the authority to decide how delegates will be chosen—whether by caucus, a meeting or meetings of party members, or by a primary election, in which the voters cast their ballots either for a slate of delegates pledged to one of the presidential candidates, or merely express their preference among presidential candidates. In the latter case, delegates are actually selected in caucuses or conventions and they need not be pledged to candidates in the same proportion as the primary vote. In 1984, twenty-five states had decided to use primaries, while the remainder used the caucus system or some combination of the two.

Political parties decide how many delegates will be allocated to each state and the criteria for their selection. In 1984, the 20-percent threshold rule was used by some state parties, while others maintained the winner-take-all rule. In any case, the principle of one person, one vote has never been a part of the American system of democracy.

While giving lip service to the democratic ideal, the American public has tacitly accepted the rules that determine its own disenfranchisement. This is reflected in the commonly heard expression "all politicians are corrupt" and in the low rate of voter participation—the lowest in the Western world. In fact, the United States is second only to Botswana in voter turnout.[6] In 1984 only 55 percent of the potential voters voted for president, and of these, only 59.1 percent voted for Reagan. Nearly 70 percent of the American public, therefore, *did not* vote for Ronald Reagan (that is they voted for another candidate or they stayed home), an insight neither the press nor the parties have been willing to share with the American public. In addition to the low voter turnout, the class character of the American electorate is dramatically skewed. The poorer and less educated sectors of the population vote at rates considerably lower than the more affluent and educated. In 1980, for example, an estimate 70 percent of those with annual incomes of over $25,000 voted, while only 25 percent of those with incomes of less than $10,000 did. Eighty-one percent of those with college degrees cast ballots, while only 51 percent of those with a grammar school education voted.[7]

Democratic Party Reform: The Lessons of the McGovern Commission

In 1968, as a result of the social ferment of the 1960s, white elites within the Democratic party inaugurated a period of reform of party rules that was the most extensive in party history. The new rules instituted by the McGovern Commission of 1972 and two subsequent cycles of party reform were designed to streamline and regularize party rules and thus break the stranglehold of backroom deals and party machines.

The most publicized set of reforms mandated a broader demographic base, requiring the party to open up to women, minorities, and youth in proportion to their representation in the population of each state. These rules gave the McGovern Commission the reputation among the New Left of being the source of the party's democratization.

In fact, the McGovern Commission signaled the end of the old party system, but it did not result in the democratization of the electoral process. Instead of the party machine controlling the presidential nominating process, corporate political action committees, (PAC), polling, media, and advertising experts now began to dominate the process. "Personality" and "Image" became the criteria for political office. In loosening party controls over the candidate-selection process, the reforms led to further impediments on the ability of ordinary citizens to gain access to the system.[8] This was reflected in a steadily shrinking electorate throughout the 1970s.

After the debacle of Carter's defeat in 1980, elements of the old party leadership—notably AFL-CIO leaders—sought, through the creation of the Hunt Commission, to reverse the rules changes that had made possible the party's nomination of "outsiders" such as McGovern and Carter, which they saw as responsible for the party's defeat, and to restore the regular party's control over the presidential delegate-selection process. The move was a desperate attempt to shore up both a declining labor movement and an almost moribund party.[9]

Among the McGovern rules that were modified were those that had limited the number of "add-on" or "super-delegates" who could be appointed by the party—these were expanded from 10 percent of all delegates to 14 percent; the winner-take-all rule, which was reinstated for some states after it had been eliminated; and an increase in the use of caucuses—since caucuses were most useful to *organized* electoral constituencies, such as unions.

The Jackson Campaign and the Second Era of Party Reform

The Jackson campaign marked the beginning of a second great period of party reform, but one quite different in players, ideology and tactics from the first, with the outcome more likely to be realignment (or, more accurately, party replacement) than reform.

The Jackson campaign's attempts to reform the party differed in two major respects from the earlier reform movement. First, it was a truly insurgent movement of the locked-out and disenfranchised trying to gain political power through rules that were stacked against it. Second, it raised the most basic questions about the nature and extent of American democracy, and called for the institution of the concept of one person, one vote as the fundamental premise of American democracy, a rule change that the McGovern and subsequent reform commissions had studiously avoided.

The McGovern reform era represented a struggle between a rising class of white middle-strata professionals (lawyers were heavily represented) and the old party leadership composed of big-city machine politicians, labor officials, party office-holders, and black elected officials. At the time, black office-holders were fairly well represented within the party. They had been used to bargaining for their interests within the old rules, and were somewhat reluctant to shake up the power base they had built by aligning themselves with the insurgent faction, even though the new rules mandated greater participation of women and minorities. Because of this, the rules adopted by the McGovern Commission were more slanted toward guaranteeing the representation of white middle-class feminists than of minorities, the working class, or the poor. The white middle-class bias of the McGovern reforms was borne out in 1976 when the explicit quota provisions applying to women expanded, while the quota provisions applying to blacks were dropped.[10] It was clear that the McGovern Commission reforms were based on a pluralism of demographics, not a pluralism of class or even of ideology. Such issues as civil rights enforcement, economic justice, peace, or even voting rights were not of paramount concern to the reformers.[11]

As the Jackson campaign evolved, it became clear that the Rainbow Coalition stood for more than a pluralism of ascription. Jackson himself had stated that the rainbow was not a "color" but a "point of view." In ideology and intention, at least, if not in actual representation (Jackson delegates were more highly educated than Mondale's and only slightly less affluent), the Jackson campaign represented the class interests of the unemployed, the marginally employed, blue-collar workers and small farmers, and the constituencies of "conscience"—peace activists and environmentalists and civil rights and human rights activists. They were also among the locked-out, for they had been battering at the doors of Congress for decades with little response.

The white middle-class bias of the party factions associated with the McGovern reforms—white middle-class feminists, neoliberals (even McGovern himself)—would become apparent as the Jackson campaign pushed against the limits of both the earlier reforms and the efforts of party regulars to take back the party from the reformers. In a sense, the Jackson campaign was a "plague on both your houses."

The Jackson Campaign and the Third Party Route

Most other movements that have represented the politically and economically marginalized have attempted to penetrate the U.S. political system either through creating mass social unrest so that the party in power would be forced to concede to some of their demands in the interests of social stability, or through the formation of third parties, which could represent class interests directly in the electoral arena in a way that the two major parties were unprepared to do. Though their domestic policies were sometimes to the left of Jackson's, third parties have always been the strategy of last resort. Significant deterioration of the two major parties had to occur before a third-party route was undertaken.[12]

In 1984, the black community was the only group with both the indigenous resources and the ideological coherence capable of launching a major challenge to the class rule of the two-party system. One might wonder, then, why it did not seek the third-party route. Unquestionably there had been a deterioration in party loyalty throughout the 1970s, indicated by the rise in independent registrations and crossover voting.[13] The black community's leaders and resources, however, were still heavily dependent on Democratic party fortunes, and many of the black politicians assumed that because of the party's dependence on the margin of the black vote, the party would have to concede some of their demands. They were badly mistaken. Black politicians, inured by the status they had been able to achieve within the party on the basis of ascriptively defined criteria, failed to understand—

until much later in the campaign (and some, not until after the campaign)—both the endemic racism of significant portions of the Democratic party elite and the class interests of which it was a function.

By running within the party Jackson was forced to challenge rules—both official and tacit—that had effectively limited both the political discourse the ruling class allowed to be determined at the polls and the participation of the vast majority of the people in the processes of governing.

The Rainbow's Challenge

Elite political strategy maintains that the best way for a candidate to gain (or maintain) political office is to stick to vague, ambiguous, or contradictory policy statements.[14] By limiting political debate, the ruling elite is able to assert its interest as the "national interest" and to label all those who oppose the national interest "anti-American." Party platforms, therefore, are not taken seriously, and successful candidates are not bound to abide by them.

By running within one of the two major party primaries, which afforded him free access to the mass media, Jackson was able to challenge these assumptions with one of the most ideologically coherent and serious campaign platforms in recent history. Jackson thus reached masses of people who could not be reached in any other way with the message that political values and ideas are to be taken seriously, that ordinary citizens have a right to engage in political debate, and that candidates must be held accountable for their campaign promises.

Jackson used his access to the media brilliantly, and his artful delivery of this message meant that it was bound to be heard at some level by the American public, even if he did not get their votes. A local New Hampshire reporter, listening to Jackson's speech to a rally of the disabled, commented: "Whether joking or serious, . . . he speaks about what he calls the higher ground. It is a place where any sensible person would like to be."[15]

The substance of Jackson's message was threefold. First, it was a message that the needs and concerns of racial minorities were not to be swept under the rug, but must be attended to for the good of the nation. The context in which this message was delivered must be noted again. It was a time of federal retrenchment of, if not assault on, most of the civil rights gains of the last twenty years. The Civil Rights Commission had been stripped of any effective power; the federal government was moving to challenge in the courts the entire body of affirmative action legislation it had formerly supported; voting rights enforcement had come to a halt; and the social welfare programs so necessary to racial minorities and the poor had been cut drastically. The Democratic party, retreating from its previous commitment to civil rights, had proposed a platform plank that opposed the use of goal-oriented remedies to alter structural discrimination. Full employment as a national goal had long since ben abandoned. The Ku Klux Klan and other white hate groups had been given a green light from the highest level of government.

Jackson brought these issues back from obscurity and made them topics of respectable debate, forcing the Democratic presidential contenders to deal with them or be forced to account for their failure to do so. Mary Berry said as early as August 1983 that the mere threat of a black presidential candidate "has forced literally every white aspirant to speak favorably to traditional Black concerns."[16]

There is no doubt that Jackson's presence in the campaign forestalled the capitulation of more of the white public to the racist and neofascist demagoguery of the Reagan administration and the religious right. Jackson had a way of converting what were traditionally considered race-specific or "left" concerns into ideas that captured the imagination of conservatives. In New Hampshire, journalist David Moberg found that "many of the converts [to Jackson] are not choosing between Jackson and McGovern or Jackson and Cranston, who are politically most similar. Often they are erstwhile supporters of Walter Mondale or even Glenn, people who had never been interested in politics before, disgruntled old-line Republicans or even soft-core supporters of Ronald Reagan."[17] The comments of one Jackson campaign worker—a retired businessman and registered Republican—are indicative of the translation Jackson was able to make.

He brought a new dimension to the primary campaign. He represents a person who can talk to the Third World and get results. Most of all, he makes us aware of society's responsibility to the disadvantaged, whether domestic or anyplace in the world. But it's linked with efficiency, rather than just throwing more money at social problems. You notice Jackson didn't say the solution to our lousy educational system was more money, but he did say teachers had to be paid well.[18]

Large groups of white farmers throughout the Midwest who were being wooed by such fascist groups as the Posse Comitatus and the Ku Klux Klan rallied to the rainbow instead, because, as Roger Allison, a Missouri farm leader explained, "here was a black man articulating our issues even better than we could."[19] White unemployed steelworkers in Pennsylvania and other areas of the "rust belt" supported the Jackson campaign for the same reason.

The second part of Jackson's message lay in his insistence that the perspective of America's leaders had to change if they were going to deal with the real world. Not only had the United States become a multinational society, but "most people in the world are black, brown, yellow or red, poor, non-Christian, and don't speak English." In televised debates, Jackson insisted on this formula, calling attention to areas of the world and to pressing foreign policy issues that the other presidential contenders had wanted to sweep under the rug: U.S. support for South Africa, intervention in Central America, the bombing of Lebanon, and the Palestinians' right to a homeland.

At several campaign stops in New Hampshire, the Jackson campaign gave a place at the podium to Arnoldo Ramos, a representative of the FDR-FMLN, the revolutionary opposition in El Salvador. Ramos used the occasion to explain the FDR-FMLN's peace plan, which was universally ignored by both the Reagan administration and the Democratic party. William Sloan Coffin, senior minister of Riverside Church, who was present at these events, told me he thought they were "the most remarkable public educational events" he had ever witnessed.

As early as February 1984, a *Boston Globe* editorial credited Jackson with moving the Democratic party debate in a more humane direction.

It is more than coincidence that at the Harvard debate the Democratic field began to articulate a broader version of Jackson's personal message: that there must be an end to the Reagan administration's attempts to "vulgarize" any racial or ethnic group, demonize the Soviet Union or trivialize the Third World.[20]

An *In These Times* editorial 18–24 April 1984 wondered if Jackson's bold initiatives on Central America had not suddenly stiffened House Speaker Tip O'Neill's spine in opposing the Reagan administration request for $21 million more for the CIA-directed contra war against Nicaragua. Randall Robinson, executive director of TransAfrica, pointed out that white Democratic candidates did not even address U.S. relations with the South African regime "until Jesse Jackson began to emerge as a potential candidate."[21] In April, pressed by Jackson's insistence that the cozy U.S. relationship with South Africa be addressed, Mondale called for a cutoff of new American investment if no progress on human rights was made, a ban on flights into the United States of South African Airways, and a ban on International Monetary Fund Loans to South Africa and the importation of Krugerrands. Even neoconservative Arch Puddington, in a backhanded appreciation of Jackson's role, admitted that Jackson's "continued espousal of a world view dominated by the image of a militaristic and racially insensitive America has not damaged his public standing."[22]

The third piece of the Jackson message—addressed as much to the peace movement as to the Democratic and Republican parties—was that in the pursuit of international peace, boldness and risk taking are essential. Jackson's peace proposals were far to the left of those of any Democratic candidate in recent history, with the exception of George McGovern. Even the mainstream white peace movements had been reluctant to make several of the issues Jackson took up the subject of public debate for fear of scaring off their white, middle-class constituency. Jackson's bold initiatives, however——the success of his trips to Syria and Cuba—proved that no breakthroughs are possible unless some party is willing to risk the optimum that is hoped for.

As controversial as was Jackson's espousal of an even-handed policy in the Middle East, his principled adherence to this position appears to have helped thaw the climate at least for a reasonable discussion of the issues among the left. Arab-American activist Abdeen Jabara told me that as a result of the Jackson campaign he was able to say things concerning U.S. aid to Israel and U.S. intervention in the Middle East at the "April Actions" rally in Washington, D.C., in April 1985 that had never been said in such a mass gathering before. Jabara's marching partner was a rabbi formerly from South Africa. "This reveals," said Jabara, "that the struggle for correct politics on Mideast issues is winning over the tendency toward accommodationism in the name of unity."

Jackson's clear positions on issues enabled his delegates in several places in the country to go to their state platform conventions armed with the ideological mandate to fight for a progressive party platform. Such platforms are usually of little consequence, but in 1984 they were seen as tools that would enable progressives to continue the fight within the party even after the primaries were over. In Washington State, for example, Jackson organizers ordered copies of all the Jackson position papers from the national office, ran training programs on the platform for their delegates, and sent delegates to the state convention armed with a thorough knowledge of the difference between the Jackson, Mondale, and Hart positions and the ability to argue on behalf of the Jackson platform. Delegates who had never been involved in anything political before found themselves able to articulate and argue the issues better than experienced Mondale and Hart operatives. The state platform that was adopted was virtually the entire Jackson program.

For the first time since the election of 1972, Democratic voters in the spring of 1984 were offered a genuine *choice*—a real peace-and-justice candidate. It was a choice the significance of which few understood at the time. Most took the "lesser of two evils" route, working for Hart or Mondale and thus forfeiting their opportunity to make a real difference in the positions of the Democratic party. The failure of that choice would become apparent after the November elections.

The Democratic Party's Response

The Democratic party responded to Jackson's enlarging of the political debate with a mixture of accommodation, cooptation, stonewalling, and outright repudiation. Because of Jackson's success in mobilizing the black community, the other Democratic party candidates were forced to treat him with kid gloves; they were fearful of alienating their own black support and of appearing racist should they criticize him directly. They were also forced to stress general themes they thought would "play" in the black community, such as fairness, compassion for the poor, and racial pluralism.

Of course, this was window dressing, and the real racism and class fears of Democratic party regulars slipped out in the press in other ways. One was in the suggestion that Jackson was a "divisive" figure who threatened the party's unity and was even responsible for creating a "white backlash" that would hurt the party in November. Typical is the comment of one unnamed North Carolina Democrat close to the campaign to re-elect Governor James Hunt who told a *Washington Post* reporter, "Politically, I'm very apprehensive about what all this [Jackson's candidacy] will mean. I really think the whole thing has a negative potential."[23] In a fit of nervous hyperbole, a senior Mondale aide told a *Newsweek* reporter, "If any candidate looks like he's sold out to get Jackson's support, he's lost 58 percent of the vote right there."[24]

Another tactic taken by Hart and Mondale was to agree with Jackson in generalities, but to ignore the substance of his proposals and to focus on each other as the genuine adversaries in the primary contest. Jackson parried this tactic brilliantly, however, by pointing out to his audiences that his opponents were not giving him—and by extension the Rainbow Coalition—the respect of being taken seriously. "It could not be more clear," he told a New York audience, "that Walter Mondale and Gary Hart would prefer to pretend that you and I do not exist." In a televised debate at Columbia University, Jackson used the occasion of his being ignored to highlight the shallowness of the debate between the two front-runners and present his candidacy as the real alternative. "There are three men in the race," he quipped, "but two directions."[25]

In the debate that followed it appeared that Hart's and Mondale's coaches had learned their lesson. Instead of focusing on each other, they targeted Reagan as the real adversary, stressing in vague generalities the themes that Jackson had been raising all along.

As the Jackson campaign gained momentum Democratic party regulars took steps both to ascertain the loyalty of their own black delegates and to limit the quality of the debate that would take place in the Democratic platform hearings and on the convention floor. Their public fears of a "divided party" rationalized their private fear of an insurgency from below that could threaten their own power within the party and the financial interests to which they were beholden.[26] In mid-April, a memo written by Chuck Dolan, executive director of the Democratic Governors' Association, was leaked to the press. The memo asserted that "it's becoming clear" that Jackson intends to use his candidacy as a lever "to bring the Democratic Party closer to his ideological creed." It suggested that the governors use their influence "to avoid special-interest planks" from any source and to give the party "a platform broad enough for most Democrats to stand on." The memo predicted that when the convention turns to platform issues on its second night,

> Jackson will deliver an emotional firestorm of a speech aimed at igniting every liberal sentiment on the floor. . . . Conventions are by their nature highly emotional events. There are a large number of party activists who under the right circumstances might vote for the sort of knee-jerk proposals which were included in the McGovern rules and platform.[27]

The memo is revealing for the fear it exposes that the "liberal" ideas espoused by Jackson might actually be the sentiments of the majority of delegates to the convention—thus the need to carefully control the parameters of the debate. Thereafter, the ideas and proposals raised by blacks, women, Latinos, peace activists, and others associated with the Rainbow Coalition—many of them ideas for which the Democratic party had stood since the New Deal—would become "special interests" that had to be cast aside in the interest of "party unity."

The idea that the real needs of working people, minorities, and women (or the universal desire for peace) had become special interests in opposition to the majority interest was a reversal the neoconservatives had first developed with regard to black concerns. Now, the Democratic party leadership was extending the pejorative label "special interests" to everything that, if public opinion polls were to be believed, the majority of the public actually wanted. The real special interests—the corporations and large financiers—had now become the majority.

The shift of the Democratic party so far to the right was a function of the decline of its labor base and the party's greater reliance on corporate and conservative PACs.[28] Mondale was caught in a no-win situation. He was constrained to try to hold on to the party's traditional constituencies, without being able to offer them a program. The party's use of blacks as mere tokens to assure the black vote for a party that offered them nothing was a shameful episode in political expediency.

As the designee of party regulars, Mondale took pains to keep both Jackson and his ideas at a distance, while trying to assure his own black supporters that their concerns were in good hands. In late April, a meeting of black politicians supporting Mondale was called by Birmingham's mayor, Richard Arrington. According to a Mondale deputy campaign manager, one of the purposes of the meeting was to focus on issues affecting blacks and to improve Mondale's performance among black voters in the remaining Democratic primaries and caucuses.[29] Another purpose was undoubtedly to make certain that there would be no defections from the Mondale position in the Democratic platform hearings or on the convention floor. The need for party unity to defeat Reagan in the fall was the weapon used by party regulars to keep Mondale blacks and women in line.

By May, even George McGovern, who claimed that he had entered the primaries to raise the right issues, capitulated to the stampede to rally around Mondale in the interest of party unity. In a stinging letter to McGovern, Jackson refused an invitation to appear at a party-unity event to retire McGovern's campaign debt. "I believe that it is too premature a celebration of party unity," he wrote.

> I believe that real party unity can only be founded on party justice. I am deeply disturbed by the lack of progress our party has made in broadening its base, in reaching out to the locked out—even to those clamoring to get in. I am deeply disturbed by the failure of Walter Mondale and Gary Hart to take up the issues of peace and justice that you and I have raised in our campaigns. . . . Our party does not need a conscience any less in San Francisco in July than it did in Iowa in January. I hoped that you would continue to play the role of conscience. Indeed, I hoped for your support for my campaign.

Then, in a lesson on political power that few black politicians or white left-liberal forces seemed capable of grasping in 1984, Jackson continued:

> [Progressive] forces could have been advanced much further if you had decided to support me. Much of the media and the party lead-

ership have tried to isolate me and the issues I have raised. . . . If you had chosen to support me, it would have been much more difficult for the Democratic Party to ignore these issues. Together we might make San Francisco in July an occasion to go down in history, an occasion when the Democratic Party might finally decide to fully learn the lessons of Vietnam, to fully commit itself to a program of peace and of jobs, of justice at home and abroad.

As the party platform hearings approached, Jackson alternately called for meetings with his two rivals to establish "areas of common Democratic agreement" and warned that unless the Democrats heeded the needs of his constituency, they faced certain defeat in the fall. Democratic party leaders took such warnings as signals that Jackson was threatening to walk out of the convention if he did not get his way and chastised him for being a spoiler. Jackson retorted: "My constituency doesn't have a history of walking out, nor have I ever walked out of a Democratic convention. I've always fought to get in."[30]

The Jackson Platform

In an address to an Operation PUSH convention on June 7, a few days before the opening of the Democratic party platform committee hearings, Jackson laid out a ten-point policy platform that he declared was a formula for a Democratic party victory in November.[31] The ten points were a summary of the positions Jackson had taken on a variety of issues along the campaign trail, as he encountered the locked-out and disenfranchised. Although written in imprecise "platform style" language, the ten-point program represented a major challenge to the basic assumptions of the Democratic party's draft platform, which would be unveiled about ten days later. The party's platform was drafted by a fifteen-member subcommittee chaired by Geraldine Ferraro and stacked with Mondale supporters.

Jackson's "New Directions Platform" called for:

1. *Fairness.* Under this heading was included a uniform primary approach based on the principle of one person, one vote; an end to all schemes to discourage political participation, including caucuses and primary front-loading; and a commitment to affirmative voter registration efforts.

2. *Voting rights enforcement.* This included full enforcement of

the Voting Rights Act to prevent schemes that disenfranchise minorities, such as gerrymandering, annexation, at-large elections, inaccessible registrars, role purges, dual registration, and second primaries.

3. *Reciprocal voting.* Under this rubric the party would commit itself to endorse and support minority candidates.

4. *Integrated slate-making.* At all levels of government the party would commit itself to reflect the racial, ethnic, and religious makeup of the nation.

5. *Peace.* A number of broad but radical proposals were offered under this heading, including a commitment to make negotiations with the Russians a first priority; a pledge that the United States would never be the first to use nuclear weapons; an immediate six-month unilateral moratorium on the production, deployment, and testing of nuclear weapons (the so-called "quick freeze"); withdrawal of all troops and military advisors from Central America, and further economic aid to El Salvador tied to peace negotiations; diplomatic and trade relations with Cuba; declaration of the Western hemisphere as a nuclear-free zone; a two-state position in the Middle East; commitment to negotiate the reduction of our military commitments in Europe and Japan; development of a coherent Asian, African, and Caribbean policy; an end to apartheid and an end to our support of dictators throughout the world; and a 20 percent reduction in the military budget.

6. *Jobs.* Development of a plan to put people to work by rebuilding America's cities; plant-closing legislation to protect workers and communities.

7. *Justice.* Passage of the ERA; support of equal pay for work of comparable worth; opposition to the Simpson-Mazzoli immigration bill; support for organized labor; an end to union-busting policies, including the Taft-Hartley Act and policies that allow corporations to file for bankruptcy as a way of breaking their union contracts.

8. *Foreign policy.* Commitment to measure human rights by one yardstick; mutual respect for other nations as opposed to the big-stick and gunboat diplomacy of both Democratic and Republican administrations; a foreign policy based on mutual economic development for aid and trade.

9. *Corporate responsibility.* Rejection of supply-side economics in favor of a demand-side policy; an end to tax breaks for runaway

corporations and tax shelters for the rich; an end to policies that allow corporations to engage in "chemical warfare" against people either here or abroad.

10. *A focus on the rejected.* A full-employment policy that focuses on those with the greatest needs: the disabled, the poor, the elderly, American Indians; an end to the bureaucracy that now dominates life on Indian reservations.[32]

Based on these general principles, the Jackson staff worked to construct a more specific set of policy options to be taken into the Democratic platform committee meetings. Among the many concrete proposals contained in the "New Directions Platform" of the Jackson campaign were the following: progressive tax reform directed at increasing the tax burdens of large corporations and wealthy individuals and directing revenues away from nonproductive to productive sectors; support for the Humphrey-Hawkins full-employment goal of not more than 4 percent unemployment; a $50 billion public works program to rebuild American's infrastructure; a $2 billion funding of the Kennedy-Hawkins Youth Incentive Employment Act; a $4.4 billion increase in funding for the Jobs Training Partnership Act; plant-closing legislation requiring firms to give prior notice and provision for worker ownership of abandoned plants; creation of a major comprehensive national manpower skills development policy; adoption of a national health insurance program that provides quality care not based on ability to pay; a national council on health care cost containment; the elimination of nuclear power and the development of alternative, nonpolluting, renewable energy sources; support for 90 percent of parity for small farmers; revision of the tax code to prohibit land speculation and exorbitant pricing by middlemen; opposition to Simpson-Mazzoli and adoption of a humane immigration policy; opposition to the subminimum wage for youth; an international economic order that seeks to redress the North-South trade imbalance and promote self-sufficiency among America's trading partners in the developing world; withdrawal of Cruise and Pershing II missiles from Europe; a 20 percent cut in the military budget; a commitment to abolish all nuclear weapons.

Jackson has been accused of having a vague, cathartic program of little more than slogans, offering nothing substantive to the constituencies for which he spoke.[33] As this brief and incomplete summary of his program indicates, the opposite was the case. In fact, it was Democratic party regulars—particularly those associated with the Mondale campaign—who kept the national policy debate at the level of vague generalities.

The platform hearings were convened on June 21 with party regulars determined to keep the lid on any substantive debate. "I'm afraid they're trying for a bland document that will offend no one," observed Washington, D.C., representative Walter Fauntroy, who represented the Jackson campaign in the platform hearings.[34] Jackson's supporters, most of whom were new to the process of party platform development, were shocked at the "undemocratic" nature of the proceedings. Participants told me that the Mondale supporters, who were in the majority, had been well primed to oppose all of Jackson's substantive platform proposals and most of Gary Hart's. At the thumbs-down signal from the Mondale whip, they would vote them down with little or no debate. The Jackson forces were clearly outnumbered and outmaneuvered. Jackson staff member Carolyn Kazdin told me that the Jackson campaign failed to get a progressive farm policy even debated by the committee because she was not familiar enough with the rules that governed debate.

An example of the overwhelming odds the Jackson campaign was up against was reflected in the committee hearing on Middle East policy. Jackson delegate Herbert Daughtry spoke passionately for a "balanced policy which supports the security of the state of Israel within internationally recognized borders and an independent state for Palestinians, with a commitment to live in peace with mutual respect for each other's rights." The Jackson position also opposed the Democratic party draft proposal to move the American embassy from Tel Aviv to Jerusalem, a proposal that many in the progressive Jewish community saw as pandering to the Zionist vote.[35] Jackson's proposal was killed by a vote of 51 to 4. Daughtry later tried to protest the cutting off of debate on a proposal put forward by a Hart delegate who described herself as a Holocaust survivor, which called for the United States to encourage Israel to freeze its West Bank settlements. When he was ruled out of order, Daughtry left the meeting in protest.[36]

The Jackson forces did manage to coalesce with Hart delegates, many of whom were equally outraged by the proceedings, to get general language in the final document that reflected the Jackson campaign's concern for racial minorities and the poor, the urgency of taking immediate steps to reverse the nuclear arms race, and a more enlightened policy with regard to South Africa and the African continent in general.

Although they may have raised consciousness, such changes did nothing to reverse the Democratic party's headlong rush to the right. The party was willing to change "illegal aliens" to "undocumented workers," but it refused to include in its platform opposition to the onerous Simpson-Mazzoli immigration bill. Jackson forces had fought hard to incorporate opposition to this bill in the platform. Resigned to an unequal fight, Jackson forces managed to emerge from the platform hearings with four "minority reports," which were brought to the convention floor. (Minority reports required 25 percent of the platform committee's vote.) These included a plank calling for "substantial real reductions in the military budget," as opposed to the increases proposed by both Hart and Mondale; support for affirmative action *with quotas* (Democratic party regulars had reversed their earlier support of quotas); a call for the United States to adopt a "no first use of nuclear weapons" pledge; and a plank calling for the elimination of runoff primaries and "all other impediments to the right to vote."[37]

Between the disaster of the platform hearings and the Democratic convention, Jackson campaign aides beat furiously at the doors of the Mondale campaign for some guarantee from the party's obvious designee that Jackson's majority black constituency would get *something* from the party for the loyalty it had shown. A jobs program for the hard-core unemployed was the least they felt the party could offer. Party regulars remained stone-faced. In a meeting to discuss the jobs proposal, black Mondale and Jackson supporters almost came to blows over the tension created by the party's intransigence.[38]

As the Democratic Convention approached with Mondale the obvious winner and still no signs of concession from the party, the Jackson campaign attempted to get delegates pledged to Hart and Mondale to vote with Jackson delegates on the four minority platform planks. The Democratic party's women's caucus, they assumed, would be the logical pool of voters for such progressive issues as peace, voting rights, and affirmative action. All of the gender-gap studies had noted the disparity between women and men on just such issues.

Several meetings were held between prominent female Jackson supporters and women associated with the Hart and Mondale campaigns and with the National Women's Political Caucus to try to find a way of shaping arguments on the minority planks that would appeal to women at the convention. The Jackson women reminded their colleagues that Jackson's strong and early support for a female vice president had provided the political leverage for Geraldine Ferraro's impending nomination. They pointed out that ending runoff primaries in the South would enhance women's abilities to achieve elected office. Without a pledge by the president not to be the first to use nuclear weapons, they explained, all other proposals on nuclear arms were absurd. Finally, women as well as minorities had been the primary beneficiaries of a strong affirmative action program.

At each of these meetings, the white women were urged to use the power of their name and the clout of their organizational machinery to back the Jackson platform planks in the interests of all women. After an urgent trip by Civil Rights Commissioner Mary Berry to the National Organization for Women (NOW) convention at the end of June, the organization voted to support three of the four platform planks.

For the most part, however, the white feminists remained politely cool to entreaties from the Jackson campaign. They had obviously made their deals with Mondale or Hart and were reluctant to jeopardize their positions with the white male hierarchy in order to support the Jackson platform.

On the eve of the convention, it was clear there was to be no public commitment of the party's white female leadership to the Jackson platform planks, or even a public outcry over the fact that Mondale had ignored black women in his search for a vice-presidential candidate. It was also clear that the whip system that both NOW and the Democratic Women's Caucus had set up in case of a floor fight over Geraldine Ferraro's nomination had been dismantled when Mondale's decision to back her was announced prior to the convention. The white women had achieved their goal—a female vice-president—and so the rest of the proceedings were to be mere celebration.

At a late-night meeting of prominent Democratic women before the opening meeting of the Democratic Women's Caucus, the Jackson women made a last, impassioned plea for feminist solidarity on the platform planks. With an eloquence born of long suffering, they argued that the convention still had an important agenda to debate. The black women urged the leadership of the women's caucus to reactivate its whip system in support of the Jackson planks, or, barring that, to hold a joint press conference announcing that the women of the Democratic party supported the planks on peace, affirmative action, and voting rights.

The white women listened with repressed, or even open hostility. They had "paid their civil rights dues," one said, and would not be pressured now into a move that would divide the party. Still others told the black women to let them (the white women) "negotiate this out with the Mondale campaign."

The meeting adjourned with no resolution to the Jackson campaign's demands. The black women left angered and disheartened that, once again, when it came to a question of political power, the much-vaunted "sisterhood" of the white feminists was only rhetoric. At a meeting of the Women's Caucus the following day, Barbara Williams Skinner, Jackson's deputy campaign manager, told the crowd that Ferraro's nomination "may have closed the gender gap, but it did nothing to close the race and class gap."

When the final vote was taken, three of the four minority planks went down to defeat, while a compromise on the affirmative action plank was passed by voice vote. The Jackson campaign had been able to pick up an additional one thousand votes for its planks, but that was not enough to pass them. Some of these were the result of lobbying with delegates representing the Nuclear Freeze movement and the Central American Peace Campaign. No doubt some votes came as a result of the discussions at the Democratic Women's Caucus meeting. But since women made up half the convention, it was clear that many had failed to support the rainbow proposals.

Jackson delegates were outraged by the reception their proposals had received. At one point, New York State Jackson delegates threatened to walk out. Al Vann, head of the New York Jackson delegation, called the party's response "extreme arrogance." Congressman Ron Dellums was heard to say angrily, "They didn't need to do us in so badly!" A delegate from Michigan, Christina Montague, told a meeting of the black women delegates, "I feel very bad that we were left out. My feeling on it is almost that they didn't see us as humans." Gwen Patton, a delegate from Alabama, exclaimed: "If Mondale cannot buy into our value system—which is not for sale—then the hell with Mondale. I am very very serious about that. This convention was a circus." Still another said, "Four years of Ronald Reagan to me is no more devastating than one more day of humiliation from Mondale."

The investment of Jackson blacks in the campaign and their sense of betrayal by the party were poignantly revealed in a meeting of New York State delegates when Al Vann, the soft-spoken but tough Brooklyn assemblyman and longtime community leader, choked up in the middle of a sentence about how the Jackson campaign was "directing our young people," and began to cry. He stopped talking for several minutes. When he started again he tried to explain his emotions: "It's just that our people have been struggling so long and so hard," he said.[39] The Democratic party platform that was finally passed was, in the words of Joseph Lowery, president of the Southern Christian Leadership Conference, "a cruel political game that engages in dangerous flirtation with flim-flam operations."[40]

Winning by a Different Name

Even before the vote was taken at the convention, Jackson had warned the Rainbow Coalition leadership that "the threshold for raising the agenda in the Democratic Party is even higher than the threshold for running. Unless you get 25 percent of the vote in the Platform Committee, you can't even raise the agenda on the floor as a minority report. So, two-thirds of our delegation has been locked out of this convention [referring to the delegates he claimed were denied him by unfair party rules], and the rest of us have been shut up."

But Jackson understood that whether the Rainbow Coalition won or lost votes on the platform was not the final measure of what the campaign had been about. He counseled his campaigners, "Their definition of winning should not be our definition of winning. . . . Our's was the poorest campaign with the richest message." And he continued, "We must [continue to] set the agenda so that we will not be judged so much by whether we won the vote, but by whether or not we raised the right issues. It's better to lose the vote and raise the agenda, than to win the vote and lose the agenda."[41]

The words were reminiscent of another presidential candidate, Eugene Debs, who had once fought the class rule of the two-party system. Debs had declared: "I would rather vote for what I want and not get it, than vote for what I don't want and get it." By their definition, Jackson said in the same speech, "we're undesirable. But if you were to ask the people—and not the party bosses—whether we should mine the harbors of Nicaragua, they'd say, 'No!' And if you ask the people if they'd like normalized relations with Cuba, they'd say, 'Yes!' And if you ask the people whether we should be investing in South Africa, they'd say 'No!' So we have an obligation to set the agenda."

Because he had been in touch with "the people" all over the country, and in many parts of the third world, Jackson understood perhaps better than most of his supporters that the debate made possible by his campaign had consequences that were far more important in the long run that what it was able to get written into the Democratic party's platform in 1984. The campaign's most significant legacy would lie in the removal of political blinders among sectors of the population that had never before been involved in national politics, in the political sophistication developed on issues by a new generation of political leaders, and in the currents of political hope it stirred throughout the world.

While the campaign unquestionably gave blacks a new sense of self-worth and political efficacy, it had other long-ranging implications for the development of new political alliances. Significantly, within months after the close of the Jackson campaign, the leadership of the country's two largest peace organizations—the Nuclear Freeze movement and SANE—made overtures to Jackson and the Rainbow Coalition. They had been among the groups that had taken the "lesser of two evils" approach in the Democratic primaries. By 1986, significant leaders of the more progressive trade unions—the Machinists, the Communications Workers of America, and the American Federation of Government Employees—were moving toward the Rainbow Coalition.

By forcing a debate on issues the Democratic party wanted to suppress, the Jackson campaign exposed the racial and class interests to which it was beholden, and it demonstrated to much of the third world that there was "another America" that was in the ascendancy—an America that wanted to live in peace, that believed in self-determination and mutuality in international relations. Jackson's call for opposition to the Marcos regime in the Philippines and the Duvalier regime in Haiti may not have had a direct affect on the liberation movements in those countries, but his prescience in detecting the historical currents at work in the world were borne out when, two years later, those regimes fell, creating new contradictions for U.S. imperialism reflected in both the Democratic and Republican parties.

Thus, the importance of an insurgent electoral campaign run within the two-party framework should not be measured in traditional terms, but viewed in terms of the wider political climate it affected. Was the debate broadened? Were the ideological differences between the candidates sharpened? Were constituencies that lacked access to political power emboldened to new levels of activism? Was the right slowed in its attempt to achieve complete domestic and global hegemony? Though the Jackson campaign's successes appeared to be minimal, most who did the judging were looking in the wrong places and choosing the wrong time frame.

9

Peoples' Power versus Backroom Deals: The Challenge to Party Rules and Voting Impediments

Whether they are Black or white, the ability to cast a vote every four years to help determine which millionaire will represent them does not bring poor people flocking to the polls. Since their votes are ineffective, their real political power is not increased by voting, and consequently their motivation to continue voting is lowered still further. . . . We in the Movement maintained a rock bottom concern for democracy. . . . We maintained a concern that civil liberties would become more than just words on paper, a concern that the Bill of Rights be truly implemented as the basic document of American freedom.[1]

—C. T. Vivian

The period leading up to the 1984 presidential election witnessed an unprecedented drive by religious organizations, liberal foundations, and labor unions to flood the registration rolls with new voters. These registration crusades were stimulated primarily by liberal alarm over the right-wing takeover of the federal government. The theory that lay behind the drives was that if those who stayed away from the polls could be induced to come out, they would vote for the more liberal of the two parties, since it was

254

known that nonvoters were generally poorer than the voting cohort. Not a few liberal funders saw voter registration drives as a way to contain potentially explosive class anger. William Bondurant, head of the Mary Reynolds Babcock Foundation, told a group of such funders that voter registration drives had to be seen as a way "to help maintain an evolutionary society, rather than fuel a revolutionary one."[2]

In using his campaign as the catalyst for a voter registration campaign, Jackson himself made a similar point. But the Jackson campaign differed in one dramatic respect from the various nonpartisan registration campaigns: in seeking not simply access to the polling booth, but political power, the campaign was forced to challenge the internal rules that governed participation in the Democratic party and the presidential nominating process.

Jackson's challenge to party rules and voting impediments was perhaps the least understood but most important of his campaign strategies, raising profound philosophical questions about the meaning, character, and extent of American "democracy." In challenging the rules, Jackson was challenging the value system that undergirds the present interest-group framework of electoral politics. In this model, based on the "economic theory of democracy," classically articulated by Joseph Schumpeter in the 1930s, individuals are seen as self-interested, atomized "consumers," who seek to maximize pleasure by attaining material goods. Like the market, the electoral arena is merely a mechanism for aggregating people's individual interests and for regulating supply (political programs) and demand (political power). The parties neither assume that people want to be involved in making decisions that affect their lives, nor do they encourage it. In fact, parties are constrained to enlarge the electorate only selectively, and to the extent that it will maintain them in office or help them regain it.

Prior to and during the 1984 elections, the Democratic party, while paying lip-service to the importance of voter registration, failed to exploit the voting-rights question as a major political issue and did everything it could to avoid registering new voters, giving credence to Walter Karp's theory that Democratic party leaders would rather forfeit the presidency than take the chance of having their own power usurped by an insurgency of new voters from below.[3]

The 1960s reasserted the traditions of social protest that conventional social science had declared dead, shattering the assumption put out by elites that the electorate was basically non-ideological and uninterested in politics. Survey-based research in the 1970s concluded that voter rationality and participation was a function of political context—that people would participate and vote consistent ideological positions if adequate choices were available and if they perceived that their participation made a difference.[4] Before the Jackson campaign, however, this survey finding had not been tested at a national level, since no real choice was offered the voters. Because African Americans have been so consistently denied even the trappings of democratic participation, the Jackson campaign's challenge to party rules and voting impediments demonstrated that, when offered a real choice, the black community is capable of demonstrating a level of political activity, participation, and sophistication that defies all elite assumptions about the disinterest of the American public in the functions of governing.

The Jackson campaign's attack on the rules was a logical outgrowth of the efforts of the Mississippi Freedom Democratic party in the 1960s to challenge the Jim Crow delegate selection process then in effect in the South. It raised this kind of challenge to a higher level by demonstrating that the entire party—North and South—exercised a similar kind of exclusionary process, based on both race and class.

The campaign's attack on party rules and voting impediments centered on three sets of problems: those that limited the participation of the majority of people in the electoral process, but were particularly discriminatory for the poor and working classes (voting impediments); those that diluted or nullified the effectiveness of individual votes (party rules and practices); and those that made it difficult for persons without the backing of large financial interests to run for office (the runoff primary).

The Challenge to the Caucus System

The caucus system is one of the most obvious devices parties have developed to limit participation in the electoral process to those who are already organized and know the rules of the game. Since caucuses are meetings of party members, only those who are regularly active in the party know how to maneuver in them. Before the 1984 elections, party regulars had organized to bring back the caucus system to all but twenty-five states, with the express intent of limiting the participation of nonactive members and newcomers. The trade union machinery was to be the means of controlling the electoral mobilization in order to secure the nomination for Walter Mondale.[5]

In order to turn out votes for Jackson, the campaign found itself having to engage in a level of voter education that strained its small coffers, taxed its inexperienced staff, and pitted it almost inevitably against organized labor in a struggle over democracy in the party.

Typical was the experience of campaign workers in Detroit. Caucus sites were set up, not in the usual polling places, but by zip codes, many of them in union halls where voters were required to cast an open ballot in front of a union official. Because it was a caucus system, the number of polling sites was reduced from approximately 1,000 during a normal election to 18, with the result that many people were required to travel out of their immediate neighborhoods in order to attend the caucuses. Moreover, the caucus was open only from 9:00 A.M. to 3:00 P.M., which meant that workers would have to take off from work in order to vote. The party did little to inform the potential electorate about where they were to go, depending instead on union phone banks to get out workers who would presumably vote for Mondale.

One of the first problems encountered by Jackson campaign workers was that of getting information to their identified voters on the location of the caucus sites. This was done a few days before the election by dropping fliers (which had to be individually printed for each caucus site) in the neighborhoods and at churches within each of the caucus districts. This was a logistical nightmare requiring masses of volunteers with cars in a city without mass transportation.

Getting people to the right place was only the first hurdle, however. Between 1980 and 1984, caucus rules had been changed by party leaders. Community organizers associated with the Association of Community Organizations for Reform Now (ACORN) had mastered the rules the last time around and were successful in beating the party bosses at their own game. This time, however, they explained in a memo to their low-income constituency, "It has taken us more than 8 months of reading the rules to figure out how they are designed to steal the Michigan caucus."

ACORN organizers, who were supporting Jackson, explained

that the number of delegates assigned to each caucus site was given a certain weighted vote based on population and the percentage of the Democratic vote in the past election. "This system steals the votes of low and moderate income Democrats who are concentrated in the inner-city," they said. "It gives extra votes to the suburbs, areas that may end up voting for Reagan in November," and "it means for the Jesse Jackson campaign that no matter how many new people he brings to the polls, he can't win his fair share of delegates."

On election day in Detroit, people spilled out of the too few caucus sites in lines that stretched for blocks. Energized by the Jackson candidacy, they turned out in numbers far exceeding the "expectations" of party officials. In Detroit's northwest district, the caucus site was finally closed at about 4:00 P.M. while hundreds of furious people remained outside. They had been unable to cast their ballots, having waited in line for three and four hours.

In Texas, voters were required to go to two different caucus meetings in one day—one in the morning and the other at night—in order to have their votes count. Those who could come only at night were not allowed to participate. The barrier posed by the two-caucus requirement, to working people, people with disabilities, the elderly, or those with family members to take care of is obvious. In spite of these impediments, blacks flooded the Texas caucuses. Expecting only about fifty attendees (as in the past), party officials were stunned when five hundred showed up. They did not have enough materials to handle the influx, and after hours of waiting, many voters got discouraged and left without casting a vote. There was evidence that Democratic party officials discouraged participation at some sites by telling people to leave because Jackson had already won all of the delegates.

Although there was not much the Jackson campaign could do about the caucus system, Jackson lashed out at it in his public appearances. "The caucus system is corrupt, it's dangerous, it's abusive," he told an ABC television interviewer. On another occasion he said: "In Arkansas Mondale got 36 percent [of the popular vote], I got 34 percent, Hart about 24 percent. Mondale won the state by only 400 votes. Mondale gets 20 delegates, Hart 9, I get 6. That's perverse arithmetic."6

In Louisiana, Jackson supporters managed to beat back an attempt by the Louisiana legislature to cancel the state's primary election. The governor had used the excuse that it was too costly, but Paul Volteau, the black sheriff of Orleans County, charged that the move was motivated by "a fear that Jackson forces would mount a serious challenge to their hand-picked candidate."[7] The primary was held, and Jackson won the state.

In Virginia, information about the caucuses and instructions on how to work them was given out over several church radio stations owned by Bishop Willis. As a result, blacks flooded the caucus meetings and Jackson won the popular vote in the state. In Seattle, sophisticated Jackson organizers used the complicated and undemocratic caucus procedures to groom a new generation of community leaders—largely low-income people—in the ways of machine politics, but with a progressive agenda. Although they got only one delegate to the convention, the education they received as a result of going through the process enabled them to take over the Democratic party in the state's largest Democratic district by November.

But Virginia and Seattle were exceptions. For the most part, the late start of the Jackson campaign, the inexperience of its organizers, and the lack of financial resources available to reach people put the campaign at a disadvantage in the caucus process. For this reason, Jackson pressed for the adoption of direct primaries and for the principle of one person, one vote as the only way to guarantee just elections. In a letter to Charles Manatt, chair of the Democratic party, written toward the end of May, Jackson stated:

> There is a difference in the democratic participation of the people in primaries and caucuses. That is one of the reasons why we oppose the caucus method of delegate selection. Of the approximately 12.5 million people who have participated in the Democratic Party's primary process and voted for one of the three remaining candidates, about 12 million have voted in the 21 primaries, while only about 500,000 have voted in the 30 caucuses held so far. Caucuses exclude the masses of Democratic voters.[8]

The Jackson Challenge to Delegate Apportionment Rules

There were four sets of rules in effect in 1984 that diluted or nullified the political effectiveness of the individual vote. One of these was the winner-take-all rule, effective in some states, which awarded all of a district's votes to the top vote-getter. The results of the voting in New Jersey where this rule was in effect demonstrated the gross disparity between the democratic ideal and the reality of the system. In New Jersey, Mondale won 45 percent of the total, Hart 29 percent, and Jackson 24 percent. Mondale won 99 of New Jersey's 107 delegates, Jackson 8, and Hart none at all. In California, it was the reverse. There, Hart won just 3 percent more votes than Mondale, but got 205 delegates to Mondale's 72 and Jackson's 29.[9] Jackson won the vote in Mississippi, with 19,000 votes to Mondale's 8,000 and Hart's 6,000, but got only 23 percent of the delegates.

The second type of rule fought by Jackson was one that awarded bonus delegates to the top vote-getter. This was a compromise between strict proportional voting and the winner-take-all rule, but still resulted in skewing the relationship between popular votes and delegate counts.

The third rule opposed by Jackson campaign was the threshold rule, which applied in those states that did not follow the winner-take-all rule. Here, in order to qualify for any delegates, a candidate first had to get 20 to 25 percent of the popular vote in a given district. Jackson districts that turned out even 19.5 percent of the popular vote, therefore, would not be awarded a single delegate. The bias in all these rules against minority candidates is clear.

The fourth party rule opposed by the campaign was the provision for a group of "super-delegates"—party and elected officials presumably unpledged to any candidate—to be added to the list of elected delegates by party officials after the popular balloting was over. Earlier reform efforts had sought to eliminate or reduce this category, but the Hunt Commission of 1981 had raised the percentage to be appointed in this manner from 12 percent of all delegates to 14 percent. It was to be the means of assuring control of the party by "regulars." In 1984 the number of super-delegates was 568, enough to put Mondale over the top on delegates, thus winning the nomination.

The Democratic Party Response

Jackson attempted to get these rules changed even before the primaries and caucuses began, by publicly calling attention to their unfairness and requesting meetings with the national and state party chairpersons in the hopes of getting some adjustment.

He warned that if the meetings failed to produce changes, his campaign would file challenges to state plans with the national party committee. If that too failed, he said, there could be a floor fight over credentials.

In January, representatives of Mondale's campaign, hoping to avoid a public fight that might place their candidate in an unfavorable light with regard to the issue of "fairness," met with Jackson and endorsed a compromise that called for lowering the threshold rule from 20 percent to 10 percent. The endorsement of a compromise represented a major concession, reported the *New York Times*, for the Mondale campaign had previously considered the party rules inviolate. Denying suggestions that he had reneged on an agreement made with both campaigns, Charles Manatt refused to endorse even the compromise, claiming it was too late to change the rules in the middle of a campaign.[10]

It was known that Manatt and the party were fearful of just such a challenge from Jackson. Manatt had fought to prevent Iowa and New Hampshire from changing the dates of the 1984 caucuses and primary. He was said to fear that any changes in the campaign calendar would open the door to Jackson to mount a much broader challenge to party rules and to use that issue to energize the campaign on racial grounds.[11]

Denied by the national party, the Jackson campaign was forced to challenge the rules on several different fronts: in the media, at the state level through legal suits and lobbying of state parties, and by threatening fights within the rules and credentials committees as well as threatening to withhold support from the front-runner should the campaign's challenges not be answered. Halfway through the primary campaign, the flurry of challenges was so intense that the *Christian Science Monitor* was moved to comment that "the Democratic race for the White House has begun to resemble a lawsuit as much as a political race."[12]

Having to mount a continuing challenge on so many fronts was taxing on both the campaign staff and legal counsel, who were trying to master a whole new set of electoral laws. As a result, some challenges that could have been made were neglected. For example, a campaign coordinator in Washington State discovered that the Mondale campaign had failed to file an affirmative action plan with the national committee in violation of the rules. She informed Jackson's national campaign office and told them to investigate every other state to see if the same thing had happened. If not, the credentials of all of Mondale's delegates could have been challenged. She was told, however, that the national staff could not handle it, and so the opportunity was missed.[13]

By late spring the national press was rife with stories headlining the "injustice" and "unfairness" of party rules and procedures and even Hart was getting into the act of charging unfairness. In late April Jackson sent a letter to party chairpersons estimating that, on the basis of the popular vote he was getting, he would be responsible for between 5 and 6 million votes in November, and asked that each state "determine a method for Jackson delegates to reflect more fairly our proportional share of the popular vote in your recent primary or caucus." Feeling the pressure of a bad press, Manatt sent a letter to the state chairmen asking them to accommodate Jackson. Few did, and in late May Jackson again met with Manatt to demand his fair share of delegates. This time he was armed with statistics that demonstrated that the popular vote to delegate count gap was widening.

"When we last met," he said, "I had earned about 18 percent of the popular vote and was receiving only about 7 percent of the delegates—an 11 percent gap." Since that time, he continued, "the Jackson campaign has increased its popular vote to about 21 percent, but awarded only 9 percent of the delegates—a 12 percent gap." Jackson stressed that this was a total violation of the essence of democracy—one person, one vote. He also argued that it was not good for the party "because it is structured discouragement to mass political participation—the key to a Democratic victory in November." He enumerated the numbers of states in which Mondale had received more delegates than the percentage of the actual vote and went on to show with figures and facts how the people's interest in democracy was being thwarted.[14]

By June, Jackson had convinced the Congressional Black Caucus (CBC), many of whose members supported Mondale, and who had done well themselves in playing by the established rules, that there was indeed a problem with the rules. New York state representative Charles Rangel, a Mondale backer, told reporters:

> Not only are the issues valid that Rev. Jackson raised, but I think they were designed to be unfair for those candidates that would not be considered front-runners. The number of votes Rev. Jackson has truly earned and in fact received makes this something that should be addressed by every Democrat, and that includes Fritz Mondale.[15]

The CBC reportedly agreed to ask the party to give more representatives to Jackson, who could "work for his positions in committee sessions and floor fights but could not be voting delegates"—a compromise that black Mondale supporters figured would satisfy both sides of the sticky situation they now found themselves in.[16]

Such a compromise was not acceptable to the Jackson campaign, which finally brought its challenge into the rules and credentials committees of the convention. At the end of June, the Mondale-dominated rules committee offered a series of concessions to the Jackson campaign's challenge designed, it was reported, "to insure that Jackson voters don't lose interest in the Democratic nominee." The committee urged the convention to agree to the formation of a "fairness commission" to study the rules and propose changes for the next election. It put the Democratic party on record against "structural barriers to voter participation" and for dismantling "unfair and antiquated systems." It added some Jackson backers as officers of the convention and allowed the Jackson supporters a forty-minute debate on a resolution calling for additional delegates for Jackson in proportion to his primary vote totals, before declaring the proposal out of order.[17]

The compromise was offered, reported Morris Udall, as a way to avoid "damaging the party and Mondale its likely nominee." Jackson, he said, has "immense potential" for affecting the November election because of his ability to either "bring [blacks] out to the polls . . . [or] sit on his hand and keep them home." He added: "If the impression is around that he [Mondale] handled this in a very weak fashion and didn't really come in and take charge of the political party it could be harmful. Jackson's got to be treated with some respect and he's earned it . . . but the nomination isn't going to be worth very much if it looks like the nominee is caving in too quickly, rightly or wrongly."

Jackson responded to the compromise with a reiteration of the themes he had hammered away at throughout the campaign:

> We cannot be so afraid of Ronald Reagan that we leave our backs wide open to the Democrats. . . . That would push us back into the bag of allowing the Democrats to take us for granted on the assumption we have nowhere to go and we'll be driven by Reagan mania. That's not right. We'll be driven by a quest for justice, which is a positive motivation, and not by Reagan mania which is a negative stimulus. I

do not want four more years of Ronald Reagan, but I do not want four more days of disrespect from the Democrats.[18]

The difference between the political expediency of party regulars—the need to control the party at any cost, to appear to be "in charge"—and Jackson's concern for justice and an involved electorate illustrates dramatically the gulf that lay between the two camps over the basic meaning of democracy in the U.S. political system.

The Challenge to the Runoff Primary

The third major area which the Jackson campaign charged limited democracy was the various administrative procedures used by southern whites to get around the provisions of the Voting Rights Act, such as at-large elections, gerrymandering, annexation, and continuation of the runoff primary. "There's been an attempt to make the voting rights issue a black issue," he told his supporters, then added that it "is not just a black issue, it's a national issue."

When the Voting Rights Act is enforced and blacks vote in large numbers, progressive whites win, Hispanics win, Indians win, peace activists win, environmentalists win. In other words, the Voting Rights Act is the trigger for the entire progressive coalition. A massive black vote means the ability to change governors, congresspersons, senators. Do not attempt to isolate it.[19]

As the campaign approached the convention, the runoff primary became the centerpiece of the campaign's attack on infringements of the Voting Rights Act. A minority plank calling for its elimination was brought to the convention floor for a vote, and a lawsuit was instituted against it in Mississippi.

The little understood runoff, or dual primary, which had come into existence in the first two decades of the century, mandated in ten southern states that where no candidate in a primary received the majority of the votes, a second primary between the two top vote-getters was to be held. The reason cited for its usefulness was the assurance it provided the party that the "best candidate" would win. It was instituted, it was averred, to provide a way for factions in the one-party South to resolve their differences.

Behind such politically neutral rationalizations, however,

lurked the real reason for its establishment: to keep blacks from winning office, as even its own author, Edmund Noel, had admitted. Racial disparities in income and education make running twice to win once virtually impossible for most black candidates and their constituencies. In addition, whites in the South consistently vote against black candidates, while blacks do not vote exclusively on the basis of race. This gives the white candidate "the freedom to campaign and spend money in poor black communities while his opponent's skin color does all the necessary [negative] campaigning in the white community," explained Mississippi attorney Victor McTeer. Studies by the U.S. Attorney General have borne out this conclusion. Since 1965, blacks have lost in more than one hundred runoff elections after winning the first time around.[20]

Southern blacks had long known the effects of the runoff, but until the Jackson campaign there had been no effort to raise it as a problem of national concern. Jackson threatened to make the runoff the "litmus test" for his support of the Democratic party in the November election, causing considerable consternation in regular Democratic party circles. The issue raised strong emotions, not only among southern Democrats, but among northern liberals and blacks who aligned themselves with the party regulars. They feared that if the runoff were eliminated, white southern Democrats would bolt the party, leaving it a party of racial minorities and their (far fewer) white allies. "That's crazy for blacks to be concerned with keeping whites in the Democratic party if those whites can't vote for black candidates," said state representative Tyrone Brooks, Jackson's Georgia state coordinator.

> What does it matter to have white voters voting Democratic if it doesn't help us elect more blacks? I'm not concerned about whether whites leave the Democratic party. I'm concerned about representation for my people. There are many Democratic officials in this state who should be Republican anyway.[21]

Not all blacks agreed with Brooks, however. Those who were now in the leadership of such black majority cities as Atlanta, Birmingham, and Memphis were nervous that the elimination of runoff primaries could backfire on blacks in elections in which a white candidate won a plurality of votes against two or more black opponents.

In pressing the little studied and largely ignored issue of runoff primaries, the Jackson campaign was compelled to present evidence for the rule's racially discriminatory effects and the biased intent that lay behind the rule; and in order to seek allies for its fight on the convention floor, the Jackson campaign also pressed the feminists in the Democratic party to engage in their own study of the effects of the rule on women's chances for elective office in the South. White Democratic party feminists at first balked at becoming embroiled in a potentially divisive issue—one they felt would surely hurt their chances with Mondale of getting Geraldine Ferraro nominated vice-president. Jackson campaign workers, however, pointed to the fact that women have had the same problem as blacks in raising campaign monies, as well as getting the votes of men. There was every reason to suspect that the runoff primary—as Jackson had suggested—was not only racist but sexist and class biased. A quickly produced study undertaken by the National Women's Education Fund showed that, indeed, more women had lost runoff primaries than had won them.

While the runoff primary may not have been the most incontrovertible example of a discriminatory voting rule, the preponderance of the evidence was with the Jackson campaign. Far from being a politically neutral device—as almost all but the Jackson supporters asserted—the runoff primary became a test of the party's continued allegiance to a racist and classist system, and a measure of the extent to which certain blacks and feminists had sold out principle for the price of being a part of the old boy's club. It was Andrew Young's pathetic defense of the Mondale campaign's efforts to suppress the elimination of the runoff primary that won him boos and hisses from black delegates on the convention floor. The runoff primary, then, exposed the fault line that ran through the middle of black politics—dividing those who still sought "influence" and "favor" within the old rules of a racist capitalist system from those who were reaching for a new definition of democracy based on universal values of justice, informed participation, access, and the free exchange of ideas. That difference was best articulated by Jackson in an interview in January, when he stated: "I am far more concerned about public negotiations for parity for the locked out, for the Rainbow, than I am about private negotiations, private brokering for a position."[22] Jackson reiterated this at the convention. While the press and black Mondale delegates were talking about "leverage" with the front-runner, Jackson asserted: "At some point in time it moves beyond a question of leverage to a higher plane of actual respect and working for the common ground."[23]

Privilege for the Few versus Democracy for the Many

The Jackson campaign's fight to eliminate the runoff primary and other infringements on the voting and political participation rights of millions of Americans was in the end unsuccessful. While winning more delegates than any political analyst had predicted he would, Jackson did not get the 400-plus delegates he asserted were denied him by unfair party rules. He had won about 20 percent of the popular vote, but was awarded only 10 percent of the delegates. The campaign had managed to get general language about opposition to voting impediments written into the Democratic platform, but a resolution of the specific rules Jackson had challenged would have to await the deliberations of the Fairness Commission, which would not meet until after the November election.

If Jackson had been awarded his due under the principle of one person, one vote, the Democratic Convention would have had an entirely different ending, as would perhaps the entire history of the 1980s. With eight hundred instead of approximately four hundred delegates, Jackson would have gone into the convention with far more clout to bargain for some of the platform issues raised by his campaign. With the one thousand extra votes he got on the platform planks, the campaign would have had over half the convention votes—enough to force the Democratic party to actively debate, if not accept, Jackson's programmatic policies. Quite possibly, Mondale would have been denied the nomination on the first ballot and the Rainbow Coalition would have been in a position to be a real power broker. Blacks would have had to be taken seriously as the bloc that could make or break the candidate in the general election.

In the final analysis, the Jackson campaign's success could not be measured by tools that were designed for its failure. By using the campaign to demonstrate the injustice of party rules and discriminatory practices, Jackson forces began to awaken the American public to the lack of democracy that it had always taken for granted. That awakening was beginning to have an effect.

In May, the Mississippi state legislature voted to end dual registration—a practice that had kept blacks and poor whites from participating in the electoral process ever since the turn of the century. The reason for the change—"Jesse Jackson," said state senator Henry Kirksey. In South Carolina, the party moved to reduce the percentage a candidate would have to win in order to avoid a runoff primary.[24] In Massachusetts, Rainbow Coalition activists pressed their state's Democratic party to adopt a platform that addressed the issues of justice within the party, pressed their senatorial candidates to take a stand on voting-rights infringements, and emerged from the process a serious force in Democratic politics in the state, even though Jackson won only 5 percent of the vote there.

In spite of the Mondale campaign's iron grip on its delegates at the convention, a *Los Angeles Times* delegate poll indicated that a majority of delegates agreed with Jackson that the rules were unfair. By a margin of 4 to 1 they voted for the establishment of a fairness commission.

The most important effect of Jackson's crusade against party rules and voting impediments was in the new generation of political leadership the campaign spawned around the country—a leadership that would be far more politically sophisticated than that which had emerged from the civil rights and black power movements of the 1960s. One campaign worker explained the effect the Jackson campaign had in her area in this way:

> As a result of the Jackson campaign, people are now seeing how to translate their community activism into the political [electoral] arena to get their needs met. . . . By the same token, change has occurred throughout the country among grassroots people—people seeing their own capabilities for asserting leadership. The old role models are now gone.[25]

The new leadership would be sophisticated, not only in detecting the new face of racism, which still gnaws like a cancer at the heart of American democracy, but in the subtle innuendos of class, which cast their shadow within and between racial groupings. For many younger blacks, loyalty to the old pluralist interest-group framework in which blacks had sought to achieve "influence" in a racial caste system they felt they could not alter was shattered for good. Typical of the emerging leadership energized by the Jackson campaign is Gwen Patton, a Jackson delegate from Alabama, who said she had demonstrated against Andrew Young at the convention when he had spoken against the elimination of the runoff primary because "he doesn't understand. We're talking about maximum inclusion. Dual primaries, at-large elections—all these are ingenious schemes used to dilute the voting power of citizens of this country."[26] Patton later ran for the Alabama state legislature in the 1986 elections.

Through the Jackson campaign many whites were also made aware of their own disenfranchisement in a system they had been led to believe was the "best in the world." The democratic bug also infected older people who had never before been politically active. Frances Crowe, a peace activist from Massachusetts, told me at the end of the primary season:

> Most people I know spend their time getting drugged or playing. I've noticed in the last few months a new kind of energy. I went to a nonviolent training to prepare people for action at a nuclear weapons company recently. Twelve people were there, most of them older—between 40 and 76. I asked them what brought them there. They said Jesse Jackson had inspired them to *do* something about their condition.

This "new generation" of leadership would carry forward a "rock-bottom concern for democracy." Its voice would begin to be heard in the November elections in such places as Vermont, Alabama, Washington, New Jersey, and Kansas, and in countless cities and towns across the country. And this "new generation" would eventually challenge even the man who had led it to open its eyes.

The Future of Race in American Politics

> Race is part and parcel of the American political experience. It is one of the prime molders and shapers of political campaigns. In many cases, it is the unspoken and hidden negative factor in American politics, a negative factor that has been used against minority candidates, especially black candidates. How does one transcend race? How do you raise issues to a level of rare and profound sophistication? How do you downplay race? Do you stress your qualifications? Do you identify with the popular issues of the day? Do you ask and pose the difficult questions? How do you modify or how do you lessen the impact of race?[1]
>
> —Leslie B. McLemore

In no other country in the world, except South Africa, does the ruling class have as durable a mechanism for keeping itself in power as the American ruling class.[2]

Whenever blacks have become too "uppity," thus threatening both the symbolic and the economic bases of white male power, new interpretations of the basic equation between blacks and all that is debased, dangerous, and contaminated are generated. We saw this in the new interpretations given to the meaning of black power and the black poor by neoconservative intellectuals in the late 1960s and early 1970s and we see it again in the reactions of the white press and Democratic and Republican party leaders to the Jackson campaign.

Because it threatened to unmask the cultural strategems that have served to secure the public's assent to the continuance of white male power, Jackson's call to form a rainbow coalition of the rejected was not only politically but psychically dangerous to those in power. Jackson proposed to unhinge powerful sectors of the white united front—namely, white women, white labor, white farmers, white issue-constituencies, and those members of other ethnic groups who had identified with the dominant value system—and to unite them into an opposition bloc that rejected the racist values that are at the heart of the American imperial enterprise and have undergirded white identity.

This chapter examines the regeneration of cultural racism during and immediately after the Jackson campaign, the responses of the black and white electorate to this regeneration of cultural symbols, and the prospects for political realignment suggested by these events.

Racism and the Fourth Estate

To an unprecedented extent, the 1984 elections—and their outcome—were a mass media product. The power of the mass media as the chief mediator of political values and symbols and thus as the maker and breaker of candidates had risen steadily throughout the 1970s, reaching its near apotheosis in the election of former actor Ronald Reagan in 1980. Reagan's ability to carefully manage the images of himself that were allowed to reach the public, as well as Mondale's awkwardness before the cameras, played a major role in the public's response to these two men in the 1984 election.[3] Although Jackson was something of a master at using the press, he was playing on a much larger stage than he was used to—a stage whose spotlight could be turned off at the whim of an editor or network president, a stage whose lighting could be manipulated to make him appear (in a reversal of roles) the Iago to Mondale's Othello, or the Willie Loman in an American tragedy of his own making.

Since he was unable to purchase air time, Jackson's ability to establish himself as a "serious" candidate was totally dependent on his ability to attract the media's attention. He did this throughout the spring, summer, and fall of 1983 by creating the appearance of a genuine draft by the black community, generating in the white press intense public discussion of whether he would or would not run.[4]

Ironically, it was Jackson's ability to command the fervor of black audiences so necessary to attract the white media that also proved to be his Achilles' heel. The more be became pegged as the candidate of the black masses, the less seriously was he taken as a candidate of the white electorate.

From the very beginning, Jackson was saddled with the double-edged stereotype of the black man in racist mythology: either he was the entertaining but dull-witted Steppin Fetchit, whose job was to deliver the black vote to the white master, or he was the menacing Black Man Rampant, that fearful figure who haunts the nightmares of the white oppressor.[5] For the first two months of the campaign, so long as Jackson's legitimacy was limited to the black community, the first image tended to predominate, with just a hint of titillating menace. As New York Daily News columnist Earl Caldwell put it, Jackson was "a provocative sideshow—a show of the ghetto, by the ghetto, and for the ghetto."[6] For New York Times reporter Howell Raines, Jackson was a character out of a blackface melodrama. With his "bugle voice, bulging eyes and fierce bandito mustache," wrote Raines, he made a "Democratic field already regarded as uninspiring seem doubly dull." "As a protest candidate for whom victory is not the primary goal," pontificated Raines, "Mr. Jackson has the luxury of raising divisive ideological points."[7] In effect, Jackson was performing in a replay of the uptown entertainment downtown whites had once come to Harlem to get. No matter that the points Jackson was raising were life-and-death issues to millions of people, the press paid scant attention to them. Said Newsweek's Jack White, "He's covered as a nuisance. Nobody cares if he wants to scrap half the aircraft carriers—it's not going to happen. It's a Catch-22."[8]

The condescension with which Jackson was greeted by the white press was in stark contrast to his coverage by black reporters, a situation that sometimes caused the same paper to convey two completely different impressions of Jackson and the campaign. On the day Jackson announced his candidacy, for example, two articles appeared in the *New York Times*. One, by white reporter Howell Raines, appeared as the front-page story under the title "A Provocative Candidate." The article was filled with negative allusions to Jackson's "provocative and perhaps divisive role," the "combative potential of his brand of politics," his "aggressive" language.[9] The other article, by black reporter Ronald Smothers, entitled "Jackson Declares Formal Candidacy," was buried on the inside of the paper's second section. It was a straightforward, upbeat account of Jackson's announcement event. The article quoted from Jackson's eloquent speech and mentioned that he was accompanied by 110 supporters, who included representatives of white farmers, Indian and Hispanic groups, and white peace and environmental activists, as well as clergy and black politicians.

From the beginning, then, coverage of the Jackson campaign exposed and at times exacerbated the difference between the way in which white media institutions and their black reporters viewed events in the black community. Said *Philadelphia Inquirer* associate editor and columnist Acel Moore, who is black:

> If you had asked all white editors at the beginning if Jackson could make a creditable showing, most would have said that he was just a preacher who talked in rhymes, that he couldn't deal with complex issues. Black reporters who had covered him over the years knew that he was a skilled orator, a scholarly man with a tough mind, and that he would surprise most white editors, reporters and the public.[10]

Essence editor Audrey Edwards was more blunt:

> It was probably to be expected that most of the media coverage of Jesse Jackson's campaign would be, in a word, racist. Only an arrogant white press, influencing an arrogant, foolish white America, would continue to think that Black Americans either can't read or can't read between the lines.[11]

The problem Jackson faced in dealing with the white media was familiar to blacks who have aspired to public office—particularly if they were the first to break the color barrier. Not only were their "credentials" continually trivialized, but it was hard to escape the characterization that they were running simply as "the black candidate." It was a familiar racist tactic, as Henry (Mickey) Michaux, who had run for Congress in North Carolina in 1982 pointed out:

> My announcement contained the only reference that I ever made to race. I did not have to make any references to race, because the

Newspaper said, "Mickey Michaux, black attorney from Durham, North Carolina, seeking to become the first black congressman. I mean every newspaper, every T.V. story. The media make an issue of race.[12]

The affixing of the word "black" to the office to which he aspired functioned to predetermine Jackson's constituency in the mind of the white electorate. As Jackson himself pointed out, the press never referred to Hart as the "white Coloradan senator," or to Mondale as the "former white Vice President."[13] Black politicians differed on how to handle this dilemma. One strategy was to make no reference to race at all in an attempt to win white middle-class voters on the pure merits of one's credentials, using a vague emphasis on "progress" and a low emphasis on economic justice issues. Tom Bradley used this strategy when he ran for mayor of Los Angeles, as did Wilson Goode in Philadelphia and Andrew Young in Atlanta. Others had found that white liberals liked to vote for the first black representative. They counseled using minimal references to the fact of race while running an issue-oriented campaign to appeal to the white left.[14]

Jackson made the best of a no-win situation. He needed to appeal to black pride and racial solidarity in order to mobilize a constituency that was disenchanted with electoral politics and alienated from mainstream institutions; but faced with a press that portrayed such appeals as "divisive," he also needed to assure whites that this presented no danger to them. His concept of the Rainbow Coalition as a combination of ethnic groups, issue groups, and entitlement groups made a place for whites in his campaign. In his announcement speech, he also sought to head off the race-baiting that he knew lay ahead of him:

I seek the Presidency because I want to affirm my belief that leadership is colorless and genderless, and that the sole hallmark of a true leader is not the skin color he or she received from God, but the ability of the person to bring competence, compassion, and fairness to the sacred trust that the people elect their officials to discharge.[15]

Jackson's message that he was in the race to win, not simply to protest, and that he sought a majority constituency was, however, drowned out in the continuous attention the press paid to his race. He needed something that would positively attract the nonblack voter—that would catapult him to a level beyond the entertainment section of the nightly news.

Serious but Dangerous

The mission to Syria to release Lieutenant Goodman became that crossover vehicle. *Newsweek,* that maker of celebrities, while trivializing the skill with which Jackson had pulled off this "Syria primary," was nevertheless forced to concede its accomplishments:

> Jackson had: (1) initially put Ronald Reagan on the defensive and underscored the diplomatic impasse over his policy in Lebanon; (2) eclipsed his seven rivals for the Democratic presidential nomination, most notably Walter Mondale; (3) rallied—indeed, positively galvanized—his core constituency in black America; (4) reopened communication between the United States and the government of Syrian leader Hafez Assad, and, almost in passing, rescued a Navy aviator from captivity. "He knocked one out of four ballparks at the same time," sighed one presidential aide.[16]

It was after the Syrian mission, according to journalist William Henry, that Jackson's specific identity as a person, beyond the mere fact of his being black, began to register with white voters.[17] One would have thought that would have ended the skepticism of Jackson's abilities to run for the presidency and his characterization as the "black presidential candidate." It did not.

It was after the trip to Syria that the second, more virulent racist image began to predominate in the media. Jackson was no longer a titillating figure whose function was to deliver black votes to the white front-runner. Now he was a political leader who threatened to pull not only blacks but other sectors of the Democratic coalition away from candidates acceptable to the ruling class. Now he was someone to fear.

There were many who had reason to fear him: the Zionist leadership in the Jewish community, who feared any U.S. rapprochement with the enemies of Israel; Jackson's Democratic rivals; the Reagan administration, which had to keep black insurgency from getting out of hand; and not least, the white media, which had already decided that Mondale would be the Democratic nominee and was embarrassed by this apparent affront to its well-orchestrated predictions.[18]

The circulation of the B'nai B'rith Anti-Defamation League (ADL) memo among opinion makers earlier in the campaign no doubt helped to set the climate for the flurry of press insinuations that followed Jackson's international coup. According to William Henry, "Reporters operate more from intuition and extrapolation than from sweeping factual knowledge. If what they see before them or hear from people they trust, consistently suggests that some version of events is true, journalists will rarely have the time or persistence to check further."[19] With its mixture of insinuation, character assassination, and words taken out of context, the ADL memo had helped to establish a menacing persona for Jackson. After his trip to Syria, the underlying fear of black power and the racist stereotypes of "Arab terrorists" combined to produce a black candidate who threatened the racial harmony that was assumed to exist in the United States. One of the most blatant examples of this symbolism was a cartoon that appeared in the *Boston Globe* on 3 February 1984, which showed a grinning, monkey-faced Jackson wearing an Arab headscarf and holding up a giant money bag.

Moral Purity: A Double Standard?

More than anything else, however, it was the taint of moral corruption suggested by Jackson's "Hymie" slur that appears to have derailed potential white support for the campaign.[20] The willingness of whites to take this incident as the overriding measure of Jackson, the candidate, and of the campaign, raises questions about media intentions. There seemed to be more than an interest in getting at the truth or even the media's traditional penchant for controversy behind the press's handling of the "Hymie" remark. As Jackson pointed out, many other public figures had made statements of a similar nature and none had received such persistent grilling. For example, as a presidential candidate in 1960 John F. Kennedy referred to blacks as "niggers," but this never appeared in print even though the remark was transmitted to *Time* magazine's home office. Presidential candidate Lyndon Johnson used the same epithet in a shouted command to a secretary for one of the top TV networks during the Democratic convention of 1984, yet that remark never reached the public. President Nixon used an endless stream of viciously racist epithets in private conversation, but the National Security Council protected his privacy. In the 1976 campaign Jimmy Carter was not constantly hounded by the press after he apologized for saying that "there is nothing wrong with ethnic purity" being maintained in neighborhoods. The remark was extremely offensive to blacks, and although Carter eventually apologized for the language, he maintained his opposition to federally subsidized housing to provide for integration. Nor was Reagan asked to apologize for his Ku Klux Klan endorsement in 1980. And the more New York's mayor, Edward Koch, used ethnic slurs and jokes, the more he appeared to endear himself to white voters.

The manner and timing of the "Hymie" remark's release not only suggests a double standard among whites on the matter of moral purity—a double standard linked to their need, in a racist society, to project their own moral turpitude onto a debased "other"—but it also suggests, as one black journalist put it, a "get Jesse attititude" by the white press.[21]

The remark appeared in the thirty-seventh and thirty-eighth paragraphs of a *Washington Post* story by white reporter Rick Atkinson that ran on February 13, a full month after the remark was made in an off-the-record meeting with black reporters. The article, entitled "Peace with American Jews Eludes Jackson," was published shortly before the New Hampshire primary and right after Jackson had polled 16 percent among white New Hampshire voters. Throughout the next two weeks, reporters continued to open up their questioning of Jackson by asking him about the "Hymie" remark. Even after Jackson's apology, the press continued to refer to the remark in what appeared to be an orchestrated campaign to fan the flames of interethnic tension. Indeed, a black journalist with one of the country's major dailies told me that he had been pulled off the Jackson campaign for a while when he refused to keep inserting references to the "Hymie" remark into his stories long after it had ceased to be newsworthy.

Similar to the way in which the "Hymie" remark surfaced, Louis Farrakhan's gangster talk about black journalist Milton Coleman aired on radio on March 11, but did not come up in the press until the eve of the New York primary, two weeks later. The controversy this generated continued to build through the next ten days and into the Pennsylvania primary on April 10.

The Media and White Voters

Whether the campaign was deliberately orchestrated or simply the result of the white press's inherent racism and its need to create sensation in order to sell its product, the appearance of racial tension was the result, as a culling of some of the press headlines over the next four months reveal. Amid Jackson's attempts to explain his behavior and Louis Farrakhan's incendiary efforts to defend Jackson, political contenders in both the Democratic and Republican parties entered or were dragged into the fray.

From February through July, the press was full of claims that the country was being racially divided. As in an earlier period of rising black political demands, the term "white backlash" began to appear in the media again, with the clear implication that Jackson was responsible for it. "White Backlash Puts Democrats on Edge" (Evans and Novak); "Racial Rift: Is the Press Soft on Jesse Jackson?" (*Wall Street Journal*); "GOP Strategists Wary of Democrats," (*Washington Post*); "Bush Blames Democrats for Anti-Semitism in Race" (*Washington Times*); "Jackson as Polarizer" (*New York Times*); "The Racism in Jackson's Racism Claims" (*Los Angeles Times*); "Mondale Finds Woe at End of Jackson's Shattered Rainbow" (Mary McGrory); "Jackson 'Alliance' Reports Threaten Hart" (*Washington Post*).

In the first week of May Jackson appeared on the front covers of *Time* and *Newsweek*. The *Time* cover portrayed a large head of Jackson, his thumb upraised in a victory signal. It was surrounded by smaller black hands in postures of applause. The headline read: "Jackson Factor: Black Pride, White Concerns." Inside, the caption was "Pride and Prejudice: For Better, For Worse, Jackson Brings Race to the Forefront of the Campaign." While the *Newsweek* story was less provocative, the cover picture was even more so. The photographer had caught Jackson in an attitude of intense emotion, sweat dripping from his face, and his hand clenched like a claw. It was just the sort of picture to evoke subliminal fears in a white public already conditioned to suspect Jackson's motives.

Perhaps the most blatant form of race-baiting by a reporter was Marvin Kalb's question to Jackson on "Meet the Press. "Are you a black man who happens to be an American running for the presidency, or are you an American who happens to be a black man running for the presidency?" "No other candidate running for governor or mayor has ever had his patriotism questioned this way," commented *Newsweek's* Sylvester Monroe. The racial crossfires generated by such coverage affected the black reporters covering the campaign. Recalled Les Payne:

> The journalists had shared Jackson's predicament when, in the wake of the Coleman affair [Milton Coleman was the black reporter who had overheard the "Hymie" remark, told a white reporter about it, and then had been threatened by Louis Farrakhan as a traitor to his race] they themselves were repeatedly asked if they were reporters, or blacks first. "I have never heard anybody asked if you are a white first or a presidential candidate or journalist," says Mervin Aubespin, president of the National Association of Black Journalists and a staff writer for the Louisville *Courier-Journal*.[22]

A more subtle but equally damaging approach by white journalists was to ignore Jackson's outreach to constituencies beyond the black base—to simply assume that he was reaching only black audiences with his message. The following exchange occurred on NBC's "Meet the Press" shortly after Jackson's impressive 26 percent showing in New York State (just one percentage point below Hart).

> MR. LEWIS: Rev. Jackson, you've created a great interest and consciousness among black voters. I wonder if you think this interest will be sustained beyond this current campaign?

> REV. JACKSON: Number one, we keep saying just among black voters. I would have you know that we began to pick up votes in Iowa. In New Hampshire, there were eight candidates running; I came in number four. We began to pick up votes there. You don't win number two in New York City, over Hart by almost 100,000 votes, just with black votes alone. The Rainbow continues to grow, it continues to flourish.[23]

To be sure, the same effort to stereotype Geraldine Ferraro as concerned only with women's issues characterized the media's approach to the vice-presidential candidate. In the case of Jackson's candidacy, however, this attitude obliged the press to willfully ignore not only Jackson's overriding interest in building a rainbow coalition but also his success in beginning to forge that kind of coalition. Not only was it commonly assumed that he was unsuccessful with white voters, but in those instances when there was clear evidence of his success with whites, the media chose to look the other way.

For example, it was not until the campaign reached Tennessee at the end of April that articles in the *New York Times* and *Washington Post* credited him with having attracted a rainbow coalition.[24] Yet all along, from New Hampshire through New York and Pennsylvania, Jackson had been drawing the same kinds of crowds that he drew in Tennessee. The Vermont story should have been given headlines. There, Jackson won 15 percent of the popular vote in the final round of caucus voting in a state whose population is .22 percent black. Yet that story was virtually ignored by the national press. At the end of the campaign, as sociologist Acie Byrd was attempting to get data on Jackson's voter profile, he called ABC to ask them if they planned a story about Jackson's large white vote in California. Jackson received about 300,000 white votes there, which amounted to about 22 percent of his total. They replied that they were more interested in Jackson's winning 85 percent of the black labor vote than his white vote.

Over and over, whites who worked for the campaign found their stories ignored and their perspectives of no interest to the press. Occasionally, a single statement about some whites in the audience or a comment that Jackson was seen as an "attractive, forceful leader" by two out of three voters in a New York Harris poll was buried deep within other articles that depicted him as the candidate of the black community. Musing on this madness, a white New Yorker, Tom Kelly, wrote:

> Another of the signs and wonders of the season: Suddenly it's possible to change race, if only for a statistical moment. For example, by the time you read this I will have hied my congenitally off-pink self to a voting booth in the New York primary, voted for Jesse Jackson— more for his Rainbow Coalition, really—and been duly reported in the press as a percentage of the black vote."[25]

The *New York Times* appeared especially determined to cast the campaign as a "black only" campaign to the point of raising questions in headlines about Jackson's ability to form a rainbow coalition, leaving out or minimizing reports of events that were clearly "rainbow" events, and cropping or choosing pictures to exclude the nonblack people in Jackson's entourage.

Typical of such distorted coverage was the *Times* coverage of a particular Sunday in Philadelphia. On one of five campaign appearances that day in local churches, a white Germantown minister, who was an enthusiastic Jackson supporter, had gathered a genuinely multiracial overflow crowd to his church. The sanctuary and the church's gym were packed, and a predominantly white crowd lined both sides of the street leading up to the church, in this quiet, tree-lined neighborhood. In the chancel, a group of black, Latino, Asian, and white clergy and children flanked Jackson. The title of the minister's sermon was: "Can Whites Build a Rainbow?" Following the service, a press conference was held in the gym at which a multiracial, but predominantly white, group of forty-seven of the city's leading peace and community activists endorsed the campaign. Jackson was embraced by the white octogenarian founder of the Women's International League for Peace and Freedom as the cameras clicked.

The story that appeared in the *Times* the next day portrayed Jackson as having visited "black churches," while the picture accompanying the story showed a sea of black faces and arms reaching out to greet Jackson. No mention was made of the multiracial crowds, the sermon theme, or the endorsement press conference, which was clearly the highlight of the day's activities.[26]

Similarly, following Jackson's receipt of an award at the Riverside Church, one of New York City's most prestigious interracial churches, which sits atop the educational acropolis of Morningside Heights, the *Times* simply noted that Jackson received an award "in a Harlem church." When twenty predominantly white groups held a press conference in Atlanta for the very purpose of trying to dispel the image of the campaign as a "black campaign," not one representative of the press showed up. In Louisville, Kentucky, when the press failed to mention that there were whites working with the campaign (at least one hundred whites in the area were active organizers), campaign workers set up a one-hundred-rainbow advisory committee and held a press conference. People from every neighborhood in the city, as well as representatives from a large number of civic groups, were there. Although the press came, there was not one line in the newspaper and only one television station covered it.[27]

There was no national coverage of events that were purposely designed to enable people to make the connections across racial lines, such as the time the Jackson campaign brought white farmers into black neighborhoods in Omaha to distribute beef to poor inner-city residents, or an event that brought Jews and Arabs together in San Francisco. While Black Muslim minister Louis Farrakhan was receiving sensational front-page headlines as a surrogate speaker, no one was quoting those white surrogates who spoke for the campaign.

More sinister was the *New York Post's* invention of a racially charged battleground between Jackson, the "black candidate," and New York's mayor, Edward Koch, popular with whites and Jews. Although Jackson never mentioned Koch in his appearances in New York, the *Post* ran stories emphasizing a slogan Jackson had used in his victory speech in New York City: "New York, your time had come," and quoted the mayor as saying that Jackson's comment was "definitely polarizing the city." Journalist Wayne Barrett observed that the *Post's* strategy "has been to use Jackson to drive Jews away from this year's Democratic presidential nominee and next year's black mayoral candidate."[28] The *New Republic* cynically asserted that Jackson "is becoming an instrument for the destruction of the very dream created by the movement . . . the dream of an America free from every form of racial division, racial hatred, and racial injustice."[29]

In contrast, the black press invariably sought to impress its readers with Jackson's crossover appeal. One small article in *Jet,* for example, included eleven photos of Jackson. Only two showed him with black people, whereas out of the seventeen photos accompanying the May 7 *Time* and *Newsweek* stories, only one showed Jackson with nonblacks—Hart and Mondale.

The function, if not the intent, of the white press coverage was to limit the nonblack vote for Jackson. "In the minds and in the public utterances of many in the press," observed William Henry, "Jackson's candidacy had already been judged a failure after New Hampshire."[30] Whites and Jews who were not able to hear Jackson directly would never have known that the content of his speeches overwhelmingly focused on reconciliation of the racial tensions that divide people, and on the need to work for justice and peace in human affairs. Those who could not hear him were ignorant of the substantive policy questions addressed by the campaign on issues that the white working class would have found compatible with its own interests, or of the consistently high moral ground that Jackson called the nation to consider. Many, even pollster

Louis Harris, admitted that had Jackson been white, he would have won the nomination.[31]

The media played a similar role in the development of an electoral white united front during Harold Washington's mayoral campaign in Chicago by deliberately avoiding reporting on the positive support Washington received from whites. Manning Marable observed:

> When, on the 27th of March Black and white trade union leaders held a rally of over 13,000 black and white workers for Washington, the media provided scant coverage. One local television station editorially criticized Washington for not campaigning among white people. Yet some of Washington's most vigorous and vocal supporters were white working class leaders.[32]

Throughout the spring, summer, and fall, with a brief respite around the time of Jackson's convention speech, the media were full of stories speculating that Jackson would hurt the Democrats' chances with whites in November.[33] Even before the polls opened, mainstream journalists such as Richard Reeves were predicting that "the greatest voter segregation this Tuesday will be between blacks and whites."[34] True to their predictions, the November elections did indicate a massive racial polarization, with whites voting for Reagan by a ratio of almost 2:1. Immediately, the journalists declared that the black vote was now a liability from which the Democrats must distance themselves. The alleged white backlash had indeed materialized.

According to Tom Cavanagh, a researcher with the Joint Center for Political Studies, most social scientists differed with this interpretation. To be sure, there were significant shifts among white voters away from the Democratic party, particularly in the South. But, said Cavanagh, "most of the votes in the South, as elsewhere, were determined by the state of the economy and Reagan's military policies, not by race. The military bloc, for example, voted 85 percent for Reagan. I have yet to see any polling data that substantiates Jackson as a negative factor for the Democrats."[35]

Cavanagh views the racial-backlash theory as a self-serving rationalization put out by white politicians who want to see blacks play a less significant role in the party. "To some extent," he explained to me, "the reading of the election was a willful misreading." As in a previous era when the white-backlash theory was prevalent, the media were not interested in the interpretations of social scientists such as Cavanagh. Though he offered his data virtually none of it made its way into the public interpretations of the event. Nor did the media point out that the racial polarization indicated in the November elections was a product of the long-term alignment of racial forces, not a new phenomenon generated by blacks' entry into the presidential nominating arena. The racial polarization indicated by the difference between the proportion of whites and blacks who voted Democratic was actually less in 1984 than it was in 1980, 1972, and 1968. In the nine presidential elections since 1952, the majority of whites have supported the Democratic presidential candidate only once—Lyndon Johnson, in 1964. Both Kennedy and Carter owed their margins of victory to the black electorate.[36]

Racism and Democratic Party De-alignment

Since 1936, when the black electorate switched from Republican to Democratic, the Democratic party has enjoyed an undeserved reputation as the party committed to civil rights for racial minorities. In reality, it has conceded to black and other minority demands only reluctantly and usually under the threat of massive black electoral defection or militant disruption. It was A. Philip Randolph's threat to bring 100,000 unemployed black workers to Washington to surround the White House during the height of the fight against Nazism that brought about the banning of racial discrimination in the war industries; it was the threat of the Progressive party to lead blacks out of the Democratic party with a strong civil rights agenda in 1948 that led Truman to ban discrimination in federal employment and to desegrate the armed forces. It was the disruption caused by the civil rights movement to the potential investment climate in the South that brought about the Civil Rights Act of 1964 and the Voting Rights Act of 1965; and it was the shock to liberal America's image of itself brought about by the series of urban rebellions between 1964 and 1967, coupled with the need to unify the population for the war in Vietnam, that caused the Kennedy and Johnson administrations to initiate the most sweeping civil rights and poverty legislation since Reconstruction.

As a result of the concessions they were able to win from the

Democrats, the black electorate remained, with the exception of the Eisenhower years, the party's most loyal constituency, providing the margin of victory in close elections for Roosevelt in 1944, Truman in 1948, Kennedy in 1960, and Carter in 1976.

The Alliance Falters

The election of 1984, however, raised new and unsettling questions for blacks' continued loyalty to the Democratic party. That election may represent the final unraveling of the fifty-year-old New Deal electoral alignment. At the least it signaled a search among many of the Democrats' traditional constituencies for new forms of political leverage and representation, inaugurating what Walter Dean Burnham predicts will be an extended period of national political deadlock and drift.[37]

The loosening of black allegiance to the Democratic party was catalyzed by the party's abandonment of much of its ostensible concern for racial minorities, the poor, and the working class. While giving lip service to its New Deal heritage and mouthing the issue of "fairness," the party had voted to increase the military budget, accept cuts in social spending, oppose quotas to achieve affirmative action, oppose a pledge that the United States would not be the first to use nuclear weapons, oppose a jobs program for the hardcore unemployed and aid to the cities, and oppose even its prior commitments to full employment and national health care. According to the *Congressional Quarterly*, the party's platform was "economically the most conservative platform in the last fifty years." Precipitating factors in the rightward drift of the Democratic party's policy orientation were the population shift from the industrial Midwest and Northeast to the increasingly affluent and conservative Sunbelt and Southwest (a reverse of the population shift that brought the Democrats to power in the 1930s, resulting in what may be a long-term Republican electoral college advantage; the increasing upper-income class skew of the electorate, facilitated by the voter abstention of low-income voters; the decline of organized labor; the ascendancy within the party of a "new class" of white male politicians whose power derived from white, suburban, upper-middle-class districts; the increasing influence of organized business interests on policy formation and the selection of candidates; and, finally, a black-led insurgency within the party that sought reforms threatening both the war economy on which Democratic fortunes have been built and the power of "new class" white males to control the party in their own interests.[38]

During the 1984 election the Democratic party had to retain the loyalty of blacks without conceding anything of substance to them. In return for Jackson's willingness to campaign for the ticket and to refrain from inflammatory remarks that would "hurt the party," he was given a fairness commission, money for a handful of staff to engage in voter education and mobilization for the Democratic ticket, a position for a close aide (Ernie Greene) on the Mondale campaign staff, meetings between Jackson and southern Democratic party chairs, and the promise of support for Jackson campaign chairman Richard Hatcher's reelection to the vice-presidency of the Democratic National Committee (DNC).[39]

The concessions hardly seemed worth the effort Jackson and his supporters had put into the campaign. At that point, he could have declared himself unwilling to support a ticket that was so obviously contemptuous of black needs—indeed, the needs of the majority of poor and working people. Jackson might have led a walkout at the convention or a massive boycott of the November elections, or declared himself an independent candidate. In fact, there were many in the African-American community who were angered by the conciliatory posture he took and questioned his motives in deciding to support the Mondale/Ferraro ticket.[40]

Yet there were realities that Jackson had to take into account, as even many of his sharpest critics had to admit. First, to have led a walkout or a boycott might have subjected Jackson to the same fate as Martin Luther King and Malcolm X when they threatened to take their supporters beyond the line of accommodation and compromise. Given the reality of African-American history, Preston Wilcox has suggested that the choices offered in 1984 could easily be read as those between being "a dead man or remaining a nigger."[41]

Second, although the black community was moving to loosen its loyalty to the Democratic party, it was not in a position in 1984 to make a complete break with the only electoral vehicle it had known. The preelection survey showing that 59 percent of blacks would have supported Jackson had he run as an independent in 1984 represents considerable movement, but it does not yet suggest that an independent bid would have been politically successful. The same survey reported that only 13 percent of blacks favored the establishment of an independent party.[42] For a third-party effort to be viable, blacks, along with a majority of Latinos and a plurality of whites, would have to be willing to abandon the Democratic party.

Third, by August 1984 the Jackson campaign was physically and financially exhausted. Its supporters had neither the energy nor the money to mount a major independent drive. A campaign debt had yet to be retired, and after the convention most of its workers had to return to jobs, political posts, and families they had neglected during the nine-month marathon.

Thus, Jackson made a calculated bid to play the role of statesman, while using the Democratic party apparatus to extend his national visibility and the Rainbow Coalition's message beyond the primaries, with the intention of becoming a force to be reckoned with in the 1986 and 1988 elections. In a meeting of national campaign workers in August 1984, Jackson argued that by working for the ticket in November they would continue to educate people on the Rainbow Coalition's platform, register new supporters, and work for progressive state and local candidates in the interest of an ongoing rainbow movement.

It was hard, however, to convince members of the Rainbow Coalition that supporting presidential candidates who had so callously denied the peace, social-justice, and democratic demands of the Rainbow Coalition was worth the effort. In many places in the country, the remnants of the campaign leadership simply refused to participate in the charade of Democratic party politics, or gave only lackluster support to the ticket. In Washington State, members of the newly formed Rainbow Institute, which had grown out of the primary campaign, ignored the national elections and concentrated on getting their supporters into precinct-level positions in the state's two heavily Democratic districts with the intention of taking over the Democratic party from the bottom up.[43] In Alabama and Mississippi, many Jackson supporters stated, "we've survived four years of Reagan, and another four more years won't be all that bad." They demonstrated their disgust with the Democratic party by sitting out the November election.[44]

In Detroit, Jackson's campaign coordinator decided to become a Republican because, as he explained, the Republicans were at least more honest in telling blacks that they had to pull themselves up by their own bootstraps.[45] Nation of Islam minister Louis Farrakhan stated, "We see nothing in Reagan or Mondale to vote for," while the National Black United Front in Washington, D.C., circulated a pamphlet attacking Jackson's "sellout to the Democrats" and called for a "clean departure from the political manipulations and false pretenses of the American electoral system."[46] *Washington Post* columnist Dorothy Gilliam noted as early as July that thousands of people Jackson brought into the political process, as well as many others, were now questioning their loyalty to the party.[47] The degree of the black boycott of the presidential election is indicated in the discrepancy between the surge in black registrations between 1980 and 1984 and the black voter turnout. While black registrations had increased by 10.2 percent, black voter turnout increased by only half that much. With the exception of major urban centers such as Chicago, Philadelphia, and New York, the participation of blacks outside the South did not show much increase.[48]

The Democratic Party's Shift to the Right

The Republican party watched in glee as the old Democratic coalition came apart. They had helped it along by playing up the black-Jewish controversy and by joining in the chorus of voices portraying Jackson as a liability for the Democrats. After Mondale's devastating defeat in November, the hope of many black politicians that their loyalty to the Democratic party would be rewarded was dashed by the Democratic party bosses' need for a scapegoat. In the postmortems that followed the debacle, party leaders claimed that it was the party's allegiance to blacks and other special-interest groups (e.g., women, Latinos, gays, peace activists) that was to blame for the party's defeat. From now on, the party would have to reorient itself to appeal to the white males who had voted for Reagan.

There were, of course, other, far more plausible reasons for Mondale's defeat. By all rights, he should never have been nominated. He had won only 38.7 percent of the popular vote in the primaries. Almost no one in the party was enthusiastic about him; he was tied to the Carter defeat in 1980, and bombed with the media. With a platform that consisted of further cuts in social-service spending, higher taxes, and an increase in the military budget, he had no program that could energize the majority of the potential Democratic electorate.

Moreover, during the course of the campaign, the Democratic party had appeared to deliberately avoid expanding its base. Not only had the party alienated Jackson's black constituency, it did everything it could to make voting difficult. Stories were rife about people who went to the party in the fall of 1984 wanting to work to defeat Reagan and were turned away. Mondale/Ferraro literature was frequently unavailable, and there was little grassroots work done to get out the vote.

In spite of Reagan's landslide, the electorate did not move precipitously to the right in 1984. The Republicans lost two Senate seats and gained only fourteen in the House, eight of which had been held by southern "boll weevils" who were already Reagan supporters. Blacks provided the critical margin of support for the Democrats in three Senate races, and at least eight House races. The president won 59 percent of the popular vote, but Democrats won 62 percent of all the elections held. Rainbow Coalition members made a strong showing. A Democratic congressional candidate in Vermont—a strong peace and environmental activist—ran the best race against a long-term Republican incumbent that any Democrat has ever run against him; seven candidates, including Jackson's Vermont coordinator, were elected to the Vermont legislature, and one was elected to the Democratic National Committee. In Kansas, a young farmer—a former president of the state's American Agriculture Movement—ran for the U.S. Congress and won 23 percent of the vote in Bob Dole's heavily Republican district. In dozens of local and state races around the country, Rainbow Coalition candidates began to win seats in state legislatures, on city councils, on boards of education, and in a few mayoral races. In Los Angeles County, where Reagan won 59 percent of the vote, the "Jobs With Peace" referendum calling for cuts in the military budget to fund jobs programs and human services passed by 61 percent.[49]

Willfully misreading the electoral verdict that was rendered in November 1984, Democratic party leaders moved to disassociate themselves from the constituencies that had formed the backbone of their once touted "New Deal coalition." One of the first postelection signals of the party's turn to the right was its repudiation of the promise made by former party chairman Charles Manatt to the Jackson forces that Richard Hatcher would remain a Democratic National Committee vice-president. In violation of the DNC's tradition of accepting the nomination of its Black Caucus, which had nominated Hatcher, the party chose Roland Burris, the moderate black Illinois state comptroller who had supported Mondale. The message was clear: only "acceptable" blacks—that is, those who do not challenge the white establishment's rules—will be given leverage within the party. Jackson responded by asserting that "if the denial of blacks continues, blacks—the party's most loyal voting bloc—will leave the party and become independents."[50]

Buoyed by the capitulation of the party's liberal wing to conservative arguments, members of the party's right wing—all white males except for black congressmen William Gray (Pennsylvania) and Alan Wheat (Missouri)—moved to consolidate their power. In February 1985 they formed a caucus called the "Democratic Leadership Council," whose stated purpose was to "move the party back to the middle" by shedding its ultraliberal, antibusiness, soft-on-defense image.[51] Senator Sam Nunn, one of the group's founders, suggested that it would go beyond policy questions to attempt to change party rules to encourage "moderate" candidates to compete for the presidential nomination. Said one Democratic party strategist close to party chairman Paul Kirk, "The fear of a lot of people is that this group wants to take the cream of the party's leadership and leave Kirk with Jesse Jackson and the single-issue interest groups."[52] In the eyes of white male party leaders, the black taint had now spread to women, gays, labor, farmers, and other minority groups. A Jackson staff person heard Rick Reedy, an assistant to Paul Kirk, actually tell a group of white farmers who had come to Washington to lobby for a farm reform bill that Jesse Jackson was to blame for the Democrats' defeat in November.[53]

The Democratic party leadership's stampede to the right was further demonstrated by a March 1985 conference sponsored by the Democratic Leadership Council, which brought 135 members of the House together to evaluate the party's future. Among the speakers were former Reagan White House communications specialist David Gergen, and a motivational psychologist and market researcher who told them that America has become generally more conservative: "People are more interested in locks on our doors than bombs over our heads."[54]

In a move to limit the future influence of rainbow-type interest groups within the party, the Democratic National Committee in May 1985 repealed the guidelines for the formal recognition of caucuses, substituting a new system that permitted national committee members to form "groups" that would have no official status. In a compromise designed to hold on to blacks, women, and Hispanics while eliminating the method by which they had achieved a measure of collective power within the party, these groups were allowed to retain their seats on the National Executive Committee, but the elimination of the caucus system would clearly prevent representation of other such groups—Asian Americans, disabled Americans, Native Americans, lesbians and gays—on the party's highest council.[55]

By the summer of 1985 Jackson's hope for a fairness commission that would modify party rules that were clearly antidemocratic, as well as racist and sexist, were dashed with the appointment of the (white) former head of the South Carolina state party, Donald Fowler, to head the commission. According to *Congressional Quarterly*, Fowler's appointment was a " 'don't rock the boat' signal that makes it unlikely that there will be sweeping changes in the rules." In return for his willingness to support the party in November 1984, Jackson had been promised that former Atlanta mayor and Jackson supporter Maynard Jackson would be named head of the Fairness Commission. Now, a year later, party officials claimed that no such deal had been made.

Weakened by press and party leaders' attacks on them as special interests, as well as by their failure to build an electoral base for party reform, black, feminist, and Hispanic party functionaries had been forced to concede to this blatant attack on the cohesion that the Jackson campaign had attempted to forge between the various ethnic and single-issue constituency groups. "The whole thing was really disastrous from a progressive perspective," reported Ellen David-Friedman, a Vermont Rainbow Coalition member who served on the DNC. "We decided not to go to the floor on these issues because we knew we couldn't get even 20 percent of the vote."[56]

At its subsequent meetings, the Fairness Commission proceeded not simply to maintain the status quo, but to undo even the reforms instituted by the McGovern Commission in 1972. While it lowered the threshold rule from 20 to 15 percent, the commission increased the percentage of House Democrats to be appointed super-delegates to the convention from 60 percent to 80 percent of the House.[57] In addition, the commission decided that all 372 members of the Democratic National Committee would be super-delegates. After only cursory discussion, the Fairness Commission, dubbed by Jackson a "farce," refused to act on resolutions passed by the 1984 convention calling for more vigorous affirmative action for minorities and women.[58] As one disgruntled feminist on the DNC said to me, "party leaders don't listen to anyone who isn't a member of Congress or a governor. It just isn't like it used to be."[59]

Such events were followed in rapid succession by the capitulation of House Democrats to a series of votes to fund the MX missile system, the nerve gas program, and programs to overthrow the governments of Angola and Nicaragua; finally, the Gramm-Rudman-Hollings budget-balancing bill in effect killed any chances of building a consensus for the retention of some form of welfare-state policies.[60] Even Ted Kennedy, once the party's liberal standard bearer, joined the march to the right. In March 1985 he told audiences: "There is a difference between being a party that cares about women and being the women's party. And we can and we must be a party that cares about minorities without becoming a minority party." Too many of the public housing, job, and assistance programs, he said, have "proved to be counterproductive" in breaking the cycle of poverty and dependence.[61]

The Reagan Administration Takes the Offensive

With a balkanized Democratic party no longer in opposition but running to catch up with the Republicans, the Reagan administration launched some of the boldest attacks on the political and economic rights of blacks since the withdrawal of federal troops from the South in the Hayes-Tilden Compromise of 1877. In early 1985 the administration announced that it would move aggressively both in the courts and by means of executive orders against affirmative action plans, many of which were working successfully all over the country. The move was a blatant reversal of the twenty-five-year commitment of the federal government to intervene on behalf of those who had historically been discriminated against. In March 1985 a little heralded but extremely chilling step was taken in the federal government's decision to stop collecting racial and ethnic data on beneficiaries of federal housing programs—data collected in an attempt to detect and prevent discrimination.

Immediately after the September 1984 primaries in Alabama, as many as two hundred FBI agents swept through the five western Alabama Black Belt countries that had given their votes to Jesse Jackson, rousing elderly people from their beds in the middle of the night, taking about one thousand of them in police-escorted buses to Mobile to be finger-printed, and suggesting that their absentee ballots may have been tampered with by the civil rights workers who had secured their vote. The offices of civil rights workers were also raided and some of the documents they needed for the November elections were confiscated.

In January 1985 indictments for vote and mail fraud were handed down against eight of the Black Belt's most experienced organizers and political leaders. In bringing the indictments, the federal government used the Voting Rights Act of 1965, the very act most of these people had marched from Selma to Montgomery to get enacted.[62]

The attack on voting-rights activists in the five Black Belt counties of Greene, Sumter, Lowndes, Perry, and Wilcox was clearly designed to forestall the growing black electoral insurgency, which threatened the ability of the all-black Alabama Democratic Conference to continue to be the broker for black interests with the white-controlled party. If allowed to grow, the insurgency could also threaten, by the power of example, the entire bipartisan system of white class supremacy in the South. The legal assault on the Black Belt activists was a bipartisan conspiracy involving blacks identified with the old Alabama Democratic Conference (ADC) leadership, white Democrats and Republicans fearful of the rise of an independent, self-determining bloc of black voters, and elected officials who would not accept the old rules of interest-group politics.

To mask the racism involved in the indictments, black-white coalitions ostensibly integrated but actually controlled by whites were established in the Black Belt as parallel organizations to those controlled by the veteran civil rights activists.[63] It was blacks associated with these paper coalitions and with the old ADC leadership who ostensibly brought the charges of voter and mail fraud against the veteran civil rights workers, so that it could be portrayed as a "black-on-black" fight and not a fight over black self-determination and political democracy.

The use of blacks as fronts for the continuance of white class power was a tactic that was being used increasingly in this post–civil rights era. Other examples included the Democratic party's choice of Andrew Young to speak at the Democratic National Convention against the Jackson campaign's platform plank on voting rights; the party's choice of Roland Burris over the Black Caucus's nomination; and the Reagan administration's use of neoconservatives such as Civil Rights Commission chairman Clarence Pendleton and economist Thomas Sowell to refute the arguments of other blacks for continued national intervention on behalf of minority rights.

The tactic was obvious to most blacks but not so obvious to most whites, who since the 1960s had come to accept a limited form of "integration" and "equality of opportunity" as a part of the American tradition of "progress." If the majority of whites could be convinced that the struggle for political democracy was merely a power struggle between competing groups of blacks, the rainbow movement catalyzed by Jesse Jackson could be killed before it had a chance to go any further.

Is "White" a Color in the Rainbow?

Jackson's call to build the Rainbow Coalition offered white people a rare opportunity to begin to undo the racism that has plagued every attempt to build a viable power base for progressive politics in this country and that now draws more and more of the world into its technocratic advance, threatening the very survival of life on the planet.[64]

Not only did the Jackson campaign offer the only program responsive to the needs and interests of the majority of Americans— as demonstrated in almost every public opinion poll—but it offered white Americans an opportunity to overcome the racial and cultural separation that has blinded them to a great deal of reality and prevented them from acting even in their own self-interest.[65]

The Jackson campaign was the first opportunity on so large a scale that whites have had to work with African Americans as equals—and even to learn from them. Since the basis of white identity in racist cultures is not positive self-affirmation, but differentiation from unlike "others"—which amounts to a refusal to identify with most of the world's people—the psychic, cultural, and political lessons implied in such an opportunity are immeasurable. It is a truism, but nevertheless worth repeating, that any subjugation of another people diminishes the humanity of the oppressor—crushes the ability to see clearly, to act honestly, to think rationally, and to create solutions to the problems that plague humanity. The legacy of racism has left the majority of whites crippled in their capacity to make rational and humane political judgments.

It was not simply black-white relations that stood to benefit from whites' involvement in the Jackson campaign, but, as veteran civil rights activist Anne Braden pointed out, white progressives' ability to involve and mobilize other white people.

> The Jackson campaign seemed to offer an opportunity to . . . make real inroads into the white community that would change people's thinking. It seemed to offer that possibility because there was a campaign that was clearly black-led-and-directed—*and* it was speaking to the most basic needs of the great majority of white people in this country. If we could organize in such a way as to get them to see that, then we would be taking the first step toward a new orientation in a sizeable section of America's white population.[66]

That so few white people seized the best opportunity they have had in years to vote in their own self-interest—indeed, that a plurality voted, instead, for a president who opposed just about every issue the American public supported—is testimony to the pervasive influence of racism in our culture and to the power of the media to control the reality to which the public is exposed.

Yet it would be a mistake to take at face value the media and party bosses' conclusion that because Jackson failed to get more than 5 percent of the overall white vote, a national multiracial progressive movement led by blacks is doomed to failure. That is, of course, exactly what they would like the public to believe, and to the extent they succeed, this becomes a self-fulfilling prophecy.

A closer look at the shape of the white vote, the perceptions of white voters, and the experience of organizers who mobilized white constituencies during the campaign gives us a more nuanced and realistic assessment of the prospects for overcoming the racial barrier that has kept the American electorate impotent.

Jackson's overall white vote does not adequately measure the diverse support he actually received. That diversity is better exemplified by looking at the racial breakdown of the total Jackson vote. White votes accounted for 22 percent or approximately 788,000 of Jackson's 3.4 million total. The proportion of his total votes from nonblacks was substantial in every non-Deep South state, ranging from lows of 18 percent and 19 percent in Illinois and Ohio to highs of 33 percent, 50 percent, and 70 percent in New York, California, and Massachusetts, respectively.[67]

Yet even this breakdown does not adequately assess the accuracy of the white-backlash thesis. What must be taken into account is the campaign's financial inability to control its own media image and message, the decision of campaign managers to concentrate their limited resources on the black base to the neglect of the white voter, and the fact that the campaign started fairly late. It can be demonstrated that in those states and municipalities where the campaign organization committed itself to broad, multiracial outreach, as did those in New York, California, Nebraska, Utah, Kentucky, Tennessee, Oregon, and New Mexico, a greater percentage of the vote came from whites and other nonblacks, but where the campaign made little or no attempt to reach out to other constituencies, the nonblack vote was greatly reduced, thus reducing Jackson's national white total. For example, in Chicago and Detroit there was no outreach to whites, nor was there much in the Deep South states of Alabama, Mississippi, and Georgia, outside of Altanta.

On the other hand, where organizers in local areas did door-to-door canvassing in white neighborhoods or tried to reach the white voter through radio spots and local institutions, the response was surprisingly positive. In white-majority Hamilton County, Ohio (the greater Cincinnati area), creative and experienced white organizers made aggressive appeals to white organizations, ran radio spots and put out fliers featuring white working-class women telling why they supported Jackson, and did door-to-door canvassing in areas where it was assumed a black candidate would never go. In a lovingly humorous but sharply critical attack on the racism of her white leftist colleagues who had, until then, failed to support the campaign, white organizer Ginger Rhodes got results with the following letter:

> I'm serious—I want to see some white progressive faces at these next Jackson meetings or don't ANYBODY talk to me for the next 10 years about multinational this and mass movement that. And don't anybody ask me where the Black activists are when it comes to disarmament, nuclear power, toxic wastes, or any of our other pet projects. This campaign is about finally building some credibility around those issues by in turn supporting the economic concerns of the Black community. No, I don't want to have a meeting at my house with herb teas and talk this over. If white leftists want to talk it out, let's do it directly with the people already active in the campaign, and in the spirit of camaraderie and common goals, not hesitancy, reservation, intellectualism, and excuse-seeking.

Rhodes finished the letter with a response form, which was entitled: "Yes, Lordy! I see the light and want to mend my ultraleftist ways!"[68] In spite of a press that continually denied the existence of a rainbow coalition, the persistence and good humor of organizers such as Ginger Rhodes and the effort they made to "think big" paid off. Jackson won the county with 35 percent of the vote and beat a 30 percent threshold in each of two congressional districts.

In Nebraska, a strong city-farmer Rainbow Coalition, Jackson's personal appearance in the state, and door-to-door campaigning in Lincoln and Omaha produced an almost 10 percent popular vote for Jackson in a state that is 3 percent black.[69]

To the amazement of the state Democratic party power brokers in Kentucky, Jackson carried two congressional districts. The third, which includes Louisville with a 14 percent black population, was won with 52 percent of the popular vote; the sixth, which includes Lexington and surrounding counties with a 7 percent black population, was carried with 53 percent of the vote. While a good part of this margin of victory was due to a high black turnout at the caucuses, white organizers brought a considerable number of whites into the campaign who had never been involved in antiracist activity before. They had a clear strategy of using the campaign to reach whites they might not otherwise have access to. Campaign organizers estimated that about 150 whites were actively involved in the campaign in each of the two cities.[70]

In Eugene, Oregon, which is less than 1 percent black, Jackson won 11 percent of the vote with a Rainbow Coalition that one campaign activist, Bonnie Souza, described as "a mixture of liberals, socialists, former hippies, blacks, whites, Asians, and Native Americans."[71]

Perhaps most surprising of all was the 18 percent Jackson won in Utah, a state that is 1 percent black and heavily Mormon. The state's campaign was headed by a young maverick member of the state senate, the first black to be elected to that body and perhaps one of the few to come out of a community-organizing background. State Senator Terry Williams put together a small but dynamic multiracial organizing core that was entirely self-funded. Jackson made no appearance in the state, but the enthusiasm of the group, and the belief that whites would vote for Jackson, paid off. As a result of the campaign, several blacks, women, and Hispanics decided to run for office.

In areas where white workers or farmers were being displaced from jobs or land, they were won to the campaign either by Jackson himself or by white campaign workers who addressed their legitimate class grievances with sympathy and righteous indignation, but who pointed out that they could not win their rights by acting alone. Populations that have traditionally been assumed to be unalterably racist became Jackson's most enthusiastic supporters.

Examples like these could be multiplied all over the country. They are supplemented by numerous anecdotal material indicating that white support was more diverse than the exit polls indicated. "What surprised me," said Willy Fluker of Montgomery, Alabama, "was to meet white people right here in Montgomery who liked Jackson and were going to vote for him!"[72] In her calls around the Deep South, Anne Braden found that some whites were involved in just about every Jackson organization. In spite of the fact that, according to exit polls, Jackson's white vote was predominantly young and college educated, there were numerous stories of people who told me that their elderly mothers who had never been involved in anything political before were going to vote for Jackson.

Surveys of white voter attitudes toward Jackson revealed at worst an ambivalent picture, at best some surprisingly positive results. For example, while a Joint Center for Political Studies/ Gallup poll taken at the end of the primary season showed that 54 percent of the white respondents thought Jackson was prejudiced—surely a result of the media campaign to paint him as a bigot—the same poll gave him a 57 percent rating for "compassion."[73] While in poll after poll few whites indicated they believed a black man in general or Jesse Jackson in particular had a chance to be president in 1984, in a New York poll, where Jackson won 7 percent of the white vote, he was given a higher positive rating as an "attractive and forceful leader" than either Hart or Mondale.[74] In a *Washington Post*/ABC News poll taken in May, one out of four white registered voters and one out of three registered white Democrats said that if Jackson endorsed another candidate, they would be more likely to vote for that candidate; yet that same poll found that 42 percent of the registered voters (black and white) thought that Jackson would help the Democrats, but 43 percent thought he would hurt them.[75]

Conclusion

Racism remains an endemic part of the U.S. political system, perhaps the most important barrier to the development of a viable political left. The two major parties have used racial minorities when they needed them to provide the margin of victory in close elections, or to give the party moral credibility when it was necessary in a time of strained international relations. Neither the white Republican nor Democratic party leaders have accepted minorities on their own cultural terms, however; nor have they treated them as peers with political insights and gifts to offer the natio drawn from their unique cultural heritages and world perspec- tives.

The Jackson campaign of 1984 represented the first major attempt in the electoral arena to project a new national consensus from the "black perspective." The campaign thus exposed more clearly than anything since the end of Reconstruction the racist scaffolding that undergirds both Republican and Democratic party rule, resulting in the disenfranchisement not only of racial minorities, but of the majority of white Americans.

The Democratic party's rejection of the Rainbow Coalition has accelerated a de-alignment process that was already occurring as a result of a number of demographic and economic forces. Blacks, heretofore the party's most faithful constituency, after 1984 signaled a readiness for other options. An ABC/*Washington Post* poll taken in 1986 indicated that 53 percent of blacks said it would be a good idea" for a black leader such as Jackson to run for president as an independent.[76]

Where blacks will take their growing disenchantment with the Democratic party remains an open question. Some of the black middle class—such as Jackson's Detroit coordinator—may concede defeat for a collective black agenda and decide to play ball with whichever party they think will advance their own careers or business interests. Others, such as Nation of Islam minister Louis Farrakhan, may retreat once more into a defensive nationalist separatism. Still others, in the absence of a viable alternative, will stick with the Democratic party, attempting in whatever ways are left to fight for a more social Democratic agenda, but with diminishing returns. Yale political scientist Adolph Reed contends that for blacks to abandon the struggle over the party's future would be to consign them to the periphery of the polity and make them that much more vulnerable to the attacks of the political right.[77] Howard University political scientists Morris and Williams foresee that black Democrats may abandon the attempt to affect national elections and place more emphasis on getting blacks elected at state and local levels, but they concede that, given the power of the federal government, such a scenario will do little to change the policies that impact so heavily on black lives.[78]

As conditions worsen in the communities over which black officials preside, the only other option—outside of mass insurrection—will be Jackson's Rainbow Coalition. For the foreseeable future, that coalition must struggle both inside and outside the Democratic party for cultural influence and some concrete measures of political power—congressional seats and offices at the state and local level—if it is to become a vehicle to which the masses of the disenfranchised will rally.

As a result of the Jackson campaign of 1984, there is now the possibility that almost a million whites, and at least a third of the Latino electorate, along with smaller numbers of Asian Americans, Arab Americans, and Native Americans would join such a coalition. The vote for Jackson was essentially a vote for a third-party movement with a broad social-democratic platform, not a vote for the platform and candidate of the Democratic party.

The most formidable barrier to building such a movement remains the racism that is so cynically manipulated by those in power and so easily evoked in an ignorant white public. It may be, however, that the objective conditions for overcoming this terrible legacy are better than they have ever been. The actions of white male Democratic party officials indicate that as the contradictions of late twentieth-century capitalism deepen, more and more of the white electorate will be tainted with the aversive stain once reserved for blacks and "dirty immigrants." As white feminists, workers, farmers, peace and environmental activists, and gays and lesbians are shunned by the institutions to which they once gave their loyalty and branded "un-American" by an increasingly jingoist Democratic party, they may begin to accept their place in that "Other America" represented by the brightly colored hues of the Rainbow Coalition—a creature half in, half out of the two-party system, part social-protest movement, part electoral machine—a political amphibian in the process of evolving. "As things get worse," C. T. Vivian told me, "we are going to find more and more whites flocking to the Rainbow—except those flocking to the crazies. They have nowhere else to come to but us."

An alternative scenario that one hesitates to broach, but that must be considered seriously given the national shift to the right, is a deepening drift into fascism—wrapped in an American flag, bearing the torch of "liberty," mouthing Christian pieties, and wearing a benign smile.[79] Such a scenario is all too easily imagined by the steps the Reagan administration has already taken, with the acquiescence of a supine Congress, to roll back civil rights legislation, subvert civil liberties through executive order, appoint an attorney general who would repeal the Bill of Rights, flout international law, and nominate as the chief justice of the Supreme Court the man who designed the Nixon administration's defense in U.S. v. U.S. District Court—that the president has an inherent right to suspend the Constitution any time he deems it necessary for national security, under the legal precedent of the "inherent power" of British kings of the fifteenth through seventeenth centuries.[80]

To avert such an unthinkable future will take political education, organizing, and mobilizing on an unprecedented scale, as well as a maturity in regard to race relations that has little precedent in American public life.

11

Whither the Rainbow Coalition?

At the beginning of our journey together, the Rainbow was just a concept. In seven months we have brought that concept to reality. . . . The campaign which we are completing is not the end, but the beginning of a new movement which can change the direction of the country. We must move now to institutionalize the Rainbow, state by state and nationally. To do this, we must have a vision of where we want to go; for without a vision, the people perish.[1]

—Jesse Jackson

Well before the 1984 primary season was over, participants in the Jackson campaign realized that the movement they had generated would have to be transformed into a sustained political organization if it were going to change national priorities in the direction articulated by Jackson. Many hoped that the 1984 campaign was the beginning of a long-term struggle to forge a new coalition—one that would not be dependent on winning mere concessions from the party in power, but one that could elect its own people to office and *hold them accountable* to a people's platform.

It was a bold and perhaps outrageous hope, which ran against the tides of U.S. history. Except for the relative success of the Socialist party in the early years of the century in electing 1,200 local officials and fielding a presidential candidate five times, no other movement has succeeded in drawing together for any sustained length of time the political power of the majority of poor and working people with those sectors of the middle class who desire peace and a new international political-economic order. Henry Wallace's 1948 Progressive party campaign, which came closest to the Jackson campaign in its ideology and tactics, collapsed with the defeat of its presidential candidate, as had every previous attempt to build a movement around a progressive presidential candidate.

This chapter traces the trajectory of the hopes invested in the Rainbow Coalition from the end of the presidential primary campaign through the founding convention of the Rainbow Coalition in April 1986. It looks not only at the fitful attempts to form a national organization, but at three regional experiments that offer unique perspectives on the prospects for such coalition-building. These experiments open up new questions for political activists regarding the relationship of the Rainbow Coalition to the existing two-party structure, the relationship of social protest to electoral politics, and the nature of leadership, political education, and political accountability.

The Fitful Labor of a New Coalition

As early as May 1984, during the presidential primary, a national gathering of key Rainbow Coalition organizers and state campaign coordinators meeting in New York drafted a call to form an ongoing Rainbow Coalition. Several proposals for how such a coalition could be formed were circulated within the campaign, and by the end of June 1984, at a meeting in Chicago called by campaign staff to prepare organizers and delegates for their role in the Democratic Convention, the idea of the Rainbow Coalition as an "independent third force in American politics" emerged.

The scope of such a third force was later outlined in an internal memorandum to the Rainbow Coalition leadership by Jack O'Dell, a key strategist:

> The Rainbow Coalition is a mass political movement committed to the expansion of the definition and practice of democracy in our

country, including the realization of economic justice. As such, it has to be *bold* enough to perceive of itself as the historic replacement for the existing two-party system: one prepared to act as a "dual authority," carrying out political education, developing the public's insights into the systemic character of many of the nation's problems, and consequently proposing solutions to these problems that are germane. . . . The Rainbow Coalition, out of a definition of its purposes and goals, must be *courageous* enough to publicly advocate a far reaching reconstruction of the present system of corporate greed, which is causing the chronic mass problems we as a coalition are attempting to address.[2]

At another meeting of coalition organizers called at the end of August 1984 to announce the incorporation of the National Rainbow Coalition and to discuss its participation in the Mondale/Ferraro campaign, the outlines of a structure for an ongoing movement began to emerge. The Rainbow Coalition would have to have its own voter education/registration arm, a public policy research institute that would develop and circulate "rainbow" policy options, a Political Action Committee to fund progressive candidates, a leadership-training component, and a public relations unit with the capacity to respond rapidly to fast-breaking news with the coalition's own perspectives on the issues.

Though far from refined, the outline of the Rainbow Coalition that was beginning to emerge was the best that the African-American tradition has offered U.S. political discourse on the nature of what is to be done. As African-American philosopher Cornel West explains it, the African-American tradition, as one of four historical "ideal types" of responses to the conditions imposed by white supremacy, "acknowledges the complex interplay between practicality and ideology, electoral politics and structural social change. It discourages ideological programs that have no reasonable chance of succeeding and practical ones that preclude the possibility of fundamentally transforming the present economic system and social arrangements."[3]

The ideological vision, however, was easier to achieve than was the vehicle to carry it out. Left at the end of the primary campaign with a debt of $1.4 million, the Rainbow Coalition had neither the financial nor the institutional resources to begin a new organization immediately after the primaries. Federal election laws required that campaign offices around the country be shut down immediately after the Democratic Convention. Thus, letters went out from the national office telling local campaigns to close up shop and to await further word from Jackson, leaving local organizers without the institutional resources to transform the local campaign into an ongoing coalition. In most places, the interracial cooperation generated by the campaign had been fragile. Without an immediate political focus for cooperative activity, the hope and energy generated by the campaign dissipated rapidly, as people returned to their old networks, associations, and cultural bonds. The resurgence of anti-apartheid activity in November 1984 helped to keep some of the movement energy and focus alive, but it did little to consolidate the necessary organization-building at the base.

The failure to consolidate such a base was tragically illustrated in the 1985 New York mayoral election. Growing out of New York's successful experience during the Jackson campaign was the hope among many activists that the Jackson forces could consolidate to defeat New York's two-term mayor, Ed Koch—long anathema to the minority communities and a disaster for poor and working-class people.[4]

Without Jackson as a focus, however, the coalition that had come together around his candidacy collapsed as quickly as it had been built. Black politicians who had been on opposing sides during the presidential primary returned to their old clubhouses and to the wheeling and dealing of interest-group politics in their search for personal political advancement, since many of them had races at stake in 1985. In the absence of a unified multiracial mass base, the search for a mayoral candidate who could unite the city's diverse communities—particularly its black and Latin core—was taken over by a self-appointed black leadership group composed chiefly of politicians. Calling itself the Coalition for a Just New York, the group was wracked with internal ideological dissension and personal political rivalries.[5]

Though some in the coalition, notably Jackson's New York State coordinator, Brooklyn assemblyman Al Vann, argued in the interest of black-Latin unity for former congressman Herman Badillo, the city's highest ranking Puerto Rican, the old pull of black nationalism won out over coalition-building. The Rainbow Coalition chose as its candidate state assemblyman Denny Farrell, a weak candidate with low name recognition, lacking a solid organizational base, and for whom there was little enthusiasm among even the black elected leadership.

Black and Latino relations were badly frayed by the bitter fight over the candidate-selection process, which appeared to many Latinos as an attempt to keep Puerto Ricans from power even at the expense of losing the election. The black, Latino, and white grass-roots organizers who had come into electoral politics for the first time through the Jackson campaign were alienated once again from electoral work by what they saw as the black political leadership's inability to see beyond its own narrow interests to the wider issues at stake: namely, interracial solidarity and progressive city reform. Said black activist Barbara Omolade, "Only the most backward notions of 'racial solidarity' could justify the Farrell candidacy."6 In the end, Koch won by a landslide, polling even 38 percent of the black vote and setting the development of a multiracial progressive movement back even further.

In many areas of the country, the vacuum left at the end of the Jackson campaign provided an opening for groups with questionable motives to move in and capitalize on the energy Jackson had aroused. The National Alliance party—a formation whose past ties to Lyndon LaRouche's National Caucus of Labor Committees as well as its divisive and cooptive tactics have aroused the suspicion of many progressive activists—was active in several parts of the country, posing itself as the independent "rainbow" movement that would carry on where the Jackson campaign left off.7

Deprived of the organizational base that had come together for the campaign, as well as of attentive media, Jackson was compelled to keep the idea of the National Rainbow Coalition alive through the sheer energy and inventiveness of his personal charisma. Thus at the end of the primary campaign and for the next two years he embarked on a whirlwind one-man publicity campaign, traversing the country to speak out on the drug epidemic at local high schools and on South African divestment on college campuses, appearing at farm protest rallies in the Midwest and as a stand-up comic on "Saturday Night Live"; calling national press attention to the festering wounds of racism and economic oppression that existed in such places as Tunica, Mississippi; preaching on New York's City's homeless scandal from the pulpit of St. John's Cathedral; leading the large "April Actions" rally for jobs, peace, and justice in Washington and the march to commemorate the twentieth anniversary of the Selma to Montgomery campaign in Alabama; walking the line with striking workers; and campaigning throughout the South for a new "economic common ground" between whites and blacks. Jackson even showed up in Bitburg, Germany, at the time of Reagan's shameful rapprochement with German fascism to present an alternative perspective, led a peace delegation to speak with Soviet leader Mikhail Gorbachev at the U.S.-USSR summit in Geneva, where he pleaded not only for an end to the arms race but for the rights of Soviet Jews, spoke to the "Rainbow caucus" of the European parliament, and addressed a large antinuclear demonstration in Great Britain.

Those who had hoped to see an ongoing rainbow movement emerge from the campaign lauded these efforts to keep the rainbow message before the American public. No other public figure was making the connections Jackson was making—pointing out the emperor's nakedness—or calling attention to the still unfinished business of the American Revolution. Without the organizational or financial resources necessary to begin the ideological conversion of the American public, Jackson was a virtual one-man propaganda machine for the Rainbow Coalition.

Yet as time went on, there was a danger that the Rainbow Coalition would be solely a function of Jackson's personal charisma. Though several meetings of the national leadership were held, an organization failed to materialize. The lack of a solid financial base with which to begin an organization was a major problem. Although by early 1985 the Jackson campaign had retired its campaign debt (well ahead of any of the other candidates), the money was not available to hire an executive director and staff commensurate with the work and responsibilities involved in such an ambitious undertaking. It was estimated that a national rainbow coalition would have to have a budget of $2 million to do the kind of job envisaged. A radiothon in March 1985 that was projected to net a million dollars fell far short of its goal.

Money was only part of the problem, however. Jackson seemed incapable of lending himself to the kind of careful, patient, systematic work involved in organization-building. As soon as colleagues pinned him down on commitments, he sabotaged their plans with others of his own. Always quick to respond to fast-breaking events or to opportunities to get media coverage, he found it difficult to commit himself to the long-range planning necessary to start up this kind of organization. Jackson was finally compelled to birth the organization when it appeared that Ron Dellums and John Conyers were moving to fill the vacuum by bringing the coalition leadership together. Nevertheless, at least one person who could have given capable executive leadership to the direction of the Rainbow Coalition, Bill Howard, was dissuaded from taking on the role of executive director because of Jackson's mercurial behavior.

There were, of course, conflicting pressures on Jackson. Forces within the Democratic party, including many of Jackson's close black political supporters, were reluctant to see an independent third force come into being. Such a movement would jeopardize their own positions within the party and create a conflict between their black base and the white political and corporate elites on whom they depended to deliver the dwindling stock of patronage necessary to their legitimacy within the black community. Other forces within the party—the white bosses—were even more opposed to the development of a mass-based movement/organization that would siphon off the party's black constituency and perhaps even a good part of its Latino and white liberal-progressive base. As long as Jackson operated as an individual, he could more easily be destroyed the next time he decided to run for national office. It was rumored that such forces were intent on creating a cult of personality around Jackson for precisely that purpose. Of course, without elective office and with no money to command the media, Jackson was almost obliged to keep his name before the public by dashing from one end of the country to the other and across the world if he were to be a viable political candidate in the future. Thus, the pressures against the formation of the ongoing Rainbow Coalition were tremendous—coming from both within and without.

In spite of the national leadership's failure to consolidate a national organization, people who had been involved in the 1984 Jackson campaign in several areas of the country did not let the end of the campaign deter them from building on the momentum the campaign had generated. In at least four states—Alabama, Washington, Vermont, and New Jersey—ongoing statewide rainbow formations were catalyzed by the Jackson campaign, and many more metropolitan regions developed permanent organizations. The three state organizations we consider here differ from each other not only in the differing demographics involved, but in the particular calculus of forces within and outside the Jackson campaign out of which they grew. What they all have in common is a commitment to the kind of democratic participation and accountability promoted by Jackson during the presidential primary, as well as to the broad peace and social justice vision articulated in the Jackson platform.

A New Model for the South

Prior to 1965 whites controlled all ten of the black-majority counties in Alabama, located in the "Black Belt." After passage of the Voting Rights Act in 1965, they continued to try to maintain control through the practice of gerrymandering black-majority districts so that blacks could not win office, manipulating the absentee ballot process by placing dead people and out-of-staters on the rolls, introducing bills in the state legislature that required re-registration only in black-majority counties where blacks were organizing for political power, and other such tactics. In spite of constant harassment and intimidation, blacks and a few whites, who had been honed in the tough and often violent organizing efforts of the 1960s civil rights movement, had by 1983 finally won control of seven of the ten county commissions, five county school boards, five sheriff's offices, and nine towns, as well as three seats in the state assembly and one in the state senate.

It was these activists and their political organizations centered in the counties of Greene, Sumter, Perry, Wilcox, and Lowndes who ran the Jackson campaign in Alabama and, as a result, emerged as the leaders of a new, progressive, statewide coalition. Jackson's campaign was neither the beginning nor the end of this movement. Rather, Jackson's candidacy forced into the open the client relationship blacks had always had to the white-controlled party through the Alabama Democratic Conference (ADC). The ADC leadership's endorsement of Mondale triggered a break with this kind of dependency, signaling the possibility of a new, more independent, black-led but biracial coalition that would relate to the white party on very different terms.[8] Montgomery activist Gwen Patton explained that the Jackson campaign had made people "a lot more observant to philosophy, as opposed to being just black. I don't think blacks can now simply run on skin color."[9]

"We are concerned with economic issues, environmental issues, and developing an analysis of the military complex, which is the biggest recipient of monies being shifted from social programs," said Patton. "The ADC has . . . shown that its program has not kept up with either the needs or desires of the people. It is time the leaders of ADC recognize that the organization has become superfluous."[10]

At the end of the Jackson campaign, Black Belt leaders recognized that it was a mistake to wait on the national Rainbow Coalition office for direction. The problems they faced in the Black Belt were regional and very reminiscent of what blacks faced after the first Reconstruction period one hundred years ago. White-owned newspapers were constantly accusing black elected leadership of malfeasance and corruption. The state was threatening to take over the administration of black-controlled school districts. If blacks were not vigilant, the gains they had made over the last twenty years could be wiped out. Consequently, the leadership that had been involved in the Jackson campaign encouraged the development of strong regional organizations, such as the Selma-based Campaign for a New South. Five representatives from each of the ten Black Belt county organizations began meeting once a month to coordinate activities and plan strategy. Five standing committees were established; namely, political organization, economics, education, reapportionment, and communication. With their own representatives in the State House and on the county commissions, these organizations had a direct line to administrative and legislative power.

In the fall of 1984, however, a new threat arose. The possibility of consolidating and extending the power of this progressive coalition came under attack with the Reagan administration's indictment of eight of the Black Belt's most experienced organizers for voting fraud. The indictments threatened not only to tie up their organizations and resources in a protracted legal battle, but to destroy their ability to hold on to the offices it had taken them nearly twenty years to secure. One of those offices, that of state senator Hank Sanders, was especially pivotal. Black Belt organizer Wendell Paris told me that "Sanders has singlehandedly changed the way that the Alabama legislature has done business since the constitution was written in 1901." As the representative of a territory 150 miles long and 50 miles wide, Sanders, coordinator of the Jackson campaign in Alabama, was the "second most powerful figure in Alabama politics," said Paris. "You can't put a bank or anything else in there unless Sanders says so."[11]

In the spring of 1986, all of the civil rights activists holding office in the Black Belt were coming up for reelection. If, through the indictments, the Reagan administration could intimidate the rural, largely elderly black constituency who had voted for them into staying away from the polls, it could break the back of this progressive insurgency whose continued success threatened not only the seats of Republicans, such as arch-conservative Senator Jeremiah Denton, but those of "boll weevil" Democrats, such as Congressman Richard Shelby, who had voted against the extension of the Voting Rights Act while representing a district that included much of the Black Belt. Also at stake was a huge military transport project—the Tombigbee Waterway—that ran through the Black Belt, and the continued ability of multinational corporations such as Chemical Waste Management to operate without regard to the communities affected by their policies. Chemical Waste Management operates the nation's largest toxic waste dump, located in Sumter County, which was in Sander's district. It handles wastes from several foreign countries and forty-four states. Sanders and state representative Lucius Black, propelled by people's organizations below them, had been trying to gain some control over the waterway's job contracts and Chem-Waste's tax revenues, as well as legislation that would provide some protection from contamination for the county's residents. It was rumored that Chem-Waste had amassed a $250,000 war chest to defeat Hank Sanders, Lucius Black, and Danny Corbett of the Communications Workers of America, a white labor organizer elected to the state senate.

Thus, with an ongoing movement to protect, those who had run the Jackson campaign in Alabama were forced to go on the offensive. They saw that national support was absolutely essential to their fight-back strategy, since they were up against the power of the federal government and multinational corporations. The national networks and visibility afforded by their participation in the Jackson campaign would enable that fight to be ultimately successful.

In late November 1984 the Campaign for a New South—the major Black Belt political organization—organized a "solidarity day" in Selma, to which about four hundred people came from across the state and several other states. They attended workshops on organizing for political and economic power and mapped out local, regional, and national strategies.

A variety of national and regional networks whose leaders had been involved in the Jackson campaign—such as the Southern Organizing Committee for Racial and Economic Justice, the National Committee for Independent Political Action, the Center for Constitutional Rights, and the Commission for Racial Justice of the United Church of Christ—were mobilized to provide legal help, to raise funds for both the legal and the organizing effort, and to help publicize and educate the nation on the Reagan administration's new attacks on the Voting Rights Act. Those networks, in turn, arranged speaking tours for Black Belt leaders in other states and involved organizations such as the Congressional Black Caucus, other networks of black elected officials, and the National Council of Churches in the fight-back effort.

The successful defense of the "Black Belt 8" by seasoned civil rights attorneys, as well as the national publicity given to the cases, resulted in the acquittal of all of the defendants, except for four outstanding counts against one—Spiver Gordon. Buoyed by that victory, the Black Belt leadership held a "Black Belt summit conference" in November 1985 to discuss the formation of an ongoing political coalition that would be statewide. In January 1986 an estimated twelve hundred people from around the state, including formally elected delegates from every election district (among whom were about one hundred whites) met in Birmingham to establish the Alabama New South Coalition as an independent political organization open to all races.

In a move that indicated a rapprochement between the rural Black Belt activists and the Birmingham machine of Richard Arrington, which had backed Mondale in the primaries, the New South Coalition elected Arrington its new president. The coalition, said Arrington, would be concerned with both political empowerment and social issues, including economic empowerment. In an oblique critique of the Alabama Democratic Conference, for which the New South Coalition was obviously a replacement, Arrington said:

> The New South Coalition is not organized to place in a position of leadership some individual who can promote his own political ca-

reer. . . . The people who have been the moving forces in trying to get this group organized are insisting . . . that this be beyond any one person, that there not be any one person set up as king who is calling the shots. . . . This organization is going to focus on issues and make candidates secondary to that.[12]

One indication of the broad progressive ideology embodied in the Alabama New South Coalition was the presence at the convention of several outside observers, including Eduardo Baez, director of Nicaragua's adult education program, who told the assembled delegates, "Your struggle is our struggle, the international struggle of oppressed people." Josh Lawrence from New York, who was there as a guest observer, said the gathering reminded him of the old days of the civil rights movement, except that the leadership was a lot more politically sophisticated. H. L. Mitchell, founder of the Southern Tenant Farmers Union, the militant biracial group that organized impoverished tenant farmers during the Depression, likened the New South Coalition to the Populist movement of the turn of the century and the multiracial agrarian grassroots movements of the 1930s and 1960s. Bill Edwards, a white Tuscaloosa activist, told the convention that he was proud to be part of the organization. He urged it to reach out to the women's movement, peace organizations, environmental groups, labor unions, and those who are concerned with welfare rights, prison reform, infant mortality, and tenant rights. "The role of whites," he said, "is to work in the white community and to strongly stand up and say the politics of the New South Coalition are right."[13]

The constitution voted by the founding convention includes several features unique to Alabama politics. Officers may serve only two consecutive two-year terms, then must sit out for two years before serving in the same capacity. (Joe Reed had ruled the ADC for twenty consecutive years, affording him near dictatorial power over black politics in the state.) Each year, county chapters elect delegates to a statewide convention that has ultimate control of the organization. Between the annual conventions, a board of directors, elected by convention delegates on the basis of the state's congressional districts, is empowered to act for the whole. At least one person from each district must be under twenty-five years of age. Additionally, each county selects two representatives to a board of governors, which advises the directors and officers on policy and gathers electoral data, thus assuring a people-controlled method of data gathering. A standing issues committee solicits platform positions from the organization's membership, and candidates from all parties may be endorsed by the organization.

In the spring of 1986, hundreds of people from all over the country, including many whites, went to the rural Alabama Black Belt to engage in what was called Freedom Spring. Coordinated by the Campaign for a New South, the event had as its purpose voter education and registration to offset the intimidating effects of the Reagan administration's attack on the Black Belt movement. Though the effort went unpublicized in the national media, it was successful. All of the incumbents won back their offices. The Alabama New South Coalition, as the state's rainbow coalition, would be a force to be reckoned with in the future.

Machine Politics in a New Mold

One of the more interesting projects to emerge from the Jackson campaign of 1984 is the Rainbow Institute of Seattle, a multiracial organization of poor and working people that used traditional machine tactics to turn the Democratic party in the state's two most heavily Democratic districts into a party that truly represents the locked-out and disenfranchised.[14]

The Rainbow Institute was the brainchild of Arnette Holloway, a veteran of the Student Nonviolent Coordinating Committee (SNCC) organizing in the 1960s and a former professor of political science at Howard University, and the Reverend Gil Lloyd, a Baptist minister who was groomed in Chicago's machine politics. Holloway, a relative newcomer to Seattle, and Lloyd met each other through the Jackson campaign. Lloyd was serving as volunteer campaign manager at the time Holloway was brought on as the campaign's political consultant.

The Democratic party in Washington has a structure that at least on paper provides for public participation and representation at the neighborhood level. Every legislative district in the state is divided into approximately 100-150 precincts (roughly equivalent to a neighborhood of 300 families). Each precinct is to be represented by a precinct committeeperson who is to be the party's eyes and ears, its get-out-the-vote captain and new-voter recruiter.

Since 1889, the Democratic party in the State of Washington has had a four-tier caucus system through which it elects delegates to the Democratic National Convention. The first caucuses are held at the precinct level in people's homes, where, presumably, neighbors elect neighbors to represent them at the next caucus level. In theory, at least, the system has enormous democratic potential.

Holloway and Lloyd believed that the greatest impediment to improvement in the lives of poor and working people was their lack of participation at a basic level in the Democratic party machinery—a party that, at least since the New Deal, had claimed to represent them. Until the Democratic presidential primary of 1984, the vast majority of people paid little attention to the party and most of the precinct committee positions went unfilled. An average of five people showed up at a precinct-level caucus during a presidential primary. Consequently, access to resources within the state eluded them.

All that changed in 1984. Spurred by the Jackson and Hart candidacies, poor and working-class people and middle-class professionals concerned about peace, Central America, environmental issues, and gay rights flooded the precinct-level caucuses, swelling the participation level to an average of three hundred people. A local television documentary on the 1984 primary demonstrated that most of the people who participated had never been involved in party politics before, had never considered it an avenue to empowerment.

Holloway and Lloyd immediately saw the potential for developing that energy and excitement into a new political force that could begin to transform the state Democratic party into one accountable to its base. As Holloway told me: "The party has always been a little social club for white middle class people, largely because we've allowed it to be."

In a caucus system, it is knowledge of the party machinery and organization that counts more than numbers, so Holloway and Lloyd began by setting up weekly Saturday training sessions for people who wished to run as Jackson delegates as well as for those who were uncommitted. They were soon deluged with aspiring political operatives. Some 375 to 400 people from all over the state turned out for the training sessions, which lasted from 9:30 A.M. to 3:00 P.M.

Political novices were taught about how the arcane caucus process and Democratic party rules and machinery actually function. They were trained in lobbying, public speaking, door-to-door canvassing, political negotiating, parliamentary procedure, and in the details of Jackson's policy platform—in short, they were given all the tools needed to become effective party operatives. In the process, Holloway told me, "more and more people became aware of how the system works and why they had been locked out of it for so long." Such knowledge is power, and as people became confident of the "rules of the game" they gained courage to do things they had never done before, such as going up to elected officials and grilling them on their positions on the issues, lobbying for Jackson's policy platform at the state Democratic convention, or negotiating with other delegates for trade-offs on positions or delegates.

As more people became aware of Jackson's program through the skillful lobbying of people who had been trained in this manner, the Jackson campaign began to pick up more uncommitted delegates and even some who had originally been for Hart and Mondale. People who were not chosen delegates were nevertheless kept involved. They were sent to the next caucus round as lobbyists or deployed at state Democratic party headquarters as receptionists because, as Holloway pointed out, a lot of good political information can be overheard by someone sitting at the reception desk.

According to Lloyd, thousands of people were involved in the training process at the precinct level. He explained to me:

> They went to their precinct caucuses with the idea that they would be heard, that their votes would count. We had a number of incidences where our votes were discounted, even though they were valid. A number of machinations were engaged in to keep them from being effective, because it was a threat to the old party system. So out of the precinct caucus process we came out with a number of delegates to go to the next level—the legislative district caucuses. This was a good number of grassroots people who had never before had the status of being a political representative with the promise of being able to make a difference for their candidate. . . . Some had never even been registered to vote. But they had caught the vision, and even if they didn't make it all the way through the caucus process, they knew they could do it next time.

The more effective the Jackson campaign became, however, the greater was the opposition aroused against it. Holloway and Lloyd not only had to do battle with Mondale's machine, they also believe they were sabotaged by some of the black middle-class people on Jackson's state committee, who held formal positions of leadership but were working behind the scenes for Mondale. What emerged in the middle of the primary campaign was a class struggle between black elites securely entrenched in the Democratic party machinery and members of the civil rights establishment whose status and ability to get patronage depended on their ties with party functionaries, versus a new multiracial cohort of previously inactive and disenfranchised poor and working-class people—the majority of them single mothers—who had been empowered by the training provided by Holloway and Lloyd. They were not dependent on anyone, nor did they owe any favors. As such they were a threat to entrenched elites.

After the Holloway-Lloyd-led insurgents were successful in getting Jackson's platform passed by the entire state Democratic convention—"We were actually running the convention, at that point," recalled Holloway—the class struggle emerged into the open, splitting the Jackson campaign into two factions and weakening its ability to fight for the optimum number of delegates to the Democratic National Convention.

In a workshop following the state Democratic platform victory, the newly trained politicos began talking about how to remain involved in the campaign, even if they did not become delegates to the national convention. According to participants, a lot of people were angry about the dirty deals they had seen go down at the party caucuses and began to ask how they could organize themselves to carry on the idealism, policy positions, and participatory thrust they had had a taste of during the primary contest. At that workshop, according to Holloway, "we began talking about long-term involvement in the party by becoming precinct committee people. By getting our people into those positions, we could eventually take over the party from the bottom up." The trainers had brought to the meeting maps of all the precincts, listing all the vacant precinct positions along with the necessary forms to be filled out to run as a precinct leader. When they asked how many people would be interested in filling those positions, almost all of the 325 people present answered in the affirmative. At that point, says Holloway, "we knew that we could overpower the system."

In spite of the fact that their faction had no delegates to the convention, Holloway brought a half-dozen of her newly trained operatives to San Francisco to give them first-hand experience in a national nominating convention. They were deployed as lobbyists for Jackson, with the variety of informal caucuses at the convention, as receptionists, and in other parts of the Jackson machine.

After the Jackson campaign, the Holloway-Lloyd group incorporated themselves as the Rainbow Institute, an ongoing independent statewide organization established for the purpose of "providing leadership development, political education, and training for grassroots people."

One of the first projects of the institute was to recruit and train new leadership to fill the empty precinct committee positions and then to get them registered as voter registrars when they learned that the Democratic party was moving to limit voter registrar positions. To prevent the kind of unresponsiveness and closed-shop nature of the traditional party structure, people who became precinct committee persons were required to establish an accountability system with their constituents. Within months, the Rainbow Institute had filled over 60 percent of the 145 vacant precinct positions in the state's two largest legislative districts, the forty-third and the thirty-seventh. Arnette Holloway began writing a regular political education column in the state's oldest black newspaper, and within months the newspaper had tripled its readership.

In the November 1984 election the Rainbow Institute ran progressive, grassroots people against incumbent committee persons, enabling them to take over the party machinery in the forty-third district and coming close to the majority in the thirty-seventh. They also helped to elect a progressive black candidate to the state legislature. By the spring of 1985 they had secured two positions on Seattle's Public Development Authority; initiated regular legislature "report-back" nights in which public officials are questioned by their constituents and held accountable for their actions; and initiated a South Africa divestment bill in the state legislature.

By 1986 Rainbow Institute–related people had taken over the Democratic party in Seattle, and the institute had become the controlling core of the city's political life, with access to the patronage that goes with such power. The Rainbow Institute had incorporated into its coalition-building key financial sectors, such as the board of directors of the city's black-owned bank, the Minority Business Association, and the Black Contractors, as well as the city's community councils and its black church association. A Rainbow Institute–related person—a young Filipino-American labor organizer—is now the executive director of the King County Democratic party; a woman who had become active through the Rainbow Institute is in charge of records and elections, with the power to give out jobs. The executive officer of the county—a black Republican—is also now a part of the institute's coalitional muscle. "We've achieved the objective," Holloway told me, "of having the kind of power to achieve pretty much of what we want. We've focused on putting our people into key positions in county and city government where we can have the only kind of influence that makes a difference: the ability to deliver jobs, money, and voters." The institute has also developed a statewide network and is beginning to work with Native Americans. In the 1986 elections it planned to field candidates for even wider offices. In 1988 it will probably be the determining factor in selecting the U.S. presidential nominee from Washington State.

The Rainbow Institute has been associated with establishing an African-American cultural center in the city, and with legislation on South African divestment, the homeless, sexual assault, drug abuse, low-income housing, and integration of the construction trades. Its base continues to be the precinct-level organization that provides it with the voters and candidates, proving that machine politics can be made to work for progressive ends. The Rainbow Institute disproves the elite notion that ordinary people are uninterested in politics. Rather, it has demonstrated that if given the tools and the know-how, working-class and low-income people are willing and capable of governing themselves and making democracy work.

From Social Protest to Electoral Politics—A New Paradigm

Prior to 1962 there had been only one Democrat elected statewide in Vermont's history, but in the late 1960s and early 1970s the state became a haven for burned-out social movement activists of the 1960s. They flocked to Vermont to set up food co-ops and engage in organic farming, and they proliferated in dozens of peace and social justice organizations. Three alternative parties were also spawned. A number of attempts over the years to bring all these separate issue groups together into larger coalitions laid the groundwork for their unity in the Jackson campaign.[15]

Prior to Jackson's candidacy, however, most political activity on the left (with the exception of the work of the Burlington Progressive Coalition, which had elected a self-professed socialist as mayor) had taken place outside the electoral arena in at least four types of issue-based movements: the peace and antinuclear movement, the environmental movement, the Central America solidarity movement, and a variety of left/progressive organizing efforts around economic justice.

Had Jackson not been running in the Democratic primary, most of these groups would not have entered electoral politics. As Judy Ashkenaz, Rainbow Coalition delegate to the Democratic Convention, points out, issue organizing in Vermont has been uncommonly successful, primarily because of the state's small size and the "town-hall" tradition of democracy that still exists there.[16] The Democratic party is weak, rarely fielding a full slate of candidates against the dominant Republicans, so before 1984 most social activists thought it not worth the bother to get involved in the energy-draining intricacies of party politics.

Some activists, however, recognized that Jackson's candidacy gave a national focus and prominence to issues they had worked long and hard to get public support for. What appealed to veteran activist Dave Dellinger who, by his own admission, was not one to shout, "Run, Jesse, Run," was that here was a candidate who combined electoral politics with social action. In his first visit to the state, Dellinger pointed out, Jackson visited a toxic waste dump in Williamstown that had been contaminating nearby homes. In the largest political gathering that has been held in Montpelier, the state capitol, since World War II, Jackson asked how many people would be willing to go out in the streets to bring the boys home from Honduras and Lebanon.

Ironically, it was the near disaster brought on by Jackson's "Hymie" remark that forced those in charge of the Jackson campaign to frame a strategy that was ultimately successful in establishing the Vermont Rainbow Coalition as a permanent independent force in Vermont politics.

Jackson forces had been hoping to bring in 25-35 percent of the vote in Vermont, but after the "Hymie" remark broke—two weeks before the first nonbinding primary vote—they were reduced to 8 percent. At that point, coordinator Stewart Meacham told me, "we decided to concentrate less on the man and more on the issues."

The campaign immediately began calling itself the "Rainbow Coalition." It approached all of the issue groups in the state, asking them to articulate their position on the issues. These were then collected into a platform package and mailings went out comparing Jackson's position on the issues with those of the other candidates as well as instructions on how to participate in the caucuses. "What we said in the call," said Meacham, "is that the Rainbow Coalition supports the candidacy of Jesse Jackson, but whether you support him or not, come out to the caucuses to support the resolutions on the issues." The result was that hundreds of activists who had never been involved in electoral politics mastered the intricacies of the several-tiered caucus system and quadrupled the participation in the Vermont caucuses. "Hart had polled 70 percent in the primary 'beauty contest,'" said Meacham, but he had no program, "so when we showed up in the caucuses, with a concrete program and issues, we scared the pee out of them!"

In the final round of voting at the state Democratic party convention, the Rainbow Coalition forces more than doubled their original vote, ending up with 19.6 percent, electing three delegates to the Democratic National Convention, and one of their number, former labor organizer and outspoken "socialist" Ellen David-Friedman, to the Democratic National Committee. Said Meacham, "We basically ran the show at the convention."

Bitten by the political bug, the coalition activists returned from the Democratic National Convention determined to run their own candidates for office. They had already registered 11,000 new voters and had discovered that the voter registration process gave them access to constituencies for their issues that they normally would not have been able to reach.

As a force that was now being recognized, coalition activists had to decide on their relationship to the Democratic party. Party members would have preferred that these activists come in and be absorbed into the party process, but coalition members decided they had to keep their independence and to maintain their issue-focus up-front. By being both *in* and *outside* the party, they could maintain their issue integrity while helping to move the Democratic party agenda to the left.

Thus, they ran "rainbow" candidates—that is, candidates committed to the Rainbow Coalition platform—in the Democratic primaries, winning all but one of the races. In the November election these candidates ran as "Rainbow Democrats."

Out of twelve candidates fielded in November, the Rainbow Coalition won two state senate seats and five state house seats. Two of those seats, including one won by Don Hooper, the state's leading environmentalist, were from districts that had never elected a Democrat before, and in another race, state representative Amy Davenport defeated the most powerful Republican legislator in the state. Twenty-two-year-old Micque Glitman, who was a college student when she became coordinator of the Jackson state campaign, was also elected to the state legislature, becoming its youngest member. The November election turned Vermont's traditional Republican tide, and while the majority of the presidential vote went for Reagan, the picture at the state level was entirely different.

A major test of the Rainbow Coalition's ability to maintain its independence and yet remain on good terms with the Democratic party came in its decision to give critical endorsement to the national Democratic ticket, but not to endorse any state Democratic candidate who was not specifically committed to the rainbow platform. This meant that they refused to endorse liberal gubernatorial candidate Madeleine Kunin. The move outraged Democratic party leaders, but others were reluctant to alienate the progressives because they had demonstrated that they could deliver in terms of votes and organizing. During the fall of 1984, Ellen David-Friedman and Burlington mayor Bernie Sanders toured the state, offering critical support for the national ticket from a left-wing perspective. The coalition, in concert with other groups, registered another 9,000 to 10,000 people.

With their own Rainbow Caucus in the state legislature, the Rainbow Coalition could now begin to bring the issues they represented directly into the state legislature. Issue activists who had formerly eschewed party politics discovered through the Jackson campaign that by entering party politics as an ideologically unified bloc, they could have a relatively fast and direct impact on national and state-wide policy out of all proportion to their numbers. Because the Democratic party is organized by congressional district, which in Vermont means the entire state is one unit, progressive activists there have greater impact on national and state-wide politics with a comprehensive approach than they could by working serially on single issues and seeking to influence the votes of individual legislators.

The Vermont Rainbow Coalition has, in effect, become the umbrella for that kind of political thrust and awareness. With an all-volunteer staff and donated office space, its thirty-member steering committee meets every six weeks in a different part of the state, drawing on the work of smaller committees that meet in between. The coalition's membership is drawn from the issue networks, from alternative parties, from Burlington's Progressive Coalition, and from the left wing of the Democratic party.

Rainbow Coalition legislators have been effective in bringing a South African divestment bill before the legislature (it lost by two votes in the state assembly but won in the senate), a bill to protect AIDS victims from discrimination, and the Fair Tax Initiative, which, in the two years of its existence has become the coalition's most ambitious project. They have also been successful in getting the state Democratic party to adopt a platform that is well to the left of most Democratic party platforms, and they have made themselves indispensable to the party's vote-getting ability.

The Fair Tax Initiative demonstrates how a progressive coalition, with entry to both a major party and the state legislature, can turn what has traditionally been the province of conservatives—the issue of taxation—into an issue that has working-class appeal and a redistributive function. While the tax debate among regular Democrats and Republicans centered on various ways of providing tax *relief*, Ashkenaz points out, the Fair Tax Initiative drafted by the Rainbow Coalition provides for a comprehensive *restructuring* of the state tax system, which in Vermont has been tied to the regressive Federal income tax policy.[17]

The Fair Tax Initiative would decouple the state tax from the federal tax, provide an exemption on property taxes for low- and middle-income homeowners, and establish a progressive property tax system that levies a higher rate for commercial and vacation property than for farm or residential property. The initiative has drawn wide support, not only from low-income and farmers' groups, but from the state PTA and the Vermont branch of the National Education Association, and it has provided the Rainbow Coalition with a handle that has enabled it to do fundamental grassroots education and organizing around the state on economic/class issues. The link between social issues such as peace and class issues has often been a difficult one for progressives to make, but the Rainbow Coalition has found a way to put them together.

Rainbow Coalition activists credit their success in remaining together, in broadening their support, and in retaining their independence on the issues while working with traditional party structures to three strategies: First, Stewart Meacham told me, "Our slogan has always been that the Vermont Rainbow is neither left, right, nor center, but 'in front.'" This has allowed activists of all stripes—socialists, anarchists, liberals, and issue-oriented independents—to work together to develop trust. Second, everything the Rainbow Coalition does, including its initial decision to get involved in electoral politics, is described in terms of an "experiment." Third, unlike Seattle's Rainbow Institute, the Vermont Rainbow Coalition has publicly stated that it does not want to take over the Democratic party. "We took the position," said Meacham, "that we had no hesitation about running for anything we wanted in the party, but we were not interested in controlling the machinery. We're partly in the electoral process, but we're also into non-violent direct action. This strengthened us immensely because it tended to reassure the Mondale dinosaur forces and at the same time really confounded them." As a result, the leadership of three county democratic committees has joined the coalition.

In 1986 the Rainbow Coalition will run an even larger group of candidates for statewide office, most of them as Rainbow Democrats, and will support the independent candidacy of Burlington mayor Bernie Sanders against Madeleine Kunin, who is viewed as a Mondale-type Democrate. This support of Sanders over Kunin is likely to fray its ties to regular Democrats, and its ability to weather this particular storm will depend on its ability to build an even bigger independent base of voters outside the Democratic party, committed to the issues rather than personality or party label.

The Launching of the Rainbow Coalition

On 17 April 1986, the National Rainbow Coalition finally came together to establish what was described as the "operational unity" so necessary to transform its platform into political reality. A total of 756 delegates from forty-three states attended a three-day gathering at the Washington, D.C., Convention Center, from which, two years before, the Jackson campaign for president had been launched. The delegates had not been formally elected because the state and local machinery for such representation had not been put in place. A formal delegate convention was planned for 1987, once state and local organizations had been officially chartered. All those in attendance had, however, been part of the 1984 campaign. They had been waiting impatiently for just such a moment to come together again.

There were many gaps in sectoral and organizational representation at this hastily called and somewhat poorly organized gathering. The most glaring was the weak representation of Latinos and Native Americans and the virtual absence of large southern constituencies—ironic particularly in view of the importance Jackson attached to the South in his political strategy.

But there were some new and potentially significant additions to the Rainbow Coalition this time around. William Winpisinger, president of the Machinists Union; Ken Blaylock, president of the American Federation of Government Employees; and Jan Pierce, of the Communications Workers of America, all appeared on the platform with Jackson, indicating a rapprochement with at least a part of the labor leadership that was missing in 1984. Also present were large numbers of rank-and-file white workers, and a group of two hundred farmers from all over the Midwest and South, who had been bussed in by the unions for the Save the Family Farm breakfast. A number of black elected officials who had not supported the Jackson campaign in 1984 were also present, including congressmen Charles Rangel of New York and Mickey Leland of Texas. Frances (Sissy) Farenthold, a prominent feminist and peace activist who had once run for governor of Texas, Texas agriculture commissioner Jim Hightower, and New Mexico governor Tony Anaya were also prominent among the dignitaries. In the diversity of its colors and regions, its class and ideological sectors, it was a gathering rarely seen in American political life. "You sure are a *stra-ange* looking group of people," Jackson quipped as he called the group to recognize the artificial barriers that have kept them politically apart.

An organizational charter and bylaws—the work of almost two years of thought, proposal writing, and testing the waters—was presented to the delegates, and after considerable debate and several amendments, passed unanimously.

The organizational and financial plan is based on organizing people into the Rainbow Coalition along congressional district lines. Congressional district organizations will then feed into the statewide Rainbow Coalition. Though there was some disgruntlement among the delegates that congressional districts were not the natural units in which people usually come together politically or socially—particularly in large cities—most admitted that the kind of organizing the plan required had the potential for changing the political calculus of the nation.

The nature of the struggle that ensued over the adoption of the plan of organization indicates tensions within the rainbow movement that only time and continued organizing will begin to shake out. The first conflict arose over whether the Rainbow Coalition would become just a left-wing caucus of the Democratic party or a truly independent organization able to operate inside and outside the two-party system. This erupted when delegates read in the statement of purpose that they were "enlightened Democrats." After lobbying by independents, the wording was changed to "Democrats and independents." Nevertheless, the tension will continue for some time, as the Democratic party begins to recognize what has been spawned in its own backyard.

For the time being, it seems certain that the Rainbow Coalition will operate primarily in relation to the Democratic party—since that is where most of its seasoned political leadership is located—but it will have the capacity to support independent candidates where feasible. Much will depend on the degree of openness the Democratic party exhibits toward the coalition's agenda. "People are becoming independent," said Jackson, "because their interests are not being served by one party with two names going in the same direction." On the local level, as in Vermont, the party may be quite open to the coalition's participation. In other areas, as was evident in both Alabama and Seattle, party regulars, particularly at the higher levels of power, may perceive the Rainbow Coalition as a threat to their economic and political interests. To be successful, the coalition will inevitably go through trials by fire, in which every conceivable form of vilification, "dirty tricks," and sabotage from within and without will be used against it.

A second debate arose over what appeared to many to be an excessively top-down and centralized bureaucracy. Many delegates raised questions about whether such an organization would be able to involve grassroots and poor people, who were supposed to be the Rainbow Coalition's natural constituencies. While the problem was not fully resolved, some amendments were made to the bylaws that allowed for more flexibility. Leaders conceded that the document was a provisional one and that at the formal convention in 1987 delegates would have the opportunity to change the bylaws based on concrete experience gained from working with them.

The third struggle arose over the kind of pluralism that would be represented on the board of directors and in the leadership of the National Rainbow Coalition. Many delegates felt that the board that had been handpicked by Jackson was too heavily weighted with men and with "leadership" types who had little grassroots experience or rapport. That, too, was modified after intense discussion to at least the provisional satisfaction of the delegates.

As important as the changes in the bylaws was the process of struggle for participation and democracy that was exhibited by delegates to the convention. Informed, disciplined, and committed to the organization's success, they established a dynamic within the Rainbow Coalition that made it clear that local activists at the base will insist on a process of organizing and internal development that reflects the new, alternative society they are working to build.[18]

In its commitment to the broad principles of justice, democracy, and peace, the National Rainbow Coalition remained steadfast. Its convention was held just a few days after the U.S. bombing of Libya, which was done unilaterally and without clear proof of Libya's complicity in the act of terrorism that was the pretext for the bombing. Flanked by leading members of the Congressional Black Caucus, Jackson denounced this bombing as "failed foreign policy" and pointed out the U.S. government's hypocrisy on the issue of "terrorism." He spoke of the Rainbow Coalition as a "new majority" that could turn the tragedy of radical economic dislocation, war, and threats of war into "treasure and triumph." "We must build a vehicle for the expression of our power," he told an overflow crowd of 2000, "and through this vehicle we will project, support, and monitor political candidates and increase voter registration and participation. With this vehicle we will challenge the course of Reagan's foreign and military policy."[19] In seeming affirmation of their majority power and in the strength of their felt unity, the multiracial crowd clasped hands and swayed together in a scene reminiscent of the early days of the civil rights movement, as gospel singer Wendell Phillips sang "We Are One."

Although the more than three hundred resolutions that delegates had brought to the convention could not be processed or voted on in the time available, the Rainbow Coalition established a broad set of priorities within which most of the specific resolutions would fit. Among the resolutions were the following:

We will organize to repeal the Gramm-Rudman-Hollings legislation.

We will fight for a humane alternative to the national budget and a fair tax structure.

We will propose a fair farm policy and a complementary urban policy that incorporates economic, social, and political opportunity.

We will fight for full employment at union wages.

We will fight for a toxic-free environment and a nuclear-free world.

We will build a constituency for a noninterventionist foreign policy based on peace, development, the right to national self-determination, and human rights.

We will negotiate new relationships with the national and local party organizations in an effort to open them up further and democratize them, thereby building a base for leadership in support of these humane policy objectives. Also, we will encourage, endorse, and support independent political initiatives and campaigns that put forward to the American people the National Rainbow Coalition platform. Our goal will be to continue to press for fair election rules, especially proportional delegate selection procedures, integrated voting and slate-making, full enforcement of the 1965 Voting Rights Act, and expanded voter participation.

We will seek to revive ethical and moral values in American domestic and foreign policy by building an ethically and culturally diverse coalition that is itself founded on the ethical and moral common ground of what is politically *right* rather than merely expedient.

Epilogue: Realizing the Constitutional Promise

The revival of ethical and moral values in the arena of national policy was perhaps the true genius of the Jackson campaign of 1984. The ability to gain wider adherence to these values and to translate them into specific policy proposals and political strategies will be the real litmus test of the Rainbow Coalition's viability. This will not be an easy task; it is easier to give lip-service to such ideals than to put them into practice within a national nexus of power that rewards opposing values. An extraordinary level of courage, altruism, discipline, and dedication will thus be required of those who would build a functioning rainbow coalition. It is a measure of the truly heroic proportions of those who forged the Jackson campaign of 1984 that they were able to come even this far.

It was precisely a coherent moral vision that was missing from the populist, single-issue, and community-organizing politics of so many white activists during the 1970s—a politics that, as sociologist Robert Bellah points out, too easily lends itself to opportunism and cooptation in the absence of a broad set of principles to which many people can commit themselves for long-term political engagement.[20]

A moral vision was always the motivating power behind the great American social reform movements, whether it was the Abolitionist movement, the early women's movement, the socialist movement, the labor movement, or the civil rights movement. When those movements abandoned the moral visions that gave them life, to focus on protecting the partial material or symbolic concessions they had won—as when the labor movement dropped its great moral vision of transforming the relations of production to settle for higher wages—the movements were greatly weakened and their ability to fulfill America's rhetoric about itself was undermined.

Political leaders have always given lip-service to moral ideals, but they have rarely proposed to use them as norms in the determination of public policy. Such policy formation is derided as "impractical" and "utopian" by those who stand to benefit from power politics. Thus they have relegated to the so-called private sphere—to the province of women, clerics, and outsiders—the great notions of compassion, love, human dignity, justice, and peace.

Rainbow politics is based on the recognition that we are now in a civilizational crisis of such proportions that we can no longer afford to relegate such questions to the private order. To continue with policies based on the ethic of *realpolitik* is to endanger the future of life on the planet.

Though its enemies will call the Rainbow Coalition impractical and utopian, the effort to apply the moral vision it enunciated is the only realistic solution to the awesome possibilities that now confront us. As it attempts to gain power, the Rainbow Coalition will undoubtedly be red-baited (as every great American reform movement has been), but it can be demonstrated that its roots are deep in U.S. political foundations.

The moral vision that informs rainbow politics is the same vision that undergirds the Constitution, and both are rooted in our Judeo-Christian heritage. American constitutional history, however, is a record of the deep contradiction that lies at the heart of the American experience—between the ideals that are embedded in its formative documents, and the class interests of those empowered to interpret and apply those ideals.

The Constitution itself is a product of the heroic struggle against hereditary privilege and imperialism. As such, it incorporates one of the most revolutionary notions known to humankind: the principle of the equality and dignity of all human beings and their inalienable right to "life, liberty, and the pursuit of happiness." Such an ideal, Supreme Court Justice William Brennan has pointed out, is a constantly evolving one, which every generation must struggle to apply based on its own historical circumstances.[21]

Yet the contradiction at the heart of U.S. history is that to guard their own privilege the Founding Fathers who enshrined this principle were not prepared to apply it to everyone. Thus they read out of the notion of humanity everyone who was not a white property-owning male.

Such is the genius of the Constitution, however, that the ideal remained to be striven for, and the subsequent history of social

Notes

Introduction

1. Theodore H. White, "New Powers, New Politics," *New York Times Magazine*, 5 February 1984, pp. 22–24.
2. Walter Dean Burnham, "The Future of American Politics," in *Election 84:: Landslide Without a Mandate?* ed. Ellis Sandoz and Cecil V. Crabb, Jr. (New York: New American Library, 1985), p. 210.

1. From Melting Pot to Boiling Cauldron: The 1960s Revisited

1. Toni Cade Bambara, "What It Is I Think I'm Doing Anyhow," in *The Writer and Her Work*, ed. Janet Sternburg (New York: W. W. Norton, 1980), p. 154.
2. Antonio Gramsci, "Analysis of Situations, Relations of Force," in *Communication and Class Struggle*, Vol. I, *Capitalism and Imperialism*, ed. Armand Mattelart and Seth Siegelaube (New York: International General, and Bagnolet, France: International Mass Media Research Center, 1979), pp. 108–12; Carl Boggs, *Gramsci's Marxism* (London: Pluto Press, 1976), pp. 52, 114–15.

3. John Lukacs, *Historical Consciousness or The Remembered Past*, rev. ed. (New York: Schocken Books, 1985), p. 184.
4. William Appleman Williams, *Empire as a Way of Life* (New York: Oxford University Press, 1980).
5. Houston's confession is cited in Elizabeth Sutherland Martinez and Enriqueta Longeaux y Vasquez, *Viva La Raza: The Struggle of the Mexican-American People* (New York: Doubleday, 1974), pp. 59–60.
6. George Kennan, State Department, Document PPS23, February 1948. Quoted in a speech by Noam Chomsky, "Intervention in Vietnam and Central America," excerpted in *Resist* 176 (May/June 1985): 1.
7. Stephen Steinberg, *The Ethnic Myth: Race, Ethnicity and Class in American Society* (New York: Atheneum, 1981), p. 47.
8. Oscar Handlin, *Race and Nationality in American Life* (New York: Doubleday, 1957), p. 142.
9. Doug McAdam, *Political Process and the Development of Black Insurgency, 1930–1970* (Chicago: University of Chicago Press, 1982), pp. 5–6. McAdam thoroughly demolishes the pluralist theory and its corollary explanations for the emergence of social-protest movements in his study of the black insurgency of the 1960s. For a thorough explication of the pluralist model, see Robert A. Dahl, *Pluralist Democracy in the United States* (Chicago: Rand McNally, 1967). For another critique of interest-group pluralism, see Marvin E. Olsen, *Participatory Pluralism: Political Participation and Influence in the United States and Sweden* (Chicago: Nelson-Hall, 1982).
10. Theodore J. Lowi, "The New Public Philosophy: Interest-Group Liberalism," in *The Political Economy: Readings in the Politics and Economics of American Public Policy*, ed. Thomas Ferguson and Joel Rogers (Armonk, N.Y.: M. E. Sharpe, Inc., 1984), p. 61.
11. *The Kerner Report* concluded that only after three generations were white immigrants who had emigrated from rural backgrounds "finally beginning to move into the middle class" (*Report of the National Advisory Commission on Civil Disorders* [New York: Bantam Books, 1968], p. 16).
12. Colin Greer, "The Ethnic Question," in *The 60s without Apology*, ed. Sohnya Sayres, et al. (Minneapolis: University of Minnesota Press, 1984), pp. 120–21.
13. Andrew Kopkind, "Black Power in the Age of Jackson," *The Nation*, 26 November 1983, p. 533.
14. C. T. Vivian, *Black Power and the American Myth* (Philadelphia: Fortress Press, 1970), p. 39. Emphasis added.
15. Ibid., pp. 55–56.
16. Sellers quoted in Harvard Sitkoff, *The Struggle for Black Equality 1954–1980* (New York: Hill and Wang, 1981), pp. 179ff.
17. Vivian, *Black Power*, pp. 87, 88–89.

18. Ibid., p. 99.
19. Vivian, *Black Power*, p. 99. In a study of black political participation in the South after passage of the Voting Rights Act, Salamon and Van Evera found that economic fear (the fear of being fired, losing one's welfare payments, home, etc.) kept many blacks from exercising their newly won rights—especially in rural counties where the local white power elite controlled the jobs, the credit system, the judiciary, and the town hall ("Fear, Apathy and Discrimination: A Test of Three Explanations of Political Participation," *The American Political Science Review* 67 [1973]). The fear of economic reprisal is not limited to the rural South. Because of the professional and economic dependence of so many urban blacks on city hall, big city machines may also use the fear of economic reprisal to keep black voters and black politicians in line. See James Jennings, "Urban Machinism and the Black Voter," in *The New Black Vote*, ed. Rod Bush (San Francisco: Synthesis Publications, 1984), pp. 242–68.
20. James Forman, *The Making of Black Revolutionaries* (Washington, D.C.: Open Hand Publishing Inc., 1985), pp. 479–80, 552.
21. Martin Luther King, Jr., "The President's Address to the Tenth Anniversary Convention of the Southern Christian Leadership Conference, August 16, 1967," in *The Rhetoric of Black Power*, ed. Robert L. Scott and Wayne Brockriede (New York: Harper and Row, 1969), pp. 161–62.
22. Martin Luther King's biographer asserts that King once confided that he lacked confidence in grappling with sophisticated economic relationships—a lack of competence, he says, that was generally shared among the ministers who were in the leadership of the civil rights movement (David L. Lewis, *King: A Biography* 2nd ed. [Urbana: University of Illinois Press, 1978], pp. 250–51).
23. James Cone, *For My People: Black Theology and the Black Church* (Maryknoll, N.Y.: Orbis Books, 1984), p. 96.
24. Martin Luther King, Jr., *Where Do We Go from Here: Chaos or Community?* (New York: Harper and Row, 1967), p. 133.
25. King, "Beyond Vietnam" (Speech delivered to Clergy and Laymen Concerned About Vietnam, Riverside Church, New York City, 4 April 1967; reprinted in *Where Do We Go From Here?*, p. 189).
26. Interview with C. T. Vivian, 21 April 1985.
27. Bernice Reagon, "The Borning Struggle," in *They Should Have Served That Cup of Coffee: Seven Radicals Remember the 60s*, ed. Dick Cluster (Boston: South End Press, 1979), p. 22.
28. Reggie Schell, "A Way to Fight Back: The Black Panther Party," in *They Should Have Served That Cup of Coffee*, pp. 56–57.
29. Vincent Harding, "The Afro-American Past and the American Present," *Motive*, April 1968, reprinted in *The Movement Toward a New*

America: The Beginnings of a Long Revolution, comp. Mitch Goodman (Philadelphia: Pilgrim Press, and New York: Alfred A. Knopf, 1970), p. 128.

30. Gene Roberts, "Dr. King Planning Protests to 'Dislocate' Large Cities," *New York Times*, 16 August 1967, reprinted in *The Movement Toward a New America*, p. 137. One of the blacks arrested in the Watts rebellion is reported to have said that "the first time in my life I felt like a man was when I was burning down that store," quoted by Paul Jacobs, "Prelude to Riot" in *Movement Toward a New America*, p. 151.

31. Reagon, "Borning Struggle," p. 22.

32. Robert Allen, *Black Awakening in Capitalist America* (Garden City, N.Y.: Doubleday and Co., 1969), p. 31.

33. Forman, *Making of Black Revolutionaries*, p. 487. SNCC's declaration of its broadened agenda came, ironically, at the very point at which it was undergoing dissolution. Its vision had grown larger than the political opportunities that were available for its implementation.

34. Ibid., pp. 485–86.

35. Philip V. White, "Blacks and U.S. Foreign Policy: Obstacles to Influence," in *Black Americans and the Shaping of U.S. Foreign Policy* (Washington, D.C.: Joint Center for Political Studies, 1980), p. 43.

36. *The Autobiography of Malcolm X* (New York: Ballantine Books), pp. 333ff. See also: George Breitman, *The Last Year of Malcolm X: The Evolution of a Revolutionary* (New York: Pathfinder Press, 1967).

37. Vincent Harding, *The Other American Revolution* (Los Angeles: Center for Afro-American Studies, and Atlanta: Institute of the Black World, 1980), p. 181.

38. Schell, "A Way to Fight Back," p. 61. Schell believes that this convention of the Black Panther party may have been deliberately sabotaged because of the threat such a gathering made to the ruling elite. That meeting, according to Schell, was the beginning of the end of the Black Panther party.

39. Ibid., pp. 58–59.

40. Dan Georgakas and Marvin Surkin, *Detroit I Do Mind Dying: A Study in Urban Revolution* (New York: St. Martin's Press, 1975), pp. 1–2. Workers' groups modeled after the Detroit Revolutionary Union Movement (DRUM) were begun in several other parts of the country— New Jersey, Birmingham, and Atlanta—and plans for a National Black Workers' Congress were made. Before this could happen, however, the movement fizzled, as a result of internal differences as well as outside attacks and lack of adequate financial resources.

41. Georgakas and Surkin, *Detroit*, p. 5.

42. Reagon, "The Borning Struggle," pp. 35–36.

43. For histories of the Chicano movement, see Elizabeth Sutherland

Martinez and Enriqueta Longeaux y Vasquez, *Viva La Raza: The Struggle of the Mexican-American People* (New York: Doubleday, 1974); Joseph L. Love, "La Raza: Mexican-Americans in Rebellion," in *Three Perspectives on Ethnicity in America: Blacks, Chicanos and Native Americans*, ed. Carlos E. Cortes et al. (New York: G. P. Putnam's Sons, 1976); and Stan Steiner, *La Raza: The Mexican-Americans* (New York: Harper and Row, 1970).

44. Vine Deloria and Clifford Lytle, *The Nations Within: The Past and Future of American Indian Sovereignty* (New York: Pantheon, 1984), p. 2. Additional histories and analyses of the modern Indian insurgency are contained in Deloria, *Behind the Trail of Broken Treaties* (New York: Delacorte Press, 1974); Alvin M. Josephy, Jr., *Now That the Buffalo's Gone: A Study of Today's American Indians* (New York: Alfred A. Knopf, 1982); and Peter Matthiesen, *In the Spirit of Crazy Horse* (New York: Viking Press, 1983) and *Indian Country* (New York: The Viking Press, 1984).

45. For accounts of the party reforms inaugurated in 1968 and 1972, see Byron E. Shafer, *Quite Revolution: The Struggle for the Democratic Party and the Shaping of Post Reform Politics* (New York: Russell Sage Foundation, 1983); and John S. Saloma and Frederick H. Sontag, *Parties: The Real Opportunity for Effective Citizen Politics* (New York: Alfred A. Knopf, 1972).

46. At a meeting of antiwar activists I attended in Berkeley, California, in 1976, Daniel Ellsberg asked the group of over two hundred if they felt their actions in the 1960s had been effective in halting the war. Only a handful indicated that they thought they had been. Ellsberg told the audience that that impression is exactly what the Nixon administration had wanted them to believe and that media coverage and government responses during those years were all calculated to portray the movement as totally ineffective. Just the opposite had been the case, he said. The movement had slowed the pace of the war and had possibly prevented nuclear weapons from being used in Vietnam.

47. McAdam, *Political Process*, provides the most comprehensive analysis of the dissolution of the black insurgency of the 1960s. See also Nelson Blackstock, *Cointelpro: The FBI's Secret War on Political Freedom* (New York: Vintage Books/Random House, 1975); Lewis M. Killian, *The Impossible Revolution, Phase II: Black Power and the American Dream* (New York: Random House, 1975); David J. Garrow, *The FBI and Martin Luther King, Jr.* (New York: W. W. Norton, 1981); and Gary T. Marx, ed., *Racial Conflict*, (Boston: Little, Brown, 1971).

2. The New Right Assault on the Second Reconstruction

1. Sidney M. Willhelm, "Equality in America's Racist Ideology," *The Death of White Sociology*, ed. Joyce Ladner (New York: Random House, 1973), p. 154.
2. See E. Franklin Frazier, *Race and Culture Contacts in the Modern World* (Boston: Beacon Press, 1957); Philip Foner, *Organized Labor and the Black Worker 1619–1973* (New York: International Publishers, 1976); and Alphonso Pinkney, *The Myth of Black Progress* (Cambridge: Cambridge University Press, 1984).
3. Marxists were always quicker than capitalist managers to detect signs of trouble in the economy. See, for example, Harry Magdoff and Paul Sweezy, "Keynesian Chickens Come Home to Roost," *Monthly Review*, April 1974; *Radical Perspectives on the Economic Crisis of Monopoly Capitalism* (New York: Union for Radical Political Economics, 1975); *U.S. Capitalism in Crisis* (New York: Economics Education Project of the Union for Radical Political Economics, 1978); and Sumner Rosen, ed., *Economic Power Failure: The Current American Crisis* (New York: McGraw-Hill, 1975).
4. Henry Kaufman, "Foreward," in Edward I. Altman and Arnold W. Sametz, *Financial Crises, Institutions and Markets in a Fragile Environment* (New York: John Wiley and Sons, 1977), p. vii; quoted in Harry Magdoff and Paul Sweezy, *The Deepening Crisis of Capitalism* (New York: Monthly Review Press, 1981), p. 9.
5. Legitimation crisis has featured prominently in the political theories of neo-Marxists associated with the Frankfurt School. See Jurgen Habermas, *Legitimation Crisis*, trans. Thomas McCarthy (Boston: Beacon Press, 1973).
6. David Held, *Introduction to Critical Theory: Horkheimer to Habermas* (Berkeley and Los Angeles: University of California Press, 1980), p. 291.
7. University of Michigan Center for Political Studies Election Surveys, cited in Samuel Huntington, "The United States," in *The Crisis of Democracy: Report on the Governability of Democracies to the Trilateral Commission* (New York: New York University Press, 1975), p. 79.
8. Huntington, "United States," p. 71; Louis Harris, *The Anguish of Change* (New York: W. W. Norton, 1973), p. 142.
9. Harris, *Anguish of Change*, pp. 12–13.
10. Huntington, ("United States," pp. 85–91) even goes so far as to raise the specter of the "end of the political party as we have known it" with his colleagues on the Trilateral Commission.
11. Pollsters Louis Harris, Patrick Caddell, and Peter Hart told Democrats assembled at a party meeting in Chicago in 1975 that the public wants

not just progressive but "radical" solutions to the economic crisis ("Full Employment: A National Priority," *JSAC Grapevine* 7, no. 6 [New York: Joint Strategy and Action Committee, 1976]).

12. Ibid. Louis Harris' findings on attitudes toward business led him to conclude that while there was a significant decline in the public's confidence in business, this did not necessarily translate into support for socialism. The reactions of most businessmen to his findings, however, were to increase their fear of socialism and communism, moving them to go on the offensive against these ideologies (See also Harris, *Anguish of Change*, pp. 151–67).

13. Ibid., pp. 142–43.

14. Ibid., p. 38.

15. Samuel Lubell, *The Hidden Crisis in American Politics* (New York: W. W. Norton, 1970), pp. 13, 17–18.

16. *The Report of the President's Commission on Campus Unrest* (Washington, D.C.: U.S. Government Printing Office, 1970), p. 1.

17. Leonard Silk and David Vogel, *Ethics and Profits* (New York: Simon and Schuster, 1976), cited in David Dickson and David Noble, "By Force of Reason: The Politics of Science and Technology Policy," in *The Hidden Election: Politics and Economics in the 1980 Presidential Campaign*, ed. Thomas Ferguson and Joel Rogers (New York: Pantheon Books, 1981), pp. 275–76.

18. Huntington, "United States," pp. 61–62.

19. Ibid., p. 105, 113.

20. Ibid., p. 98.

21. Nathan Glazer and Daniel P. Moynihan, eds., *Ethnicity: Theory and Experience* (Cambridge: Harvard University Press, 1975), p. 21.

22. Cited in *Liberation News Service*, December 1976.

23. *New York Times*, 4 January 1976, p. 27.

24. D. J. Kirchhoff, "Those Who Believe in Capitalism Must Fight Back," *Barron's*, 19 February 1979.

25. Such astute left sociologists as Frances Fox Piven and Richard Cloward, Doug McAdam, and historian Harvard Sitkoff have all accepted the assumption of a "white backlash"; see Frances Fox Piven and Richard Cloward, *Poor People's Movements: How They Succeed, Why They Fail* (New York: Vintage Books/Random House, 1979), p. 332; Doug McAdam, *Political Process and the Development of Black Insurgency, 1930–1970* (Chicago: University of Chicago Press, 1982), pp. 191–97; and Harvard Sitkoff, *The Struggle for Black Equality, 1954–1980* (New York: Hill and Wang, 1981), pp. 208–09.

26. Harris, *Anguish of Change*, p. 287. Emphasis added.

27. Ibid., p. 286.

28. Peter Steinfels, *The Neoconservatives: The Men Who Are Changing America's Politics* (New York: Simon and Schuster, 1979), p. 6.

29. Nathan Glazer and Daniel P. Moynihan, *Beyond the Melting Pot: The Negroes, Puerto Ricans, Jews, and Irish of New York City*. 2nd ed. (Cambridge: MIT Press, 1970). Colin Greer contends that ethnicity is a "facade to obscure the fragility of America's egalitarian self-image. It seems to be growing in an effort to provide an excuse or rationale for the nation's inability to honor its promises of the 60s" ("Remembering Class," in *Divided Society: The Ethnic Experience in America*, ed. Colin Greer [New York: Basic Books, 1974], p. 4).

30. Glazer and Moynihan, *Ethnicity*, p. 15.

31. Glazer and Moynihan, *Beyond the Melting Pot*. Despite many scholarly refutations, Moynihan and Glazer, in the second edition of their book, stick to their earlier assumptions about the cultural deprivation of the black community.

32. Glazer and Moynihan, *Beyond the Melting Pot*, pp. 49–50.

33. For discussions and refutations of the Moynihan thesis, see: Frances Fox Piven and Richard Cloward, *Regulating the Poor: The Functions of Public Welfare* (New York: Vintage Books/Random House, 1971), pp. 183ff.; Mary Frances Berry and John W. Blassingame, *Long Memory: The Black Experience in America* (New York: Oxford University Press, 1982), pp. 70–91; Lee Rainwater and William L. Yancey, *The Moynihan Report and the Politics of Controversy: A Transaction Social Science and Public Policy Report* (Cambridge, Mass.: MIT Press, 1967); Andrew Billingsley, *Black Families in White America* (Englewood Cliffs, N.J., 1968), pp. 199–202.

34. Quoted in Piven and Cloward, *Poor People's Movements*, p. 338.

35. For an extended discussion of the politics surrounding the Family Assistance Plan, see ibid., pp. 335ff.

36. William Ryan, "Savage Discovery: The Moynihan Report," *The Nation*, 22 November 1965, p. 380.

37. Ibid., p. 383.

38. Glazer and Moynihan, *Beyond the Melting Pot*, p. lxxiv.

39. Ibid., p. lxxxvii.

40. Moynihan, "The Politics of Stability" (Address to the National Board of Americans for Democratic Action, 23 September 1967; reprinted in Daniel P. Moynihan, *Coping: Essays on the Practice of Government* [New York: Random House, 1973], pp. 191–192).

41. Moynihan, "The Politics of Stability," p. 191.

42. Aaron Wildavsky, "Government and the People," *Commentary*, August 1973, p. 32; and Robert Moss, "Let's Look Out for No. 1," *New York Times Magazine*, 1 May 1977, p. 31; quoted in Steinfels, *Neoconservatives*, pp. 242–43.

43. Moynihan, "The Politics of Stability," p. 192.

44. Roy Persons, former education official with the Johnson administra-

tion, told a conference of graduate students that I attended in July 1985 that the managers of the anti-poverty programs knew they were not intended to make any real difference in the calculus of power for minorities, but simply to cool things out. There have, of course, been several refutations of the thesis that the Great Society legislation of the 1960s was a waste of money. A comprehensive study by Sar Levitan and Robert Taggart, published in 1976 as *The Promise of Greatness*, concludes that "the 1960s programs and policies and their continuation had a massive, overwhelmingly beneficial impact." (Cambridge: Harvard University Press, 1976, pp. vii–viii).

45. For the thesis that the white backlash was a *program*, not a spontaneous reaction to black gains, I am indebted to Michael Omi and Howard Winant, "By the Rivers of Babylon: Race in the United States," Part Two, *Socialist Review* 13, no. 6 (November–December 1983): 46–47.

46. The Wallace vote may not have been based entirely on racist sentiments. According to one survey, at least 20 percent of his vote in the 1968 election came from disaffected McCarthy primary contest voters. Such a vote may have been more a protest against manipulation of the presidential selection process by party regulars than a vote for regression in the area of race relations; Nelson W. Polsby and Adam B. Wildavsky, *Presidential Elections: Strategies of American Electoral Politics*, 3rd. ed. (New York: Charles Scribner's Sons, 1971), p. 55.

47. National Opinion Research Center Survey, cited in "The Racial Attitudes of White Americans," in *The Politics of Protest*, 3 (Staff Report to the National Commission on the Causes and Prevention of Violence, prepared by Jerome Skolnick, Washington, D.C., 1969, pp. 140–41).

48. Paul Sheatsley, "White Attitudes Toward the Negro," *Race and Poverty: The Economics of Discrimination*, ed. John F. Kain (Englewood Cliffs, N.J.: Prentice-Hall, 1969), p. 137.

49. Harris, *Anguish of Change*, p. 234.

50. "The Racial Attitudes of White Americans," pp. 157–58.

51. Sheatsley, "White Attitudes," p. 138.

52. Andrew Greeley and Paul Sheatsley, "Attitudes Toward Racial Integration," *Scientific American*, December 1971, p. 19.

53. Moynihan, "The New Racialism" (Commencement Address to the New School for Social Research, 4 June 1968; published in *Atlantic Monthly*, August 1968; quoted in Steinfels, *Neoconservatives*, p. 196.

54. Moynihan, "Democrats, Kennedy and the Murder of Dr. King," quoted in Steinfels, *Neoconservatives*, p. 128.

55. This was said at the very height of the women's liberation movement,

in the midst of a strong Native American insurgency, and in the face of polls that showed the majority of the American public favoring worker ownership of large corporations. Norman Podhoretz, The Intellectuals and the Pursuit of Happiness," Commentary, February 1973, p. 7.

56. Michael Novak, The Rise of the Unmeltable Ethnics: Politics and Culture in the Seventies (New York: Macmillan, 1971), p. 141.

57. Ibid., pp. 60–61.

58. Stephen Steinberg, The Ethnic Myth: Race, Ethnicity and Class in America (New York: Atheneum, 1981), pp. 48–49. Andrew Greeley's studies reveal "surprisingly low correlations between ethnic consciousness and the persistence of ethnic traits" (Ethnicity in the United States: A Preliminary Reconnaissance [New York: John Wiley and Sons, 1974], p. 320).

59. Greeley, Ethnicity in the United States, pp. 286–87.

60. Novak, Rise of the Unmeltable Ethnics, pp. 171, 253.

61. See Andrew Greeley, The American Catholic: A Social Portrait (New York: Basic Books, 1977), p. 4; and Martin Kilson, "Blacks, and Neo-Ethnicity in America," in Glazer and Moynihan, eds., Ethnicity, p. 259. According to Kilson, 80 percent of Jews could be classified as "middle class."

62. Michael Novak, The Spirit of Democratic Capitalism (New York: Simon and Schuster, 1982) and Toward a Theology of the Corporation (Washington, D.C.: American Enterprise Institute, 1981).

63. Richard Scammon and Ben J. Wattenberg, "Black Progress and Liberal Rhetoric," Commentary, April 1973, p. 38.

64. Moynihan, "The New Racialism," p. 204.

65. Moynihan, "The Deepening Schism," The Public Interest, Spring 1972; reprinted in Coping, p. 353.

66. In 1970 and 1971 the median black family income was 63 percent that of whites. In 1973 it dropped to 60 percent, went back up to 65 percent in 1975, and then started a steady drop (U.S. Census Bureau, cited in Alphonso Pinkney, The Myth of Black Progress [Cambridge: Cambridge University Press, 1984], p. 83).

67. Jay R. Mandle, The Roots of Black Poverty (Durham: Duke University Press, 1978), p. 102.

68. Sar A. Levitan, William B. Johnson, and Robert Taggart, Still a Dream: The Changing Status of Blacks Since 1960 (Cambridge: Harvard University Press, 1975), p. 46.

69. Bureau of Labor Statistics, Handbook of Labor Statistics, 1971, cited in Mandle, Roots of Black Poverty, p. 103.

70. Irving Kristol, "Thoughts on Equality and Egalitarianism," in Income Redistribution, ed. Colin D. Campbell (Washington, D.C.: American Enterprise Institute, 1977), pp. 41–42; Daniel P. Moynihan, "Present-

ing the American Case," *American Scholar* 44 (Autumn 1975): 577–78; and Nathan Glazer, "The Limits of Social Policy," *Commentary*, September 1971, p. 52; cited in Steinfels, *Neoconservatives*, p. 214.

71. Moynihan, "The Deepening Schism," p. 361.

72. Kevin Phillips, *The Emerging Republican Majority* (New Rochelle: Arlington House, 1969).

73. Ibid., p. 37.

74. Reg Murphy and Hal Gulliver, *The Southern Strategy* (New York: Charles Scribner's Sons, 1971), p. 2.

75. Sitkoff, *Struggle for Black Equality*, 223–25.

76. Vincent Harding, *The Other American Revolution* (Los Angeles: Center for Afro-American Studies, and Atlanta: Institute of the Black World, 1980), p. 224.

77. Manning Marable, *Blackwater: Historical Studies in Race, Class Consciousness and Revolution* (Dayton: Black Praxis Press, 1981), p. 94.

78. According to Marable, the black petty bourgeoisie has never maintained a substantial economic base. Thus, black politicians and business and civic leaders had had to depend on federal subsidies and private foundation grants as a means of providing the base for political activities (*From the Grassroots: Social and Political Essays Toward Afro-American Liberation* [Boston: South End Press, 1980], p. 33). The comparative economic well-being of blacks and whites depends on more than just income. A comparison of net wealth shows that blacks have only about one-third the average wealth of whites. Most of the black gains in wealth in the late 1960s and early 1970s occurred in house equity and car ownership, not in the kinds of investments that really affect the allocation of power (William P. O'Hare, *Wealth and Economic Status: A Perspective on Racial Inequity* [Washington, D.C.: Joint Center for Political Studies, 1983], pp. 26–27).

79. William Julius Wilson, *The Declining Significance of Race* (Chicago: University of Chicago Press, 1975).

80. Michael Omi, Book Review on *The Declining Significance of Race*, in *The Insurgent Sociologist* 10, no. 2 (Fall 1980): 120.

81. See Salim Muwakkil, "Integration 101's Many Dropouts," *In These Times*, 12–18 March 1986, p. 2. In the mid-1960s 75 percent of all black households had two parents, and only 21.6 percent of all black children were born out of wedlock. By 1982 only 53 percent of all black households had two parents and over 50 percent of all black children were born out of wedlock. More than 60 percent of the single-parent families lived in poverty (Manning Marable, *Black American Politics: From the Washington Marches to Jesse Jackson* [London: Verso, 1984], pp. 103–04).

82. Marable, *Black American Politics*, p. 57.

83. Marable, *Blackwater*, p. 100.
84. For analyses of the effect on whites of racism, see Joseph Barndt, *Liberating our White Ghetto* (Minneapolis: Augsburg Publishing House, 1972).
   York: Columbia University Press, 1984).
85. In retrospect, the exile of young whites from the civil rights movement by SNCC in the late 1960s appears a tragic mistake. In 1966 whites were told by SNCC leaders to go home and organize among the white working class where the problem of racism was. They were offered the vague hope that at some future date when whites were organized, they could come back into coalition with blacks. Contrary to the assumption of many militant black movement leaders that whites did not heed their directive, whites did just that. More organizing took place in white communities during the 1970s than in almost any previous period of history. The problem was that the organizing was cut off from what was taking place in black communities.
86. McAdam, *Political Process*, p. 160.
87. Elliott Currie, Robert Dunn, and David Fogarty, "The New Immiseration," *Socialist Revolution* 5, no. 4 (October-December 1975): 7–29.

3. The Emergence of the Rainbow Coalition

1. "Jesse Jackson's Philosophy" (campaign position paper).
2. Thomas Byrne Edsall provides a compelling analysis of the right-wing ascendancy during the 1970s and its impact on publc policy in *The New Politics of Inequality* (New York: W. W. Norton, 1984).
3. See Martin Luther King, *Where Do We Go From Here: Chaos or Community?* (New York: Harper and Row, 1967), especially ch. 4, 5, 6.
4. Rainbow political strategist Jack O'Dell has pointed out that the Poor People's Campaign of 1967 was the Rainbow Coalition in "embryonic form," because it brought together a multiracial body of the dispossessed ("Interview with Jack O'Dell," *Frontline*, 15 October 1984, p. 8). For the ruling class's reaction to the Poor People's Campaign, see Gary T. Marx, "External Efforts to Damage or Facilitate Social Movements: Some Patterns, Explanations, Outcomes, and Complications" (paper prepared for Conference on the Dynamics of Social Movements: Resource Mobilization, Tactics, and Social Control, Vanderbilt University, March 1976, cited in Doug McAdam, *Political Process*

and the Development of Black Insurgency (Chicago: University of Chicago Press, 1982), p. 219.

5. See Manning Marable, *Black American Politics: From the Washington Marches to Jesse Jackson* (London: Verso, 1985), especially ch. 3; "Foreword" to *The New Black Vote*, ed. Rod Bush (San Francisco: Synthesis Publications, 1984); and James Jennings, "Blacks and Progressive Politics," in *The New Black Vote*, pp. 201–18.

6. Jesse Jackson received an average of sixteen death threats a week during the campaign. Every black person I talked with feared that if Jackson stepped out too far ahead he would be gunned down. The memory of the 1960s and the knowledge of the precarious position of African Americans in American society weighs heavily on their consciousness and produces the anomaly of rhetoric that is often more militant than actions.

7. Manning Marable, *Blackwater: Historical Studies in Race, Class Consciousness and Revolution* (Dayton: Black Praxis Press, 1981), p. 106.

8. Interview with Ben Chavis, 7 March 1985.

9. Black politicians such as Julian Bond, Andrew Young, Coleman Young, and Richard Arrington refused to endorse Jackson for fear he would split the black vote. Others such as Marion Barry, Walter Fauntroy, and Richard Hatcher supported Jackson as a way of achieving black leverage with the white nominee. Both groups, however, accepted the traditional interest-group framework of party politics. For a description of the debate between these two groups, see "Should There Be a Black Presidential Candidate in 1984?" Editorial, *Jackson Advocate*, 30 June–6 July 1983, p. 1A; Gus Savage, "Blacks Need Political Agenda for 84," *Jackson Advocate*, 3–9 March 1983, p. 5A; and Thulani Davis, "Black Mayors: Can They Make the Cities Work?" *Mother Jones*, July 1984, p. 41.

10. Alice Lewis, "Did Jesse Jackson Cause Black Upset in Jefferson County Elections?" *Jackson Advocate*, 11–17 August 1983, p. 1A.

11. Marable, *Black American Politics*, p. 248.

12. Ibid., p. 184.

13. Thomas E. Cavanagh and Denise Stockton, *Black Elected Officials and Their Constituencies* (Washington, D.C.: Joint Center for Political Studies, 1983), p. 1.

14. In contrast to the small percentage of black officeholders at the county level in the South, more than two-thirds of white officeholders are found in county or educational offices (Kenneth Thompson, *The Voting Rights Act and Black Electoral Participation* [Washington, D.C.: Joint Center for Political Studies, 1982], pp. 12–19.

15. For accounts of the Eddie Carthan case, see Sheila D. Collins, "Revenge of the Good Ole Boys," *In These Times*, 20–26 January 1982; Teresa Rybovich, "Tchula: One Example of Black Participation in the Political Life of the United States" (masters thesis, University of Wisconsin, 1986); and Reginald Stuart, "Trial of Ex-Mayor of Mississippi Town Arouses Black Fears of Intimidation," *New York Times*, 20 October 1982.

16. Maynard Jackson, Atlanta's first black mayor, viciously crushed a municipal employees union whose members made an average of $7,400 a year. Coleman Young of Detroit gave huge tax abatements to corporations to finance downtown development at the expense of the deterioration of inner-city neighborhoods; and Richard Hatcher refused to challenge Gary's property-owning establishment. For assessments of the role of black mayors, see Bruno Cartosio, "U.S. Black Mayors—What Next? A European Perspective," *Monthly Review*, June 1985, pp. 25–44; Edward Greer, *Big Steel, Black Politics and Corporate Power in Gary, Indiana* (New York: Monthly Review Press, 1979); Davis, "Black Mayors," pp. 31–51; Sidney Lens, "A Mayor's Dilemma," *The Progressive*, June 1985, pp. 18–22; Michael B. Preston, Lenneal J. Henderson, Jr., and Paul Puryear, eds., *The New Black Politics: The Search for Political Power* (New York: Longman, 1982); and Bush, ed. *The New Black Vote.*

17. Manning Marable, "Foreword," in *The New Black Vote*, p. 4.

18. Richard Child Hill, "Race, Class and the State: The Metropolitan Enclave System in the United States," *The Insurgent Sociologist* 10, no. 2 (Fall 1980): 45–67.

19. Marguerite Ross Barnett, "The Congressional Black Caucus: Illusions and Realities of Power," *The New Black Politics*, pp. 28–54.

20. Reagan's Justice Department launched an all-out assault on affirmative action programs, declaring them "discrimination" against whites, and promising to go into court to force municipalities that had accepted affirmative action guidelines not to comply with them. The Reagan administration also gutted the Civil Rights Commission, replacing progressives with commission members devoted to the Reagan roll-back program, and removed the teeth from the Equal Employment Opportunity Commission and the Office of Contract Compliance through budget cuts, staff reductions, and new regulatory and procedural restrictions. When the Voting Rights Act came up for renewal, the administration toyed with the idea of adding crippling amendments to it. It was deterred only by a massive outcry from the civil rights community.

21. *The People's Platform* (Washington, D.C.: National Black Coalition for 1984; and National Black Leadership Roundtable, 1984), p. i. The

precipitous decline in black middle-class income during the Reagan years is related to the cuts made in social domestic spending. In 1980, 54 percent of black male college graduates and 72 percent of black female college graduates had jobs tied to federal spending (Richard McGahey, "Industrial Policy: Minority Economic Interests and American Political Response," *Review of Black Political Economy* 13 [Summer–Fall 1984], pp. 85–96).

22. Oba Simba T'Shaka, "Make the Past Serve the Present: Strategies for Black Liberation," *The Black Scholar*, January–February 1983, p. 21.

23. Manning Marable, "Black Political Party Crystallizes," *Win*, 15 October 1980, p. 16.

24. Marable, *Blackwater*, p. 159.

25. *The Black Leadership Family Plan for the Unity, Survival and Progress of Black People* (Washington, D.C.: The Black Leadership Forum and the Black Leadership Roundtable, 1982).

26. Ibid., p. 43.

27. Ibid., p. 3.

28. Miami's gross fiscal losses exceeded $250 million; 3,000 jobs were permanently destroyed, and another 3,000 temporarily lost; 400 persons were injured and 1,250 arrested, almost all black men (Marable, *Blackwater*, p. 130). James C. Smith, assistant professor of political science at Jackson State University, said in 1983 that he believed blacks were disgruntled with black leadership and that they were questioning the benefits of supporting black political platforms (Stephanie Hall, "Voter Participation: Apathy or Frustration?" *Jackson Advocate*, 16–22 June 1983). Oba Simba T'Shaka had written in *The Black Scholar* that black leaders' opposition to mass action, their unwillingness to move beyond reform, "discredits them as mouthpieces of the system" (p. 29).

29. Paul Delaney, "Voting: The New Black Power," *The New York Times Magazine*, 27 November 1983, p. 37.

30. Savage, "Blacks Need Political Agenda for '84."

31. As early as 1972 Jesse Jackson, according to Barbara Reynolds, began floating the idea of a black presidential candidate (*Jesse Jackson: The Man, The Movement, The Myth* [Chicago: Nelson Hall, 1975], p. 238). Jackson also articulated the idea of a rainbow coalition as a "progressive third force" at about the same time (John S. Saloma III and Frederick H. Sontag, *Parties: The Real Opportunity for Effective Citizen Politics* [New York: Alfred A. Knopf, 1972], p. 320).

32. *The People's Platform* was published by the Black Coalition for 1984 in cooperation with the National Black Leadership Roundtable. The National Black Coalition, begun by Reverend Joseph Lowery of the SCLC, included civil rights leaders and politicians who supported both the Mondale and Jackson campaigns.

33. Thomas Ferguson and Joel Rogers, "The Reagan Victory: Corporate Coalitions in the 1980 Campaign," *The Hidden Election: Politics and Economics in the 1980 Presidential Campaign*, ed. Thomas Ferguson and Joel Rogers (New York: Pantheon Books, 1980), pp. 26–35.
34. Ira Katznelson, "A Radical Departure: Social Welfare and the Election," in Ferguson and Rogers, *The Hidden Election*, p. 316.
35. A similar attempt in 1968 to achieve interracial unity around a common political program ended in utter failure. In the aftermath of the 1967 urban rebellions, the National Conference for New Politics was called by civil rights and antiwar activists to develop a strategy to influence the 1968 elections toward antiwar candidates. Conducted in an atmosphere of white liberal guilt and black anger, the conference ended in disaster. Blacks, who were 10 percent of the delegates, demanded 50 percent of the voting power and a thirteen-point program including such items as "white civilizing committees" to "humanize the savage and beast-like character that runs through America" (Nancy Zaroulis and Gerald Sullivan, *Who Spoke Up? American Protest Against the War in Vietnam 1963–1975* [Garden City, N.Y.: Doubleday & Co., 1984], p. 51).
36. Bayard Rustin and Norman Hill of the AFL-CIO-funded A. Philip Randolph Institute tried to limit the rally's scope and venue. A number of traditional white liberal supporters of the civil rights community refused to fund it, and other of the more right-wing elements in the civil rights community, including the National Urban League, were, according to Manning Marable, at most luke-warm toward the march. The Jewish community was split, with the American Jewish Committee and the Anti-Defamation League attacting the march for its inclusion of foreign policy issues. Marable, *Black American Politics*, pp. 109–13).
37. Ibid., pp. 116, 119.
38. According to one of the march's organizers, Rep. Walter Fauntroy, who had all of the records of the groups that had been mobilized and the people who had organized the local coalitions of conscience, just sat on the material.
39. Frances Fox Piven and Richard Cloward, "Foreword," in Madeleine Adamson and Seth Borgos, *This Mighty Dream: Social Protest Movements in the United States* (New York: Routledge and Kegan Paul, 1983).
40. At the time of the inception of the Lowndes County Freedom Party in Alabama, blacks were still largely disenfranchised and few had been elected to office. Thus, there was neither a viable base of voters nor the skills or financial resources available to build an independent party, and black electoral interests were channeled into the Alabama

Democratic Conference—the black arm of the state Democratic party, which dominated black politics in Alabama until 1984.

41. Representatives of more than eighty local and national organizations from twenty states attended the founding meeting of the People's Alliance in 1977. They represented political action and civil rights organizations, third world solidarity organizations, peace, environmental, and labor organizations, and African American, Puerto Rican, and Filipino organizations and parties.

42. James Jennings, "Black Power and Electoral Activism," *The New Black Vote*, p. 210. Jenning's essay was particularly valuable in the writing of this section.

43. In 1985, Wilson Goode badly managed a confrontation between the Philadelphia police and a radical black organization called MOVE that was terrorizing a black middle-class neighborhood in which its headquarters was located. Goode's mishandling of the situation resulted in the deaths of several MOVE members and their children and the destruction of the entire city block on which it was located from a fire set off by a bomb dropped by the police.

44. Peter Camejo and Alan Vargas, "The North Star Talks With Gus Newport," *The North Star* 2, (Fall 1985), 10–11.

45. Abdul Alkalimat and Doug Gills, "Black Power vs. Racism: Harold Washington Becomes Mayor," *The New Black Vote*, p. 161. Washington's primary victory was also due to racial bloc voting which produced a split white vote between Jane Byrne and Richard Daley (the late mayor's son).

46. Ibid.

47. Ibid., p. 166.

48. Detailed analyses of the Mel King campaign can be found in James Jennings, "The Mel King for Mayor Campaigns," in *The New Black Vote*, pp. 269–90; and "The Mel King Campaign and Coalition Politics in the Eighties," *Radical America*, 17, no. 6 and 18 no. 1 (double issue), 1983–1984.

49. Documentation on Theology in the Americas can be found in Sergio Torres and John Eagleson, *Theology in the Americas* (Maryknoll, N.Y.: Orbis Books, 1976); Cornel West, Caridad Guidote, and Margaret Coakley, eds., *Theology in the Americas: Detroit II Conference Papers* (Maryknoll: N.Y.: Orbis Books, 1982); and James Cone, *For My People: Black Theology and the Black Church* (Maryknoll, N.Y.: Orbis Books, 1984.

50. Aldon Morris, in his study of the origins of the civil rights movements, calls groups like the Southern Conference Educational Fund and the Highlander Center "movement halfway houses." In the changed context of the 1970s and 1980s, I have chosen the term

"bridge-builders" to more accurately reflect their function. See *The Origins of the Civil Rights Movement: Black Communities Organizing for Change* (New York: The Free Press/MacMillan, 1984), especially ch. 7.

4. The Voter Mobilization: Part Spiritual Crusade, Part Political Campaign

1. Jesse Jackson, "The Quest for a Just Society in a Peaceful World" (Announcement speech, 3 November 1983).
2. Howell Raines, "Pressures on Jesse Jackson—Black Leader Clears the Way for '84 Race; Now He Must Prove Candidacy's Credibility," *New York Times*, 20 June 1983.
3. Karl Marx, *The Eighteenth Brumaire of Louis Bonaparte*, in *Karl Marx and Frederick Engels, Selected Works* (Moscow: Progress Publishers, 1969), p. 398.
4. Milton Coleman, "Late-starting Jackson Campaign Begins to Gain Some Altitude," *Washington Post*, 1 February 1984.
5. "Pride and Prejudice," *Time*, 7 May 1984, p. 32.
6. Aldon Morris's work is a corrective to typical white sociology, which views black movements as chaotic and spontaneous (*The Origins of the Civil Rights Movement: Black Communities Organizing for Change* [New York: The Free Press/MacMillan, 1984]).
7. Gayraud Wilmore, *Black Religion and Black Radicalism: An Interpretation of the Religious History of Afro-American People*, 2nd ed. rev. (Maryknoll, N.Y.: Orbis Books, 1983), pp. 17–19.
8. For examples of criticisms of Jackson, see Fay S. Joyce, "Presidential Decision Nears for Jesse Jackson," *New York Times*, 27 September 1983; and Manning Marable, *Black American Politics: From the Washington Marches to Jesse Jackson* (London: Verso, 1985), pp. 267–68.
9. Myra MacPherson, "Pain and Passion: The Mystique of Jesse Jackson," *Washington Post*, 21 May 1984.
10. Wilmore, *Black Religion and Black Radicalism*, pp. 139–41; "Spirituality and Social Transformation as the Vocation of the Black Church," *Churches in Struggle: Liberation Theologies and Social Change in North America*, ed. William K. Tabb (New York: Monthly Review Press, 1986), pp. 241–42.
11. Wayne Barrett, "Is New York's Time Coming?" *The Village Voice*, 17 April 1984, p. 29.
12. Interview with C. T. Vivian, 21 April 1985. The quotations on the following pages are from this interview.

13. Wilmore, "Spirituality and Social Transformation," p. 249; confirmed by C. T. Vivian.
14. Interview with Bill Howard, 13 March 1985.
15. Anne Braden, "The Jackson Campaign in the South: A Victory Already Won," *The Rainbow Organizer*, July 1984, p. 1.

5. Politics from the Black Perspective: The Ideology of the Jackson Campaign

1. Manuel Castells, *The Economic Crisis and American Society* (Princeton: Princeton University Press, 1980), p. 196.
2. Though the civil rights movement, in effect, gave birth to the New Left, it was not that movement's intention; neither was the civil rights movement as independent of major white funding as the Jackson campaign. The fact that the majority of money for the campaign came from within the black community allowed it to take public positions far to the left of what would have been politically "permissable" had the campaign sought funding from white sources.
3. W. E. B. DuBois, *The Souls of Black Folk*, in *Three Negro Classics* (New York: Avon Books, 1965), p. 215.
4. Adolph Reed characterizes the "Jackson Phenomenon" as a "ritualistic event—a media-conveyed politics of symbolism, essentially tangential to the critical debate over the reorganization of American capitalism's governing consensus" (Adolph Reed, Jr., *The Jesse Jackson Phenomenon* [New Haven: Yale University Press, 1986], p. 1). Reed's bitter diatribe against the Jackson campaign can only be read as an effort to revise history in the service of the political right. His sources of information appear to be mostly extrinsic to the campaign, obviously reflecting no intimate experience with it.
5. Robert Scheer, "Playboy Interview: Jesse Jackson," *Playboy*, January 1984, p. 64.
6. Jesse Jackson, Remarks made at the Rainbow Leadership Conference (Chicago, Illinois, 17 December 1984).
7. This is evident from a reading of the Democratic party platform adopted in July 1984. See also: Mike Davis, *Prisoners of the American Dream: Politics and Economy in the History of the American Dream* (New York: Schocken, 1986), pp. 271–72.
8. John David Maguire, "The Necessity of Thinking Black" (Paper delivered to the Student YWCA, University of Illinois, May 1970).
9. Quoted in Maguire, "Necessity of Thinking Black."
10. McGuire, "Necessity of Thinking Black."
11. Jesse Jackson, "The Quest for a Just Society in a Peaceful World" (Announcement speech, 3 November, 1983).

12. In a *Playboy* interview, Jackson disclosed that the idea of running for president had come to him as a result of watching the Democratic party leadership snub Harold Washington, in a city that was 40 percent black, to endorse two white candidates. "Most folks looked at it and pretended it didn't happen. But it *did* happen. If Kennedy and Mondale had had their way, Washington wouldn't have won. If it had been left to them, the rise of the black political movement would have been stopped, stillborn. So what do you do? . . . Take them on in the primaries, challenge the Republicans in the general election, do all of it!" (Scheer, "Playboy Interview," p. 74).

13. Jessie Jackson, "Address to Women's Rally, Pier II Restaurant, Portsmouth, New Hampshire" (1 January 1984).

14. "An Interview with the Reverend Jesse Jackson, Civil Rights Leader," *New York Times*, 28 December 1983, p. A18.

15. Scheer, "Playboy Interview," p. 68.

16. Maguire, "Necessity of Thinking Black."

17. "Jackson on Central America," *New York Times*, 14 April 1984, p. 9.

18. Scheer, "Playboy Interview," p. 188.

19. DuBois, *The Souls of Black Folk*.

20. Martin Luther King Jr., *Trumpet of Conscience* (New York: Harper and Row, 1968), pp. 69–70.

21. "An Interview with the Reverend Jesse Jackson."

22. Interview with Carolyn Kazdin, Jackson's farm coordinator, 15 March 1985.

23. Jesse Jackson, "Environmental Policy: A Call to Action" (Speech to Citizens Conference to Stop Acid Rain, Manchester, New Hampshire, 6 January 1984).

24. Jesse Jackson, "Converging Interests and a New Direction" (Speech delivered to the National Hispanic Leadership Conference, 16 April 1984).

25. Jackson, "Address to Women's Rally."

26. Jesse Jackson, "Address to the Foreign Affairs Council" (Philadelphia, April 1984).

27. Jesse Jackson, "A Call to Trialogue" (Speech delivered at St. George's Orthodox Cathedral, Worcester, Massachusetts, 4 March 1984).

28. Jesse Jackson, "The Rainbow Coalition: An End to Racial Divisions, a New Beginning for America" (Speech delivered in San Francisco's Chinatown, 1 June 1984).

29. Maguire, "Necessity of Thinking Black."

30. Jesse Jackson, "Speech to the Wisconsin State Legislature" (6 April 1984).

31. Scheer, "Playboy Interview."

32. "An Interview with the Reverend Jesse Jackson."

33. Robert Bellah et al., *Habits of the Heart: Individualism and Commitment in American Life* (New York: Harper and Row, 1985), p. 151.

34. Reed, *The Jackson Phenomenon*, has characterized Jackson's entire career as opportunistic. Germond and Witcover's comments about Jackson's trip to Cuba are indicative of the ethnocentric bias of most mainstream political analysts: "That Cuba trip was another example of just how different Jesse Jackson was from candidates who had some genuine prospect of winning the Democratic Party's nomination for President. Serious politicians don't throw themselves into the embrace of Fidel Castro, no matter how much they may privately question U.S. foreign policy on Cuba" (Jack W. Germond and Jules Witcover, *Wake Us When It's Over: Presidential Politics of 1984* [New York: Macmillan, 1985], p. 298).

35. Editorial, "Mr. Jackson's Prisoner Dealings," *New York Times*, 6 July 1984; Gerald M. Boyd, "Jackson Flies to Cuba to Pick Up Prisoners and Take Them to the US"; Bernard Gwertzman, "Cuba Move Called Propaganda Ploy"; and Linda Greenhouse, "High Court Restores Curbs on Tourist Travel to Cuba," *New York Times*, 29 June 1984. Jackson was also criticized from the left for negotiating for the release of prisoners who had obviously opposed a "progressive socialist regime."

36. "Jesse Wins a 'Syria Primary,'" *Newsweek*, 16 January 1984, p. 14.

37. Interview with Reverend William Howard, 13 March 1985. For an insider's perspective on the Syria mission, see Wyatt Tee Walker, *The Road to Damascus* (New York: Martin Luther King Fellows Press, 1985).

38. Henry Plotkin, "Issues in the Campaign," in *The Election of 1984: Reports and Interpretations*, ed. Gerald Pomper et al. (Chatham, N.J.: Chatham House, 1985), p. 47.

39. Scheer, "Playboy Interview," p. 76.

40. Public opinion polls since the late 1960s have consistently shown the American public at opposite ends of the spectrum on almost all of the Reagan administration's proposals for eliminating the welfare state, intervening militarily in the third world, cutting back on civil rights legislation, and the like. See Thomas Ferguson and Joel Rogers, "The Myth of America's Turn to the Right," *Atlantic Monthly*, May 1986, pp. 43–53.

41. Andrew H. Malcolm, "LaRouche Illinois Drive Focused on Rural Areas," *New York Times*, 31 March 1986, p. A14.

42. "Speaking on the Issues," *Philadelphia Inquirer*, 6 April 1984.

43. Theodore H. White, "Jackson, Democratic Revolutionary," *New York Times*, 5 April 1984.

44. Quoted in Fay S. Joyce, "Jackson Tells Alabama It Will Never Be the

Same," *New York Times,* 10 February 1984.
45. An Open Letter from the Jesse Jackson for President Rainbow Conference in Chicago, Illinois, 29 June 1984.

6. Beyond the Melting Pot: Building the Rainbow Coalition

1. Jesse Jackson, 18 March 1984, Washington, D.C. Quoted in *Toward a Just Society and a Peaceful World,* campaign souvenir booklet published by the Jesse Jackson for President Committee, 1984.
2. In their study of white working-class males in Boston, Sennett and Cobb demonstrate how the economic and political impotence of these men in a society that teaches them that everyone has equal opportunity easily turns into racism against blacks and "welfare chiselers" (Richard Sennett and Jonathan Cobb, *The Hidden Injuries of Class* [New York: Vintage Books/Random House, 1972], pp. 135–50.
3. Robert Scheer, "Playboy Interview: Jesse Jackson," *Playboy,* January 1984, p. 68.
4. Theodore H. White, "New Powers, New Politics," *New York Times Magazine,* 5 February 1984, p. 25.
5. Thomas E. Cavanaugh, Lorn S. Foster, *Jesse Jackson's Campaign: The Primaries and Caucuses* (Washington, D.C.: Joint Center for Political Studies, 1984), pp. 8–9. For Accounts of the campaign in Alabama, see David Moberg, "Jackson's Bid Inspires Blacks in Selma, Alabama," *In These Times,* 14–20 March 1984, pp. 6–7; Gwendolyn Patton, "Alabama," *NCIPA Newsletter* 1, no. 2 (June–July 1984); "The Jesse Jackson Candidacy and Black Politicians in Montgomery, Alabama: The Negation of the Negation," *The Journal of Intergroup Relations* 12, no. 2 (Summer 1984): 3–17.
6. Interview with Willy Fluker, 15 February 1985.
7. Interviews with Gwen Patton, 15 February 1985; Hank Sanders, 14 February 1985; Wendell Paris, 15 June 1985; Willy Fluker 15 February 1985; James Busky, 12 February 1985; Bill Kendricks, 16 June 1985; Bessie Underwood and Bobbie Simpson, 17 February 1985; Earl Hilliard, 14 February 1985; and James Wilson, 15 February 1985.
8. Richard Arrington did not fit the description of "toms of the new type." He had run a principled campaign for Mondale in Birmingham and was considered a fairly progressive mayor. After the campaign, Arrington joined forces with the Jackson insurgents to form the Alabama New South Coalition, a statewide progressive movement that began to compete with the ADC for black loyalty.

9. Patton, "The Jesse Jackson Candidacy and Black Politicians in Montgomery," pp. 8–9.
10. Bob Sanders, "Philadelphia Story: Winner Loses and Loser Wins," *The Guardian*, 25 April 1984, p. 7.
11. Gerald A. Anderson, "A Question of Blackness," cited in Manning Marable, *Black American Politics: From the Washington Marches to Jesse Jackson* (London: Verso, 1985), p. 281.
12. Quoted in Juan Williams and Milton Coleman, "Black Democrats Seek Single Voice," *Washington Post*, 8 June 1984.
13. Juan Williams, "Black Caucus Agrees to Help Jackson Alter Party Rules," *Washington Post*, 12 June 1984.
14. Ethel L. Payne, "Few Gains for Minorities at Democratic Convention," *Jackson Advocate*, 2–9 August 1984, p. 5A.
15. Quoted in Juan Williams and Martin Schram, "Blacks Express Frustration," *Washington Post*, 21 July 1984, p. 1A.
16. Cited in David Broder, "Black Voter Dissent Grows in Democratic Ranks," *Standard Star*, 11 September 1985, p. 14.
17. Robert R. Brischetto, *The Latino Vote in the 1984 Presidential Election* (San Antonio: Southwest Voter Registration Education Project, 1985).
18. Quoted in "A Melding of Cultures," *Time*, 8 July 1985, p. 36.
19. Rodolfo Acuna, *Occupied America*, 2nd ed. (New York: Harper and Row, 1981); Elizabeth Sutherland Martinez and Enriqueta Longeaux y Vasquez, *Viva La Raza: The Struggle of the Mexican American People* (New York: Doubleday, 1974).
20. These findings came from a nine-state survey of six thousand Hispanic voters taken as they left the polls in November 1984. The study was designed by the Southwest Voter Registration Education Project of San Antonio. Other participants included the Midwest Voter Registration and Education Project (Chicago); the Hispanic Women's Center and the Institute for Puerto Rican Policy (New York); and the Cuban American Committee (Miami). See also Geoffrey Fox, "Hispanic Attitudes Will Alter Politics," *In These Times*, 9–15 October 1985, p. 11; Robert R. Brischetto and Rodolpho O. de la Garza, *The Mexican American Electorate: Political Participation and Ideology*, Occasional Paper No. 3 (San Antonio: Southwest Voter Registration Education Project and Austin: Hispanic Population Studies Program of the Center for Mexican American Studies, University of Texas, 1983); Robert R. Brischetto and Willie Velasquez, *The Hispanic Electorates* (New York: Hispanic Policy Development Project, 1984); Robert R. Brischetto, Rodolpho O. de la Garza, and Janet Weaver, *The Mexican American Electorate: An Explanation of Their Opinions and Behavior*, Occasional Paper No. 4 (San Antonio: Southwest Voter

Registration Education Project and Austin: Hispanic Population Studies Program of the Center for Mexican American Studies, University of Texas, 1984).

21. Robert R. Brischetto and Rodolpho O. de la Garza, *The Mexican American Electorate: A Demographic Profile*, Occasional Paper No. 1 (San Antonio: Southwest Voter Registration Project and Austin: Hispanic Population Studies Program of the Center for Mexican American Studies, University of Texas, 1982).

22. Survey results cited in *The Rainbow Organizer* 2, no. 1, July 1985.

23. "A Melding of Cultures," p. 38.

24. Interview with Armando Gutierrez, 14 March 1985. This opinion was confirmed by several others who knew the Hispanic community.

25. Interviews with Armando Gutierrez, 14 March 1985; Baldemar Velasquez, and Gene Royale, 20 July 1985.

26. Manning Marable, *Black American Politics: From the Washington Marches to Jesse Jackson* (London: Verso, 1985), p. 266.

27. "Jesse Jackson's Positions on Women's Issues" (Campaign position paper).

28. Judy Maclean, "N.O.W.," *Socialist Revolution* 6, no. 3 (July–September 1976): 40.

29. Two books produced during 1984 outlined the gender-gap evidence and strategy: Bella Abzug with Mim Kelber, *Gender Gap: Bella Abzug's Guide to Political Power for American Women* (New York: Houghton-Mifflin, 1984); and Eleanor Smeal, *Why and How Women Will Elect the Next President* (New York: Harper & Row, 1984).

30. Sonia Johnson expressed these views at a women's meeting I attended with her in March 1985. See also Mordecai Specktor, "Citizens' Party Sets Its Own Course," *The Guardian*, 5 September 1984, p. 7.

31. Quoted in Linda Kahn, "Ferraro—Thank Jesse Jackson," *Frontline*, 6 August 1984, p. 4.

7. A Voice for the Locked-out: Widening the Rainbow Coalition

1. Jesse Jackson, Speech to National Rainbow Leadership Conference, 29 June 1984.

2. Quoted in Caroline Wang, "A Cultural Aversion," *In These Times*, 30 October–5 November 1985.

3. Cindy Ng, speech at Harlem rally for Jesse Jackson, 31 March 1984.

4. There has been very little written about Arab Americans. Among the sources used here are Sameer Y. Abraham and Nabeel Abraham, eds., *Arabs in the New World: Studies on Arab-American Communities* (Detroit: Wayne State University Center for Urban Studies, 1983);

Baha Abu-Laban and Faith T. Zeadey, eds., *Arabs in America: Myths and Realities* (Wilmette, Ill.: The Medina University Press International, 1975); and Barbara C. Aswad, ed., *Arabic-Speaking Communities in American Cities* (New York: Center for Migration Studies of New York, and Association of Arab-American University Graduates, 1980).

5. A poll taken by the Black Muslim newspaper *Muhammed Speaks* of some 3,200 blacks in three sections of New York City in 1974 reported that 71 percent supported Arabs, while 29 percent sided with Israel or held no view (Karen Farsoun, Samih Farsoun, and Alex Ajay, "Middle East Perspectives for the American Left," *Arabs in America*, p. 74). For a history of African-American involvement with the Middle East question, see James Zogby and Jack O'Dell, eds., *Afro-Americans Stand Up for Middle East Peace* (Washington, D.C.: Palestine Human Rights Committee, 1980).

6. Among the prominent Arab Americans who supported Jackson were former South Dakota senator James Abourezk, Los Angeles disk jockey Casey Kasem, and Dr. Frank Maria, a New Hampshire businessman and educator who founded the first people-to-people diplomacy program, which was the precursor of the Peace Corps.

7. Black-Arab tension in certain large cities had been growing over the years as Arabs replaced Jews as the new merchant class in the black ghettos. In Detroit, for example, 60 percent of all of the city's "party" stores are owned by Arab Americans. Blacks, on the other hand, own only 16 percent of the food stores. In Chicago 95 percent of Arab Americans are in the grocery store business. Many Arab Americans hoped that by becoming involved in the Jackson campaign they might begin to ease such tensions (see Salim Muwakkil, "Arab Black Tensions Heat Up over Urban Business Interests," *In These Times*, 4–10 September 1985, p. 6).

8. Ward Churchill, "Indigenous Peoples of the United States: A Struggle Against Internal Colonialism," *The Black Scholar*, January/February 1985, p. 33.

9. Long before the 1973 oil crisis, many energy companies and other non-Indian interests acquired permits and leases for the exploration and use of uranium, oil, coal, and natural gas on Indian reservations. Huge tracts of land in the Northwest were slated to become "national sacrifice areas" for the exploitation of these energy conglomerates (Alvin M. Josephy, Jr., *Now That the Buffalo's Gone: A Study of Today's American Indians* [New York: Alfred A. Knopf, 1982], pp. 221, 259).

10. With the tacit approval of the Reagan administration, Strom Thurmond submitted a bill that would deny all Indian land claims in perpetuity. Under the bill, the Indian nations would not even have

recourse to lawsuits for land recovery (Mark Perry, "Indians Fight Assimilation," In These Times, 2–8 May 1984, p. 22).

11. Thomas Atkins, "The Jackson Challenge," speech to the Maryland Gay/Lesbian Alliance, 1 May 1984.
12. Andy Humm, "Lesbians and Gay Americans," The Rainbow Organizer 1, no. 1 (July 1984).
13. Jesse Jackson, speech to disabled Americans (undated).
14. Daniel Levitas, "Struggle from Unity, Progress Through Action: A Brief History of Farm Organizing," North American Farmer, 26 July 1984, p. 10.
15. Terry Pugh, "Interview with Merle Hansen: Building Alliances for Social Justice," Union Farmer, January 1984.
16. Ibid.
17. Quoted in Steve Kirschbaum, "Labor," The Rainbow Organizer 1, no. 1, July 1984. See also Paul Nussbaum et al., "Jackson Gets Union Nod in Visit to Pittsburgh," Philadelphia Inquirer, 6 April 1984, p. 8A.
18. Quoted in Anna Gyorgy, "Environmentalists," The Rainbow Organizer 1, no. 1 (July 1984).
19. John Saxton, "Peace Activists," The Rainbow Organizer 1, no. 1 (July 1984).
20. Interview with Jay Bender, 4 March 1985.
21. Jack Germond and Jules Witcover, Wake Us When It's Over: Presidential Politics of 1984 (New York: MacMillan, 1985), p. 289.
22. Quoted in Morris U. Schappes, "Around the World," Jewish Currents 38 (April 1984): 46. See also Phil Gailey, "Fears Remain on Jewish Vote as Democrats Praise Jackson," New York Times, 30 June 1984, p. A1.
23. Fay S. Joyce, "Jackson Outlines His Views to Jewish Group," New York Times, 5 March 1984.
24. A "source close to the Jewish establishment" in Framingham, Massachusetts, told a reporter: "What you've got is the Jewish agencies condemning Jews Against Jackson and [Rabbi Meir] Kahane [head of the extremist Jewish Defense League, which formed Jews Against Jackson] and then playing the same kind of politics behind closed doors" (Ben Bradlee, Jr., "Jackson-Jewish Group Meeting Off, Then On," The Boston Globe, 25 February 1984, p. 4).
25. Ellen Hume, "Racial Rhetoric Puts Farrakhan in Spotlight in Jesse Jackson Camp," The Wall Street Journal, 26 April 1984, p. 1.
26. Cornel West, "Left Strategies: A View From Afro-America," Socialist Review 26, no. 2 (March–April 1986): 44.

8. *The Poorest Campaign with the Richest Message: The Challenge to the Rules of Political Discourse.*

1. C. T. Vivian, *Black Power and the American Myth* (Philadelphia: Fortress Press, 1970), pp. 100–01.
2. Frances M. Beal, "U.S. Politics Will Never be the Same," *The Black Scholar* 15, no. 5 (September–October 1984); 17.
3. Robert Scheer, "Playboy Interview: Jesse Jackson," *Playboy,* January 1984, p. 77.
4. See Frances Fox Piven and Richard Cloward, "Foreword," to Madeleine Adamson and Seth Borgos, *This Mighty Dream: Social Protest Movements in the United States* (New York: Routledge and Kegan Paul, 1983), and Charles Victor McTeer, "Another Vestige of the Bad Old Days," *Washington Post,* 17 July 1984, p. A19.
5. John S. Saloma and Frederick H. Sontag, *Parties: The Real Opportunity for Effective Citizen Politics* (New York: Alfred A. Knopf, 1972), pp. 6–7.
6. In European democracies between 70 and 90 percent of the population votes (Joel Rogers, "The Politics of Voter Registration," *The Nation,* 21–28 July 1984; see also *Democracy in America: Toward Greater Participation,* Report of the Consultation on Citizen Responsibility, Political Participation and Government Accountability: Foundation Responsibility and Opportunity [New York: The New World Foundation, 1983]). In a study of 2,006 citizens eligible to vote in 1976, 22 percent of those who said they did not vote attributed their noninvolvement to a sense of political inefficacy: "Nothing I can say or do affects government." Another 18 percent of the nonvoters were physically disenfranchised, 13 percent were ignorant of voting precedures, and 35 percent felt their lives were going so well that voting was irrelevant. When asked what would bring them back to the voting booth, the refrainers replied: "Better candidates; someone you can trust; someone who tells the truth" (Arthur T. Hadley, *The Empty Polling Booth* [Englewood Cliffs, N.J.: Prentice-Hall, 1978], pp. 39–41; 115–16).
7. Ellis Sandoz, "Introduction: The Silent Majority Finds Its Voice," in *Election 84: Landslide Without a Mandate?* ed. Ellis Sandoz and Cecil J. Crabb, Jr. (New York: New American Library, 1985), p. 22; also Joel Rogers, "The Politics of Voter Registration," p. 47.
8. Byron E. Shafer, *The Quiet Revolution: The Struggle for the Democratic Party and the Shaping of Post Reform Politics* (New York: Russell Sage Foundation, 1983), p. 524.
9. Harold Meyerson, "Labor's Risky Plunge into Politics," *Dissent,* Summer 1984, pp. 286–87.
10. Shafer, *Quiet Revolution,* p. 491.

11. Stanley Aronowitz, "When the New Left Was New," in *The 60s Without Apology*, ed. Sonya Sayres, et al. (Minneapolis: University of Minnesota Press, 1985), p. 17.
12. Steven Rosenstone, Roy L. Behr, and Edward H. Lazarus, *Third Parties in America: Citizen Response to Major Party Failure* (Princeton: Princeton University Press, 1984), pp. 126–27.
13. Norman H. Nie, Sidney Verba, and John R. Petrocik, *The Changing American Voter* (Cambridge: Harvard University Press, 1976).
14. Nelson W. Polsby and Aaron B. Wildavsky, *Presidential Elections: Strategies of American Electoral Politics*, 3rd ed. (New York: Charles Scribner's Sons, 1971), pp. 32–33.
15. Tom Keyser, "The Jackson Energy Electrifies Two More New Hampshire Crowds," *Concord Monitor*, 6 February 1984, p. 2.
16. Quoted in Manning Marable, "Political Strategies, Jackson/NAACP," *The Jackson Advocate*, 23–31 August 1983, p. A5.
17. David Moberg, "Won't Be Water, But Fire Next Time, Here Comes Jesse with the Rainbow Sign," *In These Times*, 29 February –13 March 1984, p. 8.
18. Quoted in ibid.
19. Roger Allison, head of the Missouri Rural Crisis Center, made this observation at a Save the Family Farm Breakfast at the National Rainbow Convention, 18 April 1986, Washington, D.C.
20. *Boston Globe* editorial, "The Impact of Jesse Jackson," February, 1984.
21. Quoted in Marable, "Political Strategies, Jackson/NAACP."
22. Arch Puddington, "Jesse Jackson, the Blacks and American Foreign Policy," *Commentary*, April 1984, p. 20.
23. See Haynes Johnson, "Jackson and the South: What Happens When the Emotion Dies?" *Washington Post*, 19 February 1984, p. A2.
24. See "What Jesse Jackson Wants," *Newsweek*, 7 May 1984, p. 44.
25. Gerald M. Boyd, "Jackson Assails Rivals on the Issues," *New York Times*, 30 March 1984.
26. In a provocative article written before the Democratic Convention, Walter Karp theorized that the Democratic party bosses—based on their behavior from 1981 onward—actually conspired with the Republicans to lose the November 1984 elections in order to preserve ruling-class control of the party ("Playing Politics: Why the Democratic Bosses Conspired with Reagan, and Do Not Care if They Lose in November," *Harpers*, July 1984, pp. 51–60).
27. See David S. Broder, "Jackson, Platform Foes Begin Lining Up Forces," *Washington Post*, 12 April 1984, p. A12. Gary Hart was not above using the "special-interest" label to play to racist and classist sentiments. "Political parties," he told the Alabama legislature, "must free themselves from the grasp of special interests and once

again address the country's national interest" (Murray Hausknecht, "Special Interests and the City on a Hill," *Dissent*, Summer 1984, p. 264; in the same issue, see " 'Special Interests' and American Politics," pp. 270–74).

28. As recently as 1974, Democratic representatives received $3 from labor for every $1 from business. In 1984, the contributions from labor were about evenly matched by contributions from corporate and conservative PACs (Harold Meyerson, "A Too-Loyal Opposition?" *Democratic Left* 13, no. 6 [November–December 1985]: 4).

29. See Milton Coleman and Eric Pianin, "Blacks for Mondale Face 'Jackson Factor,' " *Washington Post*, 20 April 1984.

30. Jesse Jackson, Letter to George McGovern, 25 May 1984.

31. Jesse Jackson, "The Keys to a Democratic Victory in 84," speech before the thirteenth annual convention of Operation PUSH, 7 June 1984.

32. "New Directions Platform" of the Jesse Jackson for President Campaign.

33. Adolph Reed accuses the Jackson campaign of failing to develop a political program and of settling into a "fundamentally racial strategy onto which overtones toward a broader public were affixed desultorily." (*The Jackson Phenomenon* [New Haven: Yale University Press, 1986], p. 71). Reed was obviously ignorant of both the substantive platform of the Jackson campaign and of the political constraints imposed on its discussion by the Democratic party elites. Harder to understand is Williams and Morris's contention that Jackson's issue focus narrowed as the campaign progressed, contracting just before the Democratic convention into a focus on electoral inclusion (Lorenzo Morris and Linda Williams, "Jackson and the Rainbow in the Primary and General Elections," *Jesse Jackson and the 1984 Presidential Campaign*, ed. Lucius Barker [Urbana: University of Illinois Press, 1987]). Just the opposite was the case. As the campaign progressed, Jackson picked up a wider and wider issue focus as he encountered groups of the disenfranchised on the campaign trail.

34. T. R. Reid, "Mondale Delegates Squelch Hart's Specifics for Platform," *Washington Post*, 19 June 1984, p. A6.

35. Interview with Jay Bender, a member of New Jewish Agenda, 4 March 1985.

36. The amendment was defeated by a vote of 41 to 9 with 5 abstentions. Abstaining Mondale delegates confided that they were in favor of a freeze on West Bank settlements, but felt politically pressured to "follow the Mondale Line." Many delegates later confessed that they had not even known that such figures as former Israeli Foreign Minister Abba Eban had called for a freeze on settlements. Several dele-

gates said they supported the settlement freeze on moral grounds but wanted to avoid controversy and debate on the Middle East at the Democratic convention. This information was reported to the national rainbow desk by Diane Rosenblatt and Andrea Barron, Hart delegates from Michigan.

37. T. R. Reid, "Hart and Mondale Delegates Find Common Ground on Foreign Policy," *Washington Post*, 21 June 1984, p. A10. Hart supporters at first voted with Jackson delegates on the "no first use of nuclear weapons" plank. When they found out that their candidate opposed it, they voted against it.

38. Jesse Jackson reported on this meeting to campaign workers, 29 June 1984.

39. James Ridgeway, "'The Hell With Mondale' Bitter Minorities Threaten Coalition," *The Village Voice*, 31 July 1984, pp. 11–12.

40. Press Release, Southern Christian Leadership Conference, 18 July 1984.

41. Jesse Jackson, Remarks made to National Rainbow Leadership Conference (Chicago, Illinois, 29 June 1984).

42. The South Africa issue led to the formation in the late summer of 1985 of the Conservative Opportunity Society, a group of younger Republican conservatives who differed with the Reagan administration over its policy of "constructive engagement." Some led a fight for sanctions against Pretoria within the Senate (Salim Muwakkil, "South Africa Is Now Threatening to Divide the Republican Party," *In These Times*, 11–17 September 1985, p. 3).

9. People's Power versus Backroom Deals: The Challenge to Party Rules and Voting Impediments

1. C. T. Vivian, *Black Power and the American Myth* (Philadelphia: Fortress Press, 1970), p. 98.

2. Quoted in Maxine Phillips, "Voter Registration: New Hopes, New Roadblocks," *Christianity and Crisis*, 14 November 1983, p. 423.

3. Walter Karp, "Playing Politics: Why the Democratic Party Bosses Conspired with Reagan, and Do Not Care If They Lose in November," *Harpers*, July 1984, pp. 51–60.

4. Norman H. Nie, Sidney Verba, and John R. Petrocik, *The Changing American Voter* (Cambridge: Harvard University Press, 1976); and Michael Parenti, *Democracy for the Few*, 4th ed. (New York: St. Martins Press, 1983), pp. 216–18. Parenti points out that in the 1980 presidential campaign 51 percent of the voters said there were "no

important differences between the candidates and parties."

5. See Thomas Byrne Edsall, *The New Politics of Inequality* (New York: W. W. Norton, 1984).

6. George Lardner, Jr., "Jackson Sees Bright Future for 'Rainbow Coalition' and Its Agenda," *Washington Post*, 1 April 1984, p. A3.

7. See Akinsiju Ola, "Jackson Has Already Won More Than an Election," *The Guardian*, 25 April 1984.

8. Jesse Jackson, Letter to Charles Manatt, 19 May 1984.

9. Joseph F. Sullivan, "Mondale Won 18 of Jersey's 21 Counties; Jackson Strong in Essex," *New York Times*, 6 June 1984; Martin Schrom and Jay Mathews, "States Show Vagaries of Delegate Allocations," *Washington Post*, 6 June 1984, p. A17; and Robert Lindsey, "Votes from Most Areas Give California to Hart," *New York Times*, 6 June 1984.

10. Howell Raines, "Democrats Reject Compromise Plan on Delegates Rules," *New York Times*, 20 January 1984, p. 1A.

11. Howell Raines, "Jackson Drafts Plan for Changes in Electing Democratic Delegates," *New York Times*, 4 December 1983, p. 1.

12. John Dillin, "Legal Briefs Mix with Press Releases on the Campaign Trail," *Christian Science Monitor*, 25 May 1984, p. 1.

13. Interview with Arnette Holloway, 27 November 1984.

14. "Jackson urges Rivals' Meeting to Discuss 'Areas of Disagreement,' " *Washington Post*, 2 May 1984; Jesse Jackson, Letter to Charles Manatt, 19 May 1984; and Juan Williams, "Manatt, Jackson to Confer Again on Vote-Delegate Disparity," *Washington Post*, 22 May 1984, p. A6.

15. T. R. Reid and Bill Patterson, "Platform Building: Hart, Jackson Hammer Own Issues," *Washington Post*, 12 June 1984, p. A1; Juan Williams, "Black Caucus Agrees to Help Jackson Alter Party Rules," *Washington Post*, 12 June 1984, p. A4.

16. Ibid.

17. Warren Weaver, Jr., "Democratic Panel Yields to Jackson Backers," *New York Times*, 27 July 1984, p. A23.

18. Quoted in Juan Williams, "Jackson Won't Pledge to Support Mondale," *Washington Post*, 6 July 1984.

19. Jesse Jackson, Speech to National Rainbow Leadership Conference, 30 June 1984.

20. Charles Victor McTeer, "Another Vestige of the Bad Old Days," *Washington Post*, 17 July 1984, p. A19; and *Working Paper: The Runoff Primary, Blacks and the Democratic Party*, Joint Center for Political Studies, Washington, D.C., 1984.

21. Quoted in David Moberg, "Unease Rises with the Runoff as an Issue," *In These Times*, 9–5 May 1984, p. 3.

22. Quoted in Lally Weymouth, "Sticky Questions for Jesse Jackson," *New York Times*, 9 January 1984, p. 38.

23. Quoted in Juan Williams, "Jackson Mixes His Party Ambitions with Refrains of 'Fairness,'" *Washington Post*, 13 July 1984, p. A4.
24. Moberg, "Unease Rises with the Runoff."
25. Interview with Holloway.
26. Quoted in *San Francisco Examiner*, 18 July 1984, p. A4.

10. The Future of Race in American Politics

1. Leslie B. McLemore, in *Race and Political Strategy: A JCPS Roundtable*, ed. Thomas E. Cavanagh (Washington, D.C.: Joint Center for Political Studies, 1983), p. 3.
2. For a comparison of institutional racism in the United States and South Africa, see George M. Frederickson, *White Supremacy: A Comparative Study in American and South African History* (New York: Oxford University Press, 1981).
3. For descriptions of the media's role in the 1984 elections, see Jack W. Germond and Jules Witcover, *Wake Us When Its Over: Presidential Politics of 1984* (New York: Macmillan, 1985); and William A. Henry, III, *Visions of America: How We Saw the 1984 Election* (Boston: The Atlantic Monthly Press, 1985). For a more general discussion of the role of the media in recent presidential elections, see Joseph C. Spear, *Presidents and the Press: The Nixon Legacy* (Boston: MIT Press, 1984); and Alexander Cockburn and James Ridgeway, "The World of Appearance: The Public Campaign," in *The Hidden Election: Politics and Economics in the 1980 Presidential Campaign* (New York: Pantheon Books, 1981).
4. Journalist William Henry observed that "the more churchgoers and ralliers chanted, 'Run, Jesse, Run,' the more reporters for the mainstream media described Jackson to their audiences as a serious candidate. And the more Jackson's candidacy was legitimized by the media, the more young and poor blacks felt impelled to support him" (Henry, *Visions of America*, p. 80).
5. The concept of the Black Man Rampant was used by Clive Leeman, a white South African humanities professor whose piece on racism in the media appeared in the Washington Post ("Just Who is Spreading the Racist Tension?" *Washington Post*, 15 April 1984).
6. Quoted in Les Payne, "Black Reporters, White Press—And the Jackson Campaign," *The Columbia Journalism Review*, July/August 1984, p. 34.
7. Howell Raines, "Jackson Poses Some Difficult Questions for Other Democrats," *New York Times*, 6 November 1983, p. E5.

8. Quoted in Payne, "Black Reporters," p. 36.
9. Howell Raines, "A Provocative Candidate," *New York Times*, 4 November 1983, p. 1A.
10. Quoted in Payne, "Black Reporters," p. 33.
11. Audrey Edwards, "Winning with Jesse," *Essence*, July 1984, p. 74.
12. Henry (Mickey) Michaux, in McLemore, *Race and Political Strategy*, p. 6. Michaux was the candidate frequently cited by Jackson as the example of someone who, having won the election, lost it in the runoff primary.
13. Gerald M. Boyd, "Jackson Bids for Black and Hispanic Consideration," *New York Times*, 16 April 1984.
14. Lorenzo Morris and Linda Williams, "Jackson and the Rainbow in the Primary and General Elections," *Jesse Jackson and the 1984 Presidential Campaign*, ed. Lucius Barker (Urbana: University of Illinois Press, 1987); McLemore, *Race and Political Strategy*, pp. 8–12.
15. Jesse Jackson, "The Quest for a Just Society in a Peaceful World" (Announcement speech, 3 November 1983).
16. "Jesse Wins a Syria primary," *Newsweek*, 16 January 1984, p. 14.
17. Henry, *Visions of America*, p. 123.
18. Ibid., pp. 75–76. According to Henry, media moguls had decided, by the time Kennedy left the race, that Mondale was unbeatable. At a representative party at the home of CBS commentator Bill Moyers, Mondale's apparent invincibility was agreed on by anchors, top news producers, and their bosses, the news division chiefs of two networks.
19. Ibid., p. 74.
20. This conclusion is based on numerous interviews with white campaign workers as well as by the results of a Joint Center for Political Studies/Gallup survey of white perceptions in which Jackson was rated as prejudiced by 56 percent of the white voters surveyed.
21. Kennedy and Johnson's racial slurs are cited in Victor Lasky, *It Didn't Start with Watergate* (New York: Dell, 1977), pp. 22, 184. Nixon's racist language is cited in Seymour Hersh, *The Price of Power: Kissinger in the Nixon White House* (New York: Summit Books, 1983), pp. 110ff. Carter's remarks about "ethnic purity" are described in "Candidate Carter: I Apologize," *Time*, 19 April 1976, p. 14. Jack E. White, a black reporter with *Time*, complained of the "get Jesse" attitude among white editors (Payne, "Black Reporters," p. 33).
22. Both remarks quoted in Payne, "Black Reporters," p. 36.
23. "Meet the Press" transcript, 8 April 1984.
24. A tiny, two-paragraph story in the *Washington Post* was entitled "Jackson Adds Some Hues to His 'Rainbow Coalition'" (23 April 1984, p. A3). A longer article in the *New York Times* pictured Jackson with some of his rainbow supporters. It was one of the few *Times*

photos that showed him surrounded by nonblacks (Gerald Boyd, "Tennessians Pushing Jackson Effort," *New York Times*, 30 April 1984).

25. Tom Kelly, "In Dreams Begin Responsibilities," *Christianity and Crisis* 44, no. 6 (16 April 1984): 128.

26. The *Philadelphia Inquirer's* coverage of this day, in contrast, headlined the endorsement press conference and pictured Jackson talking with the "rainbow" of children in the Germantown church (Joe Logan and Tom Infield, "Jackson Endorsed at Philadelphia Church," *Philadelphia Inquirer*, 9 April 1984, p. 7A). See also Phil Gailey, "Philadelphia Vote is Seen as a Factor in Jackson's Influence," *New York Times*, 9 April 1984, p. A1.

27. Interview with Anne Braden, 13 April 1985.

28. Wayne Barrett, "Is New York's Time Coming?" *Village Voice*, 17 April 1984, p. 5.

29. Editorial, *The New Republic*, 30 April 1984, p. 7.

30. Henry, *Visions of America*, p. 123.

31. Cited in "Pride and Prejudice," *Time*, 7 May 1984, p. 32.

32. Manning Marable, *Black American Politics: From the Washington Marches to Jesse Jackson* (New York: Schocken Books, 1985), p. 236. Washington's opponent, Bernard Epton, used blatantly racist appeals and never once campaigned in black neighborhoods, yet the media did not focus on this the way they did on the myth of Washington's total focus on the black vote (see John E. Jacob, "Race and Politics," *Jackson Advocate*, 28 April–4 May 1983, p. 5A).

33,. As far back as December 1983, John Chancellor had stated that Jackson would pull black Democrats away from the front-runners, so that Reagan would win by a landslide (cited by Alfreda Madison, "Presidential Candidate for all the People," *Jackson Advocate*, 8–16 December 1983). See also Martin Schram, "Jackson 'Alliance' Reports Threaten Hart," *Washington Post*, 1 June 1984, p. A5.

34. Richard Reeves, "America's Choice: What It Means," *New York Times Magazine*, 4 November 1984, p. 36.

35. Interview with Tom Cavanagh. See also Tom Cavanagh, "The Meaning of the 1984 Election: What the Media Didn't Tell You" (Address presented to the ninth annual mid-winter meeting of the Urban League, Bal Harbour, Florida, 4 December 1984).

36. Monte Piliawsky, "The 1984 Election's Message to Black Americans: Challenges, Choices and Prospects," *Freedomways* 25, no. 1 (1985): 19; and Warren Miller, "What Realignment?" *Focus* 12, nos. 11 and 12 (November–December 1984): 6.

37. Walter Dean Burnham, "The 1984 Election and the Future of American Politics," *Election 84: Landslide Without Mandate?* ed. Ellis

Sandoz and Cecil V. Crabb, Jr. (New York: New American Library, 1985), pp. 252–53.

38. In 1984 the difference between black and white support for the Democratic party was 54%. It was 56% in 1968; 57% in 1972; 48% in 1976; and 56% in 1980. *Congressional Quarterly Weekly Report*, 1984, p. 1739; cited in Mike Davis, *Prisoners of the American Dream* (New York: Schocken, 1986), p. 279. Because the increasingly populated Sunbelt has become more Republican the country as a whole, Walter Dean Burnham contends that there is now a built-in bias against the Democrats' enlarging their share of the electoral vote. It is conceivable, says Burnham, that we could elect a Republican president who would lose the popular vote but win the electoral vote ("The Election and After," *New York Review of Books*, 16 August 1984, p. 33). For an analysis of the shifts in electoral participation underlying the present realignment of power within the two parties, see Norman H. Nie, Sidney Verba, and John R. Petrocik, *The Changing American Voter* (Cambridge, Mass.: Harvard University Press, 1976); and Thomas Byrne Edsall, *The New Politics of Inequality* (New York: W. W. Norton, 1984), ch. 5.

39. At one point it appeared that Mondale's aides were willing to cast Jackson as a communist sympathizer, a dangerous anti-Semite, and an ego-maniac if he did not go along with the Mondale campaign (Juan Williams, "Mondale, Jackson Weigh Their Reciprocal Needs," *Washington Post*, 5 July 1984).

40. For an expression of one militant's criticism of Jackson's support for the Democratic party, see Amiri Baraka, "Reagan: The State of Black America, the State of the U.S.A. What Now?" *Forward* 4 (January 1985): 1–11.

41. Preston Wilcox, "The San Francisco Compromise," *National Newport News*, August–September 1984, p. 12.

42. David Broder, "Black Voter Dissent Grows in Democrat Ranks," *Standard Star*, 11 September 1983. The survey of 1,150 blacks was conducted by the University of Michigan's Institute for Social Research.

43. Interviews with members of the Rainbow Institute, Seattle, 15–16 May 1985.

44. Interview with Gwen Patton, 15 February 1985. Also, "Criticize Walter Mondale, But Defeat Ronald Reagan," *Jackson Advocate*, 20–26 September 1984, p. 5A.

45. Interview with Rev. Gary Douglas, 17 April 1985.

46. "Criticize Walter Mondale, But Defeat Ronald Reagan."

47. Dorothy Gilliam, "Breakthrough," *Washington Post*, 16 July 1984.

48. Thomas E. Cavanagh, "Election Round-Up," *Focus* 12, nos. 11–12, November–December 1984, p. 4.

49. For refutations of the assumption that the electorate was becoming more conservative, see Thomas Ferguson and Joel Rogers, "The Myth of America's Turn to the Right," *Atlantic Monthly*, May 1986, pp. 43–53; Manning Marable, "Race and Realignment in American Politics," *North Star* 3 (Spring 1968): 8; and Vicente Navarro, "The 1980 and 1984 U.S. Elections and the New Deal," *Socialist Register 1985/86*, ed. Ralph Miliband, et al. (London: The Merlin Press, 1986), pp. 158–209. Walter Dean Burnham saw the 1984 election as a maintenance of the status quo, but concludes that the electorate "seems to be becoming generally more Republican and more conservative," with a 5 percent increase in both categories between 1980 and 1984. Burnham, however, also acknowledges widening class polarization that was not reflected in the choices offered in the 1984 election because of the Democratic party's refusal to represent its class base. According to Burnham, Jackson could become the prophet of a new class-based electoral movement if the economy began to turn worse for more of the middle class (Burnham, "The 1984 Election and the Future of American Politics," pp. 204–60).

50. Quoted in Juan Williams, "Jackson Assails Democratic Leaders," *Washington Post*, 11 February 1985, p. A13.

51. Organizers of the Democratic Leadership Council included Missouri Representative Richard Gephardt, Governors Charles Robb of Virginia and Bruce Babbitt of Arizona, and Senators Sam Nunn of Georgia and Lawton Chiles of Florida.

52. George T. Church, "Moving Toward the Middle," *Time*, 18 March 1985. See also Phil Gailey, "Dissidents Defy Top Democrats, Council Formed," *New York Times*, 1 March 1985.

53. Interview with Carolyn Kazdin, 15 March 1985.

54. Kevin J. Kelley, "Will Anybody Poop the Party's Rightward Whirl?" *The Guardian*, 10 April 1985, p. 3. See also Jonathan Fuerbringer, "Democrats Hear Frank Advice on Problems," *New York Times*, 3 March 1985, p. 27.

55. "Democrats Cut Four Caucuses," *San Francisco Chronicle*, 18 May 1985, p. 6.

56. Quoted in Kelley, "In Dreams Begin Responsibilities"; see also Frances Frank Marcus, "Jackson Criticizes Democrats on Party Rules," *New York Times*, 25 August 1985, p. 27.

57. As a result of McGovern Commission reforms, the percentage of House Democrats appointed as superdelegates had fallen to 15 percent by the end of the 1970s (Edsall, *New Politics of Inequality*, p. 52).

58. Kevin J. Kelley, "Democrats: Back to Backrooms," *The Guardian*, 30 October 1985, p. 1.

59. Conversation with Michelle Eisenberg, member of the Democratic National Committee.

60. Kevin J. Kelley, "Rudderless Liberals Drift Left with the Tide," *Guardian*, 24 July 1984, p. 7.

61. Quoted in Fay S. Joyce, "Kennedy Says Democratic Party Must Change to Regain Support," *New York Times*, 31 March 1985, p. 24; and John Herbers, "Democratic Chiefs Divide on Ways to Rebuild Party," *New York Times*, 1 April 1985.

62. For accounts of the Alabama Black Belt voting fraud cases, see Sheila D. Collins, "Voting Rights: Justice Department Undermines Act," *In These Times*, 10–23 July 1985, p. 5; and "Alabama Trial for Rainbow Activists," *Guardian*, 8 March 1985, p. 9.

63. Interviews with Bobbie Nell Simpson, 17 June 1985; Wendell Paris, 15 June 1985.

64. For a history and analysis of how racism has destroyed every white reform movement in American history, see Robert L. Allen, *Reluctant Reformers: Racism and Social Reform Movements in the United States* (Garden City, N.Y.: Anchor Books/Doubleday, 1975).

65. For reviews of the findings of public opinion polls on the range of issues addressed by the Jackson campaign, see Navarro, "The 1980 and 1984 U.S. Elections," and Ferguson and Rogers, "Myth of America's Turn to the Right."

66. Interview with Anne Braden; memo from Anne Braden to Donna Brazile, 13 April 1985.

67. Morris and Williams, "Jackson and the Rainbow in the Primary and General Elections."

68. Interview and materials from Ginger Rhodes, 29 June 1984.

69. Interviews with Barb Steinheider and David Steinheider, Donna Polk, 27 September 1984.

70. Interview with Anne Braden, 13 April 1985.

71. Bonnie Souza, "Jesse Jackson Campaign in Eugene," unpublished paper in author's possession.

72. Interview with Willy Fluker, 15 February 1985.

73. The JCPS/Gallup poll is cited in Morris and Williams, "Jackson and the Rainbow in the Primary and General Elections."

74. Morris and Williams, "Jackson and the Rainbow in the Primary and General Elections." The New York poll is cited in "Pride and Prejudice," *Time*, 7 May 1984, p. 32.

75. Barry Sussman, "Survey Finds Whites Like Jackson More Than Primary Votes Indicate," *Washington Post*, 29 May 1984.

76. Cited in Morris and Williams, "Jackson and the Rainbow in the Primary and General Elections."

77. Adolph L. Reed, Jr., *The Jackson Phenomenon* (New Haven: Yale University Press, 1986), p. 133.

78. Morris and Williams, "Jackson and the Rainbow in the Primary and General Elections."

79. The prospect of fascism in the United States has been the subject of considerable debate during the Reagan administration. While most analysts use the term cautiously, they detect ominous signs. See Bertram Gross, *Friendly Fascism: The New Face of Power in America* (Boston: South End Press, 1982); and Marable, "Race and Realignment in American Politics."

80. According to Arthur Kinoy, who litigated this wiretapping case before the Supreme Court, William Rehnquist, appointed in 1986 as Chief Justice of the Supreme Court, was the architect of the Watergate affair, with its frightening implications for the subversion of constitutional government. Rehnquist is the only one of the Watergate conspirators never to have suffered from public scrutiny as a result of his actions in this case (Kinoy, *Rights on Trial: The Odyssey of a People's Lawyer* (Cambridge, Mass.: Harvard University Press, 1983), ch. 1.

11. Whither the Rainbow Coalition?

1. Jesse Jackson, Speech to the National Rainbow Leadership meeting, 29–30 June 1984, Chicago.

2. Jack O'Dell, "The Rainbow Coalition Organizational Principles," internal memorandum.

3. Cornel West, *Prophesy Deliverance! An Afro-American Revolutionary Christianity* (Philadelphia: The Westminster Press, 1982), p. 90; also, ch. 3, pp. 69–91. The other "ideal types" of responses to white supremacy found in black culture as described by West are the exceptionalist tradition, which lauds the uniqueness of Afro-American culture and personality; the assimilationist tradition, which considers Afro-American culture and personality to be pathological; and the marginalist tradition, which "emphasizes the suppression of individuality, eccentricity and nonconformity within Afro-American culture."

4. Accounts of the New York experience are drawn from my conversations with David Dinkins, a member of the Coalition for a Just New York; Roberto and Nellie Marrero, organizers of Latinos for Jackson; and New York activist Suzanne Ross, as well as from newspaper accounts.

5. The Coalition for a Just New York was, according to black activist Barbara Omolade, a "Black Old Boy network" representing few constituency-based organizations, little trade union leadership, and almost no women (Omolade, "Strike-Out in New York City, But . . ." *NCIPA* Newsletter 3, no. 1 [January–February 1986]: 9–13). Trade

union leader Bill Lynch, on the other hand, felt that the coalition was representative enough of the black community and that at this point in history, blacks had as much right as anyone else to decide on a candidate that other groups could buy into. He disagreed, however, with both the choice of Farrell and the process by which he was chosen. Lynch was a member of the Coalition for a Just New York ("Electoral Politics in New York City . . .: An Interview with Bill Lynch," *Against Racism* 3, no. 2 [May–June 1985]: 3–12).

6. Omolade "Strike-Out in New York City," p. 10.

7. The National Alliance party (NAP) positions itself as an independent left-populist alternative to the two-party system. It has been successful in recruiting low-income and working-class blacks in New York City and Jackson, Mississippi, among other areas of the country. Although it claims to be black-led, its core leadership appears to be a small group of whites clustered around the personality of Fred Newman. A series of exposés of NAP by Ken Lawrence were run in the *Jackson Advocate* on 16–22 and 23–29 May 1985; 27 June–3 July 1985; 4–10 July 1985. The National Rainbow Coalition's official organ, *The Rainbow Organizer*, was forced to disassociate itself from two NAP fronts, "The National Rainbow Alliance," and the "National Rainbow Lobby," through which NAP has been trying to capitalize on the rainbow idea and to recruit its natural constituency. The repudiation appeared in the June–July 1986 issue of the *Rainbow Organizer*.

8. The Alabama story is drawn from the interviews with the following people: Hank Sanders, 14 February 1985; Wendell Paris, 15 June 1985; Gwen Patton, 15 February 1985; Bill Kendricks, 16 June 1985; Willy Fluker, 15 February 1985; Rose Sanders, 15 June 1985; Larry Wofford, 15 June 1985. Accounts can also be found in *Power in the Black Belt: The Battle for the Ballot and the Case of the Perry County Three*, pamphlet published by Worker's Press; Wendell H. Paris et al., "Repression in Alabama," *NCIPA Newsletter* 2, no. 2 (May–June 1985): 1–6; "Assault on Democracy in the Alabama Black Belt," and "Black Belt Fights Back," fact sheets published by the Southern Organizing Committee; *Vote Fraud Trials Threaten Democracy*, pamphlet published by the Alabama Black Belt Defense Committee; Gwendolyn M. Patton, "The Jesse Jackson Candidacy and Black Politicians in Montgomery, Alabama: The Negation of the Negation," *The Journal of Intergroup Relations* 12, no. 2 (Summer 1984): 3–17; Sheila D. Collins, "Alabama Trial for Rainbow Activists," *The Guardian*, 8 March 1985, p. 9; idem, "Voting Rights: Justice Department Undermines Act," *In These Times*, 10–23 July 1985, p. 5; Paul Holmbeck, "Black Power on Trial, But the Jury Wasn't Fooled," *The Guardian*, 24 July 1985, p. 3; and Akinsiju C. Ola, "Progressive Black Belt Coalition

Formed," 5 February 1986, p. 10. After the Jackson campaign, ADC leader Joe Reed made a rule that anyone who supported Jackson could not hold office in the ADC, thus making certain that the Jackson forces would have to go outside the ADC to consolidate their power.

9. Interview with Gwen Patton, 15 February 1985.

10. Patton, quoted in Ola, "Progressive Black Belt Organization Formed."

11. Interview with Wendell Paris, 15 June 1985.

12. Richard Arrington, interviewed by Wade Marbaugh, "Arrington Heads New Black Political Group," *Greene County Democrat*, 29 January 1986, p. 1.

13. Quoted in Wade Marbaugh, "Hundreds Rally at 'New South' Convention," and H. L. Mitchell, "Letter to the Editor," *The Greene County Democrat*, 29 January 1985. Remark made by Josh Lawrence in a meeting with author, February 1986.

14. The Seattle experience is drawn from interviews with the following people: Arnette Holloway, 18 July 1984, 27 November 1984, 15–16 May 1985, 21 July 1986; Rev. Gil Lloyd, 15–16 May 1985; Jolinda Stevens, 15–16 May 1985; Stan Shikuma, 15–16 May 1985; William Garling, 16 May 1985; Rev. Sam McKinney, 16 May 1985.

15. The Vermont Rainbow experience is drawn from interviews with the following people and from my attendance at a state Rainbow Coalition meeting on 31 March 1985: Stewart Meacham, 17 December 1984, 20 March 1985; David Dellinger, 17 December 1984; Micque Glitman, 31 March 1985; Terje Anderson, 31 March 1985; Kit Andrews, 31 March 1985; Tom Smith, 31 March 1985; Ellen David-Friedman, 14 March 1985. Accounts are also found in Judy Ashkenaz, "Grassroots Organizing and the Democratic Party: The Vermont Rainbow Experience," *Monthly Review* 38 (May 1986): 8–21; Fox Butterfield, "Vermont Shifting to Left in a Flow of Newcomers," *New York Times*, 31 January 1986; Nick Garneau, "Burlington, VT Elections," *NCIPA Newsletter* 2, no. 2 (May–June 1985): 11.

16. Ashkenaz, "Grassroots Organizing," p. 8; Ellen David-Friedman, "Independent Vermont Governor's Race," *NCIPA Newsletter* 3, no. 2 (March–April 1986): 8.

17. Ashkenaz, "Grassroots Organizing," pp. 14–15.

18. Ted Glick, "Rainbow Coalition on the Move," *NCIPA Newsletter* 3, nos. 3–4 (Summer 1986): 1.

19. Jesse Jackson, "The Rainbow Coalition: A New Course, a New Coalition, A New Challenge" (Founding convention speech, 18 April 1986).

20. Robert Bellah, "Populism and Individualism," *Social Policy*, Fall 1985, p. 31.

21. William J. Brennan, Jr., "The Constitution of the United States: Con-

temporary Ratification" (Presentation at the Text and Teaching Symposium, Georgetown University, Washington, D.C., 12 October 1985).
22. Ibid.
23. This is the clear implication of a speech by Attorney General Edwin Meese to the American Bar Association, July 1985.

Index

374

peace and environmental activists, 217–18; platform and rhetoric, 146–47, 239; Rainbow Coalition and, 304, 316–17; reaction to Jackson campaign, 241–43

Monroe, Sylvester, 279

Montague, Christina, 251

Moore, Acel, 273

Moore, Howard, 40

Morial, "Dutch," 178

Moss, Robert, 66

Moynihan, Daniel, 57–58, 60–64, 66, 69–70, 73, 74, 75, 80

Mulhauser, Karen, 218

Municipal elections, 110–15

Nation of Islam, 88, 173

National Alliance party, 306

National Anti-Klan Network, 118, 133

National Black Political Assembly, 86, 93–94, 97

National Black United Front (NBUF), 93, 101–102, 110, 176, 187–88, 204

National Black Women's Political Conference, 198

National Committee for Independent Political Action, 107, 116

National Hispanic Leadership Conference, 157–58, 190

National Organization of Women (NOW), 147, 193–95, 249

National Rainbow Coalition: efforts to organize, 302–332; financial requirements of, 307; launching in 1986, 325–29; leadership of, 325; and moral ideals of American democracy, 329–32; new model in Alabama Black Belt for, 309–314; and ongoing statewide coalitions, 308–324; opposition of Democratic party to, 308; principles of, 327–28; priorities of, 328–29. *See also* Rainbow Coalition

National Women's Political Caucus

of Democratic party, 198, 248–51

Native Americans, 26–27, 98, 101–102, 162, 205–208. *See also* American Indian Movement

Neoconservative intellectuals: attacks against commitment to racial minorities, 60–75; and ideology of New Right, 60; impact on white liberals and social activists, 79–80; reassertion of cultural and political control by, 19–20. *See also* New Right

New Deal coalition, 22, 84, 147

New Jewish Agenda, 222, 226

New Right: assault on Second Reconstruction, 51–82; and Carter administration policies, 98; impact on civil rights movement, 77–79; reasons for growth of, 58–59. *See also* Neoconservative intellectuals

New South Coalition, 313–14

New York City: Jackson campaign in, 187–89; mayoral election and Jackson forces in, 305–306

New York Times, 58, 66, 150, 156, 163, 272, 273, 280–81

Newport, Gus, 111

Newsweek, 163–64, 272, 278, 279, 282

Ng, Cindy, 201

Nicaragua. *See* Central American policy

Nixon, Richard, 76, 277

Novak, Michael, 70–73

Nuclear Freeze movement, 217–18, 250, 252

Nunn, Sam, 290

O'Dell, Jack, 19, 132, 303–304

O'Neill, Tip, 239

Obledo, Mario, 191

Operation PUSH, 122, 131–32, 204

Palestinian issue, 204

Paris, Wendell, 310–11

Patton, Gwen, 176, 177, 198, 251, 309–310